T0244322

How Coppola Became Cage

How Coppola Became Cage

ZACH SCHONFELD

OXFORD
UNIVERSITY PRESS

Oxford University Press is a department of the University of Oxford. It furthers the University's objective of excellence in research, scholarship, and education by publishing worldwide. Oxford is a registered trade mark of Oxford University Press in the UK and certain other countries.

Published in the United States of America by Oxford University Press
198 Madison Avenue, New York, NY 10016, United States of America.

Library of Congress Cataloging-in-Publication Data
Names: Schonfeld, Zach, author.
Title: How Coppola became Cage / Zach Schonfeld.
Description: New York, NY : Oxford University Press, 2024. |
Includes bibliographical references and index.
Identifiers: LCCN 2023021254 (print) | LCCN 2023021255 (ebook) |
ISBN 9780197556375 (hardback) | ISBN 9780197556399 (epub)
Subjects: LCSH: Cage, Nicolas, 1965– | Motion picture actors and actresses—United States—Biography. | LCGFT: Biographies.
Classification: LCC PN2287.C227 S36 2024 (print) | LCC PN2287.C227 (ebook) |
DDC 791 .4302/8092 [B]—dc23/eng/20230714
LC record available at https://lccn.loc.gov/2023021254
LC ebook record available at https://lccn.loc.gov/2023021255

DOI: 10.1093/oso/9780197556375.001.0001

Printed by Sheridan Books, Inc., United States of America

For my mom and dad, who instilled in me a love of movies ever since
The Silence of the Lambs

Contents

Author's Note

This book is drawn from more than 125 interviews with people directly involved in the making of these movies, all conducted by the author between May 2019 and December 2022. The book also incorporates quotes from archival sources, such as newspaper articles, magazine profiles, television interviews, and DVD commentary tracks. All quotes from original interviews are delivered in the present tense (i.e., "says," "recalls"). All quotes from preexisting sources are delivered in the past tense (i.e., "said," "recalled") and cited accordingly.

A portion of this book (Chapter 7) incorporates elements of the article "Truly Batshit: The Secret History of 'Vampire's Kiss,' the Craziest Nicolas Cage Movie of All Time," written and reported by the author and published by *The Ringer* in 2019.

Lastly, note that this book contains some significant spoilers pertaining to films that Nicolas Cage appeared in between 1982 and 1995.

Introduction

Nicolas Cage's first great performance took place on a school bus in the fourth grade. He was Nicky Coppola then, a skinny kid from a troubled family, but the character he was playing went by the name of Roy Richards. Or maybe Roy Wilkinson. The name changes depending on the telling, but the gist of the tale—a treasured chestnut of an origin story, which Cage offered up frequently to interviewers during the early years of his career—is always the same:

Cage was attending a school for juvenile delinquents after being expelled from elementary school for pranking his classmates by hiding bits of fried grasshoppers in egg-salad sandwiches.[1] On the bus to school, he was routinely beaten up by a belligerent bully, who forced Cage to hand over his Twinkies. One day, Cage grew tired of submitting to the bully's abuse. He devised a plan.

"I put on my brother's jeans and a pair of cowboy boots, slicked back my hair, and put on some shades," Cage told *Playboy* in a 1996 interview. "I got on the bus, went up to the bully, and told him I was Roy Wilkinson, Nicky Coppola's cousin. I said, 'If you mess with him again, I'm going to kick your ass.' He bought it, and the next day, when I got on the bus as Nicky Coppola, he left me alone."[2]

If this were a hacky Hollywood biopic, this would be the part of the screenplay where the words "Seven Years Later" flash onscreen and the narrative jumps ahead to Cage in early eighties garb, wandering into some audition. And sure, the story of ten-year-old Cage warding off a bully by sheer force of performance *does* seem like readymade fodder for an Aaron Sorkin script. (It really did happen, Cage insisted.)

And yet, for all intents and purposes, Cage's acting career began on that bus. Hamming it up for an audience of one, he sensed the power of transformation and absorbed the lessons that would power his ascent to stardom: most crucially, "that I could act and that there was power in being able to act."[3]

Perhaps even then, Cage, a sensitive young boy sponging up pop-culture influences and ephemera swirling around him, sensed that his superpower lay in his imagination. That giving a great performance meant you had to risk looking ridiculous—barking the whole alphabet, flipping over blackjack tables, screaming "The Hokey Pokey" at the top of your lungs. That if your own birth-given identity wasn't working out, you could discard it and carve out a better one.

Or, who knows, maybe he was just happy to keep his Twinkies.

* * *

Nicolas Cage was an unusual baby—or so said his father, a man with a flair for literary embellishment. "When he was born, he lifted his head, looking around like an old soul who wondered how he ever landed on this planet," August Coppola, the late literature professor who fathered and mostly raised Cage, once said. "He was impish, but besieged by nightmares."[4]

Any account of Nicolas Cage's early life is contractually bound to mention that the man was born under the sign of show business. His uncle—August's younger brother—is one of the world's most celebrated filmmakers, the director behind *The Godfather* and *Apocalypse Now*, Francis Ford Coppola; his aunt is Talia Shire, the actress best known as Connie in *The Godfather*; and his grandfather was the composer Carmine Coppola, whose 78s he heard on the phonograph as a child.[5]

Yet at the time Nicolas Kim Coppola was born in early 1964, none of his famous relatives had achieved much success. Francis was a budding twenty-three-year-old filmmaker being mentored by Roger Corman. Carmine was a long-struggling musician and composer who, despite having served a stint as first flute in the NBC Symphony Orchestra, was full of resentment and frustration.[6]

Cage's father, August—or Augie—was the star of the family, an academic whiz kid who taught literature at California State University in Cage's hometown of Long Beach and later became Dean of Creative Arts at San Francisco State University. August was popular with women—"He was Mr. Casanova," says his son Christopher—and his relationship with and eventual marriage to dancer and choreographer Joy Vogelsang produced three boys, of whom Cage was the youngest.

August Coppola was the kind of eccentric professor cherished by adventurous students and feared by dull ones. A book-jacket bio from 1978 described him as "a teacher, environmental artist, and creator of innovative educational programs."[7] After observing the way his fingers interacted with the texture of a pencil, he became obsessed with researching the dimensions of touch and nonverbal communication. "Then he locked himself up for three days in a room in complete darkness, just to feel around," says Christopher Coppola. This led to the Tactile Dome, an interactive exhibit at the Exploratorium in San Francisco, which the elder Coppola designed in 1971.[8]

Occasionally, August Coppola would begin courses with an exercise: He would ask his students to close their eyes, then open them and tell him what they saw. When some students said "Nothing," August would ask them to leave his class until they saw something.

The man took a similarly professorial approach to raising his three boys—Marc (b. 1958), Christopher (b. 1962), and Nicolas (b. 1964)—whose minds he stimulated with a steady diet of literature and great art. Cage described his father as an intimidating figure and the source of his passionate nature. "[H]e's an imposing-looking figure—white sideburns, a combination of Sean Connery and Beethoven," Cage once told *Playboy*. "When I was a kid, the other kids were seeing Disney and he was showing us movies like Fellini's *Juliet of the Spirits*. This was before video, so he would take us to the art-house cinemas."[9]

Imagination was encouraged in the household. During one Thanksgiving dinner, August handed his boys crayons and paper plates and required them to draw their meals.[10]

Cage's childhood took a turn for the traumatic around 1970, when his mother began suffering from severe mental illness. She was in and out of institutions for years, and August became the boys' primary caretaker. "My brother and I share the same pain, growing up with a sick mother. I had to grow up really fast, because he was a little bro, so I had to cook for him," says Christopher Coppola. "We had a very, very stressful childhood. And it wasn't my mom's fault. She was ill. My dad—great teacher, great thinker, but not the strongest father figure in terms of the nuts and bolts of what you do."

A lonely child haunted by fearsome nightmares and an absent mother, Cage became increasingly aware of his differences from others. "I was always shocked when I went to the doctor's office and they did my X ray and didn't find that I had eight more ribs than I should have or that my blood was the color green," he once told *Movieline*.[11]

Amid this trauma, Cage searched for transcendence and escape, and he found it in movies and television: *The Monkees*, *Captain Kangaroo*. One anecdote illustrates just how inevitable was his life's path: At age six, he fantasized about escaping into his television. "I wanted to get *into* the set," he told *Details*. "Amazing things happened there: Dinosaurs were inside the TV, and Jerry Lewis. I remember being on my living room floor on a red carpet, a round throw, and we had an oval-shaped '65 Zenith. . . . That was the reason I wanted to act, because I was so mystified by the tiny people."[12]

Cage's creativity emerged at a young age. Christopher Coppola recalls watching his brother sing in an elementary school talent show. "He went up and sang 'Yellow Submarine' all by himself a cappella," Christopher says, "but when he did the 'We all live in a yellow submarine' refrain, he would sing it with a really high voice like Jerry Lewis because he loved Jerry Lewis. And the whole frigging audience went nuts. They were jumping up and down, screaming. One little kid, second grade, on a stage, not afraid of anything."

Several years later, Christopher and Cage invented a homespun radio show called "Junkery Jack." Cage was always the guest speaker on the show. "Once he played a German scientist," says Christopher. "He played all these different characters. He was doing that at eleven, even earlier!"

Cage was fourteen when he saw Elia Kazan's *East of Eden* at the New Beverly Cinema. In interviews, he has described how James Dean's performance changed his life and made him want to be an actor. Before seeing the film adaptation of John Steinbeck's novel, the teenager liked making his friends laugh; now he was certain he wanted to be a dramatic actor, like Dean. He refused to be funny anymore. "Nothing affected me—no rock song, no classical music—the way Dean affected me in *Eden*," Cage later said. "It blew my mind. I was like, 'That's what I want to do.' "[13]

In the film, which came out in 1955, James Dean plays Cal, a disaffected youth vying for his stern, Bible-thumping father's love. At the story's climax, Cal attempts to give his father a large sum of money—which he earned by capitalizing on wartime food prices—in a desperate bid for the man's affection. When his father rejects the gift, regarding it as blood money, the boy is devastated. Dean weeps and clutches his character's father in a pained embrace; then he emits a guttural moan of sheer, bottomless anguish.

This was the scene that astonished fourteen-year-old Cage the most: the raw and heightened emotion; the deep desire for acknowledgment and love from a father, a desire Cage understood. "I was sitting in the audience crying along with him, really blubbering out some sobs," Cage told the *Baltimore Sun*. "Maybe I was on the outs with my father at that time. Maybe I was just overwhelmed by Dean's performance and how much his character wanted to get through to his father. But I realized that no other art form can engulf you the way movies can."[14]

There are traces of Dean's influence, particularly *East of Eden*, in many of Cage's early roles: the way he vacillates between rebellious disaffection and a searching vulnerability in *Valley Girl*; his wartime fervor in *Racing with the Moon* and contentious sparring with an abusive father in *Birdy*. The Dean fixation certainly explains Cage's attraction to playing rebels and outcasts, characters who tremble with a visceral sense of alienation and nonbelonging in polite society. Even *Moonstruck*—despite its vastly different tone—has curious echoes of *East of Eden*'s storyline: two brothers embroiled in an acrimonious relationship, one of whom falls for the other's fiancée.

It's strange that Cage was most influenced by an actor who died years before he was born. But this was also emblematic of a childhood under the tutelage of an academic father who cultivated in his sons an interest in literature and films from long ago, and of a career in which Cage has borrowed freely from Japanese Kabuki theater of the eighteenth century, silent cinema of the 1920s, and Jimmy Stewart performances from the 1940s alike.

Drawing on the distant past, trying to "experiment and fast-forward into the future of acting," as he put it in his 1996 Academy Award acceptance speech, Cage is always looking behind or ahead. He has always been out of step with the present. In interviews, he has sometimes been asked why he doesn't do theater. His answer: "I want a permanent record. I want to be there forever."

And if James Dean's performances are still swirling around the ether nearly seventy years later, who's to say people won't be trying to figure Cage out in 2093?

* * *

In 2018, I was interviewing Ethan Hawke for a *Newsweek* feature when Nicolas Cage came up in conversation.

Actually, I deliberately steered the conversation to Cage. A few years earlier, Hawke had generated some attention by stating that he believed Cage was the only actor since Marlon Brando who had "actually done anything new" with acting. I wanted to ask Hawke to expand on this thought, and as soon as I mentioned Cage's name, he began passionately soliloquizing.

"I think Nicolas Cage is one of the few people in the history of acting that has really changed [the form]," Hawke told me. "Stanislavski came up with this idea of naturalism and pursuing life as it is, moving away from a more performance-oriented Shakespearean style of singing roles. Brando and Lee Strasberg and the Group Theatre and all these people push it forward. Gene

Hackman and De Niro and Meryl Streep—we've all been dutifully falling in line. Except for Nick Cage.* He's doing something *else!*"[15]

Even Cage's detractors would have to concede Hawke's point: Cage *is* doing something else. For much of his forty-year career, the actor has instilled his performances with a woozy intensity that dissolves irony and indifference, transcends boundaries of good taste, elevates bad movies, and absorbs peculiar influences like a DustBuster gone berserk. Never settling for easy or predictable creative choices, Cage has made a career out of defying the accepted wisdom of what makes an acting performance "good" or "real."

You can call his style operatic, expressionistic, larger than life, or—to use a term Cage coined, reflecting a perceived connection between modern actors and the ancient shamans—"Nouveau Shamanic." But Cage is operating in a category of one. As Hawke told me, "I'm just locked into a kind of seventies style of truth-seeking. Nick comes at it from some other angle that's more mysterious to me."

That mystery was one of the animating questions inspiring this book: What is the source of the unknowable power that drives Cage whenever he is on camera? How did the shy, gawky teenager known as Nicolas Coppola transform himself into the wild-eyed, mesmerizing icon capable of lighting up the screen in films as varied and genre-spanning as *Moonstruck*, *Vampire's Kiss*, and *Face/Off*? How did he develop this unquenchable muscle for portraying misfits and wackos? When did he veer away from the more conventional path of his Brat Pack contemporaries? And just how far is he willing to go for a great performance?

My own interest in Cage began in 2004, when my mother took my brothers and me to see *National Treasure*, the dizzily fun, admittedly hokey adventure film that restored Cage's box-office standing after several years of creative risks (*Adaptation*, *Matchstick Men*) and expensive bombs (*Captain Corelli's Mandolin*, *Windtalkers*). I knew none of that at the time, of course. A teenage history buff, I was simply enthralled by the idea of secret codes on the Declaration of Independence leading to lost treasure. And Cage was good at embodying the obsessive zeal of a treasure hunter determined to solve 200-year-old secrets before Harvey Keitel tracks him down.

* A quick note on spelling: Throughout his career, Cage's shortened first name has varyingly been written as "Nic" or "Nick." While fans often use "Nic," Cage himself confirmed in a 2020 interview with *LA Weekly* that he spells it with a "k." In the interest of consistency, I use that spelling in this book.

My Cage appreciation deepened in high school, when a Coen brothers obsession led me to his zany performance in *Raising Arizona*, and then college, when I attended packed screenings of *Bad Lieutenant: Port of Call New Orleans* and *Face/Off* at the on-campus movie theater. Back then, conventional wisdom seemed to suggest that Cage was a lousy actor who had gotten lucky with some fluke performances, but *Face/Off* stunned me with its high-concept, identity-swapping acrobatics. I couldn't imagine any other actor convincingly portraying the madness that John Travolta might experience trapped inside of Cage's face. (If you ever have the chance to watch *Face/Off* with a theater full of stoned college kids, I recommend it.)

By then, Cage's erratic lifestyle and outrageous purchases had become a topic of fascination. Friends and I would trade links to news stories about Cage's extravagant purchases of foreign castles, or the white pyramid tomb he bought in New Orleans as a final resting place for his future afterlife, or the time he awoke to find a naked stranger eating a Fudgesicle in his bedroom. Cage inspires public fascination in part because he seems to live his daily life like he is living in a Nicolas Cage movie: Did Cage really pay $276,000 for a stolen dinosaur skull which he later had to return to Mongolia, or was that a character he played in a movie?[16] It can be hard to separate Cage's onscreen exploits from his outrageous off-screen life.

After college, I tumbled deeper down the Cage rabbit hole, particularly after I had a chance to interview the man himself for *Newsweek*, where I was working as a staff writer. Cage was promoting a since-forgotten horror thriller called *Pay the Ghost*. We spoke about that film and the unlikely cult appeal of 2006's *The Wicker Man* and the time Cage turned down a role in *The Lord of the Rings* franchise. The interview took place on Yom Kippur, and I was woozy and lightheaded after having fasted all day. (If you ever have the chance to interview Nicolas Cage on Yom Kippur, I do not recommend it.) But Cage was good-natured and thoughtful, even when I brought up a seemingly sore subject: the proliferation of internet memes involving his face.

During the years that followed, I spent much of my free time filling in holes in my Cage education: reading books about Cage, chipping away at the man's filmography, marveling at his go-for-broke performances in lesser-appreciated films like the war drama *Birdy*, the dark Martin Scorsese gem *Bringing Out the Dead*, or the con-man comedy *Matchstick Men*. Of course, I spent time watching his indefensibly bad ones, too, many of which have inscrutable one-word titles, like *Next* or *Rage* or *Arsenal*. But whenever Cage seemed to be falling too far into the straight-to-VOD cesspool, he would surprise us with something great, like 2018's psychedelic revenge spectacle *Mandy*.

The idea for this book grew out of two experiences toward the end of the decade. The first was that conversation with Ethan Hawke, which got me thinking about the roots of Cage's unorthodox approach to performance. The second was an article I wrote for *The Ringer* about my favorite Cage movie, the 1989 cult classic *Vampire's Kiss*, on the occasion of its thirtieth anniversary. In this film, Cage portrays a yuppie literary agent who goes insane and believes he is turning into a vampire; famously, Cage went to outrageous lengths, even eating a live cockroach, for the sake of the role.

For the piece, I tracked down a range of people who worked on *Vampire's Kiss*—the screenwriter, director, producers, cinematographer—and chronicled the untold story of the film's genesis and the remarkable fervor which Cage brought to the role. It became clear to me that the stories of Cage's commitment to the role—and his unlikely influences, such as German Expressionist cinema—were as captivating as what unfolds onscreen. And there seemed to be a dearth of reliable, well-sourced reporting separating fact from myth when it came to *Vampire's Kiss*, and the early years of Cage's career in general.

That's what seeded the idea of a book examining Cage's early career and rise to fame. Crucially, by researching *Vampire's Kiss*, I got to know that film's producer, Barbara Zitwer, who left the film industry to become a literary agent. Barbara encouraged me to expand my interest in Cage's early years into a book. This seemed like kismet: a movie in which Cage played a deranged literary agent connected me to an actual literary agent interested in a book on Cage. Without Barbara, *Vampire's Kiss* would not exist. And neither would this book.[†]

* * *

"Why write a book about Nicolas Cage's early career?"

I've been asked this question a lot. In focusing on Cage's early years—this book spans from his earliest performances, circa 1981, to his performance in 1995's *Leaving Las Vegas*—I am not examining the full, forty-year trajectory of his work. This is not a conventional biography. It does not encompass

[†] Full disclosure that Barbara Zitwer is both my agent and one of many sources quoted within the chapter about *Vampire's Kiss*. My *Ringer* article about *Vampire's Kiss*, upon which that chapter is based, was written and reported entirely before Barbara became my agent.

Cage's life story, nor does it linger on the man's colorful personal life, except where relevant to the performances.

Instead, I aim to investigate Cage's origin story: to tell the stories behind the films that first made him a star, and the ways he set about testing the limits and stretching the contours of that stardom. Zooming in affords me the luxury of depth: instead of writing a little bit about every Cage movie (he has more than 100 credits to his name, some woefully forgettable), I am exploring his early films in unprecedentedly rich detail and with direct insight from many of the directors, producers, and others who helped make them. The goal is to trace the actor's rise, his creative self-discovery, and the development of his rebellious approach toward acting.

Cage often refers to independent films as his "roots"; when asked to name his favorite entry in his filmography, he is far more likely to say *Vampire's Kiss* or *Pig* than *National Treasure*. It was in independent film where Cage first made his name and received the greatest degree of creative freedom. In this book, I focus on Cage's pivotal work in independent and mid-budget projects before he ascended to action-hero immortality.

The central focus is the story of how a young Nicolas Coppola *became* Cage. How the goofy teenager from *Fast Times at Ridgemont High* and *Valley Girl* transformed into an icon. How he simultaneously abdicated and benefited from his family name. How he threw himself into a misguided phase of Method-inspired masochism before rejecting the very pretense of cinematic realism. How he excelled at romance, drama, low-budget comedy, big-budget comedy, road-movie pastiche, and neo-noir all by age thirty. And what made him tick behind the scenes of his formative roles.

The concurrent goal is to unearth revealing and untold stories about Cage's early years and the movies that launched him. To that end, this book is rooted in original interviews with more than 125 people who worked with Cage during the first fifteen years of his career—from well-known filmmakers such as Mike Figgis, Amy Heckerling, and David Lynch, to fellow actors such as James Caan, Matthew Modine, Eric Stoltz, and Elisabeth Shue, to Cage's brother Christopher Coppola, who directed him in *Deadfall*. That list also includes many producers, casting directors, screenwriters, cinematographers, and crew members whose names are not famous but whose contributions to filmmaking are significant.

Cage himself respectfully declined, through a manager, to participate in this book; I will not speculate as to his reasons for turning down multiple interview requests. Instead, his perspective is represented by way of archival quotes. I have spent hundreds of hours combing through old newspaper, magazine, and television interviews with Cage (particularly interviews conducted during the era of this book) in order to accurately represent his insights into his early life and work.

Most of all, I've sought to demythologize Cage. As the internet has both heightened and complicated Cage's fame, the actor is too often reduced to a joke or viral phenomenon—he's the guy who screams "Not the bees!" in *The Wicker Man* and bellows the alphabet in *Vampire's Kiss*, his bulging face and flowing *Con Air* hair easy fodder for memes and sequin pillows and YouTube highlight reels. To skeptics, he's a punchline, a sentient self-parody; to fans, he's a genius or the "one true God"; either way, he's stripped of some essential humanity. In this book, I seek to peel away the layers of mythology—to portray Cage not as an icon or meme but simply as a person, a talented young actor finding his voice.

Perhaps the memes and GIFs rankle because they saddle Cage's appeal with a veneer of irony or insincerity. In reality, Cage's sincerity is a defining quality: sincerity in his love of film, and sincerity in how he pours himself into every character. "No one else can project inner trembling so effectively," Roger Ebert once wrote. "However improbable his character, he never winks at the audience. He is committed to the character with every atom and plays him as if he were him."[17]

In turn, these characters—the rogues' gallery of misfits and delinquents Cage has portrayed throughout his career—always seem so sincere in their desperate and dangerous yearnings for redemption. Take Ronny Cammareri, the hopeless romantic Cage played in 1987's *Moonstruck*. "We aren't here to make things perfect," Ronny implores Loretta in one of Cage's most beloved monologues. "The snowflakes are perfect. The stars are perfect. Not us. Not us. We are here to ruin ourselves and to break our hearts and love the wrong people and *die!*"

This is a shadow thesis for Cage's early performances. Like Ronny, Cage was willing to make a fool of himself for love. He was willing to ruin himself (or his reputation, or his trailer, or the life of an innocent cockroach) for the sake of a great performance.

Cage is never perfect. Rarely has he strived for perfection. But his failures are often more interesting than other actors' successes.

Now, I want you to come upstairs with me and get in my bed.

1

From Coppola to Cage

A floppy-haired teenager boxes an imaginary opponent at a beachside gym. He is shirtless and pumped full of testosterone, punching the air wildly while raving about *Rocky* and pretending to be Sylvester Stallone. "*Hit! Smash! Hit!*" he exclaims, narrating his punches to an unengaged friend. He wears nothing but jean shorts, and with every punch, his hair flops up toward the horizon line.

It doesn't look like a historic moment, but this is a muscular, seventeen-year-old Nicolas Cage—Nicolas Coppola, as he was known then—in his screen debut. The scene is from *The Best of Times*, a long-forgotten 1981 television pilot in which the young actor's talents are lost in the haze of an endearingly quaint sitcom glow.

The Best of Times aimed to be a wholesome variety show about the lives of eight teenagers, replete with chirpy theme music, peppy musical numbers, and scripted sketches about messy rooms, part-time jobs, and the trials of finding a date to the dance. A canned laugh track follows every punchline, and every cast member looks like they're at heightened risk of breaking into song at any moment—which occasionally they do, singing "9 to 5" while prancing around a carwash. (Baby-Cage struts around in overalls, holding a gas pump for a microphone.)

Everybody gets their start somewhere, and Cage got his in this proto-reality-show fever dream. He appeared in the pilot alongside a teenaged Crispin Glover (Cage's high school classmate), who stars as the All-American-Boy host, breaking the fourth wall and addressing viewers from his bedroom as his mother yells out of frame. Glover seems disturbingly gleeful in every scene, as if overjoyed by the thought that anybody would cast Crispin Glover of all people as a normal, well-adjusted teen.

"It was everybody's first job," says actress Jill Schoelen, who co-starred as Jill (the show used all the teens' real names). "There's a certain joy in just that experience alone."

* * *

The Best of Times was the brainchild of George Schlatter, an influential television producer and the man Cage has credited with first discovering him.[1] Schlatter made a name for himself in the late 1960s, when he created the zany sketch comedy show *Rowan & Martin's Laugh-In*. He gave Goldie Hawn her start on *Laugh-In*, and later discovered Robin Williams in a comedy club in 1977.[2] Schlatter's philosophy is that what television needs is more spontaneity, more happy accidents.

Around 1980, he conceived an idea for a humorous variety show centered on the world of teenagers. *The Best of Times* was intended to be "a reflection of all the things that were happening then, as seen through the eyes of a group of very talented young people," Schlatter says. He took it to a new production company, Carsey-Werner Productions, which had a deal with ABC, and hired his mentee, a television director named Don Mischer, to helm the pilot. "He described it as a 1980s-style teenage *Laugh-In* kind of thing," Mischer recalls. "With one-liners and short pops and all that."

In March 1981, they began auditioning teenage unknowns. "Nicolas came in, and he was an innocent seventeen-year-old guy that I think could bench-press a jeep," Schlatter says. "He was a delight!"

Schlatter sensed in Cage a raw talent combined with innocence. "At seventeen, he hadn't been in the arena long enough to be painted or formed or shaped. Everything we did with him was an adventure."

"He was gung-ho, eager to try anything," says Mischer. "I remember the first time we auditioned him and he started doing push-ups with one hand. It impressed us. And he had a real energy. He put his heart and soul into everything he did."

Cage got the part, and after some rehearsals at Schlatter's offices on Beverly Boulevard, the young cast filmed the pilot in April 1981. Cage quickly bonded with the other actors.

"Nick really wanted to do a great job. He was so earnest," recalls fellow cast member David Rambo. "Everybody was really green, with the exception of Julie Piekarski. But Nick was great. He was the class clown and leading man all in one. I remember early on he got the script and he looked at me in the rehearsal building and he said, 'David, how do I memorize all this? This is a lot!' "

Cage was among the youngest of the teen actors who landed a role, though with his ripped physique and enviable height, he didn't seem that way to the others. "He looked so mature," says Schoelen. "I just remember thinking, 'Oh, he's so much older-looking than all the other boys I knew in high school.' "

Evidently the writers agreed, since *The Best of Times* opted to present Cage (playing Crispin's best friend, Nick) as a buff, body-building surfer type. Little of the actor's brooding eccentricity comes through. In most of his appearances, he is shirtless, working out on the beach. In one sketch, he trains a dorky friend on how to attract girls, strutting across the sand and stroking his hair, like a *Playgirl* centerfold come to life.

Just one scene offers a glimpse of Cage's vulnerability and range. In a serious turn, the actor speaks directly to the camera, talking about the Reagan-era military build-up and his fears of being drafted. "I just hope we don't have a war," he admits, his boyish face crumbling in concern.

"We weren't using cue cards or anything," Mischer says. "He just spoke it. He spoke it because I think he felt it. To me, that was the thing that stood out the most in the show—hearing him honestly explain how fearful he was about the possibility of going to war."

"It wasn't fame that was driving Nick. It was artistry," says Rambo. "He wanted his work to be real and authentic. He didn't want anything fake. I think that's why he was so worried about the big monologue on the beach. There were a lot of performers in that cast, but Nick was a real artist."

* * *

Cage's pedigree was common knowledge among the cast of *The Best of Times*, who knew him as Nicolas Coppola, "but he didn't play that card," says Mischer. "He never pulled 'You know who my family is?' "

Nor was he eager to reveal his troubled home life. Because he lacked a car, Cage let David Rambo drive him to set one day. But he instructed Rambo to wait outside and steer clear of his father. "He said, 'He's not a very happy man. Don't come up. I'll come out,' " Rambo recalls.

During the shoot, Cage developed a lasting friendship with Crispin Glover. Both came from Hollywood families—Glover's father was the character actor Bruce Glover—but were eager to make it on their own terms. And Glover's wackiness began rubbing off on Cage.

"Crispin was a character," says Cage's high school classmate and friend David Kohan, the future co-creator of *Will & Grace*. "He drove a 1940s cab; he would dress on even the hottest days of summer in these big, wool, 1940s thrift-store suits. He had a crazy, nervous energy that he would just generate into this manic, comic persona, and he was also really sweet, really smart, and self-aware."

"Crispin probably was his closest friend," says Christopher Coppola. "Crispin was a very eccentric kid, and obviously a very eccentric actor and artist. I think there might have been a little competition about how eccentric one could be over the other. Maybe that's another reason why my brother really liked to push it."

* * *

After the shoot wrapped, Cage and his castmates celebrated at an Italian restaurant in Westwood. They all squeezed into a circular booth table, excited about their pilot. "We thought we'd be seeing each other for the rest of our lives," says Rambo. "And then we didn't."

Mischer describes *The Best of Times* as "way ahead of its time," and he may be right. The show's gestures toward unmediated realness—actors using their real names, talking to the audience—predated the rise of reality TV by a decade. "It mixed variety with reality, in a sense," Mischer says. When Glover excitedly addresses viewers from his bedroom, he looks like the distant cultural ancestor of a teenaged YouTuber.

But such elements juxtapose awkwardly with the show's reliance on sitcom punchlines, squeaky-clean one-liners, and hokey song-and-dance numbers. The show failed to tap into the Gen X zeitgeist the way the John Hughes classics of the mid-eighties would, a few years later. "It was just very, very clean-cut," says Schoelen. "Probably a little too clean-cut."

Cage himself rarely acknowledges his first professional gig. "My dear friend Crispin would hate it if I mention that job, because it was not good," he remarked in 1994. "It didn't get picked up, thank heavens."[3]

Maybe there's an alternate universe where *The Best of Times* took off and Cage and Glover spent the early eighties toiling as sitcom regulars before drifting off into anodyne obscurity. In reality, *The Best of Times* failed to generate much enthusiasm when it aired as an ABC special during the summer of 1981—one reviewer called it "simplistic to the point of inanity"—and it never got picked up as a series. Cage's first role was a bust.[4]

* * *

The Best of Times introduced Cage to the world as a muscle-popping, weight-lifting ladies' man, but that wasn't who he really was in high school. Sports gave him anxiety.[5] He was a misfit, a dreamer—a middle-class kid at a rich-kid school, Beverly Hills High, where his classmates included Glover, future *National Treasure* director Jon Turteltaub, and plenty of celebrity kids.

"Nick was a man in high school," says classmate David Kohan. "He was tall and strapping and had hair on his chest. But he was still a theater kid—he was not an athlete. There were jocks and nerds and brains and fuck-ups and surfers, like in *Fast Times at Ridgemont High*, and Nick definitely fell in the theater category. Room 181 was where all the theater-y people hung out, with their leg-warmers and their bandanas and their jazz shoes. That's where he felt at home, it seemed to me."

Kohan first observed Cage's eccentricity when the two were in an ancient history class together freshman year. The homework was to write a short paper on Cro-Magnon Man. "For most of us, the assignment was to write a dry, fact-based regurgitation of stuff we had learned. Nick wrote ten pages, at *least*, just from the perspective of Cro-Magnon Man waking up in the cave and what he saw," Kohan recalls. "I just filed it away, like: This is a person to note."

Cage was an outsider at the school from the start. At Beverly Hills High, most students came from one of four feeder schools. "The kids in those elementary schools all knew each other, so they came to Beverly with a full, solid social foundation," Kohan says. "Nick came from someplace else, God knows where—he just kind of showed up one day and he wasn't from one of the four elementary schools."

Moreover, Cage's home life was different from his new classmates'. Cage lived on the fringes of Beverly Hills, near a car dealership. August Coppola, now divorced from Cage's mother, moved the family there so his son could attend Beverly Hills High, but Cage felt inadequate at the school, surrounded by flashy displays of wealth.[6] Although he sometimes spent summers at his uncle's Napa Valley estate (tantalizing glimpses of a more lavish existence), he did not grow up with his uncle's riches. His father supported the family on a professor's salary. Cage did not even have a car—an emasculating indignity in Beverly Hills, and one which likely influenced his later passion for acquiring expensive sports cars—which meant he couldn't take girls on dates.[7]

"It was frustrating, because kids there had a lot of money, and I couldn't really compete," Cage recalled in a 1994 interview. "I was a nerd who took the bus to school while a kid driving a Ferrari was taking the girl I liked for a ride. I had a difficult time."[8]

"He seemed like a poor kid at Beverly," says Kohan. "He had a name that seemed to signify a lot of money, but he didn't seem like he had a lot of money."

Cage considered that acting might be one way to get the opposite sex to notice him. He later claimed that, at fifteen, he was walking down a street, frustrated that girls weren't paying attention to him. He thought to himself: "If I was Scott Baio, they would."[9]

Relations between Cage and his father were fraught during the actor's high school years, which spanned 1978 to 1982. August Coppola apparently suspected that Cage wasn't really his son—a lie Cage's mother had once told August during an argument—and treated the boy coldly as a result.[10]

At fifteen, Cage sought his father's approval by telling him he wanted to be a writer.[11] August took his sons' intellectual development seriously, devising entire curricula for them outside of school. "He set up a reading program for me at home," Cage recalled in 1985. "He'd give me a book a week, like *Siddhartha* or *The Loneliness of the Long-Distance Runner*, and tell me to write the missing chapter from the middle of the book." A voracious reader, Cage studied Latin and even took kung fu lessons at his father's encouragement.[12]

"He wanted me to become a writer," Cage later said, "because to him writing was—and I agree with him—the root of all creativity."[13]

But the more August tried to steer Cage toward writerly ambitions, the more his son was drawn to acting instead. No art form brought Cage the transcendence that film did. After seeing *East of Eden*, he was certain he wanted to be like James Dean—to be a serious actor, to make audiences feel things as deeply and profoundly as Dean did for him.

Cage's career path solidified when, in the middle of his high school years, August Coppola took an academic leave* and sent his youngest son to live with Uncle Francis in Northern California for a year. Cage has identified this as the moment his ambitions became motivated by spite. More attuned than ever to his uncle's success, he seethed with jealousy at the glitzier lifestyle his cousins enjoyed. "I was affected immensely by my uncle's riches," he recalled in 1994. "And it was like a golden key, you know? It made me a little bit angry, but in a positive way, because it made me want to go out there and get it for myself."[14]

During this stretch, Cage took a summer course in acting at the American Conservatory Theater in San Francisco.[15] When he returned to Beverly Hills High, he was determined to prove his worth. School plays (which, at Beverly, were scouting grounds for managers) became the beneficiary of his budding

* "He just took time off to write his novel," says Christopher Coppola of this period in his father's career. "He wasn't on sabbatical."

talent. Kohan recalls Cage as a talented and sometimes mischievous presence in their Theater Arts class: "It was fun goofing off, fucking around onstage, and trying to make each other laugh."

Cage's brash humor sometimes collided with the school's drama teacher, Andrew "Andy" Grenier, a Svengali-like figure who fancied himself a molder of creative minds. Grenier was an eccentric reared at the Herbert Berghof Studio in Greenwich Village. At Beverly, he hosted guest speakers like Milton Berle and once organized a school production of *Hello, Dolly!* with sets that cost $15,000 to build.[16]

Kohan recalls Cage pulling a sophomoric prank during a rehearsal for the 1981 school production of *The Crucible*. "I'm sure it was a dare," Kohan says, "but there's a line at the very end in *The Crucible* when Judge Danforth says, 'State your name, sir,' and the line is 'John Proctor, sir. Elizabeth Proctor is my wife.' And he gets out there and says, 'John Schmuck, sir. Elizabeth Schmuck is my wife.' Andy went ballistic on him. He said, 'Godammit, Coppola! You'll *never* be that good, *never!*' "

"He and Nick would occasionally have a *mano a mano* that would erupt," says singer-songwriter Maria McKee, another of Cage's friends at Beverly. "He was threatened by Nick."

As a denizen of what she calls the "far out, experimental drama department," McKee grew close with Cage and Glover. Her best friend became Cage's girlfriend; the four of them became a little gang, catching David Lynch films at the Nuart Theatre and hanging out at Damiano's Mr. Pizza. McKee recalls being struck by Cage's spontaneity. "When you hung out with him and Crispin, you never knew what was going to happen."

During their junior year, Cage and McKee were members of Grenier's Theater Arts class. For the class final, each student was required to perform two monologues: one classical and one contemporary. Cage performed a monologue from *Hamlet*, but he did not prepare a contemporary one. He told McKee he would just make it up as he went—and that's what he did.

"He improv-ed and made up this bizarre, stream-of-consciousness poetry monologue," McKee says. "And afterwards Andrew Grenier quizzed him on it—'So, what is this monologue?' 'Oh, it's a really obscure Russian playwright'—and he made up some name. 'I've never heard of it. When was it produced?' 'Oh, you know, the sixties.' He just totally winged it. It was fascinating. He pretended it was a real play."

Grenier had esoteric tastes of his own. In early February 1981, he directed a school production of *Fables Here and Then*, an obscure play written by

David Feldshuh (Tovah's brother). Cage and McKee appeared together as husband and wife.[17]

"We always had these far-out, experimental warm-ups before rehearsals, where we would go back to, like, slime and primordial being," McKee recalls. "And Nicolas would always try to get us all to break character. He would put his sweatshirt hood over his head until just a tiny part of his face was showing, and he would just make the most bizarre sounds. He was just so wild and hysterically funny."

* * *

Around 1980, during his junior year at Beverly Hills High, Nicolas Cage starred in a student film called *The Sniper*. The director was a classmate named Larry Law (then known as Larry James), an aspiring filmmaker who met Cage in English class. The two boys bonded over their interest in movies—Cage told Law about a strange Italian horror film he had seen called *Suspiria*—and they decided to collaborate.

Law liked making Super 8 movies with his friends. But he wanted to make war movies, and his friends looked like kids. "It just never looked convincing," Law says. "And Nick was the only person I knew that already looked like a man at that age. He was bigger, he was buff, he had stubble. I think I first used him in some tiny movie about an executioner with his shirt off and a hood on and an axe. He had a perfect body for that."

The Sniper—a more serious effort—came later. Set during the Irish Civil War, it was based on Liam O'Flaherty's short story of the same name and starred Cage as a sniper on a rooftop. According to Law, the film was shown as part of a Beverly student film contest and won several awards.

Cage acted in more traditional productions at Beverly, too. In October 1980, he had a small part in the school production of *Our Town* while his classmate Jon Turteltaub got the lead.[18] He landed a bigger role as Jud Fry in a May 1981 production of *Oklahoma!*, where he was spotted by Christopher Viores, a small-time Hollywood manager who signed Cage as his client. Viores had an eye for undeveloped talent, spotting potential clients waiting tables or acting in local plays. "He was the one in that play who had the most possibilities," Viores later recounted. "He had the talent. And we signed him."[19]

Then, in October 1981, Cage received raves for his performance in Beverly's fall play, *The Crucible*. "Nicolas Coppola's John Proctor, the central figure in the play, was also superb," wrote classmate Jack Weiss in the school paper. "Coppola presented a vivid, three-dimensional character."[20]

Cage seemed to be amassing confidence and swagger offstage, too. Larry Law remembers wandering around Westwood Village with school friends on the weekends. "We'd go with Nick, and he'd be wearing some leather jacket and snakeskin cowboy boots or something badass-looking. We didn't know what to do with women at the time, and he would just approach a beautiful woman that he fancied and ask her if she wanted to go to a museum."

Cage's eccentric impulses were contagious. One afternoon, he and Law were swimming at the Santa Monica State Beach. There were some girls nearby, and Cage was eager to make an impression. "With his hands, he just grabbed a fish that happened to be swimming around, a little four-inch fish," Law says. "He grabbed it and bit its head off. And then offered it to me, so I was obliged to take a bite out of the fish. That's how we became fish brothers."

* * *

In 1981, Cage finally bought himself a car, a Triumph Spitfire, using half the $5,000 salary he had received for *The Best of Times*. But he couldn't get the convertible registered; when he finally did, his father wouldn't let him drive it. Instead, Cage would sit in the parked car and imagine himself driving to the beach.[21]

August's disapproval of his son's ambitions only hardened Cage's determination. Once, Cage was so desperate to be taken seriously by his father that he told August he was the singer on Joe Jackson's hit song "Is She Really Going Out With Him?" "I needed to believe he believed in me," Cage later reflected. August bought it.[22]

On another occasion, he returned home late after auditioning for a play. The father–son confrontation that ensued is the stuff of a biopic writer's dreams. August was annoyed that the dishes hadn't been washed. In Cage's telling, his father told him, "Nicolas, you are never going to be an actor, so don't even bother to try." Cage exploded: "You're wrong. I am going to be an actor. You are going to wish you hadn't said that to me."[23]

By the winter of his senior year, Cage was fed up with rejection and fed up with Beverly Hills High. The final straw was a slight from the drama department. Cage's old friend, Kohan, beat him out for the part of Riff in their spring musical, *West Side Story*.

"You'd think I could play somebody in *West Side Story*, wouldn't you?" Cage told an interviewer in 1985. "Anyway, I didn't get cast, so I split."[24]

Cage took the proficiency exam and left school without graduating. He was eighteen.[†]

"He knew what he wanted to do," says Kohan. "At Beverly Hills High School, everybody graduates and goes on to college—that is just the assumption. The fact that he didn't made him a little bit of a rebel."

* * *

Fast Times at Ridgemont High was supposed to be Cage's big break. The mother of all high school sex comedies, that movie seemed to be everybody's big break, a kind of hormone-heavy incubation center for eighties movie stars. *Fast Times* helped establish the careers of Sean Penn, Jennifer Jason Leigh, Forest Whitaker, and Judge Reinhold, and it marked the feature film debut of future *Pulp Fiction* drug dealer Eric Stoltz.

It marked the film debut of Cage, too, though it feels like a technicality to say so: he appears onscreen for all of twenty to thirty seconds, delivers no real lines, and was credited as "Nicolas Coppola" for the second and last time.

Fast Times at Ridgemont High arrived in 1982, one of the historic transitional years for American cinema. Plenty of great movies came out in 1980 and 1981, but 1982 was when the cultural category of the "eighties movie" really began. It was the year the dream of the New Hollywood era collapsed in the flaming wreckage of Francis Ford Coppola's overpriced passion project *One from the Heart*. It was the year an aspiring filmmaker named John Hughes landed his first film credit (albeit as writer, not yet director). And it was a moment when teenagers were beginning to dictate, more than before, the kinds of movies that studios would make.

As the critic Dana Stevens writes, 1982 was "the dawn of a new golden age of what were then referred to, with some derision, as 'teen exploitation movies.'" Hit comedies like *Animal House* and *Caddyshack* had helped bring a raunchier sensibility to the box office, and younger audiences were ripe for targeting. The genre's commercial potential had been revealed by *Porky's*, a comedy about the "sexcapades" of teen boys in Florida, which became one of the highest grossing movies of 1982.

[†] It's not clear exactly when Cage left Beverly Hills High. In several interviews, he claimed to have left during his junior year because he didn't get the part in *West Side Story*. But Kohan says he left during his senior year, and newspaper listings confirm that *West Side Story* was the spring musical at Beverly in March 1982—Cage's senior year. See "High Steppers." *Los Angeles Times*, March 18, 1982, p. 7. Newspapers.com, https://www.newspapers.com/image/389046344. Accessed July 17, 2022.

Fast Times, with its frank depictions of horny high schoolers learning fellatio techniques and exploring sex with each other (and, in one unforgettable scene, themselves), soon followed. It seemed primed to be another teen exploitation bonanza but turned out to be much more: a quotable classic, an unexpected star-maker, and the rare film that neither elides nor glamorizes the awkwardness of early sexual experiences. For this reason—and the film's empathy with its female characters' discomfort—Stevens argues that it's "the polar opposite of exploitation."[25]

Fast Times at Ridgemont High is an ensemble comedy, chronicling a year in the lives of teenagers at a fictional California high school, including the sexually inexperienced Stacy (Jennifer Jason Leigh), her well-liked older brother Brad (Judge Reinhold), and the delinquent, perpetually stoned Jeff Spicoli (Sean Penn, lightening up for once). The screenplay was written by *Rolling Stone* journalist Cameron Crowe and based on his 1981 book. Crowe posed undercover for a year at a San Diego high school, pretending to be a student while secretly lapping up character ideas.

After writing the screenplay, Crowe offered the project to the director everybody associates with upbeat sex comedies: David Lynch. The *Eraserhead* director read the script and politely turned it down, correctly surmising that this wasn't his type of movie.[26] Crowe found a better fit in Amy Heckerling, a punk-rock fan from the Bronx who had recently graduated from the American Film Institute. He watched her thesis film, about a girl desperate to lose her virginity before turning twenty, and liked her sensibility.

At the time, teen movies weren't regarded with much respect, and Universal Studios was pressuring Crowe to include more grown-up characters in *Fast Times* so it would appeal to adults. He resisted. In Heckerling, he found someone who shared his vision of a movie entirely about young people and *for* young people, an unmediated glimpse of Southern Californian adolescence, where social status is defined by what car you drive and where you work at the mall. "It was like, here's that world they function in," Heckerling later reflected. "Here's what you grown-ups don't see."[27]

Cage was seventeen—an ideal SoCal specimen—and desperate for a breakout role when the movie entered production in 1981. He became a leading contender to play Brad Hamilton, the cocky high school senior who works a demoralizing fast-food job and fantasizes about his sister's attractive best friend. "I must have auditioned for that part 100 times and I thought I was going to get it," Cage recalled in a 2021 interview.[28]

So did casting director Don Phillips. "A lot of people read for that part," Phillips says. "But Nick was head and shoulders above all the Brads." Phillips interviewed Cage early on and was impressed with what he saw: a good-looking kid, tall, very polite. "At that time, he was Nick Coppola," says Phillips. "Of course, I think that's the reason he got in to see me, because he had no credits except in some play at Beverly Hills High."

Inexperience wasn't a problem. With minimal budget for cast salaries, Phillips, a casting guru later credited with launching the careers of Mary Steenburgen and Matthew McConaughey, was determined to find unknowns. "I saw something in Nick that was special. And I thought he could be the perfect Brad," Phillips says. "Brad was a little inexperienced with girls, with studies, with work. I saw that [Cage] had a lot of those qualities. He was new and he was young and he was ambitious."

"He wasn't a traditional, good-looking American boy," says Heckerling's then-assistant, Carrie Frazier. "But there was something that was so engaging and so soulful. I felt like he was somebody who could [play] wounded very easily."

Phillips told the film's producer, Art Linson, that they had found their Brad. The next step was for Cage to read for the part in front of Linson and Heckerling. "Nick came back and he read great," Phillips says. "He was wonderful. I said, 'He's the one! I'm right!' Amy kept hesitating." Cage returned and auditioned again. "Amy kept rejecting him. She really wanted Judge [Reinhold]," Phillips says.

Heckerling, however, maintains she wanted Cage, too. "There was no other contender. He was the only one I was considering," the director says. "There was something so lovable and goofy about him. The part was somebody that thinks they're hot shit, but you would sense the vulnerability. I felt like that was just there perfectly."

So, why didn't he get cast? Heckerling is deliberately vague on this question. She was told, "after seeing many people and calling back Nick repeatedly, that I couldn't use Nick." (She won't say who issued this decree or why.) "And then I was desperate," Heckerling adds. "I was like, Oh God, let's call in Judge." Reinhold was a friend. He lived in her building and was dating her close friend and assistant, Carrie Frazier. Like the stars of many era-defining high school movies to come, he was in his mid-twenties—practically a lifetime removed from high school—yet willing to play a teenager.

Cage had come within inches of his first big role, but despite Phillips's protests, Reinhold got the part. Heckerling would later say this was a practical decision: Cage was underage. "We wouldn't be able to work with him as many hours as we could with people that were eighteen and over," the director said in a 1999 featurette.[29] Today, though, the director maintains that Cage's age wasn't a factor because he misled them into thinking he was eighteen. (Cage has denied that he ever lied about his age.[30])

As a kind of consolation prize, Heckerling gave Cage a smaller role as "Brad's bud," a nameless side character who works alongside Brad in the fast-food joint (Figure 1.1). "He was wonderful," the director says. "He did want to do a bunch of improvs, and some of them were a little kooky. He'd say something, and the crew would look at each other like, 'What?' "

Eric Stoltz recalls messing around with Cage and other actors outside their makeshift trailers. "We were a bunch of young teenagers, most of us doing our very first movie," Stoltz says. "Just like high school, we settled into our various cliques. The lead actors were working most of the time. But us smaller roles, we spent a lot of our days sitting around the honeywagons. And while we were hanging out and waiting, we would take the piss out of each other and goof around."

The shoot proved formative for the film's stars, but it was miserable for Cage. Other actors mocked him for being a Coppola. The experience helped

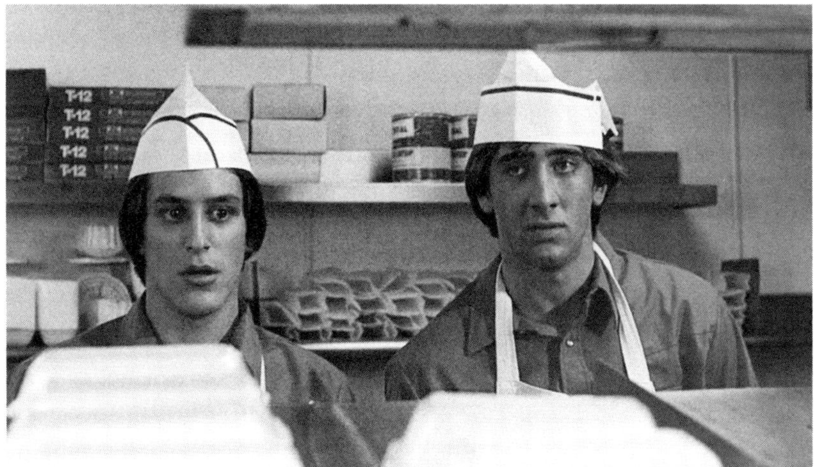

Figure 1.1. Nicolas Cage (then Nicolas Coppola) made his film debut in the raunchy teen classic *Fast Times at Ridgemont High* (1982, Universal Pictures). But instead of winning the lead role of Brad, for which he auditioned, he was cast as a nameless side character who works in a fast-food restaurant alongside him (played by Judge Reinhold).

motivate his decision to shed his troubled surname. "I was pretty much the nerd to everybody," Cage later told *Entertainment Weekly*. "I was the brunt of jokes because my name was still Coppola, so there'd be a congregation outside my trailer quoting lines from *Apocalypse Now*, like, 'I love the smell of Nicolas in the morning.'"[31]

In multiple interviews, he singled out Stoltz as a source of particularly merciless teasing.[32] Forty years later, Stoltz is surprised to learn that he's part of Cage's origin story, but he does have regrets.

"Nick was one of the younger ones," Stoltz says. "He was big for his age, and he was quite bold and animated. In the midst of all this hanging around, on occasion he would drop his uncle's name. Which isn't a crime, but it didn't feel very good. So we would give him guff about it until he stopped.

"I remember us all laughing and having a good time," Stoltz continues. "In retrospect, we were undoubtedly envious of his God-given Hollywood access. And he was probably a bit insecure behind all that bravado. But I certainly didn't have the maturity to understand any of that. So yeah, I did take part in the teasing and I'm sorry I did. I do hope that didn't cause him too much pain."

Stoltz and Cage never worked together again, but they both went on to star opposite Cher in Oscar-winning films. Stoltz played Cher's son; Cage played her lover.

* * *

Disappointingly, *Fast Times* didn't give Cage a chance to prove his worth. Most of his appearance (including a scene where his character sagely informs Brad, "Your sister's turning into a fox") was cut from the film.[33] In the theatrical version, his character is visible onscreen for mere seconds, most prominently in the background of a scene in which Brad disputes with an irate customer. Presumably, no one who went to the movies in the summer of 1982 took much notice of the blue-eyed fry cook lurking in a silly hat.[‡]

Studio executives disliked *Fast Times* and didn't plan to give it a wide release, thinking it was doomed to flop.[34] But with its alternately titillating and mortifying depictions of teen life, it became an unlikely sleeper hit, defining

‡ Cage can be briefly glimpsed in a few other scenes, if you squint. Early on, there's a quick shot of his character taping an "I AM A HOMO" sign to a classmate's back at school. Moments later, Cage high-fives Brad on his new 1960 Buick, then is seen standing next to Brad in the school gymnasium. See Lewandowski, Joey. "Fast Times at Ridgemont High (1982): Seven Shots of Cage [Joey's Review]." *The CageClub Podcast Network*, August 5, 2015, https://www.cageclub.me/fast-times-at-ridgemont-high-1982-seven-shots-of-cage-joeys-review/.

the nascent high school movie genre and launching half a dozen careers with it. "It's a favorite movie of mine, because of what I did for those kids," says Phillips, the casting director. "They were unknowns, all of 'em. I gave 'em a life."

Except for Cage, who was left behind, wondering if his only chance of a career in movies was his part-time job selling popcorn at the Fairfax Theatre.[35] "I would just stand in the back of the theater and dream," Cage told the *Los Angeles Times* in 2022. Just like in his childhood living room, Cage yearned to be *inside* the screen—not behind a concession stand.[36]

* * *

After the *Fast Times* shoot, Cage, still known as Nicolas Coppola, went to audition after audition. Nothing seemed to pan out.

It was a time of possibility and disappointment. There were close calls. At one point, he tried out for a low-budget horror movie called *Time Walker*, about an alien unleashed from King Tut's tomb. The casting director, Johanna Ray, happened to be the mother of Cage's former schoolmate. "The first thing he said to me was, 'I was in Continuation at Beverly Hills High with your son Eric,'" Ray says. "I don't know if you know what Continuation is. That is where . . ."—she pauses, laughs—"the bad kids go."

She had him read a scene. "I was totally blown away by him," Ray says. "In my mind, he had already got the lead role. But then, when I scheduled him to come in and meet the director, he had just gotten back from a skiing trip and he had broken his leg. His leg was in a huge cast and he couldn't come in."

The role went to someone else. The movie was a flop.

Often, Cage found that casting directors were more interested in asking him about his uncle's work than his own. "When I first started going to auditions and was still using my real name, it was obvious that people were thinking about twenty years of someone else's history," the actor recalled in 1988.[37] Having a name as prominent as Coppola, he once remarked, felt like having *U.S. Steel* stamped on his forehead.[38]

What Cage longed for was an identity of his own, a reputation not contingent on some casting director's opinion of *The Godfather*. He became frustrated by his inability to escape the shadow of his uncle's fame.

"You could see something had switched, where he was really fighting for his own identity," says Cage's high school friend E. G. Daily, who briefly studied acting with him at Peggy Feury's Loft Studio. "You could tell that he had this visceral need to conquer his own thing—not be enmeshed in the

Coppola [family], but create his own success. Which is what he did. That was the part of him that was just very strong and very quirky and able to manifest some pretty powerful things."

Cage's identity crisis was compounded by the fact that, although he resented being defined by his uncle's success, he was not above taking a role in his uncle's films. A moment of reckoning arrived in early 1982. Coppola was in preproduction for *The Outsiders*, his picturesque adaptation of S. E. Hinton's coming-of-age novel. Cage auditioned for a big role. According to one oft-repeated (and possibly apocryphal) story, he spent two weeks downing beers and staring at a photo of Charles Bronson to psych himself up for the part.[39]

The audition went badly; Cage's nerves got the better of him. He was rejected by his own uncle. Like Michael Corleone in *The Godfather Part II*, he did not take kindly to familial betrayal. He was distraught. "I was ready to forget acting," Cage told a newspaper in 1985. "I went into the hospital with everything wrong with me. Heart, lungs, liver, tonsils—they all went bad. I was ready to go to sea and become a novelist."[40]

Cage had friends who were going to Alaska and making good money working on crab boats. He resolved that he would try one more audition. If it didn't work out, he would give up and go live "a Melville-like existence at sea."[41]

But redemption arrived from the same source that had spurned him: Uncle Francis. By the spring of 1982, Coppola had decided to shoot a second Hinton adaptation, *Rumble Fish*, immediately after *The Outsiders*, retaining much of the same crew. Both films chronicled loss of innocence against the backdrop of street gangs in Tulsa, though stylistically they were day and night. As *Rumble Fish* entered lightning-speed preproduction, Cage got a call from Coppola asking if he would help "read" the actors auditioning at Coppola's Zoetrope Studios. "I would play the other characters while they did their auditions," he said in 1985. "The minute I wasn't me auditioning, I began to show them something."[42]

The next day, Cage was stunned to learn he had a supporting part in *Rumble Fish*. He had not even realized he was in consideration.

So, instead of going to sea, Cage flew to Tulsa in the summer of 1982 for his first major role. His identity crisis had not abated. Around the same time that he accepted the ultimate career boost from his uncle, he began considering the ultimate break with family.

* * *

Nepotism is ancient tradition in Hollywood, but Cage's desire to rid himself of a famous surname was unusual. Many of Cage's contemporaries were willing to embrace or at least passively accept the benefits of a prominent family name: Drew Barrymore, Laura Dern, Bridget Fonda, Charlie Sheen, and Ben Stiller, to name a few. A devout individualist, Cage calculated that he would rather fail on his own terms than succeed on the merits of his uncle's fame. "He said it was a bigger anchor than it was a benefit," says Chip Miller, a film producer who was friends with Cage in the 1980s.

Cage was unusually close with his maternal grandmother, Louise Vogelsang (affectionately known as "Divi"), who supported her grandson's talents with fierce enthusiasm. "She resented the Coppolas," says Christopher Coppola. In 1982, after demoralizing experiences on the sets of *Fast Times* and *Rumble Fish*, Cage decided to lose the Coppola name for good. It was Divi to whom he turned for guidance.[43]

The two sat down at Divi's table and discussed potential new monikers. "Nicolas Blue"? "Nicolas Faust"? Both were considered, then discarded. So was "Nicolas Vogel," a play on Cage's mother's surname, Vogelsang.

They considered "Nicolas Mascalzone"— an Italian phrase for "bad boy," his great-great-aunt's pet name for him—but that wasn't right either. He wanted something succinct, "a very simple, exotic name that would be unusual but that you could say in one syllable," as he later explained.[44]

That he found personal liberation in the name "Cage," a word that suggests enclosure and confinement, is an enduring irony of Cage lore. As with most things Cage, there's more meaning to the name than appears. In countless interviews, he has explained that he selected it as a tribute to his favorite comic-book character, Luke Cage. Cage loved comic books as a child. Around six, a scrawny, troubled child, he was haunted by intense nightmares and insomnia. He took comfort by retreating into what he called "an imaginary world where I could go to and be these other characters"—many inspired by his beloved comic-book characters.[45]

Yet occasionally Cage has mentioned a second inspiration for the name he chose: John Cage, the pioneering avant-garde composer whose work Cage's father admired.[46] Hence, Cage fashioned himself an identity defined by two distinct poles: one commercial, the other defiantly avant-garde. "I thought it was interesting you had both sides, you know, you have the popcorn side and the more thoughtful side," Cage said in a 2014 interview.[47]

In her book *National Treasure: Nicolas Cage*, author and Cage expert Lindsay Gibb argues that this duality is a lens for understanding Cage's entire career and body of work. He is forever vacillating between his Luke Cage and John Cage instincts, veering from action-movie bombast to art-film credibility and back. Much of Cage's career has been an attempt to strike a balance between the big-budget payouts, like *The Rock* or *Con Air*, and the more subdued, art-house achievements, from *Bringing Out the Dead* to *Pig*. What other actor would star in Werner Herzog's unhinged *Bad Lieutenant: Port of Call New Orleans* (2009) and low-grade Disney slop like *G-Force* (2009) in the same year?

This dichotomy is not absolute. As a child, he preferred the superheroes whose powers emerged from deep suffering.[48] In Cage's world, superhero gallantry has always been mingled with a certain vulnerability. This quality has sometimes interfered with Cage's commercial aspirations—most notably in the late nineties, when he was under contract to star in a $190-million Superman movie directed by Tim Burton. Cage planned to play the Man of Steel as "a beautiful freak," a character who, despite his superhuman strength, is not afraid to acknowledge his loneliness and alienation.[49] But the portrayal never happened. After sinking at least $30 million into the project, Warner Bros. grew nervous about its commercial prospects and pulled the plug.[§]

Crucially, Gibb observes, Cage is often drawn to roles that enable him to explore duality within the realm of a single film. In 2002's *Adaptation*, for instance, Cage simultaneously portrays two twin brothers, Donald and Charlie, screenwriters with vastly different sensibilities: one self-assured and eager to please commercial audiences, the other anxious and arty (a fictionalized version of the film's actual writer, Charlie Kaufman). "Here, Cage's duality—his popcorn side and his thoughtful side—is made flesh in Donald and Charlie," Gibb writes. Spike Jonze, who directed *Adaptation*, once said that directing Cage in each role felt like directing two different actors.[50]

The overarching, eternal duality is the Jekyll-vs.-Hyde divide between Cage's birth name and his stage name. By taking the name of a superhero, Cage was also living the superhero fantasy: parachuting out of his drab life into a more powerful, more potent persona. "I was a skinny, kind of weak kid who had a dream of being the Incredible Hulk," Cage said in a 1999 interview. "And on some minute level, I still use those fantasies to try to transform myself from that skinny little kid."[51]

[§] Cage reportedly still earned his full $20 million salary, thanks to an enviable pay-or-play contract.

Nicolas Coppola was the nerdy adolescent who couldn't get girls. As Nicolas Cage, he lived a wilder, freer existence, modeling himself after outlaws and rockers. Cage was the character who, at eighteen, smashed a ketchup bottle against the wall in a deli to impress a date.[52] Cage was the angst-ridden eccentric who spent Halloween 1984 getting a lizard tattoo on his shoulder blade in order to look more dangerous, then decided that the lizard was too serious-looking and added a top hat and cane.[53]

These are true stories, but they are also legends of Cage lore, examples of how Nicolas Cage is as much a character, a creation, as Sailor Ripley or Benjamin Gates. Cage understands this. In 1996, asked if he might reinstate his given name, he answered, "It's nice to have two names. One is *me* me, the other is an invention of me. Being Nicolas Cage, it's almost like an alter ego." Perhaps it was inevitable that Nicolas Cage would agree to play the ultimate Nicolas Cage character, a fictionalized version of himself, in the 2022 film *The Unbearable Weight of Massive Talent*. He was playing with the idea that his entire identity is a performance.

In 1982, of course, this alter ego was purely theoretical. "Nicolas Cage" was a blank canvas, a name which, unlike Coppola, carried no preexisting baggage. "When I altered my name," Cage later reflected, "it was like this weight came off me."[54]

It was a pivotal moment of creative self-actualization. Cage did not undergo a legal name change, but for all personal and professional purposes, he became Nicolas Cage by the early fall of 1982** and signed with his first talent agent, Ilene Feldman, under that name.

Members of the Coppola family were upset, and Cage's uncle was taken aback by the decision. "I think people were pissed. Even my dad was, even though he said, 'OK, I get it,'" says Christopher Coppola. "[Francis] was surprised and didn't understand why. . . . It didn't bother me. I get it. You do what you have to do for your art, and that's what he told me he had to do."

Vindication came faster than expected. As Cage told an interviewer in 1988, "I took the name Cage, and the first audition I did under that name was the best audition I'd ever had."[55]

** The exact date is unknown, but Cage seems to have changed his name sometime between the start of principal photography for *Rumble Fish* (July 1982) and auditions for *Valley Girl* (September or October).

2

Punk Romeo

"I'm gonna make you a star."

Those are the words filmmaker Martha Coolidge remembers saying to Nicolas Cage one fall day in 1982, when he auditioned for her film *Valley Girl*. They are not words one usually hears outside of cheesy rock biopics or meetings with overzealous drama teachers. That Coolidge used them suggested a fierce confidence in the as-yet-unproven talents of the goofy eighteen-year-old actor standing before her.

That Coolidge said it to Nicolas *Cage*, not Coppola, made all the difference to him: she did not know he was a Coppola.

An endearing teen rom-com about a girl from the San Fernando Valley who falls for a punk from Hollywood, much to the disapproval of her Valley-speakin' friends, *Valley Girl* was never meant to be an enduring classic. It was never meant to be *anything*, really, other than another high-school exploitation flick, shipped off to theaters like frozen burger patties ordered in bulk for the cafeteria. "It was sort of a B-movie back then," says co-star E. G. Daily, Cage's friend from high school, who played one of the girls in the Valley crew. "It wasn't trying to be a big film. I think that added to the magic. Nobody had expectations for it. And then it just blew up."

That it transcended such expectations is a testament to the sharp direction by Coolidge, an enthusiastic supporting cast, and an era-defining soundtrack—not to mention a certain eighteen-year-old hunk with a rebellious gleam in his eye. *Valley Girl* was pivotal for Cage not just because it was his first starring role and breakout performance, but because it was his entrance to a new identity, his first time carving out a taste of stardom on his own terms and under a new name. *Valley Girl* wound up establishing Cage's knack for portraying impulsive rebels, and it introduced audiences to his hangdog handsomeness and bad-boy romantic appeal.

But Cage's breakout role would not have existed without a concept initiated and financed by a savvy film executive named Tom Coleman. In the 1970s, Coleman founded the film distribution company Atlantic Releasing Corporation, which made a name for itself buying and distributing foreign art-house titles in the United States. It even nabbed an Oscar for a French drama called *Madame Rosa*. "Suddenly, we were the art kings," Coleman says. By the early 1980s, Atlantic Releasing was pumping along and making acquisitions, but the market was growing crowded. The company needed a way to distinguish itself. Coleman began developing some commercials films of his own, with the idea that the company could expand into a production house.

One morning in 1982, Coleman came into the office with a *Newsweek* article about the "Valley girl" phenomenon. Earlier that summer, the iconoclast musician Frank Zappa had scored an unlikely radio hit with "Valley Girl," a goofy tune that satirized the ditzy speech patterns of teenagers in the San Fernando Valley. Valley girls—or "Vals"—spoke to each other in "Valspeak," a distinctly Californian dialect peppered with gratuitous "likes" and "totallys" and exclamations like "I'm so sure!" (Basically, the female equivalent of the surfer-dude lingo Spicoli deploys in *Fast Times at Ridgemont High*.) Zappa's song featured his fourteen-year-old daughter, Moon Zappa, delivering a hysterical impression of the Valspeak she heard at parties and at the Sherman Oaks Galleria—"Like, oh my *God!*" "Encino is, like, so bitchin'!" "Gag me with a spoon!"—and it brought the Valley slang to national prominence. "It was sort of what we today call a meme," says the film's co-producer Andrew Lane.

By August, this youth phenomenon was being chronicled in *Newsweek*. "[A] bitchen new single from southern California has been riding the airwaves *to the max* this summer, providing parody-rocker Frank Zappa with his first mainstream hit and, more to the point, inspiring adolescents around the country to adopt a bizarre new kind of slang," wrote *Newsweek*'s Lynn Langway. Zappa's song had been intended to mock Valley girl vernacular, but its popularity seemed to flatter Vals and inspire legions of imitators. The magazine reported that "the usual spin-offs are whirling into stores: Val posters, beach towels, bumper stickers and T-shirts—even a 'Valley Dudes' record."[1]

Coleman's interest was piqued. The article made him realize that "Valley Girl" wasn't just a hit song; it was a cultural phenomenon happening in the Valley and in the larger world of the suburban Californian middle class. "It put it in a cultural perspective," Coleman says. "I walked in. I said, 'Boom. This is a movie.' "

Coleman's idea—a low-budget teen flick cashing in on the latest youth fad—wasn't the height of sophistication, but he assembled a quality team to see it through. He was friendly with a young producer/screenwriter named

Wayne Crawford, who had produced several independent features with his collaborator Andrew Lane. Coleman had been developing a movie with Crawford called *Miami Beach*, which was going nowhere. Coleman told him to forget *Miami Beach* and handed him the article about Valley girls. "I said, 'Drop what you're doing. I want it quick. Basic story. *Romeo and Juliet*.' Boom," Coleman recalls.

Crawford and Lane banged out a screenplay in ten days. Lane had a day job at Warner Bros., so they wrote at night. The working title was *Vals*. The concept? A star-crossed love story between a suburban Valley girl named Julie and a punk from the grittier side of town (namely, Hollywood), Randy. Julie must decide between the alluring bad boy and her preppy ex-boyfriend, Tommy. "There was just this whole Valley rivalry that seemed pretty ripe for stories," Lane says. "We immediately gravitated towards the *Romeo and Juliet* angle, using the Valley and the city as the Capulets and the Montagues."

The challenge was twofold: learning enough Valley slang to write authentic dialogue, then threading the slang into the script without rendering it incomprehensible. "Our strategy was to establish the Valspeak at the beginning of the movie and back off," Lane says. Indeed, it's only during the opening sequences—which show Julie and her friends hanging out at that holy nucleus of eighties teen movies, the shopping mall, giggling and saying things like "Totally gnarly!"—that the Valspeak is played up for laughs. It is a credit to the filmmaking that Julie becomes a complex character, her regional vernacular more an earnest character quirk than a cheap punchline. While Julie's friends are snobby and clique-minded—necessary to facilitate the movie's predictable lessons about embracing nonconformity and people from differing backgrounds—*Valley Girl* does not regard the subculture with the parodic scorn of Zappa's song.

Indeed, Martha Coolidge insisted on portraying these horny teenagers with nuance and sensitivity. "I never ever took it as a non-meaningful movie," Coolidge says. Although Crawford and Lane wrote and produced *Valley Girl*, they wanted to have a woman direct the film, since it was presented from Julie's perspective. Lane knew Coolidge socially and recommended her for the job.

In the early 1980s, the Connecticut-raised Coolidge was among a rising wave of talented female filmmakers, such as Penelope Spheeris and Amy Heckerling, who were straddling the line between independent and commercial filmmaking and working twice as hard to establish themselves in a male-dominated industry. Despite the success of Heckerling's *Fast Times at Ridgemont High*, studio heads remained reluctant to grant serious opportunities to female filmmakers. In interviews, Coolidge was frank about the difficulties of being taken seriously. "I spent twenty years getting to where I am, which is at the beginning of my career," she quipped in 1985.[2]

Her path was far from conventional. Coolidge studied film at New York University's Tisch School of the Arts, where she was warned in an entrance interview that a woman should not plan to be a director.[3] She spent much of the 1970s working as a documentary filmmaker in New York; her feature debut, *Not a Pretty Picture* (1976), was a profoundly original feminist statement that flitted between documentary and narrative form while interrogating Coolidge's own teenage experience with date rape.

Not a Pretty Picture caught the interest of Francis Ford Coppola, who was impressed enough that he hired her to be a director at his production company, Zoetrope, a kind of laboratory developing young filmmakers. "He said, 'I've looked at your early films and I think you are the woman we want to bring in as the Zoetrope woman. And I want you to do a film for us and develop it,'" Coolidge recalls.

The experience turned sour when Coolidge spent years at Zoetrope developing a rock & roll love story called *Photoplay*, only to find it mired in script conflicts and scrapped around the time *One from the Heart* plunged the company into financial turmoil. "It was terrible, because the promises had been so serious," Coolidge told the *New York Times* in 1983. "At Zoetrope, they said: 'We're not like the rest of the industry. We don't cancel projects.'"[4]

More disappointment followed when Coolidge left Zoetrope to direct a film called *City Girl*, which shut down when the production ran out of money. Peter Bogdanovich, famed director of *The Last Picture Show*, took an interest and put up his own money to pay for its completion, but *City Girl* never wound up being released. It was while she was still immersed in that heartbreak that Coolidge's luck began to change. She went to dinner with her friend Andrew Lane, and he told her about a new script he had written.

Lane spent an hour selling her on the project before Coolidge realized he wanted her to direct it.[5] "He said, 'The title is *Valley Girl*,' which of course made me practically throw up. I thought, 'Oh God, what does *that* mean?'" Coolidge recalls. "I took the script home, and much to my great pleasure, it was a good script! They took it seriously. It's funny, but they didn't laugh *at* the people. I came in and said, 'Look, it needs two scenes that are critical.' I said it needs falling in love—they just never showed it—and then breaking up. So I sat with Andy and Wayne and we wrote it, and then I had basically two weeks to prep the whole picture and get started shooting."

Coleman, ultimately credited as the film's executive producer, admits that he fought against hiring Coolidge. He considered her too inexperienced, too unproven—a common catch-22 for female directors. Then he got a call from Peter Bogdanovich, "who was a very big deal in those days," Coleman says. Bogdanovich gave him a pitch on Coolidge.

Coleman was eager to begin shooting in a matter of weeks, so he agreed to let Coolidge direct. "I gave her the first-time director speech: 'Do not try to direct this movie. Cover it! Just get your shots,'" Coleman recalls.

Accounts differ as to the terms of this agreement. Coolidge says that the studio made her promise to include at least four shots of naked breasts, to which she reluctantly agreed. "I said, 'That's great. Can I make the acting justify it?'" Coleman says he may have requested some nudity, presumably to compete with the success of *Porky's* and *Fast Times*, but "would never have gotten into the granular like that."

Valley Girl's budget was paltry and Coolidge's salary abysmal (Coleman says around $1,500, Coolidge says $5,000). Yet at thirty-six, she had finally gotten a big break. Coolidge found herself in the rare position of accepting a studio assignment while receiving considerable freedom to strengthen the script and bring her own feminist sensibility to the project. "I would not settle for cliché female characterizations," Coolidge later told author Christina Lane. "We pursued relationships which were deeper. And we took the material which was, for *Valley Girl*, simple, and we deepened it."[6]

* * *

When Cage auditioned for *Valley Girl* in the fall of 1982, he was eighteen and newly wrestling with the contradiction that would define the first few years of his career. He had just changed his name to set himself apart from Francis Ford Coppola, and yet he had accepted a supporting role in Coppola's *Rumble Fish*, all but ensuring that people would learn of his relation to the director. He didn't even have his own apartment: he was living with his brother Christopher behind their maternal grandparents' home, in a guest house built by their grandfather. Cage became sheepish about his pedigree and sensitive to charges of nepotism.

Given Coolidge's own connection to Coppola, one would reasonably assume that she deliberately gave the role to her former mentor's nephew. But the truth is more serendipitous: she had no idea who Cage was. She had met many members of the Coppola family during her time at Zoetrope, but never Cage.

Casting for *Valley Girl* occurred in the frenzied span of two weeks. "[The producers] were in a rush because they wanted to capitalize on the whole 'Valley Girl' thing," Coolidge says. "But it was also because it was going into winter, and this is a beach movie, in a way."

The director drew on her Zoetrope connections as she hastily cobbled together a cast and crew. Many of the young actors she auditioned had either appeared in or been considered for Coppola's *The Outsiders*; Colleen Camp and Frederic Forrest, cast as Julie's ex-hippie parents, had both appeared in *Apocalypse Now*. Lee Purcell, who played Julie's friend's attractive stepmother, signed on because she was friends with Camp, and because she had never worked with a female director before. "It was glorious to have a female director," Purcell says. "And somebody as skilled as Martha."

As for Julie, Coolidge selected Deborah Foreman, a twenty-year-old blonde from Texas who knew nothing about Valley girls, though she faked the accent convincingly.[7] "I'm the only one in the film that grew up in the Valley," says Heidi Holicker, who was waiting tables when she landed the part of Julie's best friend, Stacey. Holicker related to the regional rivalry; she remembered going to Zuma Beach as a teenager and seeing messages like "VAL GIRLS GO HOME" scrawled on the brick wall.

Nobody seemed right for the part of Randy, the sexy rebel from Hollywood. "We interviewed everybody in the Brat Pack," Coolidge says. She liked Judd Nelson, and even offered him the part, but he was unavailable. Others were all wrong. Sick of auditioning boring hunks, Coolidge remembers telling her casting director: "Look, please don't bring me any more pretty boys. I really need somebody who's quirky but attractive, and smart."

In a moment of frustration, Coolidge walked over to the reject pile. Lying on top was a striking headshot of a young Nicolas Cage. He looked goofy and handsome and manly: soulful eyes, floppy light brown hair, slashing eyebrows, chest hair poking out of his shirt. "I picked him up and I held him up. And I said, 'Bring me somebody who looks like *this*,'" Coolidge recalls.

The casting director obliged.[*] Cage came in for an interview, a tall, lanky kid with piercing blue eyes and not much to say. "He was very shy," Coolidge says. "That's not a bad sign for an actor. But he wouldn't talk about himself at

[*] Annette Benson, the casting director in question, disputes Coolidge's version of events. She does not remember anyone finding Cage's photo in a reject pile. "I didn't have a reject pile," Benson says. Instead, Benson says she was friendly with Cage's then-manager, Christopher Viores, and agent, Ilene Feldman, who told her, "You gotta meet Nick!" Benson in turn brought Cage in to read for the director and producers.

all. So then I said, 'Yes, I like him,' and the producers said, 'Is he good-looking enough?' The casting director and I looked at each other and said yes."

Cage returned for a more formal audition. He read opposite Foreman, and now Coolidge was confident he was the guy. It was one of the most exciting auditions she had ever seen.

"The first time he read, I thought Elvis Presley," says casting director Annette Benson, who noticed a certain depth in Cage's eyes. "I remember looking at Martha at the time. We had made eye contact, like, This guy is *good*."

Lane was impressed, too. Cage wasn't conventionally handsome, but he had presence. "We met dozens of young actors," the producer says. "Nick and Judd [Nelson] were the only two guys who could look a girl in the eye and say 'I want to fuck you' with sincerity. All the other kids were, 'Aw shucks, gee whiz.' Nick had real, genuine sexuality, which he was able to convey, radiate—it was real with him."

When Coolidge offered Cage the part, he said he needed to check his availability; he had already committed to a role in *Rumble Fish*—directed by one Francis Ford Coppola—which was in the midst of reshoots. Coolidge was still unaware the actor was himself a Coppola. Cage seemed to want to keep it that way. She put her arm around him and said, "Nick, look, I want to make you a star. I'm gonna make you a star. You're gonna be a star anyway, but why not be a star with me? I want you to be in this movie."

The director assured Cage that she would talk to Coppola and work out a shooting schedule that would accommodate both films. "I said, 'Look, Francis is like a relative of mine. I was years with him.' He got this strange look on his face," Coolidge says. "I say, 'Please, I'm going to call up Francis.' He doesn't say anything."

What happened next was a kind of Hollywood farce. Coolidge went to call Coppola, not knowing that the actor about whom she was calling was Coppola's own nephew. Coppola was occupied, so her call was answered by Doug Claybourne, a producer on *Rumble Fish*, who informed her that there wasn't anybody with the name Cage in his film. "This went on for twenty minutes," Coolidge says. "I'm saying, 'Look, he said he played Iago.'[†] He finally said, 'Well, I don't have anybody named Cage. But I do have somebody named Nick. It's Nick Coppola.' I was so embarrassed, oh God!"

[†] Cage's character in *Rumble Fish*, Smokey, is sometimes compared to *Othello*'s Iago because of his sneaky scheme to steal his best friend's girl.

Coolidge then realized whom she was dealing with. Having been assured that the conflict could be worked out, she went back and told Cage everything was fine: crisis averted. "But why didn't you tell me?" she added. Cage asked her not to tell anyone he was a Coppola.[8]

The anecdote illustrates just how desperate Cage was to escape the shadow of his family name. In subsequent years, he would emphasize to interviewers that Coolidge cast him without knowing of his dynastic background. "It's a little sad," wrote one journalist who interviewed Cage in 1986, "this boy's need to separate himself from his famous uncle, to convince us that Martha Coolidge cast Nicolas Cage without having any earthly idea that he was, in reality, Nicolas Coppola."[9]

The actor often claimed *Valley Girl* was the first audition he ever did as Nicolas Cage. That he landed the job felt like validation from on high, a rush of confidence that he could win roles on his own merits. "I felt like I was floating, like all this baggage was gone," Cage reflected in 1996.[10]

Yet Hollywood nepotism, like most forms of privilege, operates in less overt ways than one can see. Would Cage have landed an agent if not for his family connections? Would his headshot ever have wound up in Coolidge's pile in the first place? Would she have taken a chance on him had he not already been cast in *Rumble Fish*?

The twist here is that Cage's pedigree did help him secure the role in ways he probably never knew. Coleman, whose company financed *Valley Girl*, insists that he knew Cage was Coppola's nephew and only agreed to his hiring for that reason. "Frankly, that is what got him the job," Coleman says.

Most producers and studio heads interviewed for this book like to say they knew Cage was perfect for this or that role right away. Not Coleman. He remembers meeting Cage and dismissing him within five minutes. He freely admits he was the studio boss who tried to stop Coolidge, Crawford, and Lane from giving Cage his big break. "They were convinced this was the choice. Passionate about it," Coleman says. "I'm going, 'Oh my God, how are we getting this money back?' "

In an era when teenagers were often played by twenty-somethings, Coleman thought Cage—who really was eighteen—looked too old to play a high schooler. "The character is supposed to be seventeen," he says. "'To me, he looks like he's thirty years old. Look at the movie, the guy has got chest hair like a fifty-year-old Greek! I said, 'He's the strangest guy. Never looks anybody in the eye. Doesn't say anything!' "

Coleman was concerned about protecting his investment. He begged his producers to "just bring me a regular teen-perspective heartthrob." But Coolidge and the two producers were insistent: Cage was their star. "When I finally agreed to move forward with Nick, I said, 'Well, at least his name is Coppola. And that's gotta be worth some publicity,'" Coleman says. Instead of worrying about giving a lead role to a nobody, Coleman knew Cage's big secret: he wasn't really a nobody at all.

* * *

The first time the actor Cameron Dye spotted Nicolas Cage on the set of *Valley Girl*, Cage had a simple request: "Call me Randy."

No matter that the film was a hastily prepared low-budget endeavor. Cage was determined to try some of those Method techniques which until now he had only heard about secondhand. Staying in character, for instance. "He was of the school 'Call me Randy' and all," says Dye, whose character was named Fred. "I walked in the first day of rehearsal and he was like, '*Fred!*' 'Yeah! Randy?'" Unable to fully commit, Dye got around by addressing Cage with "hey man."

He and Cage had first met several months earlier, when both auditioned for *The Outsiders*. "I think we both recognized the outsider in each other, and that kind of drew us together," Dye says. Neither had landed a role, but now their careers were taking off in symmetry, cast as best friends Randy and Fred in *Valley Girl* (Figure 2.1). (Dye sported some of the film's most distinctive punk looks, with his funky necklaces and bright streaks of magenta-dyed hair.)

It was obvious that *Valley Girl* did not have the resources of a Coppola film. Sources place the budget at a paltry $350,000. Many crew members were unpaid volunteers. The entire shoot encompassed twenty-two days. "There was no money to make this movie," says Purcell. "All the wardrobe came out of our closets. It was very much a homegrown, grassroots kind of movie." Coolidge remembers fighting with Coleman just to get a second camera.

Yet for the young actors, the shoestring production afforded a certain looseness, a freedom to make the characters their own. "It was really like, 'Hey kids, let's put on a show,'" says Holicker. "That's one of the critical things that made that film work. Because we had no perks. We had no trailers. We had no dressing rooms. We had one makeup artist; we had one hair person for all of the cast."

Figure 2.1. Randy (Cage) and Fred (Cameron Dye) arrive in enemy territory: a Valley party. Cage became a star virtually overnight after playing a punk with a sensitive side in *Valley Girl* (1983, Atlantic Releasing), his first starring role.

The main cast first met at a table read, and then they had two or three weeks of rehearsal and prep time. With no budget for a rehearsal space, Cage and Deborah Foreman would run lines in the guest house where Holicker was living. Once or twice, Coolidge took the young actors dancing at nightclubs. She also sent them to a high school in the Valley for a day, encouraging them to hang around and meet real Valley teens.[11] (Her conclusion: nobody actually says "Gag me with a spoon.")

Cage, however, chose a more extreme method of bringing authenticity to his performance: he decided to sleep in his car throughout the shoot, apparently believing this would help him relate to the gritty background of his character, Randy. The choice was puzzling. While Julie's family and home life are extensively depicted in *Valley Girl,* Randy's home life is never shown; nothing suggests that he lives in a car. Like a bargain-bin Robert De Niro, Cage was nonetheless attracted to grand Method gestures. "He was into going deep," says Dye.

Cage's co-stars were impressed by this show of commitment. Coolidge was concerned. She warned him about the dangers of living in a car in Hollywood.

She also fretted about the logistical complications. "He wanted to be like his character. I said, 'You can't do that, Nick. If you do that, how do we call you if we change the call time?' Because we didn't have cell phones," Coolidge says. But Cage was insistent and said he would call in from pay phones. The episode was a harbinger of more intense Method stunts on subsequent films.

It also provided context for Cage's sometimes chilly behavior toward colleagues. Heidi Holicker, who played Stacey (the best friend who disapproves of Julie's romance with Randy), recalls that Cage was charming and sweet to her when hanging out off-set. While shooting, he seemed to flick a switch. "Once he was on set, he was Randy, Method actor, completely in character at all times. And Randy did not like Stacey," Holicker says. When they were about to film the scene in which Holicker's character unhappily rides in a car with Julie and the two punks, Cage began goading her, mockingly saying things like, "What's up, Stacey? What's wrong?" Holicker was taken aback. Then it clicked: "He was just in character! By the end of the night, I got it."

Whatever frustrations Cage's Method indulgences caused were far and few between. "He was filled with ideas," Coolidge adds. "I just found him incredible to work with."

Indeed, even at his most inexperienced, Cage was never shy about bringing his own flourishes to the script. When Randy mimics Julie's Valley slang as he storms off during their breakup scene? Cage's improvisation. When he crashes Julie and Tommy's date disguised in sunglasses and a chef's hat? Cage's idea. When Randy, gazing out at the Valley, pulls an edible wax whistle from his pocket and blows it like a forlorn harmonica? All Cage's idea. "He hadn't been in movies enough to know how many props you have to buy," Coolidge remembers. "So he bought one set of wax whistles and then ate part of it. And I cut!"

Throughout the shoot, Cage's Coppola heritage was an open secret, but cast and crew members were warned not to bug him about it. "The first day Nick was on set, we were all told, 'Don't mention the family,'" says Lee Purcell. "But it was so hard not to mention that. I came from nothing. Nowhere. Nobody. And he came from Hollywood royalty. I was really curious. But every time I would talk to him, I would just bite my tongue."

Fortunately, Purcell did not find Cage to be entitled or snooty. "[He was] just so polite. 'Yes ma'am, yes sir.' He was really raised well."

***

Cage struts into frame at the start of his first starring role, shirtless and wet, his chest hair shaved into a "V."[‡] The girls giggle and swoon from across the beach ("My God, what a hunk!"). Cage—well, Randy—drapes a towel over his shoulder and gazes back, his sensitive blue eyes making contact with Julie. Forget *Fast Times*. This is, for all intents and purposes, Cage's grand entrance on the silver screen.

Cage is rarely described as a great romantic lead, but in *Valley Girl* he embodies a breed of character which he would return to again and again throughout his early career: the forbidden love interest. Cage excelled at playing the bad boy, the corruptive influence, the more dangerous half of a star-crossed romance. He's shined as the impulsive ex-con in love with a cop (*Raising Arizona*), the tortured baker who tumbles into a forbidden romance with his brother's fiancée (*Moonstruck*), the lawless boyfriend whose girl's mother goes to homicidal lengths to end their union (*Wild at Heart*), the sex-crazed painter determined to seduce his best friend's wife (*Zandalee*). And what is *Leaving Las Vegas* if not a deeply dark, untenable romance? Even *Con Air* intersperses its shoot-'em-up sequences with tender moments in which hero Cameron Poe pines for his wife and calls her "my hummingbird."

The actor excelled at making love look dangerous. He delighted in portraying men who do crazy things for love, perhaps because Cage *was* a person who did crazy things for love. "I've made a romantic fool of myself many, many times, by performing grand gestures when I'm not wanted," Cage admitted in 1997.[12] This was a guy who, in his real life, went on a wild quest, chasing down rare treasures like a black orchid and J. D. Salinger's autograph, to win the hand of future wife Patricia Arquette.[13] As David Lynch once put it, "Nicolas Cage makes it cool to be in love."[14]

This pattern began with *Valley Girl*. Cage's sexiness in *Valley Girl* is intrinsically tied to his forbidden aura: he and Julie are pulled apart by class and social status, yet remain drawn to each other. It is not a wordy performance. Cage was shy in real life, and he is shy in the movie. But his expressive face fills in all the emotion we need. At the pivotal party where they first speak—she on her home turf, he a crudely dressed intruder on Val territory—Randy communicates his attraction with soft glances, his pensive blue eyes piercing across the room.

[‡] Cage was an unusually hairy teenager. Worried that he looked too old, Coolidge instructed him to shave his body hair. It was Cage's idea to shave his chest into a tight "V," modeled after the Superman logo.

Julie is transfixed. Already, Randy's sex appeal is taboo: Stacey (Holicker), who disapproves of Julie dating outside her social sphere, mutters "*Gross!*" and walks away, later dismissing the two guys as "hoods." From the beginning of his career, Cage is introduced to audiences as a bad influence, his James Dean idolization finally paying off.

While *Fast Times at Ridgemont High* keyed in on the awkwardness of early sexual experiences, *Valley Girl* pushes sex to the background, instead emphasizing the innocence and intoxication of first love—one of many ways it transcends its exploitation-movie origins. Cage balances rebel swagger with a touch of vulnerability. Surprising Julie in the bathroom, he asks her out and melts her uncertainties with brooding intensity and sustained eye contact.

From there, we get the usual teen romance beats: the shadow-lit first kiss at a Hollywood punk club, the parked-car make-out session, the blissful falling-in-love montage (set against a backdrop of neon Hollywood signs and Modern English's indelible 1983 hit, "I Melt with You"), the tearful breakup, the creative efforts to win back the girl. *Valley Girl* falls into some unfortunate eighties clichés (like portraying stalkerish behavior as quirky and romantic), but it cleverly defies others. Julie's parents, for instance, aren't your usual Reagan-era authoritarian scolds. They're caring, dorky ex-hippies who run a health-food store and reminisce about Woodstock.

Cage lights up every scene he's in with a goofy, youthful aura that he'd soon leave behind. He revels in playing the outsider, the misfit, a theme which he would *not* leave behind. In one scene, he wanders into the health-food store—jeans skintight, hair sticking up wildly—in search of Julie. He looks like he has just been beamed down from Mars. Yet he is also in full control of his romantic appeal.

"His emotional sensitivity was perfect," says Coolidge. "He understands it and he has the power. If you don't have the power at eighteen, you may have it five years later. But he did."

Cage and Foreman have an easy chemistry, and he plays off her bashful innocence (Figure 2.2). In truth, he really was in love with Foreman. "I had a massive crush on her, and I would write her poems. I wrote her one called *American Girl*," Cage admitted in a 2018 appearance at the Sundance Film Festival. "I adored her. So I didn't really have to act."[15]

The shoot was a whirlwind of hormones and romantic energy. "Everybody was making out with everybody," E. G. Daily says. So it's not surprising that some onscreen attractions crossed over into real life, nor surprising that

Figure 2.2. Cage was eighteen when he filmed *Valley Girl* (1983, Atlantic Releasing), but his chest hair and manly features made him look like a grown man. Director Martha Coolidge gave him the role because she wanted someone "quirky but attractive."

Cage (who candidly told an interviewer in 1985 that he became an actor "to get laid") took an interest in his co-star.[16] Coolidge says she learned that Cage and Foreman had become romantically involved near the end of the shoot, when they were filming the breakup scene. Coolidge didn't understand why Cage and Foreman were struggling with it—they had performed the same scene well during auditions—until she realized they had taken a sincere romantic interest in each other.

The director had to separate them and coach them individually. She told Foreman to imagine she was breaking up with someone else. And she gave Cage a note that he never forgot, and which influenced his subsequent performances for years to come: "Your character is sad but not defeated."[17]

For Cage, the film's goofy climax (in which Randy crashes Julie's prom, slugs his rival, and whisks her away to the euphoric tones of "I Melt with You") was a kind of fantasy fulfillment. He had been shy in high school. His own prom had been a disaster: he tried to kiss his date but became so nervous that he vomited all over his shoes and tuxedo.[18] Now he could distance himself not only from his uncle but also from his nerdy past identity. "The frustration that I felt in high school," he later admitted, "went right into the character of Randy."[19]

But whatever feelings he had for Foreman did not pan out into a relationship. "We absolutely were fond of each other, but Nick and I never dated," Foreman told the *New York Times* in 2020, when the release of a dismal *Valley Girl* remake reignited interest in the original. "After the film wrapped, he invited me up to his uncle's home in Northern California. And it was in that period of two or three days I knew we were not a couple."[20]

* * *

Cage's life changed quickly when *Valley Girl* came out. Perhaps more quickly than he realized.

Tom Coleman recalls an early screening at the Sherman Oaks Galleria, a popular Valley haunt. Although Atlantic Releasing planned to distribute the film, this was a sneak preview to test the waters and build buzz, maybe see if a big studio might want to pick it up. The movie played to a packed house, with studio reps lurking among the masses, and it played great. Coleman was happy: he had a movie, a real shot at making his money back. He was relieved to see that the audience seemed to like Cage.

Cage, though, missed the screening.

While driving home that night, Coleman saw an old Firebird on the side of the road, its hood up. To his surprise, he recognized the driver. "I go, 'Holy shit! That's Nick!'" Coleman immediately pulled over. There was Cage, standing next to the car, smoking a cigarette. "Totally low-key. Even though he's out in the middle of nowhere," Coleman says. "I go, 'Nick! It's Tom! We just screened *Valley Girl*!' And he goes, 'I know, man! I wanted to come see it! But it was sold out.'"

Coleman found this endearing: Cage didn't seem to realize that he didn't need to buy a ticket to his own movie. Stardom was new to him. "We had a whole roped-off section," Coleman says. "He didn't think to take advantage. He was standing in line to buy a ticket to his own premiere showing."

Valley Girl didn't seem primed to be a hit when it opened on the West Coast in April 1983. Atlantic Releasing, which distributed it themselves, marketed the film so cheaply that they didn't even have the correct stars on the movie poster: a shirtless Cage is standing beside a girl who is clearly not Foreman.[§] Coleman claims that Cage eagerly posed for the poster but Foreman refused; Coolidge says Foreman simply wanted to be paid for the poster and the company said no. (Foreman declined to be interviewed for this book.) Meanwhile, Coleman had to fend off a trademark-infringement suit from Frank Zappa, who unsuccessfully sued to block *Valley Girl*'s release.

The cast figured the movie would sink without a trace. "We thought, OK, it'll go straight-to-video or whatever," says Purcell.

Instead, *Valley Girl* became a modest hit, earning around $17 million—many times its measly budget—and turning Cage into a minor star overnight.[21] Suddenly, Lane was fielding calls from other producers, wondering who this kid was. "It seemed the word was out," Lane says. The film had beat *Rumble Fish* to release, which was just as well, since *Valley Girl* consummated Cage's years-long struggle to climb out from beneath the Coppola shadow.

Valley Girl got decent reviews, but it was young people, not critics, who crammed into theaters to see it. They were drawn by the Valspeak phenomenon, perhaps, or maybe the buzzy music component. Coolidge had spent several years immersed in rock clubs while prepping her aborted Zoetrope project. With *Valley Girl*, she put her knowledge of the scene to work, building a potent soundtrack steeped in the burgeoning new wave and post-punk of the era. "I Melt with You" became the de facto theme song after Coolidge heard it on the radio and, not knowing the title, sang it to her music supervisor. West Coast punk acts The Plimsouls and Josie Cotton also landed prominent cameos. Like many things about *Valley Girl*, the soundtrack is dated, but in a fun, pleasurable way.

One of the film's young fans was a twenty-year-old Quentin Tarantino. An aimless high school dropout at the time, he went to see it multiple times at a Redondo Beach movie theater called the Marina 3. One day he noticed that, while most movies lasted at the theater for one or two weeks, *Valley Girl* had been playing for five. He saw it again, in a screening full of young people laughing and cheering, some back for their second viewing. "That's when I realized, Oh! This movie really is talking to the subculture that it's making the movie for," Tarantino recalled in a 2019 podcast interview. "And it ended up playing there like nine weeks. People kept going to see it."[22]

[§] The girl on the poster is model Tina Theberge, who has a small role as Randy's ex-girlfriend Samantha. To be precise, Theberge says that the image is actually her face, but not her body. She was never informed that her image would be used for the poster. "I only knew when I saw it on the billboard above the restaurant where I worked," Theberge says. "I was very shocked."

Over time, Tarantino came to appreciate how deftly *Valley Girl* used music to capture a hyper-specific time and place. "The thing that's so special about *Valley Girl* is the music that plays is exactly the KROQ lineup when that KROQ new wave music just broke," the filmmaker said in the same interview. "They used it at that time! When you went and saw *Valley Girl*, those songs were still on the radio."[23] Tarantino drew on this influence by threading KHJ broadcasts throughout 2019's *Once Upon a Time . . . in Hollywood*, incorporating period-specific commercials and radio air checks to capture the aural ambience of 1969. That film and *Valley Girl* both contain intoxicating montages of neon signs around Hollywood, and they both spotlight cinemas advertising *Romeo and Juliet*—a subtle callback on Tarantino's part.

Lane remembers having dinner with Tarantino and his producer Lawrence Bender during the 1992 Cannes Film Festival, where *Reservoir Dogs* was being screened. "Quentin was sort of waxing poetic to me about *Valley Girl*," Lane recalls. "He said to me, 'Name any scene in the movie.' So I named a scene or two, and he knew the dialogue for pretty much any scene on demand. I don't know how much that speaks to his love of the movie or being a little maybe autistic about movies. I know he had an affectionate place in his heart for the movie."

Tarantino later cast Michael Bowen (who played Cage's preppy rival, Tommy) in three of his own movies. He has, however, never worked with Cage. "The two of us could really do something quite special," Cage told me in a 2015 interview. "But I remain positive and hopeful that it will eventually happen."[24]

* * *

Watching Cage's performance in *Valley Girl* forty years later is like seeing an egg hatch in slow motion. You can catch fleeting glimpses of so many Cage performances to come: his romantic glow opposite Foreman foreshadowing the operatic swoon of *Moonstruck*; his drunken, self-destructive spiral pointing the way to *Leaving Las Vegas*. His protests in the breakup scene are our first glimpse of "Cage rage"—those bellowing outbursts deployed everywhere from *Vampire's Kiss* to *The Wicker Man*—while the scene where Randy hides in the bathroom, conveying his inner monologue with nothing but mime-like facial contortions, hints at Cage's love of silent cinema.

Valley Girl was always an underdog, but its influence is undeniable. Along with *Fast Times at Ridgemont High*, it established the primacy of the suburban mall in the teen-movie canon and set a blueprint for the John Hughes classics of the mid-eighties and other, bigger-budgeted high school movies to come. Its immersion in the regional vernaculars and cliques of catty teens is embedded in the DNA of *Encino Man*, *Clueless*, *Mean Girls*, and countless others.

By the time it came to DVD in 2003, *Valley Girl* was a nostalgic throwback, its cult appeal solidified by years of regularly playing on television. Holicker often attends *Valley Girl* screenings and reunions, where fans of the movie will sometimes hug her and cry. Cage has maintained a certain affection for it, too. In 2018, he referred to it as "one of my best movies."[25]

All these years later, Coleman admits he was wrong about one thing: Cage was the right guy for the role.

"In hindsight, the fact that he wasn't the conventional type is pretty much the critical ingredient in that film that sets it apart from the many *My Tutors*** of the world," Coleman reflects. "There was a richness and uniqueness to the character you just didn't see."

** A widely panned 1983 sex comedy featuring Crispin Glover in his film debut.

3
Pulling Teeth

In his two starring roles of 1984, Nicolas Cage dove into Method acting with masochistic zeal. Drawing blood on set, inflicting bodily pain—all was fair game in his quest for De Niro–esque authenticity. Abandoning the new-wave peppiness of *Valley Girl* as eagerly as he had discarded the family name, Cage starred in two coming-of-age dramas released that year: both period pieces; both mid-budget dramas centered on young, male friendships in working-class neighborhoods. Most strikingly, both were wartime films—though not war films per se—exploring the effects of major American wars on the young men shipped off to die before they were old enough to vote.

Yet in tone and story, *Racing with the Moon* and *Birdy*—Cage's second and third starring roles—are as different as World War II and Vietnam. *Racing with the Moon* is a nostalgic coming-of-age film tinged with romance and boyish adventure. *Birdy*, the darker and more complex of the two, is a troubled exploration of war-borne trauma and mental illness and what it means when friendship is not enough to overcome psychological deterioration. Its production process plunged Cage into difficult questions about how much pain you must feel to play a man in pain.

Racing was the first movie Cage made after achieving some semblance of stardom. Change came quickly. The *Los Angeles Times* spotlighted him as "one of the young, hot new faces" of the summer of 1983. "It seems that he's being brought up for every project that is coming around these days," his agent, Ilene Feldman, told the newspaper.[1]

But Cage himself retreated from the spotlight after *Valley Girl*. He refused to do press, placing Feldman in the odd position of not only landing him roles but having to give interviews on his behalf. Instead of focusing on his performances, journalists began fixating on his unwillingness to talk. The *Los Angeles Times* profile, for instance, described Cage as a man of mystery:

> Cage, 19, does not give interviews . . . period. In the style of Robert De Niro, Al Pacino, Harrison Ford and Sean Penn, he "just wants to work," says his agent, Ilene Feldman.

In the same article, Feldman explained that Cage "doesn't acknowledge any of this new popularity" and chastised journalists for focusing on his family name: "He's not trying to capitalize on it, and it's extremely unfair when people mention it. When he graduated from Beverly Hills High School, he signed with our agency under the name Nicolas Cage." The average reader would have learned little about Cage's acting style (barely mentioned), but would have been informed that he had recently acquired a pet monitor lizard named Smokey, a detail Cage specifically instructed Feldman to mention.[2]

Cage's intensity and refusal to play the press game reminded journalists of Sean Penn for good reason. In 1983, he and Penn became close collaborators, cast as best friends in the period drama *Racing with the Moon*, which also featured Cage pal Crispin Glover in a small role.

It's a cliché to observe that onscreen dynamics between young actors sometimes cross over into real life, but you'd be hard-pressed to find a better case study than *Racing with the Moon*. Here is a movie in which Penn and Cage, who became close friends while shooting the film, play Hopper (Penn) and Nicky (Cage), close friends in 1943 small-town California, chasing girls and pondering their futures during the final weeks before they are shipped out to war (Figure 3.1). Hopper is the all-American boy, a gravedigger's son with a romantic side, sensible and smart. Nicky, who works with Hopper in a bowling alley, is more impulsive and volatile (as Cage certainly was offscreen). Elizabeth McGovern sweetly plays Hopper's love interest, Caddie, a beautiful and seemingly wealthy schoolmate who falls for his charms. By the time the movie hit theaters, Penn and McGovern were actually engaged.[3]

Such tenderhearted material was unusual for Cage. Saturated with a warm, nostalgic glow, *Racing with the Moon* began life as a script by a twenty-two-year-old screenwriter named Steve Kloves.* Kloves, who was not yet born during World War II, took influence from one of his favorite films, the similarly tender *Summer of '42*. His screenplay became the passion project of producer Alain Bernheim, who took it on and found a willing director in actor-turned-filmmaker Richard Benjamin.

Benjamin was struck by the script right away. "I sat down and read it. Immediately, when I finished it, I read it again," Benjamin says. "Then I called my agent and said, 'I love this thing. I want to do this.' It happened very fast."

* Yes, the same Steve Kloves who later achieved fame as the screenwriter behind most of the *Harry Potter* movies.

Figure 3.1. Sean Penn (left) and Cage bonded while starring in the coming-of-age drama *Racing with the Moon* (1984, Paramount Pictures). Penn's Method intensity and insistence on remaining in character rubbed off on Cage.

Benjamin liked the feeling it evoked—the small-town setting, the last moments of innocence before the war changed everything. And he liked the symbolic image of the boys chasing after a steam train, the same train that would take them to war.[4] Though he had been a successful actor for years, Benjamin had only just completed his first film as a director, the well-received 1982 comedy *My Favorite Year*. Now he had found his second, much sooner than expected.

Persuading a studio to finance it was not simple. Bernheim, the producer, pitched it to different studios without success. According to a 1983 *New York Times* account, "they considered it too 'soft' to make a profitable movie," a common concern in the dawning era of edgier teen movies like *Porky's* and Blockbuster franchises like *Star Wars*.[5] Hollywood was changing, and budgets were tightening for traditional, character-driven dramas.

Finally, Sherry Lansing, the president of production at 20th Century Fox, fell in love with the script and acquired it for Fox. That was the good news. The bad news was that, weeks later, in late 1982, Lansing left Fox. The new bosses were less excited about *Racing with the Moon* and wanted to cut its budget. "I said to them, 'Look. Can I take this somewhere else if you don't want to do this?'" Benjamin says.

Conveniently, Lansing had formed a new production company, Jaffe-Lansing Productions, based at Paramount. Lansing's company was willing to cover the necessary budget (around $6.5 million), which included expensive period sets, such as constructing a replica of a 1940s bowling alley on a soundstage. So *Racing with the Moon* transferred from Fox to Paramount less than two weeks before principal photography was scheduled to begin.[6]

The transition was hectic: Richard Benjamin had just gotten off a small flight to Mendocino County, California, where Fox construction crews were already building sets, when he got the news from producer Stanley Jaffe. "The picture was still at Fox while I was on the plane," Benjamin says. Upon arrival, he went to an airport phone booth. "It's Stanley on the phone. He's saying, 'We've made the deal. It's no longer a Fox picture, it's a Paramount film.' So I turn around and wave at the pilot on the plane and say, 'Don't go! I think I'm coming back.'"

He had already assembled a remarkable cast of emerging stars. Cage was among the last to be cast. Lansing was impressed with his abilities. "You saw this giant talent," she says, "but what I also saw was this incredibly nice human being who was dedicated to doing good work."

When Cage came in to audition, Benjamin could tell the actor had more than a name in common with the Nicky character. They shared a certain wildness, an attraction to danger. "Almost from the moment he walked through the door, I knew that [he] was right," Benjamin says. "Yes, they have to be actors and be good actors and all that. But for me, you cast for *who* they are. What they are. It's almost casting for their soul."

The timing was good. *Racing with the Moon* entered production in the spring of 1983, around the same time *Valley Girl* hit theaters and Cage's star power rose exponentially. When the latter film opened in Mendocino during the *Racing* shoot, Cage went to see it with a group that included Penn, McGovern, and the actress Shawn Schepps, who played Caddie's best friend. They were falling all over themselves, telling Cage how good he was, Schepps recalls.

"He was just so psyched," Schepps says. "He got to see himself in a movie theater."

* * *

Few actors who worked with Cage in the 1980s had a greater impact on his craft than Sean Penn. The two first met on *Fast Times at Ridgemont High*. Penn was the star. Cage would watch him work.[7]

Despite portraying a goofball—quotable stoner Jeff Spicoli—Penn approached the role with the hot-blooded seriousness one might bring to a Holocaust drama. He attempted to live as Spicoli for months, and he insisted on having the character's name on his trailer instead of his own.[8] His tendency to remain in character garnered him the nickname "Sean De Niro." At rehearsals, he would mess around and harass his co-stars the way he thought Spicoli would.[9] "Everybody had to call him Jeff, not Sean," recalls Amy Heckerling. "Some of the crew was like, 'Why do I have to make a chair that says Jeff on it?' I was like, 'Just do it.' "

Naturally, some of this influence rubbed off on Cage. "When studio heads were coming to the set to talk to Sean Penn, obviously whatever Sean is doing, others will say, 'What did he do? I wanna do that, too,' " Heckerling says.

By 1983, Penn was a star—a *Rolling Stone* cover declared him "the next James Dean"—and directors were willing to tolerate his brooding demeanor and Method quirks if it resulted in performances on par with *Fast Times*. On *Racing with the Moon*, he again insisted on being called by his character's name. "I remember he blew up a couple of times with the camera operator when he inadvertently called him Sean," says cinematographer John Bailey. Producer Stanley Jaffe joked to Lansing that if Penn ever played a mass murderer, real bodies would start turning up.[10]

Filmed on location in Mendocino County, where film crews recreated the storefronts of 1943, *Racing with the Moon* reunited Penn and Cage (four years Penn's junior, though Penn's baby-face made him look younger). They spent time studying how to manually set pins in a pre-automated bowling alley. The two quickly bonded. "Sean and Nicky were really close on this thing," says Benjamin. "They kind of are cut from the same place. Sean, too, was intuitive—a terrific actor, but also unpredictable. It comes out of some kind of physical and emotional loose place. That's what you're looking for."

Bailey, the cinematographer, recalls that Penn had a more internalized approach to his character. Cage was the more physical actor; it was somehow easier to photograph his movements. "There was something dance-like and balletic in the way he moved," Bailey says.

Inevitably, Penn's Method intensity began rubbing off on Cage like pot fumes from Spicoli's bedroom. A reporter for the *Los Angeles Times* visited the set and observed that Penn had forged deep bonds with both Cage and

McGovern. "All three were so absorbed in their roles that their on-camera and off-camera identities often seemed to merge," the journalist wrote. Only McGovern was willing to talk to the reporter, though Penn cut short the interview by banging on her trailer when he heard his name mentioned. "Despite pleas from their publicists, neither Penn nor Cage would step out of character long enough for an interview," the newspaper reported.[11]

As production began, Cage could be so impulsive that it was difficult to tell where he ended and his character began. During rehearsals, he inhabited Nicky's character with uncanny ease. "He was so loose and so intuitive and so unpredictable, in such a good way," Benjamin says. "That's exactly who that character is. He acts before he thinks it through. That's what causes everything to happen in the film. You didn't want to direct him or tell him how to do anything. That all came out of him."

It was during the 1983–1984 era that Cage, hungry for authenticity, first amassed a reputation for extreme methods bordering on masochism. Taking inspiration from reigning kings of taking-it-too-far like Robert De Niro, he would eagerly inflict pain or discomfort on himself if he thought it might help his performance.

Perhaps he was eager to one-up Penn with his own commitment to character. By his own account, Cage clashed with Benjamin when he tried drawing real blood as preparation for an emotionally intense scene. "I was looking for hyper-realism, that kind of visceral aura," Cage said in 1996. "And I took out a pocket knife and basically cut my arm open. I wanted the blood to flow on film." According to Cage's telling, the director objected and said, "Wrong movie, Nick, let's cool it."[12]

"Everybody heard about it after the fact," says Shawn Schepps, who did not witness the incident firsthand. "I know Richard Benjamin was horrified. Any adult would be horrified. Probably the Sean Penn shit was rubbing off on [Cage]. He was trying to be as intense as Sean. But no one can be as intense as Sean."

Curiously, Benjamin has no memory of the knife incident. "As far as I am concerned, this never happened," he tells me. (Duncan Henderson, the second AD, does remember it, but says "it wasn't a big issue because neither Nick or Richard Benjamin made it into one.")

Yet there were other times Cage was willing and eager to put himself in harm's way for the sake of a little excitement. Like the train, for instance. *Racing with the Moon* takes its title from Hopper and Nicky's favorite drunken pastime: hanging around train tracks as a speeding locomotive approaches, then racing alongside and grabbing onto the rail. Nicky is the reckless instigator. "We're drunk!" his friend protests as the train barrels toward them. "Who cares, I wanna race it," Nicky says, a wicked grin on his face.

That reckless camaraderie spilled over into the real-life antics of Cage and Penn. They wanted to shoot the sequence without stuntmen, and as the roaring train sped toward them (an antique steam engine that had been specially reassembled for the film), the two young actors reveled in the most dangerous game: waiting until the last possible moment to jump out of the train's path. "We got into this standoff—who was going to jump first?" Cage later told *Entertainment Weekly*.[13]

Naturally, Benjamin was terrified. "I had them on the train tracks. And there's no stopping that train!" he says. "Because of who they are, I thought: 'Ehh, this is really dangerous.' They stayed there longer than I would have liked. That was a little scary. But that was the characters, and that was also *them*. They didn't want any stunt people." Cage and Penn wanted to run and jump onto the moving train themselves, too—just like James Dean does at the beginning of *East of Eden*—but Benjamin insisted on stuntmen for that.[14]

Yet the qualities that made Benjamin nervous were the same that confirmed that Cage and Penn had been perfectly cast. "It was almost like when we weren't shooting, they *were* these two guys," the director says. "It's the way they work. It was really good for me and good for the film."

The film's best moments draw from the two actors' chemistry. Even when Hopper and Nicky's friendship is strained by the latter's recklessness and desperate need for money (his girlfriend is pregnant and he needs $150 for an abortion), they sink into an unspoken intimacy and understanding.

Cage's job is to bring a certain volatility to a film otherwise heavy on sentiment. It was the first time he displayed his knack for portraying unstable, explosive characters riven with potent combinations of machismo and torment. Everything we need to know about these boys is revealed in their attitudes toward the war. Hopper keeps his feelings locked away; he can't bring himself to attend funerals for fallen acquaintances or talk about the fact that he might not make it back for Caddie. Nicky is a blustering hothead who *only* talks about the war, boasting about his juvenile fantasies of "killing japs." Like many Cage characters, Nicky is a misfit in polite society; the war is a naïve outlet for his yearning for escape.

In one of the best scenes, Nicky is piss-drunk, babbling about some war movie, as he and Hopper stagger into a tattoo parlor. Nicky pulls up his shirt and demands an eagle tattoo "clear across my goddamn chest." Cage revels in the character's wild-eyed grandeur, bringing his signature intensity to these outbursts of patriotic bloodlust. "They were making some of that stuff up right then and there," Benjamin says of Nicky and Hopper's drunken banter before they enter the tattoo parlor.

The scene parallels a 1984 incident from Cage's real life, in which he got a tattoo of a dancing lizard etched on his shoulder as a symbol of his rebellion.[15] In some tellings, the tattoo was a revolt against his shirtless-stud image in *The Boy in Blue*, a way of signaling that he didn't want his muscular physique to overtake his acting abilities. (Or, as *Rolling Stone* put it: "He got the tattoo because he felt his soul was leaking out of his body and he figured the tattoo might burn it back in."[16]) Cage and his character both had a visceral need to immortalize their wild emotions in ink and flesh—except Nicky channels his rage into a sophomoric war fantasy, while Cage found an outlet for his pent-up energy in acting.

Cage is equally good during the pool-game scene, a high-stakes, *Hustler*-style sequence in which the actor displays the full gamut from brash cockiness to sweaty panic. And in a memorable sequence at the bowling alley, he gets a chance to show off his vocal chops. Nicky, clutching a broom as a microphone, croons along with the jazz standard "Tangerine," then gyrates wildly on the squeaky-clean floor like a lost Elvis progenitor. It's Cage's first time singing onscreen, a glimpse of the vintage showmanship he would later display in *Peggy Sue Got Married* and *Wild at Heart*.

Cage and Penn remained close long after *Racing with the Moon*. "They loved each other. They had secret codes and handshakes, secret sayings," says *Fast Times* casting director Don Phillips, who was a longtime friend of Penn. For years, Cage and Penn often seemed like character actors disguised in movie-star skin, high earners willing to work for scale if they believed in a movie enough. Both emerged in the thick of the Brat Pack, yet radiated a stubborn individualism that defied categorization. In interviews, Cage sometimes cited Penn as an inspirational figure.[17]

Their friendship soured in 1998, when Penn publicly criticized Cage's pivot to big-budget action blockbusters. By then, Cage had long since veered away from the realist tradition of screen acting that defined Penn's approach. "Nick Cage is no longer an actor," Penn told an interviewer. "He could be again, but now he's more like a . . . performer."[18] Cage was hurt by the remark and soon declared their friendship over.[19]

* * *

Racing with the Moon is not particularly well-remembered among Cage fans. There is a nostalgic melodrama to the film that's at odds with Cage's then-preference for punk-rock gestures. Maybe it's too soft. Maybe it's simply overshadowed by the performances that followed it.

But I'm willing to argue that *Racing with the Moon* is underrated. It's a warm, compelling drama—a bit sentimental, occasionally treacly, but elegantly shot and buoyed by three excellent performances pitched just between innocence and heartbreak. At its best, it's rich with period specificity: small, evocative glimpses of how totally the war pervaded daily life for young men well before they arrived overseas. And Cage is good at injecting some recklessness into the story.

For Richard Benjamin, who remains exceptionally proud of the film, *Racing with the Moon* was a labor of love. As the March 1984 release approached, all the ingredients seemed to be in place for success. The critical response was good. Vincent Canby, the *New York Times* critic, called it "an exceptionally appealing movie about subjects you may think you've already had enough of."[20] Roger Ebert, of the *Chicago Sun-Times*, was effusive. Both singled out Cage's performance for praise.[21]

Yet the film failed to connect with audiences. It was a kind of *Valley Girl* in reverse: despite established stars and a major studio backing, it sank at the box office, not quite recouping its $6.5 million budget. "I was heartbroken," says Sherry Lansing. "The movie gods didn't shine on us." In retrospect, *Racing with the Moon* was perhaps too traditional to woo young moviegoing audiences. "It doesn't have explosions," Lansing says. "It's a slice of life."

In 1984, though, there was an easier scapegoat for the film's failure: the stars simply refused to promote it. Their shunning of interviews became the story itself, a cautionary tale for film studios. "Penn, McGovern, and Cage are all notoriously publicity-shy," explained the *Los Angeles Times*, which quoted Lansing speaking on their behalf: "These particular performers feel that they fulfill their obligation to a film when they leave the set."[22]

Thus, promotional duties fell to the producers, Lansing and Stanley Jaffe, a less glamorous draw for media spots. Lansing appeared on *CBS Morning News*, *Good Morning America*, and the *Today Show*, and did a few joint interviews with Jaffe, but it wasn't enough to draw out moviegoers. "Let's face it: Stanley Jaffe and Sherry Lansing are not Elizabeth McGovern and Sean Penn," Lansing told the *Los Angeles Times*, hardly concealing her frustration. She estimated that the three actors' promotional moratorium would cut opening weekend gross by 30 percent.[23]

Publicists were exasperated. *People* magazine offered Penn and McGovern a cover story and photo shoot, but Penn said no, suspecting that the story would emphasize their engagement instead of the movie. Penn was wary of press, wary of questions about his "process," and wanted his performance to speak for itself.[24] McGovern granted one interview to the *New York Times*, but Cage followed Penn's lead, perhaps realizing that interviewers would likely ask about his uncle.

Cage remained reticent about interviews for years. In 1986, when he finally grew more comfortable with press, he all but disowned *Racing with the Moon*, expressing his growing discontent with anodyne expressions of sweetness. "Everybody said it was a nice little movie," Cage told *The Cable Guide*. "I didn't like it myself. I felt it was a Hallmark card, to tell you the truth. I would have made it a little more dangerous."

Bizarrely, he offered one proposed revision: "I would have made my character a circus clown going to war. That would have made it real dangerous. Clowns really freak me out."[25]

* * *

Rarely does an actor star in two films within the same year that speak to each other the way *Racing with the Moon* and *Birdy* do. *Racing with the Moon* is the before, and *Birdy* is the after. *Racing with the Moon* is the prewar fantasy, *Birdy* the postwar trauma. In the former, Cage plays wide-eyed and innocent, intoxicated by the escape and promise of war. In the latter, he plays broken—and nearly broke himself in the process.

Released at the end of 1984, nine months after *Racing*, *Birdy* is a film so meditative and strange, so haunting in its depiction of war-borne trauma, that it's a wonder it got made at all, much less with a $12 million budget and a well-regarded director.

Its story centers on two friends, Al Columbato and Birdy, growing up in Philadelphia during the 1960s, both from lower-middle-class families. Al, played with a cocksure sensitivity by Cage, is outgoing and interested in scoring with girls, yet has an abusive father to contend with. Birdy (Matthew Modine), his best friend, is quieter and more withdrawn. Birdy's great obsession is birds. He fantasizes about becoming one. He has an aviary in his bedroom, inhabited by two canaries, and instead of pursuing girls of his own species, he retreats to a bizarre, elaborate fantasyland in which he is the female bird's mate. His dreams of birdlike freedom become more real to him than the outside world.

Al indulges Birdy's obsession at first, the way close friends often do, but grows frustrated when Birdy's fantasies consume his life. Both Al and Birdy would like to fly away from their depressing surroundings, but Birdy is the only one who *literally* tries to fly, clad at one point in a feathered pigeon suit.

This is all told in flashbacks, interwoven into the film's nonlinear telling. The present narrative unfolds in a mental hospital after the boys return, both traumatized, albeit in different ways, from the Vietnam War. Al has narrowly survived a bomb explosion, his face disfigured and heavily bandaged. When an anguished Al mutters in voiceover, "We didn't know what we were getting into with this John Wayne shit, did we?" he could be speaking directly to the war-hungry kid Cage played a year earlier in *Racing with the Moon*.

Instead, Al speaks to Birdy. But now Birdy does not respond. After being missing in action for a month, Birdy returns from Vietnam in a mute, catatonic state. He is traumatized. He spends his days in a grim hospital room, silent and detached, perched in strange, birdlike positions, his body and mind seemingly engulfed by the spooky shadows that illuminate his cell. He appears to believe that he has become a bird.

Al visits him, desperate to bring his friend out of this psychosis. It's rare for Cage to play the more normal of two friends, but here he gives one of his most emotionally draining performances as a beaten-down kid clinging to the belief that companionship and shared memories can pull a friend out of debilitating mental illness.

Birdy began life as a peculiar, unexpectedly successful 1978 novel by a first-time author known as William Wharton. Wharton had fought and been disabled in World War II, and he set his novel during that war. British filmmaker Alan Parker read the book at his agent's urging but considered it impossible to adapt for the screen.[†] Parker, whose career had blossomed with the success of the nightmarish Turkish prison ordeal *Midnight Express*, sent a note to his longtime producer, Alan Marshall: "Great book. Don't know how to do it."[26]

The trouble was that Wharton's book lacked a conventional narrative flow. Instead, it flitted back and forth between both boys' perspectives, with lengthy stream-of-consciousness passages that took the reader deep into Birdy's troubled mind. "So much of the story happened inside the boy's head, and the poetry of the book was literary," Parker later told the *New York Times*. "To make it cinematic—I didn't know if I could make the jump."[27]

[†] For insight into Alan Parker's thought process, I've relied on his essay about the making of *Birdy*, published with the 2019 Blu-Ray release, as well as his comments in a 1984 *New York Times* article. Parker died in 2020.

Parker moved on and directed three other movies, including the celebrated musical *Fame*. He established himself as a versatile filmmaker whose movies spanned genres but seemed united by emotional intensity and evocative visuals. Meanwhile, two Los Angeles–based screenwriters, Jack Behr and Sandy Kroopf, became enamored with Wharton's novel. After their producer friend David Manson made an informal arrangement with Wharton's agent, they spent months pitching *Birdy* to bewildered studio heads. Finally, they interested the film division of A&M Records, which optioned the rights in 1982.

Behr and Kroopf wrote a screenplay, bringing a new structure to *Birdy* by fleshing out flashback scenes fleetingly mentioned by Al in the book and discarding many of the lengthy subconscious passages, which seemed "too novelistic," Kroopf says.

"We were mainly interested in the relationship between the characters and the friendship aspect," Kroopf says. While Wharton had inserted clues (missed by most readers) that Birdy and Al were secretly the same person—alter egos somehow split apart—Kroopf and Behr treated them as two distinct characters whose friendship becomes a through line.[28] (Neither writer had thought Birdy and Al were one person when they first read the book.)

The screenwriters also chose to modernize the story, setting it during the more recent Vietnam War rather than World War II. "[We felt] it would make it a little more relevant to people," says Kroopf.

Jonathan Demme was in talks to direct, but A&M wanted to move quickly and Demme was committed to 1984's *Swing Shift*. So, in 1983, the *Birdy* screenplay made its way back to Alan Parker. He had once thought the book unfilmable. After reading Kroopf and Behr's screenplay, he changed his mind. "I immediately liked what they had done. They had minimized the internalization inside Birdy's head and cunningly interwoven the past and present," Parker wrote.[29] Parker signed on to direct, found a willing distributor in TriStar Pictures, and soon began scouting locations in the decaying neighborhoods of Philadelphia—"a background of hopelessness that anyone would yearn to soar above," Parker thought.[30]

Casting took place in San Francisco, Philadelphia, and New York, where Cage spent the latter half of 1983 wreaking havoc on the set of *The Cotton Club*. Determined to find young actors capable of playing Al and Birdy—both difficult roles—Parker held open casting calls, sometimes auditioning more than a thousand actors in a single day. He soon became frustrated with "pseudo method-actor weirdos bringing in stuffed pigeons and photos of dead relatives for motivation."[31]

Cage and Matthew Modine, who was five years Cage's senior and had brothers who had served in the Navy during Vietnam, both auditioned to play Al.[32] Modine was shooting another film in Toronto when he got a call from Parker telling him he got the part of Birdy. He thought it must be a mistake. "I'm six-foot-three and I imagined Birdy as a very fragile, bird-like person," Modine says. "I'd recently finished the film *Vision Quest* and was in quite good shape. Not at all what I imagined was physically correct for Birdy."

Parker, though, saw something of Birdy in Modine's introverted, sensitive nature and held firm. "I tried to explain that I had auditioned for Al, and Parker just brushed me off saying, 'You're going to play Birdy and you're going to be great!' " Modine says.

After rejecting countless others (including Rob Lowe), the director settled on Cage to play Al.[33] "The first time he came in to read for me, he seemed so strong, so assured, that I was never sure if he could reveal the vulnerable side of his persona," Parker later wrote. "The more he came in, the more he looked like Al, who swaggered through life with big enough shoulders for the frail Birdy to lean on, but, deep down, he needed Birdy more than Birdy needed him."[34] (Parker, like Martha Coolidge, was oblivious to Cage's family name when casting him: "It was a very sensitive issue with him," the director told an interviewer in 1985.[35])

By now, Cage had a proven knack for portraying gritty, streetwise bad boys of the underclass (he did *Valley Girl*, *Rumble Fish*, and *Racing with the Moon* all in the span of a year), roles which appealed to him because they distanced him from the rich-kid-from-Hollywood-royalty image he loathed. *Birdy* would continue this trend. It would also provide Cage with the most emotionally demanding role of his young career.

* * *

When Matthew Modine met Cage for the first time, Cage asked him a question he found shocking: "Are you one of those actors that tries to mess the other actor up when you're off-camera doing a scene together?"

Modine was baffled. Who, he wondered, had Cage worked with who had behaved in such a way? "Suffice to say, the scenes Nick and I had were about telling the characters' truths," Modine says.

Indeed, so much of *Birdy* unfolds in a bare cell with only Modine and Cage (one mute, the other despondent) to hold the audience's interest that it was crucial for them to work closely together, Cage's bravado and frustration attuned to Modine's disassociation. Parker instructed the two actors to get to know each other before the shoot began.

So, in the spring of 1984, Modine, who lived in New York, flew west and spent a few days bonding with Cage. Modine was intrigued by Cage's celebrated family. Modine had grown up in a working-class city near the Mexican border, the youngest of seven kids. "My uncle wasn't one of the most respected filmmakers alive. Having that type of fame so close to you has an impact," Modine says.

Yet the two actors hit it off. Modine took Cage to a popular burger spot called Fatburger, after which Cage took Modine to one of his L.A. haunts, Pink's Hot Dogs. "We both ate way too much and felt sick," Modine says. "It was funny." They drove to the Santa Monica Pier, reveling in the amusement park attractions and posing in the photo booths. "We sent a strip of the photos to Parker to prove that we were getting to know each other," Modine says.

In one image, Cage is grinning goofily, his floppy hair long and parted in the middle. Modine stands behind him in a button-down shirt, a more reserved smile on his face.

For both boys, the difficult work lay ahead. Cage had arduous quantities of dialogue to memorize, including Al's desperate monologues in Birdy's cell. Parker, a notoriously exacting director, had no patience for actors who didn't know their lines.[‡]

"Parker would rip you apart as an actor," says crew member Jon Guterres, who worked on *Birdy* as a camera grip. "He'd rip anybody apart. We always said, if you have an opportunity to contribute to an Alan Parker movie, don't fuck up. Because the English have a real tricky way of making you feel like shit, and remaining proper." (Modine puts it more diplomatically: "He was quite tough on set, and this was only out of his love and passion to create the best art he could.")

Cage could memorize his lines without trouble, but trouble was what he often caused when not delivering lines. Parker heard stories about him trashing his trailer during *The Cotton Club*. "His reputation kind of preceded him," says Kristi Zea, who designed costumes for *Birdy*. "Alan was nervous

‡ Case in point: Danny Glover had a small role as a bird breeder, but Parker cut the scene because Glover couldn't remember his lines. "I'd never seen an actor die before," says Jon Guterres. "He walked off the set and Parker said, 'I don't know whether to make him cry or be easy on him.'"

about him. And apparently said to him, 'If you trash your trailer, you're out of here.'"

On *Birdy*, though, Cage turned his destructive energy inward. He approached the role with a kind of monastic focus. To study his lines, he dismantled the script and taped his monologues to the wall of his hotel room.[36]

Modine had the opposite challenge: portraying Birdy for major stretches of the film *without* language, playing a character whose trauma is profound but never expressed in words. While Cage became obsessed with remaining in character at all times, inhabiting Al in the physical realm, Modine took a more spiritual tack.

"I never imagined myself playing a role like Birdy," Modine says. "As we got closer and closer to filming, I got on my hands and knees and asked for all the women, men, and children that had been misunderstood, abused, and beat up by life to help me play this role. I'm not religious, and I won't lie—I felt like a thousand souls lifted me up and guided me on my journey."

* * *

On May 8, Parker and the two stars began a week of rehearsals at a church hall in Philadelphia. Principal photography began a week later, with most of the flashback sequences being filmed in Philadelphia and along the Jersey Shore. Shooting sequentially, Parker believed, might help Cage and Modine absorb their character arcs.[37]

Crew members noticed that Cage stayed in character and eschewed casual chit-chat. "He had a bit of madness in him, which suited the character," says cinematographer Michael Seresin. "When I first met him, his reactions were a little bit slow. I would say, 'Very nice to meet you, how're you doing?' And there's like a beat before he would say, '. . . Yeah.'"

Both actors came to set well-prepared—a saving grace, given the numerous technical challenges Parker had to navigate. First was the matter of shooting with live canaries, eighty of which had been trained specially for the film and happened to give Parker the jitters. "Alan had a phobia about birds," says Seresin, who had worked with Parker since the filmmaker's early days directing TV commercials. "I said, 'What the fuck are you doing a film about birds for?' He said, 'Oh, I can't stand them.'"

More onerous was the use of the Skycam, a newly invented cable-suspended camera system allowing Parker to shoot a sweeping aerial shot in which Birdy imagines himself to be a bird. Much was made in the press about *Birdy* being the first movie to use the Skycam. In reality, the untested technology caused so many technical headaches that Parker took to calling it "Sky-Scam."

When the shoot resumed later that summer in Northern California—most of the postwar scenes were shot at the Agnews Developmental Center, a historic psychiatric hospital in Santa Clara—Cage seemed like a different person. In Philadelphia, he had been playing a kid: horny and eager, bounding with life. Now he was playing a wounded veteran, reeling from the horrors of war. Parker observed that the actor "bore no resemblance to the cocky youth who swaggered through the streets" earlier in the shoot. "As we tackled the scenes in the cell, you could see Nick/Al's vitality drain from him as it was transferred, almost sucked in, by Birdy."[38]

"Once we began filming the hospital scenes, post-Vietnam, Nick and I pretty much only communicated as our characters," Modine says. "That meant me silently existing inside of my/Birdy's mind and body, and Nick/Al trying to encourage me out."

Cage disappeared inside of the character. He became obsessed with trying to feel Al's anguish. Even his face looked different: two teeth were missing. Cage told people that he had the teeth pulled so he could absorb the pain of an injured vet. "If he'd been given this job six months before and there was a war on, he would have gone off to the war—so he could live the part," says Seresin.[39]

Cage's determination to remain in character absorbed his life for months. His boldest sacrifice was deciding to wear Al's bandages on his face full-time, on and off the set, as though he had really been wounded in Vietnam (Figure 3.2). "I could have taken those bandages off, but I didn't," Cage said in 1984. "I left them on for five weeks. I slept in them. I'd wake myself up in the middle of the night and say, 'Don't sleep on that side; that's the side that was hurt.' "[40]

He became conscious of the stares he got in public, such as teenage girls giggling at him, which paralleled the ones his character experiences on a train.[41] He also lost around fifteen pounds, in part because the bandages made it difficult for him to eat.[42] Cage determined not to even look at his unencumbered face: "Each morning as fresh bandages were applied Nick would keep his eyes closed," Parker wrote.[43]

British directors sometimes bristle at the more ego-driven American style of Method acting, but Parker was respectful of Cage's sacrifice and considered it a brave decision. What really mattered was that Cage came well-prepared for his dialogue and didn't stray from the script; "too often," Parker wrote,

Figure 3.2. While playing a wounded Vietnam veteran in *Birdy* (1984, Tri-Star Pictures), Cage was so determined to emulate Method techniques that he insisted on wearing his facial bandages continuously during the five-week stretch of the shoot.

"young American actors use rambling improvisation as a smokescreen for not knowing their lines." Cage never had that problem.[44]

Others, though, were vexed by Cage's stubbornness. "I remember the makeup lady was pulling her hair out, because he refused [to remove the bandages]," says Zea, the costume designer. "He just wanted this thing to stay on. It was a tough thing for her to keep continuity going. But obviously, for him, it really helped."

Cage's masochistic indulgences were extreme, but they can be understood as aspirational exertions of an era in which Method acting (or what the press sometimes misunderstood to be Method acting) was prominently glamorized by Hollywood legends. This was a perversion of the concept. In its original form, Method acting grew out of the teachings of Russian actor and theater director Konstantin Stanislavski (1863–1938) and his "system" of training actors. Rising to prominence in prerevolutionary Russia, Stanislavski was preoccupied with a quest for theatrical truth. His dilemma, essentially, was this: How could an actor project inner truth while surrounded by the inherent artifice of a play?

Stanislavski arrived at his own "system," in which actors were trained to internalize their characters' emotions and respond "as if" the fictional occurrences of the play were real. Feigning the character's emotions wasn't enough. As Stanislavski wrote (speaking through the voice of Tortsov, a fictionalized version of himself) in his book *An Actor Prepares*: "In our art you must live the part every moment that you are playing it, and every time."[45]

Stanislavski's teachings were introduced to American film actors by way of prominent instructors like Lee Strasberg and Stella Adler. By the 1960s, Method acting, or "the Method," was heavily associated with Strasberg, whose teachings advanced Stanislavski's pursuit of psychological truth by encouraging actors to summon memories and emotions from their own lives. At the Actors Studio, Strasberg's students included some of the greatest American actors of the day—Al Pacino, Marlon Brando, Jane Fonda, Dustin Hoffman, Robert De Niro. He trained them to go deep into their characters, even to discuss and understand their characters' backstories and childhoods.[46]

The goal was for actors to infuse their performances with an elusive authenticity. Emotion was king. As Strasberg wrote in his book *A Dream of Passion: The Development of the Method*:

> I have already pointed out that in life, if we believe something is true, we behave as if it were literally true. The actor's task is to create that level of belief on stage, so that the actor is capable of experiencing the imaginary events and objects of the play with the full complement of those automatic physiological responses which accompany a real experience.[47]

In other words, Strasberg understood Method acting as an inward identification with character. Yet his most successful students surely deserve some blame for distorting the popular understanding of the term. In modern culture, Method acting is associated with physical feats of endurance and self-abasement—"an extreme commitment to erasing the boundary between character and self . . . that is in many respects the opposite of what Stanislavski and his American followers espoused," film critic A. O. Scott wrote in 2021.[48]

Is it any wonder Cage conflated Method with masochism? During his formative years, Cage swallowed up legends of his idols and their attempts to live the part. In that era, such stories were everywhere. There was De Niro working twelve-hour shifts as a cab driver for *Taxi Driver*, then gaining sixty pounds for *Raging Bull*.[49] There was Al Pacino going so deep into *Serpico* that he tried to arrest a truck driver during the shoot.[50] There was Dustin Hoffman staying up all night to play an exhausted character in *Marathon*

Man (to which Laurence Olivier supposedly quipped: "Why don't you try acting next time, dear boy").[51]

And of course, there was Marlon Brando—the actor most associated with the Method's arrival in America—who lived in a veterans' hospital to prepare for his role as a paraplegic in *The Men*.[52] Cage idolized Brando; in a 1996 interview, he recalled hearing that Brando had lain on a real block of ice so that he could shiver "the shivers of death" in *Mutiny on the Bounty*.[53]

This wasn't what Stanislavski had taught, but they were flashy and impressive stories. Cage tried to emulate those sacrifices on *Birdy*. He met with war veterans and watched videos of them speaking, but believed he needed to go further. He needed to live like one.[54] "At the time, my idols were people like Robert De Niro, who I heard lived the part and gained the weight," Cage said in a 1994 interview. "So I thought, 'Well, why not just do that? Why act? *Be!*' I learned quickly that it's very hard to have a life when you do that."[55]

Method acting is often perceived as an advanced level of acting prowess, but in Cage's case, the approach stemmed from a lack of formal training. Modine, on the other hand, had only a few degrees of separation from the master: he had studied in New York under Stella Adler, who had studied intensively with Stanislavski himself in 1934. Adler famously rejected Strasberg's emphasis on "affective memory" and encouraged actors to draw on their imagination instead. She told students: "Your talent is in your imagination. The rest is lice."[56]

Modine took heed. He threw himself into the role of Birdy with passion. But he didn't need to remain in character constantly to arrive at the performance's truth.

"My approach to acting was very different from Nick's," Modine says. "Working from your imagination affords you the freedom to step out of the character. I'm not criticizing another actor's approach, just pointing out the difference. There is no right or wrong. I lost almost thirty pounds before and during the filming for the hospital scenes. I just didn't talk about it because what does it matter to the audience? Does it make my performance better having knowledge of it?"

The contrast between the two actors was readily apparent to crew members. "Matthew Modine would act like a crazy person, and once they'd yell 'Cut,' he'd go play volleyball with us or basketball with us," recalls Jon Guterres, the camera grip. "Nicolas was always in his role. He never came out of it."

Guterres remembers a tense day on set when Cage and Modine were filming one of the wrenching scenes at the hospital. The crew member holding the clapperboard was wearing a cast on his injured foot. Each time he walked out of frame, the cast would repeatedly knock against the floor, making a goofy tapping sound. "Now everybody starts laughing," Guterres says. "And Parker says, 'OK, come on, you guys. Get it together.' "

Guterres put his fingers in his ears to block out the tapping, but he couldn't stifle his laughter. Parker dismissed him from the set. Guterres felt awful, knowing he had disrupted a sensitive scene between Cage and Modine. The next day, he went to Cage's trailer to make amends. "I want to apologize for wrecking the mood of the scene yesterday. I just lost control," he remembers telling Cage. The actor responded, "Well, when this movie is over, maybe I can laugh, too."

Guterres realized then how tormented Cage was by the role. "I felt really bad for him," he says. "It was very emotional, what he had to go through on that movie."

* * *

Let's talk about the teeth.

If you read a newspaper or magazine profile of Nicolas Cage published between, say, 1985 and 1999, there's a good chance it will mention Cage's teeth. Specifically, it will tell you—as an example of Cage's ruthless commitment to roles—that this crazed actor had two teeth removed in order to connect with the pain of his character in *Birdy*. Or to simulate shrapnel damage. Or both.

This alluring detail seems to have been first mentioned in a December 1984 *New York Times* story, which reported that Cage had "two of his front teeth pulled out" to play Al. "I wanted to look like I was hit by a bomb," Cage told the newspaper. "I felt this was a once-in-a-lifetime part, and it deserved that much."[57]

A month later, the *Daily News* published one of the first sizable profiles of Cage. The story zeroed in on the teeth extraction:

> To put himself in character, to feel the shame and the pain and the revulsion of that macho kid from Philly who comes home with a mangled face and a twisted psyche, Cage had two of his *own* teeth pulled, on either side of his jaw.[58]

The story is only partially true. Cage did have two teeth removed, but they were baby teeth that needed to be removed eventually for dental reasons; Cage simply timed the procedure so he could use the pain as fodder for the performance.

"The fact is, he had tiny baby teeth with no adult teeth behind them," says Modine. "He used the opportunity of the character he was playing to remove them for his portrayal. To the world, Nick removed the teeth to play his character. It's a splashy news story. The world loves a story about suffering to create art."

The dental work altered Cage's facial appearance when he arrived on set for the postwar scenes. "It made his mouth swell so it looked like he had injured himself in the war," says sound recordist David Macmillan. "He could hardly open his mouth in the beginning. He was in quite a lot of pain." So noticeable was the alteration to Cage's mouth that on his next film, *The Boy in Blue*, an assistant director was tasked with visiting Cage's trailer before scenes to remind him to put his teeth in.[59]

Back then, Cage seemed to deliberately encourage the perception that he had undergone a painful dental procedure purely for the sake of art. In subsequent years, the story hardened into myth, top-tier Cage lore; in many tellings, we are to believe that Cage had the teeth removed without anesthesia (he didn't). And why not? The details were exaggerated, but the message—here's an actor hellbent on taking every performance to the physical or psychological extreme—wasn't untrue.

Cage subscribed to a belief system in which authenticity was linked with masochism and self-mutilation. This was juvenile, but Cage's attitude then stemmed from a mix of inexperience, hero worship (that burning desire to emulate De Niro or Pacino's Method feats), and guilt. "I felt a little guilty about playing a guy who was in Vietnam, never having experienced anything like that, so I guess I became slightly masochistic and took it out on myself, to try to put myself through some sort of pain, to feel somewhat of a connection," he admitted in 1986. "But it didn't happen. How can you possibly know what Vietnam was like?"[60]

In October 1986, during one of his first television appearances, Cage finally admitted that the teeth had been blown out of proportion, that he had needed the surgery anyway. "It makes good press, but it's not true," he informed a bewildered Dick Cavett, who had brought up the teeth as his first question.[61]

But it was too late. The story had become legend. By the mid-nineties, when Cage was an Oscar frontrunner, he was still being asked about his post-adolescent dental exploits. By then, Cage, older and wiser, chalked it up to inexperience. "I thought it would be a way to connect with some kind of physical pain," he told *Playboy*. "I don't know what I was doing. I found myself, at nineteen, in a demanding role without proper training."[62]

The teeth became an eternal emblem of Cage's intensity. As recently as 2021, reputable sources like Vox.com repeated the enduring myth that he had his teeth pulled out without anesthesia.[63]

Fixating on dental pain, sleeping in bandages—these were undeniably pretentious indulgences. They had little discernible effect on Cage's performance, but they helped the actor accrue the mystique and attention he craved. Cage did not want merely to emulate the De Niros and Brandos of the world; he wanted to join their ranks, to create legends that would be passed down to the next generation. That dental surgeon gave him more than she ever knew.

* * *

Nicolas Cage could never truly understand the pain of a war veteran. But he could understand the pain of trying to reach a loved one in the throes of mental illness. The physical and emotional terrain of *Birdy* was closely linked to his own childhood trauma.

Cage was six when his mother, Joy Vogelsang, was first institutionalized for chronic depression and schizophrenia. He sensed that something was wrong when he saw his mother talking to a wall. "I remember saying, 'Mom, walls don't talk,'" Cage later recalled. "And she thought that was really funny. She's a very gentle person who is quite jolly, but like anybody who goes into these states, what they're seeing is real."[64]

Cage's upbringing was profoundly affected by his mother's illness. Vogelsang was away for long stretches of his childhood. "She was institutionalized for years and went through shock treatments," Cage told *Playboy*. "She would go into these states that lasted for years. She went through these episodes of poetry—I don't know what else to call it. She would say the most amazing things, beautiful but scary."[65]

Vogelsang's institutionalizations continued on and off through Cage's high school years and the start of his career. She and August divorced in 1976, and though Vogelsang wanted custody, she was unable to raise the kids. Occasionally, when Cage visited her, she seemed to lose her memory; she would forget major occurrences, such as the fact that her father had died. "[When] I started working as an actor, she had been there for many years, so when she came out it was like Rip Van Winkle," Cage told *Movieline*. "She didn't know what the hell was going on. 'What do you mean, Nicky's an actor?' "[66]

One memory remained engraved in Cage's mind. It was the memory of going to visit his mother at the institution as a child. He would walk down a long hallway, past other inmates grabbing at him, yelling things. "At the end of it," Cage told *Playboy*, "she was always there, sitting, waiting."[67]

During the eighties, Cage never discussed his mother's illness in interviews. He kept this aspect of his past hidden; perhaps it was too recent, too raw. While promoting *Birdy*, he mentioned to one interviewer that he had drawn upon "emotional experiences in his own life," but refused to say what they were.[68] It was not until the mid-nineties, by which time Vogelsang had recovered, that Cage opened up about his mother. He credited her as a source of his creativity—"she's been a huge inspiration in my work," he told the *New York Times*, "because she just naturally was kind of surreal"—and confessed to past fears that he might inherit her illness.[69]

Given these stories, it's possible to view Cage's performance in *Birdy* (Figure 3.3) with fresh eyes. Cage spent weeks shooting his scenes at a real psychiatric hospital in Santa Clara. While there, he was surely reminded of those visits to a different psychiatric ward in Southern California. Cage spends this performance fighting and pleading to reach a friend who seems to have lost touch with reality, and eventually, a breakthrough arrives. But he also knew that, in real life, long-term mental illness does not cohere to linear narratives or Hollywood resolutions.

And yet, despite the pain, Cage has described his troubled childhood as a deep emotional well to draw on for his characters: "It gave me an insight and a sensitivity that I don't think I would have had." Even at the worst of his mother's illness, he said, he was able to "detach and look at it with a scientific curiosity."[70]

Christopher Coppola believes that many of his brother's performances pull from their mother's influence. "I think anything he brings when he's trying to understand his existence and embrace it and his morality, or *mortality* maybe, and you can't hide from it—when he feels that, I think that's when he brings in his mom," Christopher says.

Accordingly, mental illness is a persistent theme in Cage's filmography. Cage is often drawn to characters afflicted with one psychiatric disorder

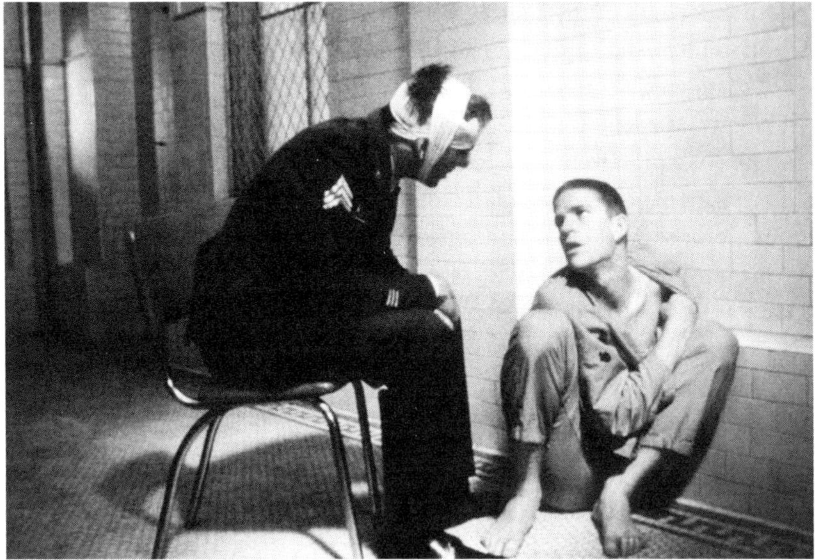

Figure 3.3. In *Birdy* (1984, Tri-Star Pictures), Cage plays a young veteran who tries to bring his traumatized friend (right, Matthew Modine) out of a catatonic state. The film's themes and setting were reminiscent of Cage's childhood experiences with his mother's mental illness.

or another. In *Vampire's Kiss*, his character is suffering from some sort of loneliness-induced psychotic break; in *Leaving Las Vegas*, it's alcoholism and suicide ideation; in *Adaptation*, anxiety and social phobia; in *Matchstick Men*, obsessive-compulsive disorder. And in both *Bringing Out the Dead* and *Bad Lieutenant: Port of Call New Orleans*, he portrays (very different) characters descending into paranoia and hallucinations.

But in *Birdy*, he plays something else—a witness to mental illness, fearful and powerless to rescue someone he cares about from a grim existence within the country's woefully inadequate mental health system. He plays someone more like the little boy he once was.

* * *

By the time *Birdy* wrapped in August 1984, Cage was physically and emotionally exhausted. There was no time to recover. Within days, he traveled to Canada to begin work on *The Boy in Blue*, a lackluster sporting drama about the real Toronto oarsman champion Ned Hanlan.

"I was a wreck right after *Birdy*," Cage recalled in 1985. "I was fifteen pounds underweight and I limped. I had a week to become one of the world's greatest athletes."[71]

Skinny and spent, Cage began bulking up and training with an Olympic sculling champion to build muscle. He was a baffling fit for the role, being neither Canadian nor particularly interested in sports, and in press materials promoting *The Boy in Blue* he seemed to regard the film more as a post-*Birdy* detox than a serious role: "One of the reasons I really wanted to do [*Boy in Blue*] was that I needed a crash course to get me out of that guy in *Birdy*. That was an emotionally draining experience; I don't think I'll play another guy who thinks he's going crazy for a long time."[72]

While Cage spent the fall parading his rippling triceps up and down the Rideau Canal in Ontario, Parker was speeding *Birdy* through postproduction so it could be released in time to qualify for Oscar consideration. Gerry Hambling edited it, seamlessly weaving together past and present vignettes, while Peter Gabriel delivered an exceptional last-minute score, a tapestry of synth textures in the key of psychic dread.[73] (The highlight: "Birdy's Flight," which brings a keening sonic intensity to the mesmerizing sequence in which the camera swoops over and above Birdy's neighborhood, taking flight like the bird he imagines himself to be.)

Birdy was always going to be a tough proposition at the box office: a war movie with few war scenes; a period piece nearly bereft of nostalgia; a coming-of-age film whose most erotic moment depicts, with trembling sincerity, a character having a wet dream about birds. Parker was insistent on adding such scenes: "I think the sexual weirdness is a very important ingredient in the film," he wrote his producer in 1983.[74]

"It is a strange little movie," says producer Alan Marshall. "This was a hard sell. It was a film in somebody's head and mind."

The film was rushed into a limited release in December 1984. Reviewers responded with considerable enthusiasm. *Newsweek* veteran Jack Kroll praised the film's two leads for delivering "marvelous performances that call for a team nomination for Academy Awards."[75] *New York Times* critic Vincent Canby was equally rapturous. He described *Birdy* as a film "so good and intelligent and moving—and so difficult to categorize in any succinct way—that it may be time for an upward reevaluation" of Parker's filmography.[76]

Establishment critics hadn't taken Cage seriously in *Valley Girl*. Now they praised him for revealing a deeper dramatic range—an early foreshadowing of the refrain that periodically pops up whenever he excels in a quieter, character-driven drama (see *Bringing Out the Dead*, *Pig*).

Audiences, though, failed to take much notice of *Birdy*. It was buried amid the Christmas movie rush; two months later, it had grossed only about \$500,000.[77] Strange and dreamlike and unabashedly heavy-handed, *Birdy* couldn't compete with the blockbuster franchises of 1984.

The problem was TriStar's release strategy. Rushing the just-finished film into limited theaters with enough time to qualify for awards but not enough to mount a proper publicity campaign proved a colossal misjudgment. The hope was that *Birdy* would build buzz on the back of some Academy Award nominations, but the film received none.[78] By March, TriStar had canceled a planned national release and Marshall was lamenting that *Birdy* would have gotten Oscar nominations had it been released in October. "We took a risk and we got nailed," the producer told the *San Francisco Examiner*.[79]

Cage and Modine—"still-emerging talents," in the euphemistic parlance of the *Los Angeles Times*—were not big enough stars to move ticket sales, yet both were getting the best reviews of their young careers. Cage began granting his first interviews, a process he found nerve-wracking. Prudence Emery, a unit publicist on *The Boy in Blue*, recalls watching Cage do an interview with *Seventeen*. "He was shaking," she says.

A *Daily News* profile, the first to delve deep into his ambivalent Hollywood heritage, captured his nervousness: "He's tall and slender, bearded and friendly, but fidgety and ill at ease, not at all comfortable about giving interviews." Yet when the conversation turned to acting, "the young scamp is reincarnated as a serious and mature artist . . . and one begins to understand just how deeply Nic Cage cares about his craft."[80]

Meanwhile, *Rolling Stone* jointly profiled him and Modine and captured their bracing contrast:

> In contrast to Modine, the twenty-one-year-old Cage has little reserve. Ever since he walked into his first big part, in *Valley Girl*, he has exhibited the strangest mixture of threatening sex appeal and goofiness. . . . Whereas Modine is graceful as a dancer, Cage seems to lug his body around as if he's self-conscious of its size. They're a lot like Birdy and Al in the movie.[81]

It was during this period that the media fascination with Cage's Method intensity started. Cage sensed an opportunity to build up a mythology. In multiple interviews, he boasted about the bandages and the teeth extraction. The

Kansas City Star heralded him as "an actor who lives his parts to a dangerous degree."[82] The *Daily News* summoned Cage's then-manager, Christopher Viores, to bear witness:

> One of the things that struck Viores about Cage was his willingness to totally immerse himself in a role, a characteristic he shares with such Hollywood heavyweights as Robert DeNiro [sic] and Dustin Hoffman, and Cage's own personal favorite, Marlon Brando. "He likes to think things through very carefully and become a character, even off the set."[83]

As for *Birdy*, it's not uncommon for an arty film to sink at the box office and land a cult following later on. What is unusual is how quickly *Birdy* found redemption.

In March 1985, after revising their marketing campaign to emphasize the "uplifting friendship" between Al and Birdy, TriStar gave the film a wider release.[84] *Birdy* never came close to recouping its budget, but with the help of Cage and Modine's promotional efforts, word of mouth began to pay off. In May, the film screened at the Cannes Film Festival—unusual for a movie already in American cinemas for months—where it won the Grand Prix Spécial du Jury prize. Cage made the trip to France, hamming it up with his director and co-star at a black-tie dinner party where four white doves flew out of a large cake.[85]

"That experience was amazing and, at the same time, odd for all three of us," says Modine. "There's video of a press conference where you can see we were all heading off on different paths. The experience we shared after the Cannes screening is still a highlight of my life. We received a standing ovation and applause that just went on and on and on. It was magical."

All these years later, Modine speaks of *Birdy* with a kind of reverence. It is, he believes, the greatest role he's ever had, and a film unlikely to get made today. "Film financiers are less adventurous and audiences today are cynical and more impatient than ever," Modine says. "*Birdy* unfolds like a bird's wings and is lyrical."

The film's quiet influence rippled into view when Parker died in 2020. Directors as varied as Edgar Wright and James Gunn expressed deep affection for *Birdy*. A few months later, when Seresin began working with Noah Baumbach on 2022's *White Noise*,[§] Baumbach made a point of telling him how much he loved *Birdy*.

§ Michael Seresin was hired as *White Noise*'s cinematographer in 2020, and then was replaced mid-shoot in 2021.

* * *

In *Birdy*, Cage's performance is steered by a raw torment that's unique in his filmography. Maybe it's not the torment that's unique—he's played tormented many times—but the rawness. In Birdy's cell, he trembles and begs for connection. Cage's voice is strained and desperate, always on the verge of tears. "I'm scared, Birdy," Al moans at the film's climax, emptied out like the suitcase of stray balls he brought to try to jog Birdy's recognition. He fears for his friend's debilitating trauma, and his own.

We have never seen Cage so vulnerable and pained, operating on such a primal level. There are no layers of surrealist flourish (an accent, a voice, an exaggerated movement style) separating him from his character's pain. He is essentially playing himself, or what he imagined he would be, had he been in Vietnam.

What gives the performance depth is its duality. In playing Al before and after the war, Cage almost plays two distinct characters. He communicates this difference with sheer physicality. In the flashback scenes, Al moves through the world with gusto: we watch him hop over fences, strut down the Atlantic City boardwalk. His hair is long, his face undamaged. Cage delivers his dialogue with youthful zeal. Dress him in 1940s garb and he's Nicky from *Racing with the Moon*.

The postwar Al speaks more slowly and uncertainly. Smiling or laughing seems like it would take great effort. In one scene, he limps onto a train car, peering out from his bandages like a stranger entering unfamiliar territory. His physical wounds are obvious; the spirit-crushing effects of the war are revealed more gradually.

Cage has a knack for playing dual roles. Later came *Peggy Sue Got Married*, in which he plays Kathleen Turner's love interest both as a teenager and as a middle-aged man, and the mischievously meta *Adaptation*, in which he plays opposite himself as twins Charlie and Donald Kaufman. Cage relied upon physicality to delineate between the two roles, as Lindsay Gibb writes in *National Treasure: Nicolas Cage*: "Cage made Charlie hunched over and tense while Donald was more upright and loose."[86]

But Cage's greatest feat in duality belongs to *Face/Off*, John Woo's 1997 action epic in which Cage's character, a sadistic terrorist named Castor Troy, surgically trades faces with John Travolta's character, FBI agent Sean Archer. As the cat-and-mouse plot unfolds, Cage gives an exhilarating dual performance in which he switches mid-film from one character to another: from Troy with Troy's face to Archer with Troy's face.

Cage carefully studied how to mimic Travolta's mannerisms and vocal rhythms—an acting challenge he later described as "acrobatic" and "a cubist mindfuck."[87] His stand-in at the time, Marco Kyris, found it remarkable to watch Cage switch between the two roles. "The characters are so different, and he dove into both characters," says Kyris. "He could bounce back and forth. He *did* bounce back and forth. It was completely different people. And I didn't see the same face. I saw Archer's face on Nick because I believed in it. I was completely engulfed in what he was doing."

In both *Birdy* and *Face/Off*, Cage's character undergoes a drastic facial transformation. Both movies have a dramatic scene in which he first glimpses his new appearance in a mirror. In *Face/Off*, Cage, enraptured by the stylized intensity of action movies, squeezes every ounce of absurdity out of this moment: he laughs, he sobs, he smashes the mirror in a wild rage. In *Birdy*, though, Cage was still grounded in naturalism, and his reaction to his self-reflection is more understated.

Birdy is not flawless. Cage dials up the melodrama too heavy at times, and the ending, an attempt to wring some urgency out of Al's conflict with a military doctor (John Harkins), is abrupt and silly.[**] But it's a very good film, enriched by the complexity of its performances, the evocative nature of its cinematography (Seresin and Parker studied old prison movies and composed remarkable shots of Birdy perched amidst shadows in his cell), and Parker's accentuation of duality and contrast: innocence vs. trauma, Birdy vs. Al, freedom vs. confinement. Birds obsess Birdy because they can fly away from the daily indignities of life on the ground. Al is the realist, and Cage's performance was accordingly rooted in a kind of extreme realism.

For years, Cage felt embarrassed by how much of himself he had exposed in *Birdy* and worried that he was being typecast as "the Italian thug from the wrong side of the tracks."[88] "[T]hat role was so close to home, so bare that it's embarrassing for me to watch," he said in a 1990 interview. "There wasn't a lot of thought behind it. It was just a stripped down character bleeding."[89]

Cage's immersion in what he understood to be Method acting coincided with his brief commitment to cinematic realism, a style which, as A. O. Scott notes, took hold in American filmmaking right as Stanislavski's influence

[**] The end of *Birdy* is jarring in its comic relief. Co-writer Kroopf notes that in the script, there was more after Al finds Birdy safe on a lower level of the roof, but Parker chose to cut the ending short and exploit the rather cheap sight gag. Kroopf worried that this ending dulled the film's impact. "I had mixed feelings the first time I saw it," he says, but he grew fonder over time. As for Cage's work in the rest of the film, "I found his performance really moving," the writer says.

arrived in Hollywood.[90] With *Birdy*, Cage took realism as far as it could go. He soon realized there were creative limits to naturalism (and practical limits to living the part) and spent the latter half of the eighties carving out a more surrealistic approach. If you split his career into eras, *Birdy* surely represents the culmination of Cage's realism phase.

"I really beat myself up for that part," Cage recalled in a 1996 interview. "And when I saw the movie, I thought, Well, gosh, I didn't give it enough thought or shadings. At the time, I referred to it as emotional vomit. But I look at it now and I feel better about it."[91]

After all, it's the movie he cut his teeth on.

4
Uncle Francis

To study Nicolas Cage's rise is also to study Francis Ford Coppola's fall from grace. You cannot write about one without the other. In the early to mid-eighties, their trajectories were almost conversely linked—Cage siphoning power from his uncle's desperate need to work, like Michael Corleone growing stronger with the Godfather's faltering health.

Except it wasn't Coppola's physical health that was faltering. It was his career and finances. In simplest terms, Coppola helped launch his nephew's career by giving Cage three significant early roles: *Rumble Fish*, *The Cotton Club*, and *Peggy Sue Got Married*.* Two of those were teen pictures. Coppola was making multiple teen pictures in quick succession largely because he needed money. Coppola needed money because the flop of his 1982 dream project, *One from the Heart*, had plunged him and his studio into deep debt. See how it's all connected?

Forced to work himself out of debt, Coppola pivoted to a nimbler style of filmmaking, making four feature films in four years (by contrast, he directed just four during the entire 1970s) and calling upon a new generation of stars, such as Ralph Macchio and Matt Dillon. Nestled in some dark crevice of that new generation was Coppola's own nephew.

Even as a child, Cage had a complicated relationship with his uncle's fame and fortune. He was eight when the indelible gangster epic *The Godfather* established Coppola as an icon of the New Hollywood era. Tension grew between Francis and August. Francis sent Cage's family a package of *Godfather* promotional T-shirts, but August wouldn't let Cage wear one. Cage eventually saw the film and was aroused by the scene in which Michael's Sicilian bride undresses while kissing him.[1] When *The Godfather Part II* came out, August took him to see it, but said, "Don't tell your uncle we went to see the movie."[2]

* As of this writing, Coppola is one of just two filmmakers who have had the distinction of directing Cage more than twice. The other: Cage's high school friend Jon Turteltaub.

When production began on *Apocalypse Now*, "Francis wanted us to go to the Philippines, because we were very close with his kids," Christopher recalls. "And my dad said, 'Absolutely not, are you kidding me? They're in school.' He refused."

Cage once described the Coppola family as "loaded with grudges and passion"—perhaps not unlike the Corleone family.[3] Growing up, Coppola had always been conscious of Cage's father's good looks and academic success. August was the golden child: brilliant, handsome, passionate about the arts. Francis, five years younger, was a comparably mediocre student.[4]

"He was like the star of the family and I did most of what I did to imitate him," Francis recalled in a 1983 interview. "Tried to look like him, tried to be like him. I even took his short stories and handed them in under my name."[5]

Coppola liked to imagine that his brother would be a famous novelist someday and he would be a playwright. Even Coppola's screen credit was modeled after August: he went by Francis Ford Coppola, middle name and all, because his brother was August Floyd Coppola.[6]

The Godfather changed the family dynamic for good. Francis's success and fame far eclipsed his brother's achievements in academia. The Coppola family was full of artistic accomplishment, but suddenly everybody else's careers seemed to orbit around Francis. Talia Shire was a gifted actress whose greatest acclaim arrived when her brother cast her in *The Godfather*. Carmine Coppola was a long-frustrated composer—frequently unemployed, resentful of those more successful than him—but finally won an Academy Award when his son hired him to write music for *The Godfather Part II*.[7]

Between 1972 and 1974, Francis directed three masterpieces back to back—*The Godfather*, *The Conversation*, and *The Godfather Part II*—two of which won Best Picture. These years of greatest acclaim coincided with rough years for Cage's family. August was raising three sons on an academic salary; his wife was enduring long periods of hospitalization. They divorced by 1976.[8]

August poured himself into his work, which grew ever more eccentric. He wanted to be a great American novelist—one who wrote books, not screenplays. "That was important to him, to be recognized as a novelist," says Cage's brother Christopher. In 1978, he published an experimental erotic novel called *The Intimacy*, about a man and woman who choose to live in total darkness in search of "a rehabilitation of the soul." The book was the culmination of the professor's obsession with touch, and it was filled with passages of gooey erotic exploration (typical sentence: "He pumped all the harder, his testicles slamming up against her, his temples aching").[9]

While the book apparently resonated with August's female admirers, it was not a success. By 1985, it had sold fewer than 2,000 copies.[10]

"We lived with him while he was writing it," says Christopher Coppola. "He thought the book would be a huge success. It was a major flop. It hurt him deeply. He got mad when they wanted to capitalize Coppola and make August small and was furious."

Such blow-ups were common in the household. "We're very difficult," Christopher says. "My dad was incredibly high-maintenance. Little things could happen that would trigger him and you would wonder why."

Meanwhile, *The Intimacy* fermented bitterness when some members of the family believed August had based a villainous character on Francis. As Christopher puts it, "That book has a lot of ugliness around it." Though the book jacket stated that August was working on "two succeeding novels," he never published another.

* * *

By 1974, Francis Ford Coppola was among the most celebrated and well-paid filmmakers in America. Soon he owned a twenty-two-room Victorian mansion in San Francisco, a Manhattan apartment in the Sherry Netherland Hotel, and a Napa Valley estate and adjoining vineyard.[11]

Into this world of fame and fortune stepped the adolescent Cage—always a visitor, never a belonger. Cage and his brothers spent summers at Uncle Francis's house, where they encountered Hollywood legends walking the halls. The San Francisco house had a screening room, and once, at fourteen or fifteen, Cage was permitted to attend an early screening of *Apocalypse Now*, which amazed him with its horrific scope.[12]

"He had a long conversation with Dennis Hopper, who was there at that screening," says *Apocalypse Now* co-producer Fred Roos, a longtime Coppola collaborator. "He was so impressed that Dennis Hopper would talk to him about movies and art and acting. It was a watershed experience for him." When Cage told Hopper that he liked classical music, Hopper took the boy seriously and recommended an opera by Prokofiev.[13]

At the same time, Cage's relationship with his famous uncle was straining under the weight of jealousy and resentment. The stories Cage has told are grandiose enough to have been rejected from a *Godfather* screenplay. A few choice anecdotes:

(1) Cage, around twelve or thirteen, was in the backseat of his uncle's car. Coppola was driving over the Golden Gate Bridge, listening to the Beatles song "Baby, You're a Rich Man." "I was thinking, 'Yeah, he really deserves to listen to this, doesn't he?'" Cage later told the writer Eve Babitz. "He was right at the height of *Godfather II*, and I vowed to myself that one day I'd be able to listen to that song, too, as a reward to myself."[14] (When *Valley Girl* was a hit, Cage fulfilled this wish by taking his Triumph Spitfire for a joyride on Sunset Boulevard and savoring every word of the tune.[15])

(2) Another car ride with Coppola, late 1970s. Cage told his uncle, "If you want to see acting, give me a screen test and I'll show you acting." No answer. His uncle simply ignored him.[16]

(3) Cage and his father were at his uncle's house. August and Coppola were talking about something James Joyce supposedly once said to his literary idol, Henrik Ibsen: "You were great, but I hold the mantle now." Years later, after *Valley Girl*, Cage was at his uncle's house again. "He was lighting a cigar and I just said it: 'You were great, Francis, but I hold the mantle now.' He got upset and flustered," Cage recalled in 1996. (Cage reflected that there is "a fundamental competitive edge amongst the men in my family."[17])

Cage has insisted these stories are true (this seems like a place to note that multiple attempts to interview Francis Ford Coppola for this book were not successful), but they feel like origin myths, peaks into the damaged psyche of someone who grew up hungry and ambitious in the shadow of an artist whose ambitions were fulfilled beyond anyone's imagining.

"We were the Southern Coppolas, sometimes called the poor Coppolas, because we weren't rich," Christopher reflects. "So he had a lot of anger. He wanted to make it big. And he did, because he's goal-oriented."

Cage grew up in proximity to vast wealth but not with vast wealth, and there lay the distinction. Like many Italian-American patriarchs, Coppola was known for his hospitality—cooking extravagant dinners, entertaining guests. Cage was often a beneficiary of this hospitality. But when the young Cage spent a year living at his uncle's house—riding around in his uncle's cars, marveling that his cousins had a movie theater in their basement—he stewed in the knowledge that this opulence did not belong to him. He vowed that someday he would return and buy a palatial mansion in San Francisco of his own. "I said, 'You know what? I am going to get back. I am going to get even somehow.' And I think I turned into Heathcliff," Cage later recalled, referring to the jealous hero of *Wuthering Heights*.[18]

But Cage's true revenge was not in accruing wealth of his own. It was in relinquishing the family name, a proud name stretching back generations. Surely Coppola of all people understood that this was not personal; it was strictly business. Still, he did not like his nephew's decision. When *Valley Girl* came out, Coppola sent Cage a congratulatory telegram. He signed it: "from Francis Cage, Eleanor Cage and all the other Cages."[19]

* * *

If Nicolas Cage inherited one quality from Francis Ford Coppola, it was his willingness to gamble everything for a movie. Coppola was a beacon of the New Hollywood era, not just because of *The Godfather*'s success, but because of his willingness to take creative risks.

Such risks do not always pay off. Indeed, Cage was eighteen when he watched one of his uncle's dreams come crashing down.

The musical romance *One from the Heart* was supposed to be Coppola's dream project. In 1980, Coppola bought a Los Angeles lot and sunk his fortune into his own film studio, Zoetrope Studios, where he could employ talented actors and filmmakers in-house (Martha Coolidge among them) and make his own movies with creative autonomy. Instead of being at the mercy of studio heads, he *was* the studio head. Besides, after spending four years making Apocalypse *Now*—shooting in the jungles of the Philippines amid raging typhoons and nearly going mad—Coppola relished the idea of making his next movie on his home turf, his own studio, where, as biographer Peter Cowie notes, "the sun would rise and set to his command."[20]

The idea was for *One from the Heart* to be shot entirely on extravagant Zoetrope sound stages—including a scale model of Las Vegas—instilling the film with a sheen of deliberate artifice.[21] Like Martin Scorsese had done with *New York, New York*, Coppola sought to break away from gritty seventies filmmaking and bring a touch of Old-Hollywood glitz and glamour to his stylized Vegas fantasia. At the same time, he was filling his studio with cutting-edge technology and experimenting with new methods of what he called "electronic cinema," such as directing actors remotely from within an Airstream trailer (dubbed "Silverfish") outfitted with Betamax recorders, monitors, and sophisticated editing equipment.[22]

"Francis was making his own version of an old-fashioned Hollywood studio, where you have an in-house production designer, an in-house casting department," says Aleta Chappelle, who worked in casting at Zoetrope. "It was a real, true entity."

Naturally, Coppola's fantasy of total control spiraled out of control. While Zoetrope was struggling to meet payroll, *One from the Heart*'s budget ballooned from $12 million to $23 million to just under $27 million, much of it spent on enormous set construction costs. Coppola took out a series of large bank loans in order to finance the production himself, putting up his real estate as collateral.[23] When the *Los Angeles Times* profiled him in early 1982, the filmmaker was described as desperate and overstretched, "a man who feels hurt and isolated, spurned by establishment Hollywood." If *One from the Heart* were to fail at the box office, "our studio couldn't survive it," Coppola declared.[24]

The film more than failed at the box office. It belly-flopped, grossing a humiliating $804,518 during its original run.[25] Although visually exquisite (sleek and brightly colored, heavily inspired by Coppola's love of theater) and wonderfully scored by Tom Waits, *One from the Heart* was thin on character and plot, the elements that had elevated Coppola's seventies masterpieces.[26] Coppola was due for a backlash. Critics, responding as much to the undeniable hubris that had toppled his empire as to the film itself, were not kind.

"It was a bitter disappointment, the reception of *One from the Heart*, because people just didn't get it," says Coppola's longtime producer, Fred Roos. "*Why did you create those sets? Why didn't you just go to Las Vegas?* Well, that was the whole point. It was not to be a real Las Vegas; it was a fantasy Las Vegas."

The failure of *One from the Heart* was devastating for Coppola. In mere weeks, he had gone from being one of the most powerful, hailed directors in the world to a struggling artist. He was more than $20 million in debt. He was soon forced to put the Zoetrope studio facility on the market and become that dreaded thing he had escaped, a director-for-hire.[27] "It was traumatic," Coppola later told *GQ*. "I felt I had fallen from grace, that I was a failure."[28]

This event, along with the disastrous bomb of Michael Cimino's *Heaven's Gate* in 1980, is often regarded as emblematic of a larger sea change in Hollywood. The failure of *One from the Heart* didn't just mark the end of Coppola's winning streak. It marked the end of the New Hollywood era as a whole, that transformative period when ambitious young "movie brats" like Coppola and Spielberg (most of them white and male) were regarded as American auteurs and were granted remarkable degrees of creative freedom to make era-defining movies with minimal studio interference.

That all changed circa 1980–1982. Power shifted away from auteurs, with their swelling budgets and unquenchable ambition, and back to studio executives. High-priced passion projects like *One from the Heart* would now fall under suspicion—a lesson even Martin Scorsese learned the hard way when Paramount pulled the plug on *The Last Temptation of Christ*. As the critic Noel Murray writes, "the balance shifted to younger movie stars, dazzling special effects, and easily understood story ideas—all often packaged together by super-agents, working in concert with studio executives, always with an eye toward maximizing profits rather than making masterpieces."[29]

Accordingly, the most inventive auteurs who rose to prominence during the 1980s largely worked outside the major studio system, and on nimble budgets. Some of the filmmakers who later worked with Cage, like David Lynch, watched and learned from Coppola's mistakes.

The ripple effect of *One from the Heart*'s failure enabled Cage's rise in odd and fortuitous ways. For one thing, Coppola's eagerness to restore his commercial standing resulted in opportunities in his films for young, emerging actors such as his nephew. For another, one of the casualties of Zoetrope's collapse was *Photoplay*, the movie Martha Coolidge had been developing there for two years, which subsequently freed her up to make *Valley Girl*.

Curiously, *One from the Heart* was also the first Coppola film whose production process Cage witnessed up close. Cage's father briefly served as an executive at Zoetrope around this time, assisting his brother on special projects, such as a restoration of the 1927 epic *Napoléon*.[30] Cage, meanwhile, was busy filming *The Best of Times*. "I remember our uncle would request that I go straight to the set of *One from the Heart* and teach Raul Julia how to use nunchaku sticks," Cage recalled in a 2020 interview.[31] Thus, the adolescent Cage was both witness to his uncle's fall from grace and a participant in his reinvention.

After the *One from the Heart* debacle, Coppola figured he had two options. One was to give up and leave the film industry. The other, as he later put it, "was to fight back to being as productive as I could be and make one film after another."[32]

He chose the latter path. Much as his nephew would later spend the bulk of the 2010s pumping out one role after another to cover personal debts, Coppola would spend the remainder of the eighties averaging a movie a year, paying back the bank.

* * *

It was convenient that the movie Coppola already planned to make after *One from the Heart* was considerably more commercial and less costly. Coppola had decided to make *The Outsiders* after receiving a letter in 1980 from a school librarian and her young students begging him to adapt S. E. Hinton's novel, about Oklahoma youths caught up in gang rivalries and violence, into a movie. When Fred Roos read the book, he agreed. Zoetrope was so cash-poor that it had to pay Hinton's option fee (only $5,000) in smaller installments.[33]

After spurning the concept of location shooting on *One from the Heart*, Coppola left his sound stages behind and chose to make *The Outsiders* on location in Tulsa, a therapeutic endeavor after his recent heartbreak.

"He just wanted to get out of L.A.," says Roos, who produced *The Outsiders* and later *Rumble Fish*. "He wanted to be around some young people and not around the business. The idea was, go far away and have a whole different kind of filmmaking experience." Roos describes it as a return to Coppola's experience making the low-budget gem *The Rain People* (1969): "You're on the road, you're out of L.A., you're a band of artists making a movie together."

The Outsiders was also Coppola's first movie centered on youth since the pre-*Godfather* days, which was good news for eighteen-year-old Cage. Its cast, filled with rising stars like Emilio Estevez, Matt Dillon, Ralph Macchio, and a young Tom Cruise, helped crystallize the generation later known as the Brat Pack.

Curiously enough, it was Roos who pushed Coppola to give Cage a shot. "I knew about Nick's acting," Roos says. "I had seen some things he had done, which Francis hadn't even seen.† I helped push him to Martha Coolidge on *Valley Girl*. I remember suggesting him to Francis for something. Francis hadn't been aware of his acting, that he'd actually started his career: 'Nicky? *Nicky?* Acting?' I said, 'Yeah. He's damn good!' "

Roos had an eye for talent. He helped cast *The Godfather* back in 1970, pulling out unknowns like John Cazale for major roles. He remembers what struck him about Cage early on: "His intensity, his focus, his daring. He never wanted to let it be boring, even at a young age."

Nepotism was hardly anathema to Coppola, who by the mid-eighties had granted roles to his sister and young daughter (Sofia Coppola's stage name was "Domino") while employing his eldest son, Gian-Carlo Coppola, as an

† Roos can't remember exactly what he had seen. Presumably, it must have been *The Best of Times*, or a student film Cage appeared in at Beverly Hills High called *The Sniper*.

associate producer. Still, Coppola wasn't convinced by his nephew's abilities. When Cage auditioned for *The Outsiders*, he was one of dozens in consideration. Coppola later recalled, "I had all the candidates—which included Nicolas Cage, Mickey Rourke, Robert Downey Jr., Patrick Swayze, Dennis Quaid, Matt Dillon, Rob Lowe, and Emilio Estevez—sitting on benches in a circle watching each other trying for the different parts."[34]

Cage was rattled by the pressure. The audition didn't go well; his uncle kept him waiting for hours, then turned him down.[35] When Coppola flew to Tulsa in March 1982 to begin shooting, Cage was left behind, ready to give up acting altogether.

It was *Rumble Fish* that changed his fortunes. While on location for *The Outsiders*, Coppola read *Rumble Fish*, a similarly themed novel by S. E. Hinton, and immediately decided to film a second Hinton adaptation. He and Hinton pounded out the screenplay on his days off during the *Outsiders* shoot. The audacious idea was in the tradition of his once-mentor, B-movie king Roger Corman: Coppola would extend his stay in Oklahoma and shoot *Rumble Fish* soon after *The Outsiders*, using most of the same production crew he had already assembled there.[36]

"We went to make *The Outsiders*, and during the course of it we got to know Susie [Hinton] really well," Roos says. "We liked the town. We liked the experience. And then we just started having conversations about *Rumble Fish*."

"I remember the conversation when Francis asked S. E. Hinton, 'Did you have any other books we should make?' " says Aleta Chappelle. "She goes, 'We can make *Rumble Fish*.' And then all of a sudden we were making *Rumble Fish*." Where once Coppola had the luxury of spending four years on one movie, now he was pumping out two in one year.

The story of *Rumble Fish* centers on a complex relationship between two brothers connected to gang life in Tulsa. Rusty James is the brash hothead, young and naïve; he idolizes his older brother, the enigmatic and philosophical ex-gang leader known as the Motorcycle Boy, but the Motorcycle Boy is disillusioned with gang life and wants to leave the rumbles behind. The film shared some cast members with *The Outsiders*—notably, rising stars Matt Dillon (as Rusty James) and Diane Lane (his girlfriend, Patty) and musician Tom Waits—but was an altogether different story which required a new audition process.

Roos remembers agitating strongly for Cage to get a role. Cage was called back to Zoetrope's offices—not to audition, but to help read other actors who were auditioning. The pressure was off. The next day, he was surprised to learn he had a supporting role in *Rumble Fish*.[37]

"We do those tricks with casting, Francis and I," says Roos. "There are a lot of stories about different movies, how we'd audition somebody without them even knowing they were being looked over."

Cage was cast as Smokey, the disloyal best friend of main hood Rusty James. He was Nicolas Coppola when he took the role and Nicolas Cage by the time the film was in the can.

* * *

Rumble Fish is often regarded as a companion piece to *The Outsiders*, but it presents itself more as that film's impressionistic photonegative. As Coppola put it, *Rumble Fish* was "the antidote" to *The Outsiders*. "As colorful and sunset-y and even saccharine as *The Outsiders* was, this was to be the opposite," Coppola explained in a DVD commentary track.[38]

It is remarkable to think the two films share a director of photography. *The Outsiders* is drenched in lavish color and swelling drama, evoking the widescreen palette of a Technicolor melodrama from the 1950s. It is hopeful despite its tragic storyline and is unabashedly sentimental. "The compositions were classical and pictorial with the camera removed and stoic," director of photography Stephen H. Burum told *American Cinematographer*. "*Rumble Fish* was exactly the opposite; we wanted to shove the camera into the faces of the characters and become more of the psychological storyteller."[39]

Though woven from the same literary cloth, *Rumble Fish*—the bolder and more interesting adaptation—is the most overtly avant-garde film Coppola has ever made. It is dreamlike and surrealistic, shot in monochrome black-and-white, an aesthetic modeled upon the German Expressionist films of the 1920s: high-contrast photography, sharp angles, dense waves of fog, heavy shadows that make a drunken teenage sex party look more like Orson Welles than *National Lampoon*. There are time-lapse shots of clouds rushing overhead like billowing smoke, shots of trees that sway and creak as though they're haunted by restless spirits. Coppola shot in deserted sections of Tulsa, eager to convey a sense that these teens were living and fighting in a wasteland.

The sound design is chaotic and disorienting—dialogue consumed by the percussive roar of Stewart Copeland's bracing, rhythm-heavy score—and the whole film cracks with a feverish energy. Some flourishes, such as the Siamese fighting fish ("rumble fish," as the Motorcycle Boy calls them) appearing in brilliant color while the rest of the movie is in black-and-white, feel like self-conscious callbacks to the European art films of Coppola's youth.

Indeed, Coppola has said he intended *Rumble Fish* to be "an art film for teenagers"—a kind of gateway drug for Gen X teens to discover cinematic treasures from decades past. "I tried to take the influences that affected me as a teenager and make a film for teenagers using them," Coppola explained in his DVD commentary.[40]

During the shoot, he screened movies for the cast and crew that he wanted to use as stylistic reference points: F. W. Murnau's *Sunrise* (1927), Orson Welles's *Macbeth* (1948), Robert Wiene's *The Cabinet of Dr. Caligari*, and F. W. Murnau's *The Last Laugh* (1924), among others.[41] "Francis was trying to get across to them, especially to Matt Dillon, how important body language was [in silent cinema]," Burum, the director of photography, explained.[42]

It's altogether fitting that Cage got his start in a film so indebted to German Expressionism. From a young age, Cage shared Coppola's enthusiasm for German Expressionist filmmaking; years later, he would cite films like 1922's *Nosferatu* (also by Murnau) as a major influence on his exaggerated performance style in *Vampire's Kiss*. Of course, this shared enthusiasm was hardly a coincidence. Coppola and Cage were likely introduced to these films by the same person: August Coppola, who taught films like *Nosferatu* in a class at Cal State Long Beach and to whom *Rumble Fish* is dedicated.[43]

And yet there is not much of the German Expressionist tradition in Cage's performance in *Rumble Fish*. He is more of a supporting player than a star in what was supposed to be his first major film role.[‡] As Smokey, Cage plays a scheming, well-dressed hoodlum, his greasy hair dyed black. He holds his own, but his performance is restrained compared to Matt Dillon and Mickey Rourke's more strenuous dramatic work as the two brothers at the heart of the film.

Smokey at first seems like a side character: a friend of the more volatile Rusty James, who yearns for a return to the gang fights of old (before drugs "ruined the gangs, man") but lacks his brother's restraint. Not until the film's latter half is Smokey's true character revealed. After Rusty James cheats on his girlfriend, Patty, at a party, she begins dating Smokey instead. Rusty James angrily confronts Smokey outside their bar hangout, Benny's Billiards. Smokey is the picture of aloof detachment, puffing a cigarette in a suave shirt

‡ *Rumble Fish* was filmed before *Valley Girl*, but *Valley Girl* came out months earlier and thus became Cage's real breakout.

and averting his friend's gaze as he confirms that, yes, he planned for Rusty James's infidelity to get back to Patty so he could swoop in.

Then, in Cage's biggest monologue, Smokey tells Rusty James that he is not smart enough to be a revered gang leader like his brother once was. "You've got to be smart to run things," he says. "Nobody would follow you into a gang fight, cuz you'd get people killed." Cage never raises his voice. No violence ensues. Smokey glances at his watch, Rusty James accepts these painful truths, and he hands Smokey the pool cue as a symbolic transfer of power.

Cage was eighteen, barely out of high school, when *Rumble Fish* was filmed during the summer of 1982. The shoot was not an easy one for him. He felt intimidated by his more experienced co-stars. "They seemed to know some secret that I didn't," Cage recalled in a 1985 interview. "I didn't know where they got their fire. So I locked myself up in my room and read books on Japanese management systems, because I thought my character would probably grow up to be a businessman."[44]

Exacerbating Cage's stress was his last name—still Coppola—which provoked murmurs and occasional teasing from other actors. Cage was convinced they thought he was only there because of nepotism, which irked him, since, if anything, Coppola was *particularly* hard on his nephew. "Once Francis made me do forty-two takes—a scene looking at a watch—and I've never had to do forty-two takes again in my whole career. I know that that was like some kind of strange trial that I had to go through," Cage later told *Rolling Stone*.[45]

Perhaps Coppola was testing his nephew, or perhaps he was attuned to the watch's thematic significance in ways Cage was not. Among the film's weightiest themes is the immensity of time: a perpetual sense of clocks ticking and youth fading. The film's high-contrast photography overflows with images that centralize time—least subtly, a memorable shot of Rusty James and the Motorcycle Boy leaning against a gigantic clock face—not to mention the use of time-lapse photography itself. Coppola's preoccupation with time becomes an explicit fixation for Tom Waits's character, Benny, the philosophizing barkeep muttering to himself while fixing drinks at Benny's Billiards. "Time is a funny thing," Waits muses in one scene, tidying in the background of the shot as a garish clock dominates the foreground. "The older you get, you say, 'Jesus, how much I got—I got thirty-five summers left.'"

Waits had entered Coppola's orbit when he was hired to compose music for *One from the Heart*, spending months cooped up with a piano in a wood-paneled office at Zoetrope.[46] Coppola soon realized the cult songwriter, with his back-alley hoodlum charm, ought to be in front of a camera, too, and gave him a bit part in *The Outsiders* and a bigger one in *Rumble Fish*.

It was during the latter shoot that Waits met and befriended Cage. Despite their fourteen-year age difference, the two hit it off—both outsiders to the Hollywood establishment, both sharing a skewed, contorted sensibility. Waits specialized in writing songs about the kinds of lowlifes and drunks ("Jitterbug Boy," "Dave the Butcher," the Frank of "Frank's Wild Years") that Cage might embody onscreen, and the two would remain close pals for years. Waits, in fact, later credited Cage with reigniting his interest in comic books, which inspired the song "Eyeball Kid." "I hadn't thought about comic books since I was a little kid," Waits told a 1999 interviewer, "but he seemed to carry that mythology with him."[47]

During *Rumble Fish*, both men were new to film acting, yet Coppola gave them considerable leeway to make their characters their own. Waits concocted most of Benny's philosophical meanderings himself. "Francis just said, 'Write your own dialogue,'" he recalled in a 2004 interview. "He says, 'I'm not even gonna tell ya what to say—man, this is your diner, this is your apron, your spatula. I'm not gonna give you any lines.'"[48]

Cage, meanwhile, was given plenty of reign with his own character, particularly during the pivotal scene in Benny's when Rusty James realizes that Smokey has stolen his girl. "So much of what he did in this scene he invented," Coppola said in the film's DVD commentary. "The idea that he gives Patty a picture of himself as a kid, the way he's decked himself out—this is all Nicolas's invention." When Rusty James hands Smokey the pool cue as a symbol of gang leadership, it was also Cage's idea to drop the cue and walk away.[49]

* * *

Nicolas Cage and his uncle both needed a hit in 1983, and they each got one. It just wasn't the movie they made together.

Valley Girl arrived that spring and propelled Cage to minor fame. Coppola, meanwhile, owed a hearty thanks to the school librarian who persuaded him to adapt *The Outsiders*. A genre film as straightforward as anything in his filmography, *The Outsiders* helped restore Coppola's commercial standing after the *One from the Heart* disaster. Yet *Rumble Fish*—released just seven months later, in October 1983—sank at the box office, grossing barely $2.5 million. (By comparison, *The Outsiders* had grossed double that in its first weekend alone.)[50]

Perhaps it was a fanciful delusion to think that this expressionistic art film would capture the youth audiences shelling out for *Porky's*. *Rumble Fish* is not the kind of film you make when you need a hit. It is the kind of film you make when you've already made your hit and now you can make the film you want to make—a one-for-them-one-for-me trade-off Coppola never had to make in the seventies. (Coppola himself admitted that he "started to use *Rumble Fish* as my carrot for what I promised myself when I finished *The Outsiders*."[51])

In an attempt to emphasize its art-house appeal, *Rumble Fish* premiered at the New York Film Festival, but neither critics nor audiences were receptive. The reviews offered more evidence of Coppola's diminished status in the industry. Critics chastised him for being pretentious and out of touch with young moviegoers. *Time*'s Richard Corliss described *Rumble Fish* as "Coppola's professional suicide note to the movie industry, a warning against employing him to find the golden gross," while the *New Republic*'s Stanley Kauffmann blasted it as "a ridiculously trite configuration of adolescent heroics."[52] Even critics inclined to like the movie seemed to regard it as more style than substance—a film that "tirelessly attempts to disguise what might have been a perfectly respectable B-movie about urban teen-agers," as Vincent Canby wrote in the *New York Times*.[53]

Yet *Rumble Fish* was never an empty vessel for flashy technical experimentation. Critics misunderstood *Rumble Fish* because they did not know—perhaps couldn't have known—that it was among the most personal films Coppola has ever made. And Cage's presence in the film was intimately linked to this personal resonance.

In essence, Coppola was drawn to the film because it is a story of two brothers, the younger of whom idolizes the older. Rusty James, who narrates Hinton's novel, yearns to be a gang leader because his older brother was *the* gang leader. Rusty James is simple-minded and inarticulate and eager for his brother's respect. The Motorcycle Boy is aloof and enigmatic, mysterious and assured. He is twenty-one, but seems much older.[§] He drops references to Greek mythology, which frustrate and confuse Rusty James, who lacks his intellect. When Rusty James tells an acquaintance in a bar that he's going to

[§] In the novel, the Motorcycle Boy is seventeen and Rusty James fourteen. Coppola chose to make both characters several years older, perhaps so he could justify casting Mickey Rourke and Matt Dillon.

be "just like him," the man shakes his head: "You ain't gonna never be like that, man."

The material resonated with Coppola because it brought him back to his own childhood, worshipping an intellectually superior older brother. In the 1940s, the Coppolas lived in a rough neighborhood by the railroad yards in Woodside, Queens. "I had a brother five years older . . . who was my idol, who was very, very good to me. Just took me everywhere and taught me everything," Coppola said in a 1983 interview. To his mind, August's presence was not unlike the Motorcycle Boy's: a mysterious and dapper figure, revered by the other kids in the neighborhood. "He was the leader of the gang and he was tremendously handsome," Coppola said.[54]

Rusty James idolizes his brother "just as I idolized my brother," Coppola said in his DVD commentary. "Everything I aspired to be—the desire to be in the arts, to know about literature, to be a person to whom knowledge and learning was important—it was all taken from my brother, August."[55]

Many of Coppola's films depict complex relationships between brothers—*The Godfather*, *The Godfather Part II*, *The Outsiders*, *Tetro*—yet none draws from his own childhood as intimately as *Rumble Fish*, a movie which Coppola has listed alongside *The Conversation* as one of his two favorite movies he has made.[56] To this effect, Coppola's decision to grant Cage a role in the film was loaded with familial significance. It was almost a kind of secret stunt-casting legible only to the director: Coppola did not just place his brother's son in the film; he went out of his way to make August's son resemble August at a younger age (Figure 4.1).

It is striking, for instance, that Cage has coiffed black hair in *Rumble Fish*, in stark contrast to his sandy-blonde mop in *Valley Girl*. Coppola specifically instructed Cage to dye his hair black because Cage's father had black hair; the director then asked actor Vincent Spano, who *does* have black hair, to dye his hair blonde in contrast to the other boys. The only real purpose this color swap served was to make Cage look more like his own father.

Coppola considered having the characters wear matching gang outfits, but chose to dress each boy in different attire. Cage wears a stylish jacket with a 2 of Spades card on the front and the words "WILD DEUCES" on the back. This, too, has familial significance. During their Woodside days, August Coppola belonged to a club known as the Wild Deuces Social Club. Cage is wearing a replica of his own father's club jacket, an artifact from thirty-odd years earlier.[57]

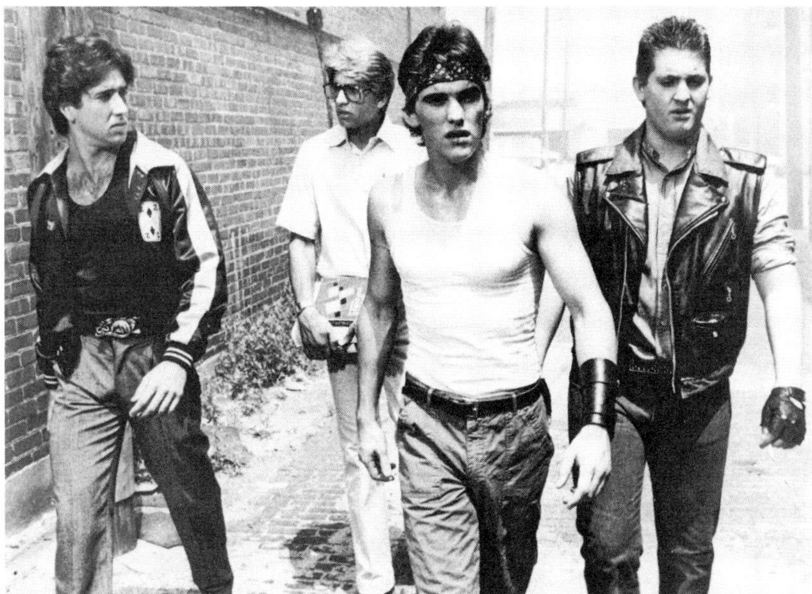

Figure 4.1. For *Rumble Fish* (1983, Universal Pictures), Francis Ford Coppola instructed his nephew (left) to dye his hair black and wear a replica of his father's club jacket. Coppola deliberately styled Cage to resemble his father, August Coppola, to whom the film is dedicated.

The decision to model Cage's look after his own father was a strange one considering that the Motorcycle Boy, played by Mickey Rourke, is the character actually modeled after August. Because August was an intellectual, always reading Sartre and Joyce, Coppola made the Motorcycle Boy look like Albert Camus.[58]

Ultimately, the Motorcycle Boy is a doomed hero. During the film's final passages, Rusty James tries mightily and fails to save his brother from his own disillusionment and seeming death wish. Coppola was reminded of a dream he once had in which his brother was trapped in a manhole and he had to run from house to house, calling for help. "I think the younger brother who feels he must save the older brother is a deep theme in my heart," Coppola explained.[59]

During the film's end credits, a dedication appears: "This film is dedicated to my older brother, August Coppola, my first and best teacher." As August himself later remarked, "The dedication was a recognition of my importance in his life, both good and bad. It's a poignant film in that Francis has often had regrets because I was supposed, in his mind, to achieve what he achieved. Our family was consecrated to success."[60]

Caught between these brothers was Nicolas Cage, a boy wearing the club jacket of his father while entering the business of his uncle. If *Rumble Fish* was intended to honor August's influence, his son's presence onscreen hardly seems in keeping with the man's wishes. August never wanted Cage to become an actor. "[M]y brother, as he got older, show business was just odious to him," Coppola admitted in 2016, several years after August's death. "He hated that all his relatives were in movies and theater."[61]

After the shoot, Cage heard through the grapevine that Coppola had not been impressed with his performance. The messenger was his own father. "You're too restrained as an actor," August told his son. "I don't think you have what it takes."[62]

* * *

Nicolas Cage was an unknown when *Rumble Fish* was filmed and a star by the time the movie hit theaters. *Valley Girl* came out in the intervening months.

"Francis saw the movie and called," Cage later told *Playboy*. "I could hear the excitement in his voice. He wanted me to be in his next two movies." In Cage's view, his uncle did not really believe in his acting abilities—despite having cast him in *Rumble Fish*—until seeing *Valley Girl*.[63]

Universal Pictures evidently hoped that Cage's newfound star power might boost interest in *Rumble Fish*. During the summer of 1983, the studio issued a press release introducing Cage and emphasizing his role in *Rumble Fish*. The document described the actor as "a self-styled teen-age intellectual" who "compares his *Rumble Fish* character to Iago and says he prepared for the part by reading books on Japanese management strategy."

After mentioning Cage's recent and forthcoming credits, the press release offers a tellingly selective account of his origin story:

> Without a doubt, his career is launched. Originally interested in writing, Nicolas began to study acting as a means of learning more about character. He ran into some obstacles with a novel he was writing, and enrolled at the American Conservatory Theatre in San Francisco. He was fifteen years old at the time. He continued acting and now studies with the noted coach, Peggy Fury [*sic*].
>
> Although accustomed to novels by writers like Kafka and Huxley, he admits reading S. E. Hinton's book upon which the film is based when he

> was thirteen years old. "A girl recommended it, and I said 'what is this, I'm reading Melville,'" young Cage recalls. "The book stood out though I would never have admitted it then," he continues.[64]

Reflecting August's influence, the press release hones in on Cage's intellectual image:

> As for the future, Nicolas thinks he will eventually continue with his education. He cites Chekhov's dictum that an artist should "study everything." For the moment, however, he will continue acting, treating his career as a job and moving straight ahead.[65]

What goes unmentioned is as telling as the information that appears. Conspicuously missing was any mention of Cage's family name. Nor was *Fast Times at Ridgemont High* mentioned, presumably because Cage was credited as Nicolas Coppola.

It's unlikely the press release did much good for Cage. As was his wont in 1983, he did no interviews promoting *Rumble Fish*. As was also his wont, he found a less conventional way of celebrating his performance. He bought a two-and-a-half-foot monitor lizard and named him Smokey, after his character. "I've always wanted a huge lizard that I could throw rare filet mignons to," Cage later explained.[66]

* * *

In 1983, well before *Rumble Fish* had been released, Coppola recruited his nephew to appear in his next movie: the Prohibition-era gangster drama *The Cotton Club*. Having grown up in the shadow of *The Godfather*, Cage found the opportunity to play a mobster under Coppola's tutelage enticing enough to override fears of nepotism charges. "I told Nick when he took the part in *Cotton Club* that the same problem would probably arise," Cage's agent, Ilene Feldman, said in 1983, referring to her client's dread of family scrutiny, yet Cage took the part anyway.[67]

For Coppola, too, *The Cotton Club* came with considerable baggage. The film's tumultuous production history, a four-year saga filled with unsavory financiers and ballooning costs, often overshadows the movie itself. This chaos, though, was set in motion long before Coppola came on board.

After the *Godfather* films, Coppola, not wanting to be pigeonholed, had little interest in directing another mobster picture. "If I just had made a career of fifteen mafioso movies, I would be very rich," he later told *GQ*, "but I wouldn't know as much as I do now."[68] Nor was he eager to reunite with Robert Evans, the notoriously erratic and drug-addled producer who, as head of production at Paramount, had presided over *The Godfather*. Back then, Evans had fought Coppola on virtually every decision—insisting that Pacino was all wrong for the film, that casting Brando was a fool's choice, conspiring to replace Coppola with Elia Kazan—then eagerly took credit for the film's success when it came out.[69]

By 1980, Evans was long gone from Paramount and his career was in a downward spiral after a well-publicized drug bust. The solution, he believed, was to spend his own money optioning James Haskins's book *The Cotton Club*, a pictorial history of the legendary Harlem jazz club where Black musicians like Fats Waller and Duke Ellington performed for a white audience that often included well-known mobsters. Evans envisioned a fictionalized film centered on real-life mob figures frequenting the club. Hiring *Godfather* author Mario Puzo to write a screenplay, he wanted to pair *The Godfather* with an immersion in African American history and music. Evans's pitch, in his own words, was "gangsters, music, pussy—how could I lose?"[70]

From there, everything went wrong. Puzo struggled to produce a worthwhile script. Evans tried and failed to nail down Al Pacino, then Sylvester Stallone for the lead role. Robert Altman was briefly attached to direct, then walked away. Evans, who had no directorial experience, decided to direct *The Cotton Club* himself.

Meanwhile, given his tarnished reputation, he failed to attract much interest from major studios (his proposed $18–20 million budget wasn't cheap) and decided to fund the picture with private investors instead. Evans raised seed money from a Saudi arms dealer named Adnan Khashoggi, and later convinced two rich casino tycoons with no knowledge of filmmaking, Ed and Fred Doumani, Sr., to finance the production in exchange for a stake.[71]

Eventually, Richard Gere signed on for the lead role (a fictitious, mob-connected musician named Dixie Dwyer), resulting in a de-emphasis of the African American characters, and Orion Pictures agreed to distribute the film.[72] Gere's contract guaranteed him script approval, and there was still not an approved shooting script. Despite their mutual animosity, a desperate Evans contacted Coppola and pleaded with him to help whip the mess of a script into shape.

"Richard Gere said, 'I'll have to have a proper writer write this script,'" recalls executive producer Dyson Lovell. "And Bob said, 'There's only one writer that I really respect. That's Francis Ford Coppola. And he's not speaking to me.' " Lovell mediated between the two men, and Coppola agreed to take a call from Evans. When Evans asked his former enemy to help edit the script, Coppola agreed, free of charge.[73]

The project spiraled out of control. Amidst this chaos, Evans's film about organized crime and murder became intertwined with real organized crime and murder. In April 1983, after the Doumani brothers cut off further funding because they disliked Coppola's rewrite, Evans struck a deal with a vaudeville show promoter named Roy Radin, who created a $35 million offshore holding company intended to back *The Cotton Club* and four subsequent films.[74]

Then Radin became embroiled in a dispute with a cocaine dealer named Karen Greenberger (also known as Elaine Jacobs), who had introduced him to Evans and now wanted a percentage of the deal. He refused. Weeks later, Radin was found dead, his body decomposing in a remote canyon outside Los Angeles.[75]

Greenberger and several associates were later convicted of Radin's murder. Evans was questioned as a possible suspect, and though he was never charged in the crime—nor did any evidence suggest he was involved—the murder destroyed what remained of his Hollywood reputation. "The Cotton Club Murder," as the incident became known, cast a dark shadow over the film long after the shoot wrapped.[76]

* * *

Coppola never planned to direct *The Cotton Club*. He was recruited as a pro bono script doctor. At the time, he was planning to direct a different gangster movie: *The Pope of Greenwich Village*.[77]

But after reading an early draft of Evans's screenplay, Coppola deemed it a disastrous mess. He summoned Evans and Gere to his estate and pitched a new vision for the story. Evans, impressed, offered him $250,000 to rewrite it; Coppola, still in desperate need of cash, accepted. Coppola soon became enthralled by the rich historical backdrop of the Cotton Club and the concurrent Harlem Renaissance and conceived of two distinct storylines—one Black and one white—woven together like *The Godfather Part II*. Evans, however, hated Coppola's unabashedly educational screenplay. Desiring a sexier, more commercial product, Evans paid him another $250,000 to rewrite it again.[78]

The movie was consumed by chaos and ballooning costs long before shooting began. The original $20 million price tag now seemed like a quaint fantasy. As Evans became preoccupied with the legal and funding complications, Coppola took over the film's creative development. Soon it became inevitable that Coppola would direct *The Cotton Club*. He didn't want the job, but Evans, who once thought he could direct it himself, needed an experienced, bankable director at the helm to keep the money flowing and both the Doumanis and Orion happy. Coppola refused, but then—recalling the endless meddling from Evans on *The Godfather*—agreed on one condition: full creative control.[79]

Coppola immediately asserted control, dismissing Evans's crew members and replacing them with his own. "Francis fired the majority of them within three weeks of taking over," says cinematographer Stephen Goldblatt. Coppola began making crucial casting decisions. He rehired multiple actors from *Rumble Fish*: Diane Lane (as the glamorous Vera Cicero, Richard Gere's love interest), Tom Waits (as the nightclub's emcee), and Laurence Fishburne.

Valley Girl came out in April 1983, the same month Coppola was immersed in rewriting *The Cotton Club*. Coppola was impressed with Cage's performance and offered him a supporting role as Vincent Dwyer, the violent, unstable younger brother of protagonist Dixie Dwyer (Gere). "Francis saw what Nick could do, and he was very right for this role—a wild, out of control young gangster," says Fred Roos. "That over-the-top thing Nick could do was perfect for it."

Like several characters in *The Cotton Club*, Cage's was based on a real-life crime figure: Vincent "Mad Dog" Coll, a sadistic mob hitman who was involved with New York boss Dutch Schultz's bootlegging operation before splitting off and forming his own gang, resulting in a bloody gang war between the two. In 1931, Coll became a public enemy after he inadvertently shot and killed a five-year-old boy during a botched hit on a Schultz enforcer. His crime career came to a grisly end in 1932, when, at twenty-three, he was gunned down in a Manhattan telephone booth shortly after kidnapping and holding a rival gangster for ransom.[80]

These events—with some names and details changed—are dramatized as a subplot in *The Cotton Club*. As Vincent Dwyer, Cage stalks around the criminal underworld with slicked-back hair and a pencil-thin mustache, his well-groomed appearance belying the chaos he unleashes and the enemies he forms. Brash and impulsive, the character was not unlike the war-hungry hothead Cage had played in *Racing with the Moon*, albeit with a more hateful, homicidal streak.

As he had on *Racing*, Cage was determined to commit to his character as uncompromisingly as possible. But with the *Cotton Club* production mired in endless delays and over-budget costs (not to mention conflicts between Coppola and Evans, who was effectively banned from his own set at Coppola's orders), this proved to be more of a commitment than Cage had planned. When he arrived in New York in August 1983, Cage had no way of knowing that the shoot would take him through Christmas. "It was like joining the army," Tom Waits later quipped, "like being Shanghaied."[81]

"But there was no real expectation," says Goldblatt, the cinematographer. "There was no script! There was no plan! It was a bunch of crooks started it off. The whole bunch of them—they were all crooks. Cash was coming in from Atlantic City and we were making the film and it was chaos, I suppose, but Francis took total responsibility."

Cast member Lisa Jane Persky recalls spending months in the basement of the Kaufman Astoria Studios, working sixteen-hour days, exhausted yet awestruck at the caliber of talent around her. "It was script after script after script, and month after month. Problems. And it got to be really grueling," Persky says. "But it was hard to lose sight of the fact that you were working with all of these great people and you were trying to make something amazing."

Waits estimated that he worked on the film for twelve weeks, a remarkable figure given that he's onscreen for a few brief moments. Cage would learn that there was a considerable difference between playing a vicious gangster for two hours onscreen and embodying one for weeks on end.

* * *

Never in the early years of his career did Cage portray a character more reprehensible than the one he played in *The Cotton Club*, and never did he behave more terribly on a film set than he did on *The Cotton Club*.

This was a matter of direct correlation, not coincidence. To play a homicidal maniac, Cage believed, was to *be* a homicidal maniac. In 1983, he was at the peak of his Method phase and operating under the influence of Sean Penn. Penn famously lived his parts. But it was one thing to live the part of a good-hearted lover boy. How do you live the part of a psychotic gangster?

Not easily, Cage learned. "I couldn't really be a madman for the six months I was filming, because I'd be in jail by now," Cage told an interviewer in 1986. "I tried it for the first three weeks. I tried to instill some horror in people."[82]

Like Penn, Cage insisted on being called by his character's name. "When Nick would scream 'Call me Vince,' it kind of put people off," says Jane Bartelme, an assistant to the producers. "He was very insistent on maintaining the integrity of the character through filming, which could be alarming. . . . He would go into a rage when people called him Nick."

Enamored with tales of how Robert De Niro had lived his parts in *Taxi Driver* and *Raging Bull*, Cage tried to emulate the approach. As he roamed around the city in character as Vince Dwyer, his antics caused chaos beyond the film's already troubled set. One day, Cage was wandering around Greenwich Village when he spotted a street vendor selling remote-control cars. He grabbed one and destroyed it. "I smashed it, and everybody started clearing the street going, 'He's crazy, he's out of his mind,'" Cage later recalled. "I remember I gave the guy fifty dollars because I felt bad, but I needed people telling me that I was [crazy] so that when I went to work I'd believe it."[83]

Other stories of Cage's unhinged behavior abound. There was, for instance, the time he trashed his trailer in an explosion of rage, tossing his lamp out the window. The damage was so significant, "they docked his pay," says Aleta Chappelle, who worked in extra casting on the film. "It was really bad. I don't remember the money amount, but it was a huge amount. It was five figures."

Cage later attributed the incident to frustration with shooting delays. "I was slated for three weeks of work," he told *Playboy*. "I was there for six months, in costume, in makeup, on the set, in case Francis got an idea that would involve my character. Meanwhile, I'm getting offers for starring roles in other movies and I can't do them. So my behavior—all the acting out—came from frustration."[84]

At times, Cage directed his destructive energies at expensive props. A crew member named Lewis Gould, who was a second assistant director during the film's reshoot schedule, recalls one instance when he was tasked with fetching Cage from his trailer. As Gould walked Cage to the set, "he was hyping himself up for the scene," Gould recalls. "His face was very intense. He was just storming down the street."

The street was dressed for the period, and Cage passed by about a dozen vintage automobiles parked along the curb. In character as Vinnie Dwyer, the actor began angrily pounding each car he passed with his fist. "He was psyching himself up," Gould says. "But he was actually denting the fenders. And this guy who had brought the cars—he freaked out. He just came running: 'Hey, what the hell are you doing?'"

Suddenly, Cage snapped out of it. "It's like he realized, 'Oh shit. I shouldn't be denting these cars!' "

* * *

Some say that, amidst a production so turmoil-ridden that Coppola at one point walked off the set because the Doumani brothers couldn't meet payroll and were threatening to reduce his earnings, Cage's misbehavior was a drop in the bucket of chaos.[85] Costs were mounting; scripts were being rewritten daily; an actual mob associate named Joey Cusumano (a pal of the Doumanis) was hovering on set to monitor Coppola's progress.

"There were enormous difficulties in production and timing," says Goldblatt. Certainly, Cage wasn't the only star embroiled in conflict and drama. At the start of the shoot, Richard Gere was so furious about production delays, he wouldn't even come to set. "He had a contract that said he had script approval," recalls Goldblatt. "And there is no script. So he didn't come to set on the first day of shooting."

Yet it's clear that Cage's antics did not endear him to his co-stars—Gere reportedly warned him, "You keep going like this and you're only going to have about five more movies in you"—nor to the lower-ranking crew members tasked with attending to his messes. "I remember him being an amazing asshole," says Chappelle. "I don't care if he was in character twenty-four-seven. I've been around the best actors in the world. He was *really* bad during *Cotton Club*. I thought he was very abusive to everybody that was around him, and it was frustrating for Francis. I just thought, 'Wow. He's an asshole.' "[86]

"He thought he could get away with it because it was his uncle directing," Chappelle adds. "I think it was also a competitive thing with Francis. It's like a teenage boy acting out in front of his parents."

One disturbing episode lingers in Chappelle's memory. While the trailer incident has become an oft-repeated bit of Cage lore, this one has been lost to history. But it is worth relaying here as evidence of just how far Cage went in playing a repulsive character on- and offscreen.

For context, *The Cotton Club* depicts the brutal racial dynamics of the jazz age. The eponymous nightclub was a segregated space, where African American music filled the stages yet Black people were never welcome offstage. The Black characters—centered on a tap dancer played by real-life dancing legend Gregory Hines—and white characters move in separate worlds; when Hines's character tries to bring his white-passing girlfriend to the club's roof, he is violently assaulted by a bouncer.

Yet the film's attempts to probe the segregation at the heart of the romanticized nightclub are perfunctory at best. In a fictionalized flourish, jazz cornetist Dixie Dwyer (Gere) is portrayed as the first white musician to play with the Cotton Club band,[**] while his brother, Vincent (Cage), stews with racial hatred. Vincent's feelings about Black people are not ambiguous: "Good thing n*****s ain't allowed," he cheerily tells a companion while ushering her into the club. Later in the film, bleeding from a gunshot graze, Vincent tells his brother he "was fighting n*****s."

Unfortunately, Cage's determination to remain in character was so extreme that he allegedly began adopting his character's racist vocabulary on set. He did so not out of genuine racial animus, but instead in an effort to remain in character—a dark and deeply misguided perversion of Method acting. Such behavior was obviously indefensible—and liable to stoke altercations on set.

Chappelle, who supervised extras casting, recalls witnessing a tense confrontation that broke out after Cage used a racial slur on the set for an all-Black club scene. "He was in character, and I guess improvised something with one of the extras," Chappelle says.

The extra, who was Black, became so upset that he tried to fight Cage, Chappelle recalls. "It was a terrible incident on set. That was just too far. Everybody knew it was too far. "It was very upsetting," Chappelle adds. "And it did stop the shooting for a while."

Cage has never publicly mentioned this incident, as far as I can tell. But he has acknowledged his use of racial slurs on set. "The character was racist, so I'd stalk around calling everybody 'n****r,' " the actor is quoted as saying in a 1998 biography, *Nicolas Cage: Hollywood's Wild Talent*.[††] "By the time I was on film, I truly believed I was a psychotic whack job gangster thug."[87]

[**] Richard Gere reportedly agreed to the role on the condition that he get to play cornet—a complicated demand, given that, in reality, white musicians did not play at the Cotton Club.

[††] All quotes in this biography appear to be from other sources, but the book does not clarify where quotes such as this one first appeared.

Given the potentially contentious nature of such a story, I reached out to Cage to let him know the anecdote would appear in this book and offer him a chance to comment. Through his manager, Cage responded to say that there were no fights on the set of *The Cotton Club* and that he has no recollection of anything like that happening.

* * *

As Cage's breakout year of 1983 drew to a close, Coppola, his relationship with Evans now soured beyond repair, was under immense pressure to complete principal photography on *The Cotton Club* before Christmas. As Evans relinquished control of the production, Coppola shot a huge portion of the film in one grueling three-week stretch—"the shoot in Grand Central went on without a break for thirty-six hours," recalls Goldblatt—and managed to complete the bulk of filming by 6:00 a.m., Christmas Eve.[88]

Cage had been in character for so long that it was no longer clear to crew members where Nicolas Cage ended and Vincent Dwyer began. "From the day he started working, he was that character in the film. He was never out of it," says Goldblatt. Throughout the shoot, Goldblatt remembers Cage being "cold and off-centered, just as he is in the movie," but the cinematographer didn't quite realize that the coldness was more reflective of Cage's performance than the actor's personality.

In fact, this revelation did not fully hit him until the end of the shoot. On Christmas Eve, in lieu of a wrap party, the cast and crew went home for the holidays. Goldblatt found himself on a private plane with Coppola, Cage, Joey Cusumano, and other members of the cast, heading back to California. "Once we took off, Nicolas Cage returned to the charming, affable, nice guy that he is," Goldblatt recalls. "We were drinking and congratulating ourselves for having survived this, and he was great company. But he had changed from being the moody method actor to a normal person."

The transformation was remarkable. Flying above the city where he had stewed and raged as a petulant gangster for four months, Cage returned to himself. "It was like coming out of a cocoon," Goldblatt says.

* * *

Cage remained on his worst behavior when *The Cotton Club* finally premiered in late 1984. On the day of the New York City premiere, he and other cast members were fêted at a cocktail party at Gracie Mansion. Mayor Ed Koch asked the different actors to say what they liked about filming in New York.

Most gave anodyne answers ("Because I'm a native New Yorker," said Diane Lane), except Cage, who blurted out: "Because I got to hold a gun on the streets of New York."[89]

Later, at the film's premiere, Cage played a prank on Carly Simon. By his own account, he rolled up a paper program, placed it to her ear, and whispered the words "clouds in my coffee" (a lyric from Simon's hit "You're So Vain"). Simon "whipped her head around, snarled, and I looked at my friend like he did it," Cage recounted.[90]

Orion initially marketed *The Cotton Club* as a star vehicle for Gere, as well as a mob movie in the spirit of *The Godfather*, and early returns were promising. The film opened at number five and ultimately grossed more than $25 million, but such a respectable showing was not nearly enough to recoup the film's outrageous $47 million budget. When some—though hardly all—critics began panning the film, Orion shifted its marketing focus to *Amadeus*.[91] *The Cotton Club* became yet another commercial disappointment for Coppola, its runaway budget and protracted production history heightening its status as a box office bomb.

Worse, the film exacerbated Coppola's reputation for financial imprudence. Evans and Coppola openly bickered in the press about who was to blame for the costs.[92]

The irony was that Coppola had made *The Cotton Club* in part to redeem himself after *One from the Heart*, yet *The Cotton Club* shared *Heart*'s biggest shortcoming: an emphasis on style over storytelling. In interspersing the club performers onstage with the brutal violence of the storyline, Coppola suggests that show business and corruption are inextricably linked. Yet despite strong performances and a lavish recreation of the Cotton Club interior, the film often feels like an expensive series of glittery set pieces without a defined center; its mobster plot doesn't deliver the urgency such a story requires. As the *New Yorker*'s Pauline Kael wrote in a particularly scathing assessment, "The way [Coppola] directs the cast here, people exist to reflect light."[93]

Some critics were more positive, yet few took much notice of Cage. As 1984 drew to a close, the actor's profile was rising but his stardom was uncertain. All three movies he appeared in that year had been box office disappointments.

Is it any wonder I've written thousands of words about *The Cotton Club* and have barely mentioned his performance? Such has always been *The*

Cotton Club's abiding curse: the turmoil that went on behind the scenes is simply more interesting to talk about than the turmoil that unfolds onscreen.

Still, it's worth mentioning that Cage is good in the film—that he instills his scenes with a certain doomed recklessness, that he flexes his muscle for portraying wild-eyed, impulsive criminals. It's a naturalistic performance, with none of the surrealistic flourishes Cage would eventually bring to maniacal characters in films like *Vampire's Kiss*. Yet he's good at showing the turmoil and neediness concealed by this character's hotheaded bloodlust. If this were *The Godfather*, Cage would be Sonny Corleone. No surprise, then, that his character gets a grisly comeuppance reminiscent of Sonny's.

None of this was enough to redeem such a muddled film, nor to erase bitter memories of Cage's antics. "It took me years to get to a point where New Yorkers in the film industry would want to work with me again," Cage told *Rolling Stone* in 1999.[94] By then, Cage had distanced himself from his wild behavior on *The Cotton Club*'s set. It was just misguided mythmaking, he told *Vanity Fair*. "I wanted to generate stories about myself. I was trying to create a mythology around myself. All my heroes had stories around them, whether they were true or false."[95]

In hindsight, he succeeded a little too well, so much so that the stories behind his *Cotton Club* role overshadowed the performance itself—a microcosm for the film's own fate.

* * *

When Cage reunited with his uncle for their third and final collaboration, it was a film neither of them at first wanted to make. The offer to direct *Peggy Sue Got Married* had fallen into Coppola's lap in the fall of 1984, when he was still wrestling with *The Cotton Club*. A nostalgic fantasy-drama involving time travel and high school, it was not typical Coppola fare.

But the director was still deep in debt to Chase Manhattan Bank. Pursuing long-simmering passion projects was no longer a luxury he could afford. He needed work—fast.

"*Peggy Sue*, I must say, was not the kind of film I normally would want to do," Coppola later said in an NPR interview. "The nature of my debts is that I have to make gigantic payments in March, millions of dollars. And so when the time starts getting closer to the payment and I'm looking around saying what should I do, the project that was ready to go that wanted me was *Peggy Sue*."

The project had been in development hell for a while, bouncing from director to director, and Coppola wasn't too keen on the script: it seemed like a television story. What persuaded him was the judgment of his longtime producer Fred Roos, who liked the script and convinced Coppola it would be a success. Coppola needed a success.[96]

The story centered on Peggy Sue Bodell, a middle-aged woman in the midst of a bitter separation from her philandering husband—and former high school sweetheart—Charlie Bodell. While attending her twenty-fifth high school reunion in 1985, Peggy Sue passes out and wakes up back in . . . 1960, her senior year of high school, the year she married Charlie, an aspiring singer whose career never took off. Much of the humor stems from Peggy Sue's status as "a walking anachronism": she jokes about going to Liverpool to discover the Beatles and teases her dad for buying an Edsel. At first mystified, and then with a renewed sense of purpose, Peggy Sue relives this fateful sliver of her past in the hopes of altering her future.

The screenplay had been dreamed up by a married couple named Jerry Leichtling and Arlene Sarner, the first film for these budding screenwriters. There were two inspirations. In 1983, the couple hosted a music party, an unforgettable evening where everyone seemed to enter a nostalgic trance, singing oldies from the doo-wop age. "People were just swept back by the music," Sarner remembers. "They were just singing all night long. The next day, we thought, 'Well, either we should start a religion around this or write a movie about it.' "

That planted the seed: the idea that music could function as a time machine. If *Valley Girl* was a celebration of then-current New Wave bands, *Peggy Sue Got Married* was to be an immersion in the golden oldies of the fifties and early sixties. It even took its name from a 1959 song by Buddy Holly.[‡‡]

The other inspiration was more personal. Like Peggy Sue, Sarner had married her high school sweetheart (music producer Bob Ezrin) and had gotten pregnant soon after graduation. Eventually, the marriage collapsed. "At the time, I was going through a really difficult divorce," Sarner says. "And thinking about how I would have lived my life differently. I decided, well, if I didn't marry my first husband, I wouldn't have had my children."

Sarner and Leichtling (her second husband) wrote a treatment quickly and caught the interest of a producer named Paul R. Gurian. He was intrigued,

‡‡ Initially, all the major characters were named after early rock & roll songs. Charlie was named after the Coasters' hit "Charlie Brown."

but thought the script needed work. Gurian describes the original draft as a collection of vignettes about a woman who goes back in time because she's listening to songs that invoke old memories. He says he told the couple: "This is charming. [But] if I'm gonna do this kind of thing, I want to do something serious and warm and American. I want to do *It's a Wonderful Life* from a woman's point of view."

Gurian worked with them on developing the script. Then he managed to sell it to the powerful Hollywood producer Ray Stark and his Rastar production company in a deal with TriStar. Disney chief Jeffrey Katzenberg had been interested, too, and even offered to double Gurian's producer fee, but Gurian turned him down.

The production was troubled from the beginning. Not *Cotton Club*–level troubled—no murders. This turmoil was of a more routine Hollywood flavor. Debra Winger signed on as the film's star, and a young Jonathan Demme, fresh off his Talking Heads rockumentary *Stop Making Sense*, was hired to direct, only to leave the project because of creative differences with Winger.

Winger recruited a new director for the film: her friend Penny Marshall. That didn't work out either. Hawk Koch, the president of Rastar, was immediately suspicious of Marshall's lack of directing experience and habit of scheduling meetings at midnight. Late one night, Koch was awoken by the screenwriters knocking on his bedroom window, distraught over Marshall's proposed changes to the script. "They were hysterical," Koch says. "They proceeded to tell me they had just come from a meeting with Penny. Penny wanted to do a whole different movie. She wanted to place it in the Bronx."

Koch resolved to fire Marshall, ostensibly because of disagreements with the writers. Sarner declines to say what those disagreements were. "It was gonna be Penny Marshall's first movie," Sarner says. "At some point, they decided it was really getting too big and wasn't quite the right thing for her. And she was gone. And then we had Debra Winger, and no movie, no director."[§§]

Now Winger was trying to quit. Gurian remembers asking her in desperation, "Debra, how are we gonna get this movie made?" Winger suggested there was only one director she would work with: Francis Ford Coppola.

[§§] In her own memoir, the late Penny Marshall wrote that she felt undermined and disrespected by the studio heads from the beginning, and described meetings with them that felt like "being in front of the KGB." Notably, Marshall later became a major box office force when she directed 1988's *Big*, a comedy whose premise—boy transforms overnight into grown adult—is basically *Peggy Sue* in reverse.

Gurian assured Winger that they could get Coppola. "Because if he doesn't do a film, it's over," he remembers telling her. "He loses his house. And he loses his vineyard."

Indeed, the director was at risk of losing his Zoetrope studio headquarters in San Francisco if he didn't make a $1.7 million payment soon.[97] Conveniently enough, Koch got a call from Coppola's attorney, Barry Hirsch. " Barry said, 'Listen, have you got anything for Francis? He *really* needs a movie,' " Koch says. "And I said, 'Have I got a movie for Francis!' "

After some initial reluctance, Coppola agreed to direct *Peggy Sue Got Married*. At the time, the director's asking price was $2.5 million a film. Aware of Coppola's reputation for extravagant spending, Koch put unique clauses in his contract requiring him to keep the film strictly within budget.

Then, in February 1985, disaster struck: Winger suffered a major back injury a month before shooting was scheduled to start. On February 13, the *Los Angeles Times* reported that the producers planned to wait for Winger's recovery: "This is a picture designed for one star," Gurian told the paper, "and we've been through a lot of rocky roads."[98] But Winger was forced to drop out when doctors said her recovery would take months. The whole film was in jeopardy again.

"And that's when TriStar wanted to pull out," Gurian says. Gurian recruited Stark and Stark's tough-minded attorney, Jerry Lipsky. "Every morning they would wake up and try to figure out how to fuck Kirk Kerkorian," Gurian says. "They and I figured out a way to force TriStar into financing the picture."

Now they needed a new star. The studio settled on Kathleen Turner, who had risen to fame after starring in the erotic thriller *Body Heat* and who, in her early thirties, could play Peggy Sue both as a middle-aged mother and as a high schooler. (While Penny Marshall had liked the idea of double-casting, Gurian was insistent that the same actors should play the characters in both 1985 and in 1960.) Turner was fascinated by the idea of bringing a feminist edge to Coppola's male-dominated work. When she met with Coppola, they bonded by driving around Los Angeles, singing songs from the doo-wop era.[99] The trouble was, Turner was already scheduled to shoot 1985's *The Jewel of the Nile*, which meant *Peggy Sue* would have to be delayed—again—until the fall.

As for the male lead, Peggy Sue's boyfriend (and future husband) Charlie, the producers didn't have to look far. Why not Coppola's nephew?

* * *

Thirty-five years later, Gurian chuckles at the mention of Cage's name, like a bemused grandparent recalling their strangest grandson with affection. "Nicolas . . . oh boy," he says. "He's wacky! But his wackiness has a certain kind of life, and a certain kind of brutal honesty. I mean, the guy is constantly doing personality surgery in front of everybody."

Others were considered for the role of Peggy Sue's boyfriend, Judge Reinhold and Martin Short among them.[100] "I thought Nick was one of the few available people who could do the job," says Gurian. "A number of the emerging stars who could be viable did not see that there *was* a serious male role in the film. As did not the studio—'Oh my God, we're gonna make a movie starring a *woman*? And she's not Barbra Streisand?' "

Gurian knew Cage was capable. He'd been impressed by his performance in *Valley Girl*. He figured Cage would bring a similarly appealing, hunk-ish energy to *Peggy Sue*. Wrong assumption.

Meanwhile, Cage was committed to a different project: an apocalyptic thriller called *Miracle Mile*, written by a first-time director named Steve De Jarnatt. In early 1985, Cage told an interviewer that *Miracle Mile* would be his next film. He described it in mysterious terms: "Imagine being a mastodon in the tar pits and being found millions of years later by aliens."[101]

After securing a measly $2 million budget, De Jarnatt was scheduled to begin shooting *Miracle Mile* in August 1985, with Cage starring as a young man who learns that nuclear missiles are about to hit his city. "Nick was turning down everything," says De Jarnatt. "This is the only thing he wanted to make."[102]

Then De Jarnatt says he received a call from Coppola's attorney, Barry Hirsch, who was also representing Cage. In a move that's instructive of how power is wielded in Hollywood, Hirsch allegedly told the filmmaker to put *Miracle Mile* on the backburner.

"He was one of the toughest attorneys in town," says De Jarnatt. According to De Jarnatt, Hirsch told him, 'Listen, kid. We're gonna slot your little movie in in a year or two, but Nick's gonna do *Peggy Sue* and a couple other things.' De Jarnatt says he replied 'Wait a sec! That's not what Nick is saying.' But when De Jarnatt tried to reach Cage, the actor was out of town without access to a phone.

Hirsch, however, disputes this story and says he has no memory of that conversation. "There is no way that I would make such a disrespectful remark to a young filmmaker," Hirsch says. "Whether I made such a call or not, I have no idea, but I have no reason to believe I would have made such a phone call."

Coincidentally, De Jarnatt had just been offered a last-minute opportunity to direct a different film, *Cherry 2000*, with a bigger budget. He decided to accept, letting *Miracle Mile* fall into development hell.

Some weeks later, De Jarnatt says he received a desperate call from Cage. "We were just bluffing!" the actor insisted. "I told Barry not to do that! We just wanted to see if you guys could wait." But De Jarnatt had already jumped onto *Cherry 2000*.***

Coppola had gotten his wish. Cage's schedule was now clear.

* * *

Cage was initially uncertain about doing *Peggy Sue Got Married*. Actually, his mind was made up: he didn't want to do it.

His last film with his uncle had left a sour taste. "*The Cotton Club* was a disaster," Gurian says. Nicky was at constant war with Francis. He said, 'I'm never working with my fucking crazy nephew again.' And Nicky said, 'I'm not working with that asshole again.' And I had to make each of them work with the other one again. It was quite something!"

Four years earlier, Cage would have killed for the opportunity to play a big role in one of his uncle's pictures. Now he was uninterested. "I turned it down three times," he told *Movieline* in 1998. "I read the script, which was a perfectly romantic film, but the character he wanted me to play was boring. He was the babe to Kathleen Turner's starring role."[103]

Cage had just shot *The Boy in Blue*, a lackluster Canadian sports drama in which the only real depth his character was allotted was the bulging of his biceps. He hated the thought of playing another pretty face, another beefcake stud. Besides, he was tired of fending off nepotism charges. After his unhappy *Cotton Club* ordeal, he didn't need another Coppola project on his résumé. He could get roles on his own now.

Coppola persisted. He told his nephew it would be just like *Our Town*—the Thornton Wilder play Cage had acted in at Beverly Hills High.††† He said, "I really need you to be in the movie."[104]

For perhaps the first time in his career, Cage had some real leverage to negotiate. It wasn't money he wanted; it was the freedom to make the character

*** De Jarnatt eventually made *Miracle Mile* in 1988. But Cage's profile had risen. When De Jarnatt tried to get Cage back on board, the actor's agent, Ed Limato, suggested other names and said Cage was all booked up. Anthony Edwards ultimately starred opposite Mare Winningham.

††† Cage hated *Our Town*. He had played the role of Constable Warren, while Jon Turteltaub—his classmate and future *National Treasure* director—won the starring role. Coppola, however, saw the play as a model for *Peggy Sue*.

so weird that it was liable to frighten his co-stars. After taking naturalism to an extreme in *Birdy*, Cage wanted to try out a surrealistic approach to acting. "Look, I'll do it if you let me go really far out with the character," he told Coppola. "How far out?" Coppola said. "I want to talk like Pokey from *The Gumby Show*," Cage said.[105] Coppola said he could give it a try in rehearsals.

Maybe modeling a high school boyfriend after a talking horse from a claymation show from his childhood was a bizarre move, but in Cage's twenty-one-year-old mind, this must have made sense. Pokey spoke in a high, tinny voice. Cage was playing a high schooler and wanted to experiment with the way teenage boys sounded just before their voices dropped. The *Gumby* inspiration arrived by chance. "I was channel surfing and I heard that voice," he told *Playboy*. "It stuck with me. That's the way my brain works."[106]

Later the actor would say he was also struck by the hopelessness of the *Peggy Sue* character: a clueless teenager trying to save a relationship with the woman who has already lived through their future divorce. "I like hopeless situations," he explained in 1986.[107] But clearly, Cage believed the voice was key. He wanted Charlie to be the sort of teen who was in the throes of an awkward, changing voice—not a self-assured jock. He wanted to veer as far away from the testosterone spectacle of *The Boy in Blue* as possible.

Unusual voices are often key to how Cage approaches a role. When he's thinking about a new character, the voice comes first. "I'll read a line in the script and play with it vocally, externally—I'll try to find a melody or a rhythm for it—and then, only after I've got that down, will I go behind the line and put in whatever other stuff it needs to make it come to life," he told *Premiere* in 1997.[108]

In his early days, Cage felt insecure about his own voice—he believed it to be boring—and so went out of his way to imbue every character with a strange new vocal mannerism: there was the nasally squeak he used in *Peggy Sue*, the *Beauty and the Beast*–inspired growl he wanted to use in *Moonstruck* (director Norman Jewison objected), the faux-British accent he affected in *Vampire's Kiss*. Many of Cage's favorite actors, from James Stewart to James Cagney, had distinct voices. "When I started acting, I did not have a good voice, so I had to actively experiment with it and see if I could find rhythms in it, or break it up, or mess with it in some way," Cage later recalled.[109]

Just like on that school bus with his fourth-grade bully, Cage was using acting to escape his own drab identity. Except now he had his uncle's backing. He would need it.

* * *

Peggy Sue Got Married was shot at an unusually brisk pace during the late summer and early fall of 1985. Coppola, determined to prove after the *Cotton Club* fiasco that he could complete a film on time and without bleeding money, subjected the cast and crew to grueling workdays.[110] "We were exhausted most of the time," says the film's hair stylist, Kathryn Blondell. "Francis would work an eighteen-hour day on Monday, and that would set the tone of the week. The pressure was really on for him to finish."

The cast members still found time to bond and form a youthful camaraderie. Principal photography took place in Petaluma, California, and some weekends Coppola would host the young actors at his nearby winery, entertaining them with lavish lunch spreads and props from *Apocalypse Now*. "This was really like being at a camp," says Wil Shriner, who had a small role as one of Charlie's high school buds.

Shriner noticed quickly that Cage was unusually devoted to his part. "He morphed into the role," Shriner says. "We'd sit around, and I don't remember Nick being Nick. I just remember him being Charlie the whole time."

Watching the film today is like flipping through a high school yearbook, peering at the young faces of stars before they were famous. Coppola assembled a formidable lineup of rising talents: there's twenty-three-year-old Jim Carrey, singing in a doo-wop group alongside Cage; Joan Allen in one of her first roles, as Peggy Sue's best friend; Helen Hunt, barely recognizable as Peggy Sue's daughter; and, of course, fourteen-year-old Sofia Coppola as the little sister.

Carrey had achieved some local fame in Canada, but he was still years away from his big-screen breakthrough in *Ace Ventura: Pet Detective*. His minor part in *Peggy Sue* came about because Coppola felt the roles of Charlie's buddies were underwritten, so he suggested casting comedians who could improvise and build out the characters. Fred Roos was tasked with finding talented comics. One night he caught sight of a young Jim Carrey. "I remember that night clearly—going into a club on Sunset, seeing this act, and thinking, 'I've never seen a comedian quite like that,'" says Roos.[‡‡‡] "I got to know him, and then I brought him to Francis."

Once filming began, Cage and Carrey became fast friends and notorious troublemakers, bonding over a mutual appetite for causing mischief. Aleta Chappelle, who worked in the casting department, puts it like this: "Jim

‡‡‡ Roos was effectively a producer on *Peggy Sue*, he says, but could not take a producer credit for reasons involving studio politics.

was funnier than hell and crazy and wild. But Nick was crazier and wilder than him."

Carrey would seem to agree. Back then, "Nick was just a little bit dangerous to be around," the comedian later told *Vanity Fair*. "He was just expressing himself. He'd stare at someone in a really weird way just to see what the reaction was. And I said, 'Well, what are you being a psycho for?' "[111]

Carrey, however, was not an innocent bystander to Cage's antics. During the shoot, the pair carried out pranks at their Santa Rosa hotel that ranged from sophomoric to reckless. They darted around the place with squirt guns, and one rumor on set claimed they sneaked into the pool and tossed all the pool furniture into the water. "Our hotel was a madhouse," Cage said in 1986.[112]

More alarming was an episode in which they allegedly pranked a room-service waiter with a prop gun and pretended to kidnap him. Cage was quick to downplay this incident years later: "We were young and fooling around, and the guy knew we were joking," he told a *Playboy* interviewer.[113]

Gurian, who still has the prop .45 automatic in his desk, remembers it differently. He says the ill-advised stunt caused chaos and nearly destroyed the production. The terrified room-service waiter was understandably upset.

"I think somebody had to make it right with that guy," says Shriner. "Those guys were screwing around, but it was way out of line. They embarrassed the guy to the point where he went back and complained. I think our production manager had to offer him a little settlement."[§§§]

For Carrey, Cage's willingness to take risks and experiment in a high-stakes situation was an inspiration.[114] The two remained close friends and drinking buddies for years. In 1996, after Carrey became a star virtually overnight, he was part of Cage's inner circle of friends who gathered at his Hollywood Hills castle for a late-night celebration after the Oscars.[115]

* * *

Peggy Sue time-travels from 1985 to 1960. Given the means, a film historian ought to time-travel instead from the present to the summer of 1985, just to be a fly on the wall during the film's rehearsal sessions. That was where Cage first activated his Gumby voice—delivering his lines in a nasally whine that

§§§ Barrie Osborne, credited as the film's unit production manager, says he doesn't remember any such incident.

resembled a record being played at the wrong speed—to the shock and consternation of Kathleen Turner.

"I went to rehearsal," Cage said in a 2019 interview, "and everybody was rolling their eyes because I was talking like that, and my co-star Kathleen Turner was very upset, because she wanted me to be Al, my character from *Birdy*, and instead she got Jerry Lewis on psychedelia. It did not go over well."[116]

Turner approached Cage on that first day and warned him, "Film is a permanent record. Be careful what you do."[117]

Other cast members were similarly perplexed. "We were kind of all, 'Is he just screwing around with us? This is not the voice he's gonna be using in the movie, is it?'" says Wil Shriner. Shriner remembers glancing around the room. Nobody was telling Cage to cut it out. "We were all looking at each other like, well, he's established. Francis isn't saying anything. Nobody's saying anything."

"It was a weird choice," says Arlene Sarner, the screenwriter, who remembers being present at an early rehearsal when the actors sat around a table and read through the script. "But that was his choice. And Francis gave him free reign." She didn't mind the voice when Cage was playing the teenaged Charlie; she found his approach earnest and adorable. "I had a different reaction to the older Charlie. I thought that was a strange choice. He just seemed older than forty."

Like *Birdy*, *Peggy Sue* required Cage to play dual versions of the same character: "present-day" Charlie as a middle-aged philanderer in 1985, "past" Charlie as a high school senior in 1960. The present-day scenes enabled Cage to slather himself in sleaze as a crass appliance salesman: when we first meet him, he's hawking VCRs in a gaudy television commercial that looks like something out of *UHF*. Then the shot unfurls backward in a dizzying feat of camera ingenuity to reveal a mirror in which Peggy Sue, still reeling from their separation, is dolling herself up for the reunion. She's trying to ignore her estranged husband, a failed musician who recently cheated on her, on the TV behind her.

This is the rare movie where Cage gets to make three distinct screen entrances. In his first, he's on the TV screen. In his second, he materializes in a doorway of artificial light at the high school reunion, swaggering down a staircase like the king of his domain. It's the first time we glimpse "Crazy Charlie" in the flesh: there he is, a flashy peacock of a man in a garish white suit, chest hair protruding out of his button-down. "So, this is the reunion?"

Cage rasps in a weird drawl that's half Marlon Brando in *The Godfather*, half sinus infection. He flashes Peggy Sue an arrogant look. Once again, she seems uncomfortable with his presence.

Cage had always looked a little old to be playing teenagers—when he met John Hughes, the director joked that he looked thirty-five—so he relished the opportunity to play an older character for once. Cage was twenty-one, playing a forty-three-year-old man, but naturally he took it too far, slicking back his hair and drawling his lines like a geriatric lounge singer. "He tried to make the older character too old," says Gurian. "And one day I almost beat him up because I said, '*Nick*. I am younger than the age you're playing right now. And I'm about to kick the shit out of you if you don't start understanding that that age is not eighty. OK? You're not eighty.' "

Cage's third screen entrance is the most striking of all. Here is where we first meet Charlie as a teenager in 1960—an aspiring singer, naïve and innocent, full of hope for a musical break that will never come. Again we glimpse him through Peggy Sue's eyes, now bewildered instead of annoyed: After fainting at the reunion in a flood of emotion, she awakes to find herself at her high school blood drive twenty-five years earlier. A visibly younger Charlie, baby-faced with a poufy blonde pompadour, crashes her reverie with a B-grade Dracula impression, flirtily pretending to bite into her neck. "I *vant* to suck your blood," Cage intones in a hybrid vampire/Pokey voice before planting a kiss on her lips.

It takes a few scenes for the audience to register that the high-pitched voice is not an extension of the silly Dracula impression. It's just how Charlie talks. When he pulls up in Peggy Sue's driveway in his blue Impala, he sounds like a jittery cartoon character. He leans in for a kiss; Peggy Sue feigns a headache (Figure 4.2). "*Headache*, huh?" Charlie responds in a voice that sounds like someone is forcibly clamping his nostrils shut.

The audience is ostensibly supposed to root for Peggy Sue and Charlie to get back together, but Cage seemed determined to complicate this proposition by making Charlie as much of a dweeb as possible. The producers grew concerned about that voice. "He brought it into the first few days of shooting and people went bonkers," says Gurian. "I had to talk to him and talk him off the ledge. You have no idea how extreme it was in the beginning."

Not knowing about the Pokey inspiration, Gurian became convinced Cage was trying to imitate old footage of fifties star Dion without realizing that the recording had been sped up, artificially manipulating the tone of Dion's voice. "I was the one who pulled him back when I said, 'OK, you saw a Dion

Figure 4.2. In *Peggy Sue Got Married* (1986, Tri-Star Pictures), Cage wore a blonde pompadour, used fake teeth, and spoke in a high-pitched voice modeled after a horse from *Gumby*. Kathleen Turner (left) was horrified.

show on television. And you got this extreme voice,'" Gurian says. "I said, 'Nicky. Some of it has to do with the fidelity of the actual show. We'll go see Dion DiMucci and you'll see Dion DiMucci doesn't talk like that. You gotta pull back.' The dailies people totally freaked out when they saw how far he had taken it."

The way Gurian tells it, Coppola "kind of shrugged his shoulders and said, 'What am I gonna do with my crazy nephew?'"

Even fourteen-year-old Sofia Coppola seemed perturbed by Cage's work. "She was always on the set with her father," says Cage's brother Christopher. "And when Nicolas was doing some of his over-the-top stuff, Sofia kept taking her hand and waving it down, like, 'Bring it down! Bring it down!' And he said, 'Cut! Can you get her out of here?' to his uncle. That really pissed him off."

* * *

Even if Cage *wasn't* riffing on Dion, Gurian was correct to sense that Cage's performance was stuffed with bizarrely specific cultural references, Pokey included, that no one would understand. Behold the scene in which Charlie, a virgin, is taken aback by Peggy Sue's sudden sexual overtures. As she goads Charlie with increasingly naughty terms for his penis—"Doesn't Lucky Chucky want to come out?"—Cage's face contorts into a strange position, his mouth sustaining a wide "O" for five seconds. Only years later did Cage reveal that he had been obsessed with Edvard Munch's painting *The Scream* and was attempting to mimic the subject's facial expression.[118]

During a dramatic confrontation with Peggy Sue, Cage channeled an even more bizarre source text: a 1983 commercial that John Stamos had done for NEET hair remover (though in multiple interviews, Cage misremembered it as a L'eggs pantyhose commercial). "In it he said, 'I *love* L'eggs pantyhose!'" Cage told the *New York Times*. "And the way he went 'love'—he expressed it with almost a rock & roll screech. I saw that commercial, and I had to put it in *Peggy Sue Got Married*." This, presumably, explains the grating way Cage's voice cracks when he asks Peggy Sue, "Did we break *up?*"[119]

These are some of the moments where Cage appears to be sailing off into an entirely different movie than his co-stars. Yet to Cage's mind, he wasn't sabotaging the film. Rather, he interpreted Peggy Sue's visit to 1960 as occurring in a dream state, an interpretation with which screenwriter Arlene Sarner agrees and which Coppola's production designer, Dean Tavoularis, and cinematographer, Jordan Cronenweth, accentuated with unusual color schemes.

"[Cronenweth] wanted a real transition in the look of the film," says executive producer Barrie M. Osborne. For the back-in-time scenes, "he went for this Kodachrome look, which was the look you would have seen if you had taken Kodak photos of people during that year. They had a book of photographs that they used to demonstrate what they were after. Doing that became complicated and difficult. For example, to get the saturated greens in the film, we painted lawns through Petaluma green. And we painted sidewalks purple."

To Cage's mind, this dreamlike visual scheme called for a dreamlike approach to performance: if the film was unfolding in some hallucinatory vision, wasn't that license to make the characters fuzzy and distorted? "I saw Francis being very adventuresome, painting the sidewalks pink and the trees yellow—getting surreal," Cage later explained to *Details*. "I thought, Why can't actors do that? I had license to do whatever I want, because in dreams, you can get as abstract as you want."[120]

* * *

One of the more sensational stories from the making of *Peggy Sue Got Married* holds that studio executives (likely Ray Stark, the powerful producer and head of Rastar) sought to fire Cage from the production because of his woozy performance, but Coppola held them at bay. Cage has told versions of this story over the years, relishing his role as the iconoclast rebel who made the suits uncomfortable.

Here he is in 1989, boasting in a *SPIN* profile: "[E]veryone from TrisStar, including Ray Stark, got in a Learjet and flew up to see my uncle fire me. But Francis always stands by anything that's a little unusual, and he told me stories about Marlon Brando on *The Godfather*—about how people watched the dailies and said, 'You can't let him do that,' and he said, 'Wait and see.' "[121]

And in 1990, talking to the *San Francisco Examiner* magazine: "Francis was my champion. He had to cook the execs from TriStar a large spaghetti dinner to keep me from being fired."[122]

And most recently, in a widely read 2019 interview with the *New York Times* magazine: "Ray Stark from TriStar[****] flew up to fire me, and thankfully Uncle went to bat and said, 'Young Nicky's doing this.' "[123]

Did this really happen? Stark died in 2004, so he can't be called upon to testify. Multiple sources say it's true that Stark was unhappy with Cage's wigged-out approach, but they doubt Stark ever tried to fire him. "Once we started seeing dailies, there was a lot of back-and-forth as to what Nick was doing," says Jeff Sagansky, then-president of production at Tristar. "Ray just didn't care for his performance. But he wasn't gonna fire him." After such a tumultuous preproduction, Sagansky says, Stark wasn't about to recast and start again.

Stark was a famously mercurial personality with a long reputation as an industry power broker. "Ray Stark wanted to have everybody fired," says Gurian. During the first week of shooting, Stark complained that Turner looked fat and sent her a box of Weight Watchers chocolates. "I had to repair that relationship because she was so upset," Hawk Koch says. As for Stark trying to fire Cage, Koch doesn't remember it. Barrie M. Osborne, the film's executive producer, says it's possible. "I know people were unhappy, or uncertain and frightened by his performance. But Francis defended Nick and supported his interpretation," Osborne says.

"Francis had a way with Ray," Roos adds. "Francis had done writing jobs for him early on, so Francis had a way to handle Ray Stark."

**** Cage presumably meant Rastar—Stark's company—rather than TriStar.

Gurian, meanwhile, describes the whole shoot as a chaotic maelstrom of ego and tension: "Nicky's running around screaming, 'I don't want to work with that fat fuck anymore,' and she's [Kathleen Turner] coming to me saying, 'If you don't get this kid to stop being nuts, I'm not coming out anymore.' It's a movie! It's people being paid to be dramatic! Could you write a better line: 'Francis had to serve a big spaghetti dinner to save me from being fired'—wow! What writer wrote those lines?"

So it's not true, then? Just a savvy bit of self-mythologizing on Cage's part? "I'm saying it doesn't *matter* if it's true!" Gurian insists, his voice rising in frustration. "It's a world of make believe. If the lines sound better, they're the ones that will be used. You're trying to find what is true in a world that functions only on what is necessary."

A reasonable point—and one that would seem to render a primary goal of this book (that is, to separate the Cage mythology from fact) a fool's errand. My teleological crisis is assuaged by the comfort that one fact about the making of *Peggy Sue* is easy to verify: Kathleen Turner really, really didn't like working with Cage. She was unnerved by his performance and feared he was ruining the movie.

No other movie star has ever been more outspoken about how much they hated working with Cage. In a 2018 interview with *Vulture*, Turner described the power struggle on set: "It was tough to not say, 'Cut it out.' But it wasn't my job to say to another actor what he should or shouldn't do. So I went to Francis. I asked him, 'You approved this choice?' It was very touchy. He [Cage] was very difficult on set."[124] (The way Cage put it, in a 1988 interview: Turner was "horizontal and I was vertical."[125])

The film's costumer, Mary Elizabeth Still, recalls one day when she followed Turner into her trailer to help her out of her dress so she could have lunch. "She went first into her trailer, then I came in and shut the door. And she immediately screamed. I couldn't even cover my ears, it was so darn loud," Still says. "She was just rattling on about him. She was *so* frustrated working with him."

Of course, film sets are volatile environments. Surely, one might assume, Cage and Turner later worked out their differences and enjoyed a rewarding friendship?

Well . . . no. In her 2008 memoir, Turner wrote disparagingly of Cage's behavior on set and his bizarre creative choices: "The problem was that once Nicolas got the role, he wanted to prove that he wasn't there as the result of nepotism. And so everything Francis wanted him to do, he went against. . . .

Nicolas had to do the opposite to everything: that stupid voice and the fake teeth—oh, honestly. I cringe to think of it." On the last night of filming, she wrote, Cage drunkenly entered her trailer and sank to his knees, asking if she could ever forgive him. She dismissed him and said she had a scene to shoot.[126]

Most controversially, Turner's book claimed that Cage had gotten arrested twice: once for drunk driving, and once for stealing a dog. ("He came across a Chihuahua he liked and stuck it in his jacket," Turner wrote.) Cage responded by suing Turner and her publisher for defamation and ultimately winning a libel action; the actress's representatives were forced to apologize and admit the passage was false.[127]

After *Peggy Sue*, Turner never worked with Cage again. The actress declined to be interviewed for this book.

* * *

Peggy Sue Got Married was named after a Buddy Holly song, and though the reference was lost on the Gen X viewers of 1986, the film is steeped in the early rock & roll and doo-wop of the Eisenhower era: "Tequila," "I Wonder Why," and other tunes that live on through diner jukeboxes and your parents' old 45s.

The bulk of the movie is set during that fleeting musical era after Holly's death but before the British Invasion: Dion is on the television set, and our fictional Charlie is an aspiring singer who wants to be just like Fabian, the late fifties teen idol whose photo hangs from his car visor. Charlie's musical aspirations become a major subplot: he is insistent that he's going to make it big. Peggy Sue, having lived their future already, knows he'll fall short and wind up blaming his musical failures on her. How can you encourage someone to follow their dreams when you've already seen where it leads?

For Cage, the role was a chance to show off his singing abilities. He'd sung a few bars of "Tangerine" in *Racing with the Moon*, but *Peggy Sue* signified the real blossoming of his musical side. Since then, singing has become a recurring motif in his most legendary performances. As Lindsay Gibb points out in *National Treasure: Nicolas Cage*, Cage "ad-libbed an a cappella version of a piece from Stravinsky's *Petrushka* in *Vampire's Kiss*, sang two Elvis songs in *Wild at Heart*, and made up his own songs in both *Leaving Las Vegas* and *Face/Off*."[128]

That's not to mention *Adaptation*, in which he sings a desperate rendition of "Happy Together" to his dying twin, or *Mom and Dad*, which includes

Cage unleashing a terrifying bastardization of "The Hokey Pokey." Given Cage's interest in transcending the limitations of drab realism, it's no wonder he often plays characters who unexpectedly break into song.

Somehow he has never starred in a proper musical, but *Peggy Sue* might be the closest he's come. Cage activates his puppy-dog sexuality during the scene where he sings the Dion and the Belmonts classic "I Wonder Why" with his doo-wop quartet (which also includes a budding Carrey) (Figure 4.3). As Charlie swivels his hips and bats his eyes in a snazzy gold blazer, Peggy Sue finds herself unexpectedly attracted to her future husband all over again.

A few scenes later, Peggy Sue watches as Charlie sings with an R&B group (the film's only glimpse of racial integration), delivering a sad-eyed rendition of "He Don't Love You (Like I Love You)" to win her back from her artsy poet crush. The crooning strains Charlie's vocal range, but when he gestures his heartbreak with plaintive eyes and outstretched hands, Peggy Sue can't help but swoon.

To prepare for these scenes, Cage trained with a vocal coach named John Merrill, who recalls being impressed with his ability to sing on tune and

Figure 4.3. For Cage, *Peggy Sue Got Married* (1986, Tri-Star Pictures) was a chance to show off his singing abilities. His crooning and stage moves were inspired by early rock & rollers like Elvis Presley and Gene Vincent, the latter of whom Cage nearly portrayed in a biopic.

with expression. Merrill shadowed Cage for days, practicing with him in his trailer, even on the bus to set. Cage learned several songs for the R&B scene and nearly went with Dion's "Runaround Sue," but Merrill felt he was better at performing "He Don't Love You."

The film's hair stylist, Kathryn Blondell, remembers trying four different hairpieces on Cage, sifting through images of popular singing groups from the era to find the right look. "Of course, he looked at all of them. And wanted to be all of them," says Blondell. "He was really kind of wonderful to work with and frustrating at the same time. We wound up in the dentist's office at midnight, dying his hair."[††††]

Cage's ability to project the look and stage mannerisms of a fifties rock & roller was impressive, but in truth, he had more training than anyone knew. That was thanks to preparation for a movie which never got made, and which has gone virtually unmentioned in existing accounts of Cage's career.

The story goes like this: During the years leading up to *Peggy Sue*, Cage was committed to starring in a biopic of rockabilly star Gene Vincent, who was best known for the 1956 hit "Be-Bop-a-Lula," and whose career later declined in a haze of alcoholism and domestic violence. The project was slated to feature a murderers' row of rising talents: Cage as Gene Vincent, Sean Penn as Bobby Darin, a barely known Tom Cruise as Eddie Cochran, and Ray Sharkey as Johnny Meeks. "We had this great little band of kids," says the film's would-be producer, a guy named Chip Miller, who befriended Cage in 1983. "We took meeting after meeting after meeting until we had really developed a solid story."

The concept originated with Cage's first manager, Christopher Viores, who pitched it to Miller in early 1983 after optioning a biography of Vincent. At first the working title was *Rockabilly*, then *Be-Bop-a-Lula*. "It is envisioned as a vehicle to star Bruce Springsteen," Viores wrote to Miller on January 26, 1983. "It can be an upbeat, authentic film that details the growth of rockabilly music in the United States and then Europe."

Miller was a development director at an independent film company. He loved the idea. Springsteen wasn't interested in acting, so Viores suggested his client, nineteen-year-old Cage, for the part of Vincent. "He brought Nick

†††† Nearly everyone who worked with Cage on *Peggy Sue* recalls that the actor was having issues with his teeth and wound up wearing fake teeth in the film. Arlene Sarner remembers watching as Cage tried out different prosthetic teeth. "I got a dentist to redo Nicky's teeth," says producer Gurian. "We had to fix three bridges that he was covering with these stupid [fake] teeth." It's not clear if these dental issues were related to the baby teeth pulled during *Birdy*.

to the office," Miller says. "He didn't have his teeth fixed yet; they were all overlapping each other, and [he had] a crazy friggin' hair-do. But we just bonded immediately." Miller was struck by Cage's shyness and physical awkwardness—he seemed self-conscious about his towering height. "He had a very serious tone to him," Miller says, but would loosen up when he was drinking.

Cage was still an unknown: *Valley Girl* had been filmed but not yet released, and he was eager to star in a rockabilly biopic. "He happened to be an early rockabilly lover," Miller says. "He loved early Elvis. Nick fell in love with the concept and said, 'I'll do it.'" Penn and Cruise, who was about to become a household name with *Risky Business*, soon joined. The three rising stars became fast friends, though Cage and Penn soon grew to dislike Cruise. "You could see the light was shining on Tom," Miller says. "Everybody was interested in him, and he had the all-American thing. Nick and Sean still wanted to do art pictures."

With a film treatment in hand, Miller began pitching his biopic to studios. His own company wasn't interested, so he started at the top. No bites. He found a receptive ear in producer Dawn Steel, then the senior vice president of production at Paramount, but she ultimately passed. Miller describes a remarkable meeting at Steel's office with Cage, Cruise, Penn, and Sharkey. "After the meeting, she gets the kids coffee and asks me to step into the hallway," Miller remembers. "And she says, 'Chip, I love the story. I love it. But I can't possibly invest money into a project with these unknown kids."

Undaunted, Miller held a party at Club Lingerie in Hollywood to announce the planned project. Among those in attendance was the real Johnny Meeks, Gene Vincent's old guitarist. Cage got drunker and drunker as the night wore on. When Meeks began performing old Gene Vincent songs, "Nick was so enthralled, he jumped onstage to sing with Johnny," Miller says.

Miller soldiered on, determined to secure financing. He even scored some press. In September 1983, gossip columnist Liz Smith spotlighted the unmade movie in her New York *Daily News* column. "Aficionados of the [rockabilly] era will find all of this riveting," Smith wrote, noting that the cast would include "the dynamic hottest name in rock today, Prince."[129] Indeed, Prince was briefly attached to play Little Richard, but backed out that fall to focus on his own starring vehicle, *Purple Rain*.[130]

Purple Rain became a monstrous success. *Be-Bop-a-Lula*, on the other hand—well, you already know how this ends. Miller never found a financier. His actors went their separate ways. As late as 1985—by which point Cage had left Christopher Viores behind—Miller was in talks with Cage's then-agent, Ilene Feldman. "Please be advised that the undersigned producers are committed to NICOLAS CAGE portraying the role of GENE VINCENT," Miller wrote to Feldman that spring. But rock biopics weren't in vogue then, not unless they were about Wolfgang Amadeus Mozart. *Be-Bop-a-Lula* died on the vine.

Instead of portraying Gene Vincent, Cage played a fictional crooner of the same era: Charlie Bodell. When Miller saw him singing in *Peggy Sue Got Married*, hamming it up in a shiny suit, he could immediately tell who Cage was riffing on. "That's his impression of Gene Vincent," Miller says. "He just decided to play Gene—dress like him, look like him, and move like him."

In fact, there's evidence that the aborted *Be-Bop-a-Lula* movie cast a surprisingly long shadow over the first decade of Cage's career. For years, the fifties rockabilly motif kept reappearing in his work. First came *Peggy Sue*, then *Wild at Heart*, in which Cage croons Elvis tunes to Laura Dern. (*Wild at Heart* also includes Vincent's song "Be-Bop-a-Lula," paired with one of the steamiest sex scenes.) Fittingly, a *Los Angeles Times* profiler described Cage as possessing the "lizard-lidded fifties cool of a rock 'n' roll rebel."[131] Two years later, Cage reprised his King fixation on *Saturday Night Live*, playing "Tiny Elvis" in a 1992 sketch.

In 2015, Vincent's old guitarist, Johnny Meeks, died. Cage asked Chip Miller for the man's address. He wanted to send his condolences to the family.

* * *

Pop culture nostalgia tends to bubble up in twenty- to twenty-five-year cycles. In the nineties, audiences were mesmerized by pop culture fetishizing the seventies as a gritty, sexually liberated wonderland, from *Boogie Nights* to the Beastie Boys' "Sabotage" video. In the late 2010s came a deluge of films (*mid90s*, *Landline*, *Captain Marvel*) set within the more innocent environs of the mid-nineties.

So it makes sense that *Peggy Sue Got Married* was part of a wave of storytelling steeped in nostalgia for the fifties and early sixties. In fact, *Peggy Sue* was a little late to the party. In 1978, the musical phenomenon *Grease* made audiences pine for the summer of 1958. A few years later, Donald Fagen revisited his suburban fifties childhood on his 1982 album *The Nightfly*. Even David Lynch, a filmmaker seemingly allergic to nostalgia, wove latter-day hits like Roy Orbison's "In Dreams" into his nightmarish suburban satire *Blue Velvet*.

Yet *Peggy Sue*'s biggest competitor in the fifties nostalgia sweepstakes hit theaters in the summer of 1985 and brought audiences back to 1955 in a time-traveling DeLorean. *Back to the Future* was a considerably louder, more action-filled spectacle, but the superficial similarities—character trips back in time to the era of doo-wop and diners, interferes with the proper progression of a fateful teen romance—were striking enough to risk making *Peggy Sue* look like a copycat. As he prepared to shoot his own movie, Coppola reportedly refused to see *Back to the Future*, which soon became the highest-grossing film of 1985.[132]

Cage, inevitably, was forced to bat away the parallels between *Peggy Sue* and *Back to the Future*. "This one is on a more mystical level. It's a romance," he insisted in one 1986 interview.[133]

Critics invariably compared the two, but any discerning viewer could recognize that *Peggy Sue* was a different film: a drama tinged with regret and bittersweet reflection, with the sci-fi elements pushed to the background. With *Rumble Fish*, Coppola had set out to make an art film for teenagers. With *Peggy Sue Got Married*, he succeeded in making a teenage film for adults. Here is the rare eighties teen comedy suffused with the malaise and disappointment of middle age, an awareness of how adult life tends to veer away from the plans that seemed so ironclad when you were a teenager.

It's not that teenagers themselves can't understand or enjoy the fantastical storyline. It's that the film bathes youth in a certain wistful glow, as if peering back at a photograph that has faded over time. No typical teenager will fully grasp the hitch in Peggy Sue's throat when she answers the phone and unexpectedly hears her grandmother's voice. *Peggy Sue* depicts youth as a memory that can be revisited and reframed, but never quite changed. And it takes as a given the psychic weight of all the regrets and what-ifs that accumulate in middle age.

In reality, most of the actors playing high schoolers were well into their late twenties (or, in Turner's case, her thirties) at the time of filming. Not Cage. Perhaps this is one reason he seemed at such a visceral remove from the others in the film. They were performing youth from a healthy distance. He was just twenty-one—only a few years out of high school, and still enmeshed in a brash youthful rebellion of his own. "My heroes were groups like The Who," Cage told an interviewer in 1994. "I really liked the idea of having that outlaw image, that rock-and-roll persona, that edge of being a wild man."[134]

A self-described punk, Cage wanted to offend. He *liked* that people hated his performance in *Peggy Sue*. He sometimes pasted reviews that panned him into a notebook.[135] "I was reading books on [Edvard] Munch[‡‡‡‡] then, how everyone hated his works," Cage later told *Movieline* , referring to the Norwegian painter whose art had attracted critical scorn during the 1800s. "I thought I had to be met with opposition, because I had this arrogant, headstrong attitude at twenty-two. I was delighted when I got horrible reviews. I even cut them out. One said I was 'a wart on an otherwise beautiful film.'[§§§§] Another, 'a poorly wired robot.' "[136]

Though he eventually learned to compromise with creative visions other than his own, Cage would retain this contrarian streak throughout the late eighties. It worked in reverse, too. When his performance in *Moonstruck* the following year *was* acclaimed by the mainstream cognoscenti, he deemed the film "too soft" and spent four years avoiding anything with the faintest whiff of romantic comedy.[137] Not until the early nineties did Cage seem to grow comfortable with the idea of pleasing the public.

It's not such a stretch to say that the dynamic between Charlie and Peggy Sue—his naïveté and romantic fantasies of being a musician, her having amassed a lifetime of experience and disillusionment—was curiously mirrored in their real-life tension. Turner was older, more pragmatic. In a 2018 interview with *Vulture*, Turner reaffirmed her frustration with Cage's performance, but acknowledged one creative benefit: "If anything, it only further illustrated my character's disillusionment with the past," she said. "The way I saw it was, yeah, he *was* that asshole."[138]

* * *

When *Peggy Sue Got Married* was finally released in October 1986, TriStar sent Cage to New York for a press tour and put him up in a hotel. The actor asked if his "incidentals" would be covered; the company said yes. Cage, increasingly susceptible to lavish spending, went nuts at the hotel, asking for a constant supply of caviar and Cristal champagne to his room.

"The next day, I planned a banquet and I wanted to invite a lot of people, so I ended up asking people on the street to dinner," Cage told *SPIN*. "The bill

‡‡‡‡ Cage had a strange fascination with Munch. A 1988 *Playgirl* profile claimed he "locked himself in his room staring at Edward [*sic*] Munch's horrifying painting, *The Scream*, to prepare him for the part [of Charlie Bodell]."

§§§§ It's not clear where this review was published, or whether Cage was quoting it accurately. A quick search turns up no results.

for room service for my two-day stay came to about $12,000. Then I got a call from my agent telling me to slow down. I said, 'Is $12,000 a lot of money for room service?' and he said, 'Nick, it's just not done.' "[139]

During his press tour, Cage seemed to be promoting not just his new movie but what he considered a wholly new approach to acting. He appeared on the *Dick Cavett Show*, chatting and toying with a trumpet onstage alongside fellow guests Carol Kane and a mumbling, spaced-out Miles Davis. Cavett introduced him as someone the show's secretaries were "dying to meet," but Cage was more interested in espousing his radical views about acting: "I go to a museum and I see a Picasso and I think, Why is it that he can get away with drawing his wife with spikes coming out of her head or having her mouth touch the floor? I envy him. I said, 'Well, why can't I do that?' "

The actor added, "There's no limits or boundaries. I think realism—that's great, but you can go further with it."[140]

If audience members were confused by Cage's far-out theorizing, Miles Davis wasn't. The musician interacted with Cage on- and off-camera, and seemed intrigued by him; Cage had the impression Davis was the only one there who understood him. "I see Miles Davis as a surrealist father of mine," Cage later claimed, recalling how, during the taping, Davis "was very considerate and he said, 'I hear what you're saying.' He kept looking at me like we had our own connection."[141]

The actor similarly expounded upon his acting views in *Playgirl*, of all places. "It's the first time I've tried to do surreal acting," he told the magazine, name-dropping Picasso and Munch in between softcore spreads of male nudes. "I've certainly seen less surreal acting than I have surreal painting, and in that sense I feel I'm a pioneer on the frontier."[142]

Cage was entering a new era, one in which he was more inclined to cite Jerry Lewis ("a pioneer of surreal comedy," he told *The Guardian*) or Peter Lorre as influences than Dean or De Niro.[143]

As Cage's fame rose, so did press interest in his private eccentricities. Journalists were entranced by his obsession with keeping aquatic life in his apartment. A *Los Angeles Times* profile began with this spectacular lede: "Nicolas Cage wanted to introduce his pet baby octopus to his visitors. Putting his hand into the aquarium, he dislodged the creature from behind a rock. Angry, it squirted ink over his fingers."[144] A *Chicago Tribune* story described him as a "frustrated marine biologist" and noted that he kept a photo of his pet monkfish in his wallet.[145]

It seemed like a bizarre put-on, but Cage's love of exotic animals was sincere. He endured a breakup around the time *Peggy Sue* came out, splitting from girlfriend Jenny Wright. In his loneliness, he found consolation in staring at his tanks full of sea creatures for hours. "I've always been fascinated by marine biology," Cage told *Playgirl*. "It's sort of like my bible."[146]

* * *

Despite Cage's efforts to the contrary, *Peggy Sue Got Married* was a crowd-pleaser, opening to good reviews and Coppola's strongest box office earnings of the decade. Those critics who were less enthused about the film tended to single out Cage's performance for ridicule. Rita Kempley of the *Washington Post* described the performance as "icky" and hit Cage where it hurt: by calling attention to his Coppola relation and writing, "Perhaps nepotism, like time, is relative."[147] Similarly, Stanley Kauffmann of the *New Republic* noted Cage's family ties and wrote, "Nothing else explains why this thin-voiced inadequacy was given the role."[148]

Oddly, critic Paul Attanasio also reviewed the film for the *Washington Post* and found potent meaning in Cage's surreal mannerisms. "Cage finds his own ingenious solution to the problem of making time travel seem real—he plays Charlie as a stylized version of an early '60s teenager," Attanasio wrote. "He affects a Fabian pompadour and a dental insert that makes him look goofy, but the cartoon goes further as Cage twists his voice with a twangy nasality and builds the insecurities of adolescence into the stuttering of Charlie's guffaw."[149]

Critics often shrug off *Peggy Sue* as "minor" Coppola, a perception all but encouraged by the man himself. In interviews, he has expressed exasperation that this lighthearted fantasy was his most commercially successful movie of the decade. "After *Apocalypse Now*, the only film I made that the public seemed to want from me—although I don't by any means think it was the best of the group—was *Peggy Sue Got Married*," he vented to *Mother Jones* in 1988.[150]

Tellingly, *Peggy Sue* wasn't even marketed as "A Francis Ford Coppola Film." Instead, the words "Directed by Francis Coppola" (sans "Ford") appeared in small font at the bottom of the movie poster. "Francis was always trying to distance himself from this film, from the start," says Gurian. "He made it for money. And he had thought he was pure and above that."

The fact that his most successful movie in years was one he did not write or even want to make must have frustrated Coppola and underlined the sense that he was out of touch with moviegoing audiences. It would have been a backhanded compliment when critics like Rex Reed declared *Peggy Sue* Coppola's "best film since *The Godfather*," and it rankled him that *Peggy Sue* earned far more than *One from the Heart* and *Rumble Fish* combined. "Because it wasn't *his* film," says Gurian. "Because he was a director-for-hire!"[151]

The irony is that Coppola had been a director-for-hire on *The Godfather*, too—a film he made reluctantly while under financial strain. But while *Peggy Sue* doesn't match the filmmaker's seventies peak, it is a compellingly bittersweet fantasy, directed with warmth and care, and a probing meditation on a theme Coppola would spend much of his later career exploring: the strange distance between adulthood and youth. (He would return to this theme with 1996's misbegotten *Jack*, which also centers on a character whose psychological age is out of whack with his body, and 2007's *Youth Without Youth*.)

For his nephew, *Peggy Sue Got Married* was a genuinely pivotal milestone: his first time risking it all for the sake of a performance destined to be misunderstood. Cage *could* have delivered a straightforward performance as a teenage hunk; maybe he would have secured himself a place in John Hughes's speed dial. Instead, he went full Pokey. *Peggy Sue* was the formative swing toward surreal expression that would define the next five years (or, arguably, four decades) of Cage's career. It was the performance that would permanently signal Cage's disinterest in playing regular American teenagers—or regular *anyone*—and, in retrospect, it was the first glimmer of Cage unleashed, the performance that consummated his transition from Method to madness. As late as 1988—after *Raising Arizona* and *Moonstruck* transformed his career—Cage insisted that he considered *Peggy Sue* "my best performance by far."[152]

And yet *Peggy Sue* also ended a chapter for Cage: his three-year collaboration with his uncle. "Francis, much as I love working with him, always manages to cast me as left-pocket weirdos," Cage complained in a 1986 interview. "In other directors' pictures I get weightier roles."[153]

He would never work with Coppola again.

Cage's brother Christopher tried to persuade their uncle to cast Cage as Vincent Corleone in *The Godfather Part III*. "I pushed for that," Christopher says. "He went with a non-Italian, Andy Garcia. That was kind of a slap in my brother's face. I think he was just worried he was going to go bonkers on him."

Cage later attributed this parting of ways to the frosty reception to his performance in *Peggy Sue*. "Francis blamed me; he hasn't asked me to work with him since," he told *Playboy* in 1996, long after Coppola had returned to commercial prominence without his nephew's help. In that interview, Cage openly expressed disappointment that he had neither been cast in *Part III* (Fred Roos says he was considered for it) nor *Bram Stoker's Dracula* (Cage: "Dracula is one of my favorite characters in literature. Much of my lifestyle is modeled after him").[154]

Maybe Cage's uncle was doing him a favor. Before 1987, nearly half of the actor's filmography were Coppola projects. After *Raising Arizona* and *Moonstruck*, the grumbles about nepotism largely subsided. Cage would achieve serious stardom only once he fully extricated himself from his uncle's shadow. No longer was he defined—or confined—by the family name.

Throughout the 1980s, Cage was invariably referred to as Francis Ford Coppola's nephew, but by the nineties, Coppola was just as likely to be identified as Nicolas Cage's uncle.

5
Baby Fever

When Nicolas Cage was a kid in the 1970s, he and his brother Christopher Coppola made amateur short films in their backyard and around their neighborhood with a Minolta Super 8-mm camera. Cage starred; Christopher, who later became a filmmaker, directed. Sometimes they even put on puppet shows for the kids on their street.

"We weren't really into sports," Cage recalled in 1986. "We were into creating. My brother got his first camera when he was eleven, and we were always making Super 8 films and putting on shows."[1]

These Super 8 movies were Cage's earliest experiences in front of a camera: surprisingly sophisticated expressions of childhood creativity at a time when both boys needed the fleeting escape. "It was a difficult childhood because we had a very ill mother," Christopher Coppola said in a podcast interview. "We were often left alone, particularly myself and Nicolas. In order to kind of make life a little less sad, because of our mother, we would do movies."[2]

Most of these films are as lost to time as Hitchcock's early silent works. Even the most devout Cage completists will never get to view *The Unknown Circus*, a short film starring nine-year-old Nicky as a sad clown who becomes entangled in a love triangle with a trapeze lady.[3] (The inspiration was Fellini's *La Strada*, the kind of film August Coppola liked introducing to his precocious sons.)

But one fleeting glimpse of Cage's childhood juvenilia has survived into the digital age. In 2016, Christopher uploaded to Vimeo a brief clip from a film called *The Scroll of the Dragon*, which he and his brother made in 1978. The film was about an ancient Roman politician who is legendary for having killed a dragon. In a tragic twist, the man's son discovers that the legend is a terrible lie, after which the father kills himself. Cage played the son, and in the grainy footage, the fourteen-year-old baby-faced actor is easily recognizable, wearing white robes seemingly fashioned from bedsheets and sparring with the father character.

The clip is only twenty seconds long and has no sound, but you can sense Cage's youthful excitement radiating through the flickers. "There's nothing like making a Super 8 film, sending it to a lab, getting it back in the mail, and projecting it at home," Christopher wrote in an introductory note. "It is pure magic."[4]

Cage was reminded of these formative Super 8 memories a decade later, in the middle of the Arizona desert, filming *Raising Arizona* with two strange brothers compelled by the same homespun passion for moviemaking that had animated him and Christopher. "That's where I first coined the phrase: 'I'm getting that Super 8 feeling,'" Cage later recalled. "That Super 8 feeling is the feeling where you're making a movie simply because you love the movie. You're not doing it for money; you're not doing it for awards."

When Cage told Joel Coen he was "getting that Super 8 feeling," the elder Coen responded with enthusiasm: "Keep that going!"[5]

* * *

Joel and Ethan Coen knew a thing or two about that Super 8 feeling. Like Cage, the Coen brothers had academic parents—their mother was an art history professor, their father an economist—and a precocious appetite for moviemaking that began early on. Growing up in a dull, middle-class Minneapolis suburb, the brothers shared a voracious interest in movies. They watched everything from Tarzan flicks to the Italian art films that aired on a Minneapolis late-night television program.[6]

Joel, three years older, was the gregarious one, while Ethan was bookish and quiet. But both caught the creative gene: as kids, they mowed lawns to buy a (you guessed it) Super 8 camera, after which "they ran around doing jungle movies in the swamp," as their mother put it in a 1992 interview.[7]

Even in their Super 8 days, the Coens liked paying homage to eclectic cinematic influences. "We remade a lot of bad Hollywood movies that we'd seen on television," Joel recalled in a 1985 interview, describing a kind of real-life *Be Kind Rewind* situation in which he and his brother amateurishly recreated sixties movies like *The Naked Prey*. When they needed a shot of an airplane, they simply stood around waiting for one to fly over their neighborhood. When they remade 1962's *Advise & Consent*, neither brother had seen it. "We just heard the story from a friend of ours and it sounded good," Joel said.[8]

By the time the Coen brothers moved to New York in the early eighties, they were creatively joined at the hip: chain-smoking, wise-cracking, bespectacled upstarts who dressed like record store clerks, chuckled at their characters' violent misfortunes, and filled their movies with cryptic symbolism they refused to explain. Joel, now a New York University film-school graduate, was credited as director and Ethan as producer, but that was just to comply with archaic guild regulations. In reality, they shared all duties. In interviews, they smoked from the same pack of cigarettes and finished each other's sentences.[9] During filming, Joel did most of the talking while Ethan paced in circles or whispered in his brother's ear.

"Ethan was the one who didn't speak," says casting director Donna Isaacson, who worked closely with them, from *Raising Arizona* through *The Hudsucker Proxy*. "Joel spoke. And then, at some point in their history, they swapped."

The Coens' first film, *Blood Simple*, was astonishingly self-assured, a cunning neo-noir caked in rural sleaze, so delightfully out of sync with the Hollywood trends of 1984 that it created its own. Filmed in Texas on a shoestring budget, the movie introduced some of the Coens' soon-to-be regular collaborators (actress Frances McDormand, director of photography Barry Sonnenfeld, composer Carter Burwell) and placed the brothers at the center of a new wave of independent filmmakers who operated outside the studio system and reveled in high culture and low, borrowing from pulpy genre pictures and Best Picture winners alike.

Blood Simple established many of the Coens' enduring hallmarks: inky-black humor, beguiling visual motifs (the iridescent fish, a hypnotic ceiling fan), exhilarating cinematography, dramatic irony so pungent you can almost smell it, a love of hardboiled crime writers like Dashiell Hammett, and a penchant for foolish characters whose actions trigger disastrous chains of violent occurrences.

Most of all, it established their ability to produce great work on their own, with minimal resources. To finance *Blood Simple*, the brothers independently raised $1.5 million from private backers, mostly wealthy Jews in Minneapolis.[10] "They walked around asking all their neighbors and friends for $500," says Isaacson. "And they paid them all back with profits."

When Joel told *Film Comment* in 1985 that "we're not afraid of making movies for cheap," it was an expression of creative autonomy as much as practicality.[11] The Coens insisted on final cut from the beginning of their career. They understood that accepting financing from the big studios would come with compromises. And the big studios did court the brothers once *Blood Simple*, which was distributed by an indie company called Circle Releasing, became a sleeper hit on the festival circuit. But the Coens stuck to their independent guns: they turned down offers to direct studio projects and signed a new deal with Circle so they could make their own movies.[12]

Paradoxically, the Coens' disinterest in courting wealth and fame helped them gain the most coveted power of all: creative freedom. After *Blood Simple* came out, they received invitations to meet with Steven Spielberg and Hugh Hefner. But making movies under Spielberg's thumb wasn't what they wanted. Big paydays weren't their objective; in 1987, Joel didn't even have a credit card.[13] As their trusted director of photography Barry Sonnenfeld told *New York* magazine, "Money isn't important to them, except to make movies. They never want to be in a position where anyone has any power to tell them what to do."[14]

In May 1985, the *Washington Post* reported the terms of their deal with Circle Releasing. Four movies were to be financed by Circle, with the Coens guaranteed "complete artistic control, including final cut." The deal crystallized the Coens' rejection of Hollywood norms:

> Typically, a successful, independently produced first feature has been used by film makers as a way to gain entry to Hollywood. The Coens, however, join a growing number of film makers who are rejecting the bigger budgets and monetary rewards of Hollywood in return for greater artistic control and profit participation.[15]

The article mentioned that the Coen brothers' next film was already in motion, with a tentative 1986 release date. It was called *Raising Arizona*.

* * *

By the time he began work on *Raising Arizona* in early 1986, Cage was in a dry spell. A year had passed since *The Cotton Club* and *Birdy*. *Peggy Sue* had already been filmed, but its release would be postponed for half a year for reasons both technical (Coppola decided to reshoot the ending) and personal (the devastating death of Coppola's eldest son, Gian-Carlo).[16]

Cage had not appeared in a box office success (*Valley Girl*) in nearly three years. Several high-profile roles he sought in the mid-eighties had not panned out. He had badly wanted a part in Oliver Stone's breakthrough *Platoon*, but Stone turned him down; he had also been in consideration to play the bully in *The Breakfast Club*, but Judd Nelson won out instead. Clearly, Cage was too old-looking, or too strange, to fit into John Hughes's Brat Pack mold. He *was* offered a part in *Top Gun*, which would have accelerated his entry into the Jerry Bruckheimer action movie orbit, but reportedly turned it down because he disliked the film's pro-military politics.[17]

The other reason Cage was in a slump was because he needed to wash off the stink of *The Boy in Blue*, the bland rowing biopic that received a limited release in early 1986 to vicious reviews and audience indifference. Cage starred as a fictionalized version of Ned Hanlan, a real-life Toronto sculling hero who won major championships in the 1880s. It was his first irredeemable flop.

The movie was perhaps cursed from the start. Screenwriter Douglas Bowie wrote it at the behest of a Canadian director named John Trent, who planned to make a series of three films about historical Canadian sporting heroes. But those plans took a tragic turn when Trent was killed in a car accident in mid-1983.[18] "He was actually working on a draft of the script the day he went out to buy cigarettes," says producer Steven North, who developed the film with Trent.

Twentieth Century Fox, which had already picked up the film, decided to proceed with Charles Jarrott, a British director of costume dramas, at the helm. Because of a dearth of young Canadian stars, the producers mulled over up-and-coming American actors and settled on Cage. "I remember the director saying, 'Oh, there's gonna be a lot of heat on this boy,'" says Bowie. North, however, doubted Cage's bankability and preferred Matt Dillon, who wasn't interested. "The second you mentioned Nicolas Cage, the next words out of everybody's mouth [were] 'Well, you *do* know he's Francis's nephew,'" North remembers.

Cage seemingly agreed to the role as a way to pull himself out of the torment of *Birdy*. He quickly realized it was a mistake. The character was conventional and plain—a cookie-cutter sporting hero in a cookie-cutter *Rocky* knock-off. During the shoot, Cage was so miserable that he thought about slamming his hand in a trunk, injuring himself just enough to get out of the movie. "I wanted to walk off," he admitted in 1988.[19]

Instead, he suffered through. In the resulting film, which follows Hanlan's rise from lower-class hooligan to sculling champ, Cage's eccentricities are flattened in a mush of sports-drama clichés. Cage spends much of the movie shirtless and ripped, muscles glistening, as he flirts with Cynthia Dale and trains for races that are inexplicably soundtracked by synth muzak, despite the fact that the movie takes place in the 1880s. The performances are leaden and bloodless, the romantic side plot tedious at best.

Cage has starred in plenty of bad movies in his career, but *The Boy in Blue* is something worse: it's just plain dull. North was disappointed as soon as he saw the rushes. Still, he doesn't blame Cage for the film's failure. "It seemed that Nicolas was stretching to make it work," North says. "He looked beautiful. My God, those ripples were unbelievable. But I found his performance very wooden."

Bowie attributes some of the movie's shortcomings to creative differences with director Jarrott. His original script was "a bit edgier," he insists—it played up Ned Hanlan's gritty roots as an uneducated bootlegger—but Jarrott took it in a more conventional direction. North agrees; the film strayed far from John Trent's original vision, and Cage had little chance of redeeming such one-dimensional character writing. "I'm convinced there's still a film to be made about Ned Hanlan," North says. "This is not it."

Cage was embarrassed by *The Boy in Blue*—embarrassed to be seen flaunting his bare chest in such a boilerplate movie, embarrassed to give a performance where his physique makes more of an impression than his acting. "When I saw that, I thought, Well, I'm never going to take my shirt off again, or at least not like that," he recalled a decade later. "I got a tattoo on my back. I wanted to go as far away from the beefcake image as possible."[20]

The film was savaged by critics upon release, and the actor distanced himself from it almost immediately, rarely discussing it in interviews. "Shame on you," he jokingly replied to one reporter who mentioned the film in 1986. "As far as I'm concerned, that picture is dead."[21] In time, *The Boy in Blue* was destined to become the first of many movies of interest to future audiences purely because of Cage.*

The point is, Cage was eager to redeem himself in early 1986. He needed a role with some edge and sophistication, a character more compelling than the flat hometown hero of *Boy in Blue*. He needed a movie that would align with his experimentalist impulses rather than squash them. He found it in *Raising Arizona*.

The role proved slyly prescient. Across his forty-year career, Cage frequently portrays characters embarking on perilous, obsessive quests: a quest to steal the Declaration of Independence and decode its treasure-hiding secrets (*National Treasure*); a quest to break out of hell and avenge his daughter's death (*Drive Angry*); a quest to solve a clairvoyant time capsule

* Letterboxd reviews of *The Boy in Blue* are often prefaced with notes like "Cage-a-thon movie #4" or "11/88 of Nic Cage Ranked," indicating that the reviewer only watched it out of completist devotion to their hero.

that holds the power to predict world catastrophes (*Knowing*); a quest to transport a woman accused of witchcraft in fourteenth-century Styria to a faraway monastery (*Season of the Witch*); a quest to locate a missing child on an island full of human-sacrificing neo-pagan wackos (*The Wicker Man*); a quest to hunt down Osama bin Laden on a mission from God (*Army of One*); a quest to recover a beloved truffle pig stolen in the night (*Pig*). Cage's unbridled intensity, his ability to project single-minded focus and obsession, lends itself to such roles.

But in *Raising Arizona*, he is a man on a madcap quest for something much simpler: the domestic comforts of family itself.

* * *

Donna Isaacson remembers the moment she first read the *Raising Arizona* script. It was Labor Day weekend. She was sitting on a chaise. "And I'm *laughing*," the casting director says. "Laughing out loud. Every. Single. Line. In that script is in that movie."

The Coen brothers could have stuck with the neo-noir terrain that first brought them success. Instead, *Raising Arizona* was the first in a career defined by abrupt genre shifts. The brothers' second feature was so different from their first that it seemed to take place in a different universe, or at least a different state: the homicidal deep-Texas brooding of *Blood Simple* supplanted by a cartoonish, almost mythical Southwest. Where *Blood Simple* drew on the hardboiled vocabulary of film noir, *Raising Arizona* reveled in the frenetic goofiness of screwball comedy: bright and lively instead of brooding and foreboding. It was particularly inspired by the work of Preston Sturges, a favorite of the Coens.[†]

In contrast with *Blood Simple*, whose byzantine web of murder and double-cross wasn't really simple at all, *Raising Arizona* is straightforward enough plot-wise. Its story centers on a pair of dim-witted but goodhearted Arizona hicks: reformed robber H. I. "Hi" McDunnough and policewoman Edwina (or "Ed"), who meet at Hi's routine mugshot sessions and marry after Hi, newly released from jail, promises his lawless years are behind him (Figure 5.1). They desperately want a baby, but find themselves unable to conceive. Ed is infertile. They sink into depression.

† They later paid more direct tribute to Sturges with *O Brother, Where Art Thou?*, which takes its title from Sturges's 1941 classic *Sullivan's Travels*.

Figure 5.1. In *Raising Arizona* (1987, 20th Century Fox), Cage starred opposite Holly Hunter (left) as Hi, a compulsive criminal torn between his outlaw tendencies and his family responsibilities.

On the news, they hear about newborn quintuplets born to a furniture tycoon named Nathan Arizona. They hatch a plan to steal one of the babies for themselves—"they got more'n they can handle!" Ed declares in her down-home drawl—but illicit parenthood goes awry when a vicious, beastlike bounty hunter (a man with "all the powers of hell at his command") comes looking for the missing infant.

Cooped up in Joel's stuffy Upper West Side apartment, the brothers wrote *Raising Arizona* in a nicotine-fueled haze during the summer of 1985.[22] "After having finished *Blood Simple*, we wanted to make something completely different," Ethan told *Positif* magazine. "We didn't know what, but we wanted it to be funny, with a quicker rhythm."[23] They wrote with a vivid command over every line and image that would eventually appear onscreen, and finished the script in three or four months.

Central to the story was a preoccupation with the sheer weirdness of parenthood. The Coens wrote about the deranging quality of parenthood (or the yearning for such) not from experience, but as strangers in a strange land. At the time, neither Coen had kids. "We're not really intimately acquainted with murder either, and we made a movie about killing people," Joel quipped to an interviewer.[24]

In late 1985, the Coens worked with a storyboard artist to map out every single shot in the film—an obsessive step which the Coens, like Hitchcock, found essential to their creative process; working on a nimble budget, they couldn't afford to waste time or setups while shooting. "We wouldn't have written the scenes if we didn't know how we were going to shoot them," Joel told *New York*.[25]

Isaacson's job was to cast the picture. She wound up working for "the boys," as she calls them, for years, introducing them to key regulars like John Goodman and Steve Buscemi.[26] The Coens wrote with remarkable specificity, and Isaacson understood that every part needed to be cast perfectly. "The thing about the Coen brothers is that they embrace a concept and a place and a world," she says. "And they are completely faithful to that world. If you don't *hear* the music of the script, you're not right for it. You have to hear it."

The Coens often wrote characters with a particular actor in mind. Ed, for instance—a brusque, Southern-fried cop with an overwhelming maternal instinct—was conceived for Holly Hunter, who had been in the Coens' orbit for years and once roomed with Frances McDormand, Joel's wife.[‡] Casting Hi was harder. Isaacson and her casting partner, John Lyons, convinced the brothers, who lived in New York, to go to Los Angeles and search far and wide. "The boys at that point hated Los Angeles," Isaacson says. "But of course we said, 'We have to go to Los Angeles to see actors.'"

It was during this trip west—where they holed up in their agent's offices, meeting with different actors—that the Coens first met Cage. The script had stirred Cage's interest the first time he read it. He felt connected to Hi, a character marked by goofy sincerity and lawless urges—one of many hapless doofuses sprung from the Coens' imagination, but with a certain endearing quality, a sweetness about him. Like many of Cage's best roles, here was a character defined by duality: a guy torn between a life of crime on one side and his strained attempt to be a family man on the other. When Hi's buddies from jail—two escaped fugitives—show up at his door, his warring impulses begin fracturing the domestic bliss in his mobile home.

[‡] Holly Hunter had a voice-only role in *Blood Simple* as a voice on an answering machine.

"I read the script, and I immediately responded to it," Cage said in a 2018 interview. "I felt connected to it. I felt I knew where the humor was, and what beats, musically, to hit."[27]

Others were interested, too. Willem Dafoe read for the part; Kevin Costner took an interest. Despite their small budgets and inexperience, the Coens had little trouble attracting top talent. As a 1989 *Premiere* profile put it, "Hollywood looks at the Coens the way it looks at Woody Allen: Their films don't make much money, but everyone wants to be associated with them."[28]

"We would get these incoming phone calls like, 'Could you rewrite this for Jimmy Woods?'" Isaacson says. "Meanwhile, the actor is supposed to be about twenty-one years old. Everybody wanted to be in it. And the biggest star who wanted to be in it at the time was Kevin Costner. The boys were not going to hire anybody they couldn't read. And Kevin was just getting at that point in his career, as was Nick."

This drama was heightened by the fact that Costner and Cage now had the same agent: Ed Limato, a flashy, old-school denizen of the William Morris Agency. Limato's junior agent, Elaine Goldsmith, had first met Cage when she signed his girlfriend, Jenny Wright. Goldsmith was Limato's emissary in the outside world, scouting fresh talent to bring to her bosses; when Cage mentioned to her that he was planning to leave then-agent Ilene Feldman, she poached him for Limato.

Limato was a mercurial Hollywood power broker who wore salmon-pink suits and guided the careers of mainstream stars like Richard Gere and Mel Gibson, whose framed headshots he kept in the living room of his Beverly Hills estate. He was openly gay and, having no children of his own, considered his clients his family, defending them and exerting immense control over their career choices.[29] When Cage signed with William Morris, so began a decade-long love-hate relationship between him and Limato. Limato often tried to steer his strangest client toward more mainstream roles; Cage, in turn, constantly petitioned his agent to let him star in low-budget films like *Vampire's Kiss*, which Limato considered beneath his clients.

Most vexing to casting directors was Limato's belief that his clients were too established to have to audition or "read" (i.e., an informal kind of audition) for parts. He was "a big Los Angeles agent, and out of his fucking mind," Isaacson says. "I mean, he was *brilliant*. But he was, oh my God, he was very disrespectful to people who were not at his level. He was also very protective of his clients. We wanted to read them, and it was very difficult."

Limato didn't quite get *Raising Arizona*. But Goldsmith read the script and thought its wild eccentricity would speak to Cage. She was right.

Limato allowed Cage to meet with the Coens while they were in L.A., but only on the condition that they wouldn't make him read. "So Nick comes in. Sits down. He's just strange," says Isaacson. Cage had yellow paint all over his shoes, and when the Coens asked why, he explained that it was from spray-painting model rockets.[30] "He was not a chatty guy," Isaacson says. "And the guys are not chatty. They're gigglers. The good thing was, there was something about him that made you curious about him. Which is always good. You don't know what's going on behind the eyes."

The meeting was cordial but inconclusive. The Coens were unsure that Cage—known for more urban characters—could fit the movie's tone of wacky provincialism. "The question was, could he fit into the world of Arizona?" Isaacson says. "And the only way we would know that would be if he would read. And he says he's not gonna read, and that's the end of it."

Then came a surprise development: Kevin Costner wanted the role badly enough that *he* agreed to read. He just didn't tell Limato. Now the stress was mounting. Every time the phone rang, Isaacson and Lyons feared it was Limato calling to berate them for having Costner read. They left and went to see one of Costner's movies so Limato couldn't reach them. "And mind you, he's the agent for both actors, and if one wasn't going to get it, the other one had to get it," Isaacson says. "Otherwise, he would implode."

Costner read opposite Holly Hunter. The brothers were unsure. When actors read for them, they typically giggled more than they spoke: *Heh heh. Heh heh.* "That was their default," Isaacson says. "You didn't know what it meant. And they didn't know what it meant." They made Costner come back and read again.

Meanwhile, word trickled back to Cage that the Coens had told his agent they couldn't see him in the role. "I was very disheartened," Cage told the *Los Angeles Times* in 1986. "I felt so close to this character that I decided I just wouldn't take no for an answer, so we kept on at them to let me read."[31]

The Coens returned to New York. No sooner had they arrived than they got a call saying Cage now wanted to read. "We literally had just touched down," Isaacson says. "The agent says, 'If you want to read him, you have to pay for his trip to New York now.'"

Cognizant of their modest budget, Isaacson agreed but requested Cage fly coach and take a simple taxi from the airport. "And what does he do? He gets into a limo in New York!" Isaacson says. "Which was eighty dollars, which was like a zillion dollars for the budget."[§]

Cage arrived at the Coens' office, where they had a sandwich waiting for him. Any frustration with his choice of transportation was smoothed over once he read. He was fantastic.

"It was right. He *got* it," Isaacson says. "It was just fabulous."

* * *

"My name is H. I. McDunnough. Call me Hi."

Cage's voice is the first one we hear in *Raising Arizona*, narrating the film's prologue and ushering us into Hi's delinquent world of lawbreaking and love.

First-person voiceovers weren't in vogue in the mid-eighties—before films like *Stand by Me* and *Goodfellas* triggered a narration renaissance, the cliché advice to screenwriters was "Show, don't tell"—but the Coens reveled in defying conventional wisdom.[32] "Write what you know"? They set their movie in far-off Arizona, where neither had lived, because the Southwest seemed exotic.[33] "Show, don't tell"? They crammed the entire plot setup into a stunning mile-a-minute introductory sequence that unfolds for eleven minutes before the title and opening credits even appear onscreen.

This pre-title sequence is exhilarating in its storytelling bravura and comic ingenuity. The film critic Chris Nashawaty has even argued it's the greatest opening to any movie ever. As Nashawaty writes, "Watching those eleven minutes back in 1987 felt like witnessing the future."[34]

At the center of it all is Hi's voiceover narration, through which we learn about his repeat-offender background, his musings on the justice system, his wily romantic side, his unconventional wooing of Ed, and his job drilling holes in sheet metal.[**] What makes the deepest impression, though, is simply his manner of speaking: a rugged, hillbilly twang that's dotted with Sirs and rich with biblical allusions ("Now, y'all without sin can cast the first stone") and oddly poetic turns of phrase (describing Ed's uterus as "a rocky place where my seed could find no purchase").

[§] *Raising Arizona* entered production with $3 million provided by Circle Releasing. During production, according to a 1989 *Premiere* article, Twentieth Century Fox contributed another $3 million in exchange for distribution rights, bringing the budget to around $6 million—four times what *Blood Simple* cost. The Coens retained final cut privilege. Their ability to have their films released by a major studio while retaining full creative control was highly unusual.

[**] Coen obsessives may notice that Hi works for a company called "Hudsucker Industries"—a subtle link to a later Coens movie, 1994's *The Hudsucker Proxy*. The brothers actually wrote *The Hudsucker Proxy* before they wrote *Raising Arizona*, but kept it on the backburner for years because they thought it would be too expensive to make right after *Blood Simple*.

The Coens are fond of exaggerated accents (see *Fargo*), and their writing evinces a playful and mischievous love of language. With Hi, they were riffing on a Southwestern dialect, but they weren't aiming for regional authenticity. "He speaks in a mixed argot," Joel explained in 1987, "influenced by all these varied things he's picked up somewhere and assimilated in a weird way. The Bible, other books, stuff he's heard on TV, all filtered through a kind of cowboy philosopher mentality."[35]

Raising Arizona was in large part a voice role for Cage, given how much of the plot is filtered through Hi's endearing narration. Cage had never done a Southern accent before, but the role found him at the right time. After *Birdy* and *The Boy in Blue*, he decided to infuse each character with a distinctly different voice or accent, and so he embraced Hi's weird vernacular fusion.

Before shooting *Raising Arizona*, Cage spent a month working with a dialect coach named Julie Adams, who was hired to help him develop a Southwestern accent. "It was really a light accent," Adams says, "but we just wanted to give it a little bit of a twang." Several times a week, Adams visited Cage in his Art Deco apartment for dialect sessions. By this time, Cage was living in the El Royale apartment complex, a historic celebrity hideout nestled in the Hancock Park neighborhood of Los Angeles. He lived with his Burmese cat, Lewis, in an apartment full of exotic décor, walls displaying rare bugs framed in Lucite, and an aquarium inhabited by sea-creature friends, including his pet monkfish and a baby octopus named Cool.[36]

This apartment had become a topic of fascination among Cage's friends. When Chip Miller visited his old friend, he was stunned by the size and oddness of the dwelling. Cage had taken over two floors. Miller remembers seeing state-of-the-art stereo equipment, a large movie screen, abstract art, a shark tank so large that it had to be specially built *in* the apartment—and puzzlingly little furniture. "This place is huge," Miller recalls. "It's like 8,000 square feet, and there's two chairs to sit in. That's when I started sensing that there was a little eccentricity and a little spending going on at the same time."

"The first thing I noticed when I walked in, he had a shark in a big tank. I was like, oh, this is going to be interesting," Adams says. Peering around at Cage's apartment, she marveled at the actor's unusual artwork and midcentury furniture. "You could tell that an artist lived there," she says. "I felt very comfortable there, even with the shark swimming around the tank."

During these dialect sessions, Cage was trying to find Hi McDunnough, and the voice seemed key to unlocking the character. The role was different than Cage's usual assortment of city-dwelling tough guys. Hi is a bundle of contradictions, a creature of the Arizonan desert—unsophisticated yet full of outlaw eloquence, lawless yet decent-hearted. While crafting the character's voice, Cage talked about his friend Tom Waits and played some of Waits's music, which is defined by the singer's gruff, gravelly vocals, for Adams. "There was a quality in Tom Waits's voice that he liked, that he wanted to add to it," Adams says.

Adams describes Cage as "a very sensitive individual" and one of her favorite clients. "[I felt] that he did not approach a character as much cerebrally as he did emotionally and intuitively," she says. "This was a guy that always wanted to find a different angle on a reading."

As the weeks went by, pressure mounted for them to present something to the Coen brothers to show that Cage could handle the accent. They wound up recording a homespun "radio show" filled with scene readings, bits of improv, and the sound of Cage racking a shotgun to give a little extra flavor. They sent the tape to the Coen brothers, who seemed pleased with it.

"We had this little $12 cassette recorder," Adams says. "I just remember him racking that shotgun and us sitting at this tiny table in this Art Deco kitchen, looking out over Hollywood. He was full-on committed. I never felt like he was acting. I felt like he was really being the character."

Two months later, in an unusually generous thank-you gesture, Cage flew Adams to Arizona for the final week of filming. When Cage picked her up at the airport, he seemed to have fully absorbed the energy of Hi McDunnough. He was clad in a Hawaiian shirt, his hair wild and unkempt—he looked like the Road Runner, she thought. "He absolutely had kind of that wild-eyed look. You could feel the character that was emanating from him."

Thirty-five years later, Adams speaks reverently about Cage's performance. "He never played crazy. I love that about him," she says. "It's like, you don't play drunk. You play trying to play sober. He never played the obvious crazy guy at all. And that's what made his expression of that character so good. It was an authentic presentation of a guy in crazy situations, trying to keep it together while the world was trying to pull him apart."

* * *

In January 1986, Cage arrived in Arizona for the twelve-week shoot, most of which was in the Phoenix area. In search of cacti-rich desert scenery, the Coens shot at picturesque locales like Lost Dutchman State Park and Reata Pass; interiors were largely filmed at Carefree Studios in Scottsdale, where *The New Dick Van Dyke Show* had been filmed.[37]

With its cartoonish genre mishmash, *Raising Arizona* was hardly a simple shoot. "Thank God they were heavy storyboard people," says second assistant director (AD) Patricia Hess. "It was a complicated movie, obviously. You have all the things they tell you you don't ever want: Children. Animals. Special effects. And stunts."

The Coens came prepared. They had storyboarded every scene, finalized every line of dialogue; they worked creatively with Sonnenfeld, who had jumped from shooting porno flicks to Coen classics, to achieve breathtaking shots on a nimble budget. At one point, they pioneered what *New York* magazine called the "blankey cam": "Sonnenfeld on his belly on a blanket, dragged along while he films."[38]

It helped that the Coens seemed to be telepathically attuned to one another. One day, Cage watched with awe as one Coen pulled out a cigarette and handed it to the brother behind him who happened to be silently reaching for one.[39] "I think they read each other's mind is what happens," says Hess. "A whole conversation will go back and forth between the two of them with very little in the way of a subject, verb, and a predicate. And they're like, 'Yeah, OK, let's go with that!' And you have *no* idea what they're talking about."

Not since *Valley Girl* had Cage worked with a director (or two) so young and independent-minded. He was exhilarated by the Coens' originality and cutting-edge spirit. "These guys are *dangerous*," he raved to a *Guardian* interviewer in 1987. "They're kind of experimentalists, trying new styles, going to the edge."[40]

But behind the scenes, Cage's creative spirit sometimes clashed with the Coens' inflexible vision. Cage arrived on set bursting with suggestions and contributions, but the Coens liked to stick to the script. Rarely did they allow actors to make changes to dialogue.

"The boys write exactly the way they want it said," says Isaacson. "If you play around with it, it actually doesn't work."

Cage found this stifling. Across his long career, the actor is happiest on film sets where he can collaborate and suggest left-field additions. Sometimes he gets his way: While filming the action blockbuster *The Rock*, Cage was insistent that he wanted to incorporate the phrase "Zeus's butthole" (as in, "How in the name of Zeus's *BUTTHOLE!* . . .") into his dialogue. He won out.[41] Others times, less so: While making 2014's *Joe*, for instance, Cage tried and failed to convince director David Gordon Green that the movie should feature a scene in which his character is playing the pan flute naked in a backyard. But Green was at least open to Cage's reasoning, which reportedly involved the ancient Greek god Pan.[42]

By 1986, Cage had spent years working with his uncle, a filmmaker who sometimes rewrote entire scenes on the fly. The Coens admired Coppola, but found that approach intolerable. "I have no idea how you can go into a movie without a finished script," Joel remarked in 1986. The Coens preferred to arrive on set with a final shooting script, emphasis on "final."[43]

When journalist David Edelstein visited the set for an *American Film* article, he found the Coens' relationship with their star to be "bumpy but respectful" and noted that Cage "praises the brilliant script and the Coens' professionalism, but he's clearly miffed that he couldn't bring more to the party." Speaking to Edelstein, Cage was surprisingly candid about his frustrations:

> "Joel and Ethan have a very strong vision," he says, "and I've learned how difficult it is for them to accept another artist's vision. They have an autocratic nature." A few minutes after the interview, Cage summons me back. "Ah, what I said about Joel and Ethan . . . with relatively new directors, that's when you find that insecurity. The more movies they make, the more they'll lighten up. The important thing is not to discourage an actor's creative flow."[44]

It is unclear whether the Coens had second thoughts about hiring Cage. During rehearsals, they made a point of mentioning to Cage other actors they could have cast.[45] "At first they were quite nervous about working with me, and during the rehearsal process they were getting scared," Cage later claimed. The way Hess puts it, "I don't think you could even tell, honestly, if they were mad or happy with you. They're so even-tempered." (Through a representative, the Coens declined to be interviewed for this book.)[46]

This is a not-uncommon source of friction. A writer-director believes they know the character best because they wrote him; the actor believes they know him best because they're playing him. At times, Cage worried that he would be fired.

Curiously, though, Cage's vision for the film does not seem to have differed all that much from the filmmakers'. His wacky, deadpan performance suited their madcap vision; his suggestions were hardly tone-altering. Edelstein reported that Cage wanted his character to pause and comically glance at his watch during the supermarket chase scene—an idea Joel politely vetoed—but detailed no serious creative differences.[47] Cage did fight with the Coens to let him watch the daily rushes (a restriction he likened to "not letting a painter look at the canvas"), but they ultimately relented.[48]

"I didn't sense that there was any animosity," says Hess, the second AD. "Nick would do things that you'd rather he didn't, like wander off into the desert in the middle of the night. But you know—we found him."

In fact, Cage's fondness for disappearing became a source of frustration and amusement among the crew. Hess recalls shooting on studio soundstages in Scottsdale. "You open the backstage door and it's, like, rattlesnakes, cactus, Gila monsters," Hess says. During late-night shooting sessions, she would ask Cage to stay inside, but "he loved to just wander out and not tell anybody where he was going." She would try calling him. No answer. The production assistants would check his dressing room. No answer.

"We're looking around, looking around," Hess recalls. "So, off I go, amongst the saguaro and jumping cholla, and sure enough, there he was! 'Nick! Gotta come inside! Gotta make the movie! You shouldn't be out here!' '*Ohh*, I'm sorry.' He didn't do it to be obnoxious. I think he was just curious."

Chitra Mojtabai, another second AD, recalls Cage's frustration over wanting to do his own stunts. "He was angry because we used a stuntman for something," Mojtabai says. "He said nobody had asked him. Which is something I never, ever heard any other actor do." The Coens clearly worried about their star getting injured, either for Cage's sake or because they didn't want to stretch their budget with medical emergencies. Minor scuffs were inevitable—Cage fell onto gravel and cut his hand while rehearsing a scene with Randall "Tex" Cobb, who played Hi's nemesis—but hospital visits were undesirable, especially when making a movie for cheap.[49] The Coens were so nervous about going over budget that when Sonnenfeld complained of excruciating pain from a kidney stone, they begged him to ignore it before reluctantly calling an ambulance.[50]

Whatever power struggles occurred between Cage and the Coens seemed to be smoothed over once the movie was finished. In a 1987 interview, Joel was effusive: "Nick's a really imaginative actor. He arrives with piles of ideas that we hadn't thought about while writing the script, but his contribution is always in line with the character we'd imagined. He extrapolated from what was written."[51]

* * *

In his screen roles, Nicolas Cage does not project the image of parental responsibility. Nobody has ever referred to him as "America's dad." While the real-life Cage became a father at twenty-six, the actor Cage tends to gravitate toward characters too damaged or erratic or cut off from society to raise children. (Would you let Ronny Cammareri babysit your child?)

It is telling that when Cage does play fathers, he often plays them like bewildered Martians navigating a Kmart: a workaholic bachelor plopped into family life by magical decree, as in 2000's *The Family Man*, or an obsessive-compulsive career criminal forced to live with the daughter he never knew he had, as in 2003's *Matchstick Men*. Sometimes his characters are separated from their children by prison sentences (*Wild at Heart*, *Con Air*), and sometimes his character is possessed by a supernatural urge to murder his own kids (*Mom and Dad*).

Simply put, there is something about Cage that radiates visceral unease with domestic life. *Raising Arizona* was the first film to exploit this quality. It is a madcap meditation on who deserves to have a family of their own, wringing comedy out of the tension between Hi's outlaw temperament and his fatherly duties.

Hi loves Nathan Jr., but hasn't the slightest idea how to model middle-class fatherhood (Figure 5.2). When he first brings the baby home, he tours him around like an overzealous motel owner. Ed is unnerved when Hi sizes up Nathan Jr. as "a little outlaw," and infuriated when Hi reverts back to his criminal ways. "I never postured myself as the three-piece suit type!" Hi protests during his getaway ride as Nathan Jr. innocently plays with his shoelaces. The baby is both the evidence of and ostensible antidote to Hi's criminal lifestyle.

The Coens preferred hiring actors who took direction well, but while making *Raising Arizona* they found themselves at the mercy of one group of actors who had no respect for their creative vision: babies. They approached casting the "Arizona Quints" with the same care and seriousness as any casting decision and mercilessly dismissed the ones who learned to walk mid-shoot. ("Ordinarily, you'd be pretty happy about something like that," Joel quipped at the time, "but in this case it got them fired."[52])

Before the shoot, the Coens put an ad in a local paper inviting parents to bring their newborns in to audition for the lead baby. "Joel was looking for a generic-looking baby that was cute," says the film's "baby wrangler," Julie Kareus (credited as Julie Asch), a nurse who spent years handling infants in Pampers commercials before being hired for *Raising Arizona*. "They had to

Figure 5.2. Before filming *Raising Arizona* (1987, 20th Century Fox), Cage had no experience handling babies. But this fact suited his character, a dimwitted ex-con who steals a baby after realizing that his wife is unable to conceive one of their own.

be a baby that would work well when mommy and daddy weren't around, [and with] a lot of men dressed grubbily."

With Kareus's help, the production evaluated as many as 600 infants in search of the perfect Nathan Jr. Joel had intended to use alternating twins for the part, but Kareus persuaded him that one baby would be better. They settled on a cheerful, blonde eight-month-old named T. J. Kuhn, who was so sweet-tempered that Kareus jokes she wanted to adopt him herself.

"They would do temperament tests and pass you around and take you from your parents to see how you would do," says T. J. Kuhn—now in his mid-thirties—whose memories of the shoot are understandably fuzzy. "I must have been the most easygoing one of them, so they ended up choosing me for the part."

Kuhn's big-screen debut arrives during the lengthy baby-snatching sequence. A sweating, visibly nervous Hi cradles the Quints one by one, trying to get them to stop crying while he decides which one to swipe. Cage's nervousness around the infants was not entirely feigned: he had no experience handling babies and found working with them overwhelming.

"There were eight babies, and there were eight stage mothers to go with them. And the babies were crying, and the stage mothers were giving me militant glares," Cage recalled in 1987. "Babies to me are very strange, because they don't appear human to me. They've got their own way of thinking. They're sort of alien. And I respect them for it."[53]

"He used to come to me and ask me, 'How do I hold them? How do I pick them up? How do I chase them?'" remembers Kareus. "What he didn't understand is that babies make their own hours."

Kareus found herself baby-training Cage years before he had a child of his own. She taught him how to crawl on the floor with the infants, how to give them Cheerios when they became fussy. "He just never had been with a baby before," Kareus says. "Holly hadn't either, but she caught right on. T. J. really took to her." When the camera was rolling, Kareus was almost always within the baby's sight, keeping him happy and calm. Only when Kuhn was being held by the two escaped convicts (John Goodman and William Forsythe) did he begin opening and closing his fist as though he wanted out of their arms.

The Coens lampooned the anxieties of Baby Boomer parenting with references to Dr. Spock guidebooks and endless pediatrician appointments, and once again found themselves ahead of the curve: *Raising Arizona* predated a flurry of baby-themed comedies, such as Charles Shyer's *Baby Boom* and Amy Heckerling's *Look Who's Talking*.

As for Kuhn, he says his family owns around fifty VHS copies of *Raising Arizona* because his father got in the habit of buying the movie whenever he spotted it. In 2004, Cage did a radio interview with an Arizona station while promoting *National Treasure*. The morning hosts contacted Kuhn ahead of time and put the former baby on-air to surprise Cage.

* * *

Critics were confused by *Raising Arizona* when it came out. The film broke too many rules, merged too many styles. It was an overwhelming hybrid—contemporary, yet steeped in the language of William Faulkner and Flannery O'Connor novels; ironic, yet buoyed by the full-throated sincerity of its stars; high-brow and low-brow all at once.

Roger Ebert, later one of Cage's great defenders, was especially harsh. In his *Chicago Sun-Times* review, he chastised the film for its manneristic dialogue ("Generally speaking, it's best to have your characters speak in strong but unaffected English") and fantasy elements:

> The movie cannot decide if it exists in the real world of trailer parks and 7-Elevens and Pampers, or in a fantasy world of characters from another dimension. It cannot decide if it is about real people, or comic exaggerations. It moves so uneasily from one level of reality to another that finally we're just baffled.[54]

Because the Coens filled their movies with flashy camera movements and stylized homages, they were often accused of being all style and no substance. Because they wrote dimwitted characters (or "hayseeds," as the Coens called them) from rural areas, they were charged with condescension. *Chicago Tribune* critic Dave Kehr described *Raising Arizona* as "consistently smug, snide, and show-offy," but still praised the film's opening sequence: "brisk, funny filmmaking, a little in the vein of a Warner Brothers cartoon."[55]

In this passage, Kehr captured the quality that intrigued and repelled critics all at once. *Raising Arizona* is not set in the real world at all, no matter the trailer parks or Pampers. It's a live-action cartoon. In other words, the film is defined by frenetic pacing, physical comedy, and a rejection of realism. And with its warp-speed action, simple-minded characters, exaggerated visuals, and the seeming invincibility of Hi McDunnough—a man who survives being chased by crazed dogs, shot at by a supermarket clerk, and beaten by an evil bounty hunter—its zany tone owes more to Saturday-morning cartoons than to the realist dramas that attracted critical adulation in the late eighties. The usual laws of gravity don't apply.

Cage understood this. During the shoot, he was fond of telling anyone who'd listen that he based his character on Woody Woodpecker, the red-headed woodpecker who was a fixture of the Universal Studios cartoons of Cage's childhood. "[I saw] the character as a kind of Woody Woodpecker come to life. An outlaw version of Woody Woodpecker," Cage recalled in 2018. "I remembered all those Thrush muffler stickers, where you had a woodpecker with the red feathers blowing in the wind and a cigar dangling out of his mouth, so I had that drawn onto H.I. McDunnough's arm."[56]

In fact, it was Cage's idea that Hi and his nemesis, the bounty hunter Leonard Smalls, have matching Woody Woodpecker tattoos, emblematic of the psychic connection that causes Hi to dream about Smalls before they meet.[57] The Coens evidently liked this suggestion. Early in the film, there is a closeup of Hi's Woody Woodpecker tattoo during a mugshot session; later, during the climactic fight scene, Hi pulls at Leonard Smalls's shirt to reveal a matching tattoo on the villain's chest. In this moment, critic and Coen brothers scholar Adam Nayman argues, Smalls is set up to be Hi's "fun-house double," thereby recasting their final showdown as an "interior struggle" for Hi.[58]

Cage was determined to look like a cartoon character: flamboyant Hawaiian shirts, thick mustache, craggy sideburns (which Hi shaves when he goes straight), and wild tufts of hair that stick up like porcupine quills (Figure 5.3). "I would rub my hair, so static electricity would make it lift up so that I was like Woody Woodpecker," Cage recalled.[59]

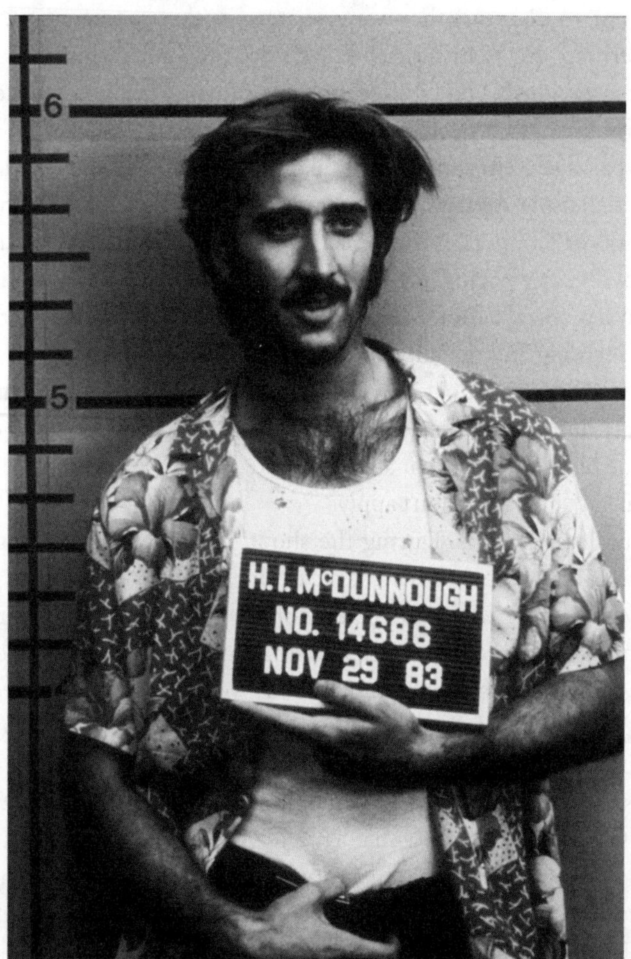

Figure 5.3. Cage's look and high-speed movements in *Raising Arizona* (1987, 20th Century Fox) were inspired by Woody Woodpecker. Ethan Coen observed that the more depressed the character grew, the wilder his hair became.

The Coens noticed that Cage was obsessed with his hair. "The more depressed the character was, the more flamboyant the tuft became," Ethan said in a 1987 interview. "There was a curious capillary rapport!"[60] (Indeed, perceptive viewers will notice that Hi's hair is at its most anarchic when he is confronted by his angry foreman Glen, who has figured out where Hi's baby came from.)

Woody Woodpecker, like Pokey, epitomized Cage's tendency to become a receptacle for oddly specific influences: cultural detritus to be chewed up and regurgitated at will in his performances. No longer leaning on Marlon Brando or James Dean, he was now culling from the cartoons of his youth. "I'm like a sponge," Cage later explained. "I could see a commercial on TV and get an idea, just the delivery somebody gave will stay in my head, and I will spew it back out."[61]

This time, Cage had found a movie that suited his anarchic visions. *Raising Arizona* puzzled critics because it was so far removed from the restrained seediness of *Blood Simple*, but its tone makes sense if you view it as a cartoon fable. The movie is full of cartoonlike flourishes. There's Carter Burwell's attention-grabbing score: an exuberant whirlwind of yodeling and bluegrass banjo. There's the extraordinary image of the two escaped cons (Goodman, Forsythe) being birthed from the slime. There's Leonard Smalls, of course, a villain wicked enough to rival Yosemite Sam. He is depicted as more beast than human, leaving a trail of blown-up rabbits and fire in his wake—in other words, a cartoon bad-guy.

At the center are two characters driven by primal urges—for Hi, it's the urge to steal; for Ed, the urge to be a mother—who bumble around in a world of absurdity, never quite in on the joke. Their adventures unfold against the cartoonlike landscape of the Arizona desert. As the critic M. V. Moorhead writes in *PHOENIX* magazine, "the desert seems, somehow, not too far from the terrain through which Wile E. Coyote chased the Road Runner."[62]

In the world of *Looney Tunes*, life moves at a higher speed. *Raising Arizona* captures a similarly kinetic sense of acceleration. In this movie, everything happens fast. Characters talk fast (Holly Hunter's "I need a baby, Hi—they got more'n they can handle!" pours out like a military bark), they run fast, and their luck changes fast. Even the camera moves fast; the Coens made extensive use of the "Shakicam," achieving exhilarating tracking shots, such as when the camera zooms up a ladder, through a window, and into Florence Arizona's screaming mouth.[63]

Cage's character is constantly in motion, always on the run: from the police, from an explosion, from a pack of dogs. Like many Cage characters, he is a man defined by his compulsive behavior, particularly when it comes to lawbreaking. During the film's opening seconds, he literally stumbles into frame, pushed by an unseen law officer. Later in the film, when he is tied to a chair against his will, he squirms and wriggles so wildly that he looks as though his head might start spinning like the girl in *The Exorcist*.

Yet never does he seem more like a cartoon character on the lam than during the chase sequence that unfolds after he returns to his old ways of robbing convenience stores. With a pantyhose on his face and some spirited yodeling on the soundtrack, Hi sprints like a bandit through the streets, the yards, and a supermarket, pursued by cops, barking dogs, and Barry Sonnenfeld's indefatigable camera. Tires screech, gunshots explode, and still our restless outlaw sprints on. Like a classic cartoon, it is high-octane action and goofy slapstick all at once.

Cage instilled these outlandish scenarios with real emotion and brought a focused physicality to the character that foreshadowed his *Vampire's Kiss*–era embrace of German Expressionism. He collected Polaroids of himself displaying gestures that he thought Hi would use, and he brought ideas of his own to the character, like having his eye start squinting when he sensed Leonard Smalls's presence.[64] "This was the first time I'd really had the chance to do action," Cage told *The Guardian* in 1987.[65]

That was a prescient remark, given that *Raising Arizona* predated Cage's action-hero ascent by a decade. In a sense, *Raising Arizona* straddles several significant facets of Cage's filmography. It solidified his affiliation with the independent filmmaking wave of the 1980s. It foreshadowed his pivot to big-budget action spectacle. It flexed his underutilized muscle for physical comedy. And it confirmed his knack for portraying criminals and outcasts, amiable characters inhabiting the less-than-amiable fringes of civilization.

Raising Arizona raised Cage in more ways than one.

* * *

Crew members have a certain way of knowing whether a movie will endure—sometimes more so than the filmmakers themselves. Those who worked on *Raising Arizona* knew it was special. The Coens' self-confidence was contagious. Chitra Mojtabai recalls people on set amusing themselves by reciting funny lines, like "Son, you got a panty on your head."

"The whole crew knew it and was saying it," Mojtabai says. "It's never happened to me on another movie that anybody enjoyed."

These crew members were unwitting guinea pigs, testers of that elusive Coen quotability quotient, and Cage shared their enthusiasm. He told an interviewer in October 1986 that *Raising Arizona* would be "the most inventive film that will come out in years."[66]

He was hardly overselling it. Released in the early spring of 1987, *Raising Arizona* is as great as any movie in Cage's filmography—exuberantly imaginative, eminently quotable, and enlivened by a poignancy and optimism so out of character for the Coens that critics seemed to think it was a put-on. The film was a moderate commercial success, pulling nearly $30 million at the box office—far more than any other pre-*Fargo* Coen movie—and solidifying the brothers' arrival as independent iconoclasts.

Critics were mixed, as were Arizonans themselves (the mayor of Scottsdale, a man named Herb Drinkwater, lamented that the film had "no redeeming social value").[67] But *Raising Arizona* was always destined to become more of a cult classic on the video store circuit than in the critical sphere. Pauline Kael, the brilliant *New Yorker* critic, did appreciate the film's cartoonish pace—a "galumphing tempo," as she described it—and heralded Cage's endearing spin on the ex-con antihero:

> Cage has sometimes been expected to carry roles that he wasn't ready for, but his youth works for him here. He's a lowlife caricature of a romantic hero, trying to do the right thing by everybody. . . . Hi's apologetic expression when he dematerializes this monster is Nicolas Cage at his most winning. (Actors have made big reputations as farceurs on less talent than Cage shows here; his slapstick droopiness holds it all together.)[68]

Few actors could hope to have a better year than Cage did in 1987. Arguably the most significant year in his filmography, it began with the minor success of *Raising Arizona* and ended with the major success of *Moonstruck.* (In between, he rebelled against his rising success by filming the low-budget *Vampire's Kiss.*) *Raising Arizona* was his coming-of-age moment, boosting his profile and signaling to audiences that this was no longer the gooey-eyed punk from *Valley Girl.* "With the exception of Sean Penn, no actor of his generation so powerfully externalizes his innermost longings," declared the *Chicago Tribune* upon the movie's release.[69]

Raising Arizona provided a lot of firsts for Cage. It was his first time portraying a full-blown grown-up (not a teenager, not a high schooler) in a starring role: a permanent crossover into onscreen adulthood. It was his first full-throated comedic performance. It was his first voiceover narration, a technique he'd later use to memorable effect in *Bringing Out the Dead* (1999) and *The Weather Man* (2005).

And it was his first, and sadly last, time working with the Coen brothers. For the Coens, this was unusual. Most actors who starred in their earlier films wound up becoming part of their self-styled repertory company.[††] "If you trace all the way back, you will see that they started with *Raising Arizona* to have a group of actors that they used over and over again," says Isaacson, the casting director. "And they never used Nick again."

Isaacson attributes this to the friction between Cage's freewheeling spirit and the Coens' stick-to-the-script ethos. "The problem was that Nick was an improvisational actor," she says. "And that was tough. It was not an easy relationship. . . . He had recommendations. And they were very polite. They also set the tone. There was never disharmony in any of the movies that I worked on. And I know there was a little bit with Nick, because they set the tone. And if you set the tone properly in the company, you're not going to have problems."

In 2001, Ethan Coen mused about wanting to work with Cage again. "We've written a Cold War comedy called *62 Skidoo* that we want him to do," the filmmaker told a *Playboy* interviewer. "It deals with amnesia, mistaken identity, and that very sixties question, 'Who am I?'"[70] Ethan likened it to paranoid John Frankenheimer classics *The Manchurian Candidate* and *Seconds*. Later, Joel told *The Guardian* that they wanted to cast the real Henry Kissinger.[71]

Twenty years later, that film has never materialized.

A lot of Cage fanatics will tell you that the greatest Cage movie never made is *Superman Lives*, the legendarily aborted Tim Burton superhero flick that would have starred Cage as an alienated Man of Steel for the Gen X set. Serious obsessives might tell you it's Elia Kazan's aborted sequel to *America*

[††] For instance, *Raising Arizona* cast members John Goodman and Frances McDormand both became regulars in the Coen universe. Trey Wilson, who played Nathan Arizona, was heading in that direction, too. In 1989, he was slated to star in *Miller's Crossing*. "I get the call from Trey Wilson's agent the night he's leaving [for the *Miller's Crossing* shoot] that he had a brain aneurysm and died," Isaacson recalls. "So now I have to call the boys and tell them Trey won't be arriving tomorrow because he's dead." Wilson was replaced with Albert Finney.

America, which in 1990 was slated to star Cage opposite Rebecca De Mornay before financing fell through.[72]

But I'm inclined to think Cage's greatest un-filmed film is *62 Skidoo*, an incredible Cold War flick that exists only in the minds of the Coen brothers.

Raising Arizona is a hell of a Cage–Coen collaboration for the ages. Still, I want another. But in the drab real world, you can't just go and steal one from Nathan Arizona's nursery.

6

A Nick at the Opera

It's September 2020, six months into a pandemic that has left New York City distressingly muted, if not exactly dead, and I'm spending another Saturday night at home. But this night is special. On this particular housebound evening, I'm watching a cascade of Nicolas Cage impressionists light up my screen as part of a telethon-style livestream called "Night of Too Many Cages." Hosted by comedian Chris Gethard, the charity event veers wildly from one Cage impersonator to the next—there's "Accounting Cage," who tabulates donations in a manic delivery, and even an appearance from Cage's former stand-in of ten years, who happily answers audience questions like "What does Nicolas Cage smell like?" (Answer: "He smells like a regular guy.")

But the evening's unexpected highlight turns out to be a DIY tribute to *Moonstruck*—the 1987 rom-com classic that elevated Cage to bread-baking, Cher-seducing, opera-loving romantic glory—performed by young children, who enthusiastically re-enact the scene in which Loretta (Cher) first meets Ronny Cammareri, the tormented baker played by Cage. A redheaded boy, around eight or nine, with a boxing glove in lieu of a wooden hand, portrays Cage's character, yelping lines like "Bring me the big knife!" in a sweet, prepubescent voice. A dark-haired girl, slightly older, delivers Cher's part. Chrissy (the bakery employee who refuses Ronny's request for the big knife) is portrayed by a very handsome dog.

It's an adorable tribute to a beloved film. And yet the segment also seems to crystallize just how much comfort and urgently needed solace *Moonstruck* brought people in 2020. As our daily lives shrank to the size of our apartments and Zoom squares, it felt good to draw succor from a film like *Moonstruck*—a film that overflows with life and love and outsized familial warmth. *Moonstruck* isn't just a movie about a big, boisterous Italian family. It portrays the whole city as a messy family, where fellow diners at the Grand Ticino restaurant might critique your marriage proposal and the familiar-looking man at the opera might just be your father. In 2020, New York lost those communal pleasures.

In fact, during the darkest days of lockdown, the romantic comedy enjoyed an improbable resurgence among the quarantined masses. "*Moonstruck* is the morbid spaghetti rom-com we all need right now," declared *Vulture* that cursed April.[1] By fall, the Criterion Collection had deemed the film worthy of its high-end DVD canon. A writer for *Esquire* declared it "one of the greatest movies about Italian-Americans ever made," praising it for depicting his culture without the usual mobster clichés.[2] And then, in a piece hailing the pleasures of the film, *New York Times* writer Caity Weaver called on the Academy to "acknowledge the unmooring from time that has become a fact of life this year" and give Cher a second Oscar for *Moonstruck*.[3]

Well, how about giving Cage his first? (For *Moonstruck*, that is.) Cage's performance is like an exhilarating pendulum, swinging between furious resentment and rapturous romantic enchantment without ever ringing false. It's the perfect balance of deranged and sexy. It's the performance that is widely revered by people who would never self-identify as Nicolas Cage fans, the performance that made the actor's smoldering sex appeal instantly legible to moviegoers too old to have registered him in *Valley Girl*.

And it's the performance that Cage would spend the next four years running as far away from as possible. To understand why, we must journey to the beginning of *Moonstruck*—or, should I say, *The Bride and the Wolf*.

* * *

Moonstruck sometimes feels like one long meditation on the communal joy and terror of dining out in New York City, so it's fitting that the movie's backstory began with a meal in New York City. John Patrick Shanley was on one side of the table, Sally Field on the other. It was 1986.

Shanley was a prolific playwright in his mid-thirties. He lived in Washington Heights, in a rundown apartment with broken windows at the center of the crack epidemic, but as far as he was concerned, he was living the dream. "I had been a writer since I was ten years old," he says. "I did a million shit jobs. And now I had finally set myself free and was able to live, very modestly, as a writer full-time. I'd been raised to be a guy who unloaded trucks. And here I was—I was a scribe! I was a poet! I was a writer!"

Field was a major star who had just won her second Oscar. When she invited Shanley to lunch to say she admired his work and thought they should work together, he was thrilled. They met at the Russian Tea Room in Manhattan, the swanky midtown spot where Madonna once worked as a coat-check clerk. "I'll write a movie for you," Shanley remembers telling Field. "But you can't pay me.

If you like it and you want to go into business, we can. And if it's not for you, then I take my screenplay and go on my way." Field agreed.

Shanley went home and wrote a screenplay, a roaringly romantic rom-com fairy tale about a gray-streaked widow in her thirties, Loretta Castorini, who lives with her parents and grandfather in Brooklyn Heights. Loretta is wearily resigned to marrying her fiancé—until she falls in love with his embittered one-handed brother instead.

The script was unabashedly long-winded and talky; defying all the norms of narrative progression, it reveled in lengthy soliloquies, morbid tangents, and a flair for the boisterous rhythms and customs of a large Italian-American household. Shanley had grown up in an Irish-American family. But as a kid, he had always been jealous of the Italian families on his street, with their great food, their lively conversation.[4] As for the swooningly romantic aura of the story, "I was living a very romantic existence, in a rundown apartment," says Shanley, who was then divorced after his first marriage. "I was king of my world."

Shanley wrote the script on spec so that a studio couldn't hog the rights while letting the project die on the vine. He titled it *The Bride and the Wolf*. Then he let Field read it. "I sent it to her and I said, 'You'll dye your hair. You'll put in a gold tooth. And I bet you'll get nominated for an Academy Award,'" Shanley says.

There are varying accounts of what happened next. According to Shanley, "She read the script. She loved it. No one would make it with her." Field, however, has said that *she* turned down the script, believing the character wasn't quite right for her. "It belonged to [Cher]," Field said in a 2016 interview. "I just didn't see myself as being, you know, an Italian, Bronx, Brooklyn. . . ."[5]

At any rate, Field was out, and Shanley's agent began shopping the script around to directors. Norman Jewison, the Canadian filmmaker whose celebrated resumé spanned from searing racial drama (1967's *In the Heat of the Night*) to big-budget musicals (*Fiddler on the Roof*, *Jesus Christ Superstar*), received it. Immediately, he was suspicious. "There was a lot of coffee stains on the cover of the script," Jewison recalled in 2006. "Which meant a lot of people had read it and passed on it."[6] Besides, he hated the title, which had confused his employees into thinking it was a horror film.[7]

But when Jewison read the screenplay, he was struck by its operatic thrall, its weighty themes of love and betrayal. He loved it. His production partner, Patrick Palmer, however, did not. "His partner called and berated my agent for sending a script that was so clearly not a film," Shanley says. "The next day, Norman called and said, 'Ignore what he said. I want to option the script.'"

Around the same time, a producer named Bonnie Palef, who had been mentored by Jewison and would soon become *Moonstruck*'s associate producer and production manager, fell in love with the screenplay. "I remember reading it in the bathtub, and the water got cold and I didn't notice," Palef says. "That's how good the script was."

Shanley went up to Toronto to meet with the director, and together they read the whole script aloud, trading off roles. Shanley was at first skeptical, but the director won him over. "Norman got it," he says. "He just got it." Shanley agreed to work with him on a rewrite.

The main issue was the title: *The Bride and the Wolf*. Jewison hated it. "That sounds like a horror picture," Jewison insisted. They began toying with titles involving the moon—a dreamlike motif in the film. Like Shakespeare, Shanley portrayed the moon as an intoxicating force, a cosmic emblem of love's trance. The screenwriter says he agreed to provide a list of potential new titles. "I sent some titles that I intentionally thought were bad," he says. "And amongst them I had the title *Moonstruck*. Which is the one that I wanted." And that was the title Jewison chose.

Palef remembers the process a bit differently. She says Jewison wanted to call the movie *Moonglow*, which she didn't care for. So she and Shanley went out for dinner in Toronto and passed pieces of paper back and forth with title ideas, and she came up with *Moonstruck*. They both loved it. The studio hated it.

"They said, 'It sounds like an action film,'" Palef says. "And we all really went to bat for it. We said, 'We're sorry. But that's what we're calling it!'"

* * *

Cher became Jewison's favorite to play Loretta early in the development process. *Moonstruck* was written during that mid-eighties stretch when, after two decades in the public eye, Cher was finally being taken seriously as an actress. Jewison had admired her performance in Peter Bogdanovich's *Mask* and knew she was perfect for Loretta: brash, pragmatic, plainspoken. After successfully pitching the film to MGM/UA president Alan Ladd, Jr., and securing a midsized budget, he set about wooing his first-choice star.[8]

The director visited Cher at her home. She was skeptical about playing Loretta.* For one thing, she had no Italian blood whatsoever. For another, she didn't think she could do a Brooklyn accent. Besides, Cher couldn't

* Another account of this conversation—from John Patrick Shanley's foreword to Jewison's autobiography—is that Cher warned Jewison, "I can be difficult to work with." Jewison replied, "I've worked with some difficult people. Are you more difficult than Judy Garland?"

imagine there would be much of an audience for a movie like *Moonstruck*.[9] Jewison assured her they could hire a voice coach. Then, he told her straight-up: "Cher, you're my first choice of any actress in the world. If you don't do this, you're going to regret it for the rest of your life."[10]

Cher finally signed on, with the producers agreeing to accommodate her busy schedule. ("We had to shoot in a very specific, short period of time," Palef recalls, "because we were lodged between these two other movies that Cher was doing.") So did an ensemble of veteran actors—Olympia Dukakis, Vincent Gardenia, the unforgettable grandfatherly figure Feodor Chaliapin, Jr.—to fill out Loretta's lively Italian family. But Ronny Cammareri, the troubled romantic lead, marinating in resentments in that dungeon-like bakery, was the hardest role to cast. The studio wanted a star. Nobody seemed right.

Plenty of actors showed interest in the part, most of them older and more established than Cage. Shanley suggested Raul Julia and John Turturro. Neither seemed like a fit. Al Pacino, in a career lull after 1985's *Revolution*, was briefly interested. When a relatively unknown Ray Liotta auditioned, Jewison was unimpressed, jotting down "needs style" and "too young" next to his name.[11]

"I'd seen a couple of other people screen test for it," says Shanley. "Some of them could do half of it. They could do the anger. Or they could do the romance. But nobody could do the anger *and* the romance: the volatile two sides of this guy. Until Nick did it."

Cage had taken a break from acting before *Moonstruck* came along. He spent the summer of 1986 reeling from the death of his cousin Gian-Carlo Coppola, who was killed in a boating accident, and reading *The Brothers Karamazov*, fantasizing about playing the violent eldest brother, Dmitri. "I don't feel very creative at the moment, so I've turned everything down," he told an interviewer that October.[12]

He was inclined to turn *Moonstruck* down, too. He was hardly an obvious fit. Cage was nearly a decade younger than Ray Liotta. He was twenty-two, going on twenty-three; he had just played a teenager in *Peggy Sue*. Cher was forty (her character is stated to be thirty-seven), upending the Hollywood cliché of middle-aged men wooing younger women onscreen. Ronny's age is never specified in the script, and Shanley had certainly not intended for him to be significantly younger than Loretta.

But once Shanley saw Cher and Cage's screen test, such details didn't matter. "You could immediately see that they had chemistry, and that they were some kind of a matched set," he says.

Cher was Cage's most forceful champion.† His *Gumby*-inspired acid trip of a performance in *Peggy Sue Got Married* may have infuriated Kathleen Turner. But it dazzled Cher, the person whose stamp of approval would boost Cage's career at a pivotal moment. "I thought that anybody who had the guts to expose his ass like that was the right person to play Ronnie [*sic*] Cammareri," Cher wrote in her memoir. "The first time I read the line, 'Give me the big knife, I want the big knife,' I could only hear him saying it."[13]

Jewison was skeptical—"Nicolas did have a darker interpretation of Ronny than I did," he admitted in 1988—but he came around to the idea.[14] With his lanky frame and hairy chest, Cage had always looked old for his age. Before the screen test, Jewison advised him not to shave for several days so he would look even older. "I tried to find the most tormented actor I could find," Jewison later reflected. "And it was Nicolas Cage! I thought he was kind of a tormented soul."[15]

The studio disagreed. Or maybe they agreed *too* much; either way, they didn't want that weirdo mucking up their movie. "The trouble with Nicolas in 1986 was that he was death at the box office," Jewison wrote in his memoir. "Most of his films had bombed."[16] That's not entirely true (*Peggy Sue* and *Valley Girl* had both done well), but it's fair to say *Birdy* and *The Boy in Blue* didn't exactly recoup.

Ultimately, the choice came down to Cage vs. Peter Gallagher, an older and certainly less volatile actor. Both screen-tested with Cher, but her preference was clear. "I think that Peter is a great actor, but in my mind, he wasn't *nuts*. Nicky was nuts, and 'nuts' is what we needed," Cher wrote in her memoir.

Palef agreed. "I thought he had the energy and also the sense of danger," she says. When studio heads pushed for Gallagher to be cast instead of "Nicky," Cher revolted: "I went against the studio and told them I wouldn't do the film without Nicky."[17]

After a week-long stalemate, Cher got her wish, and Cage got the part. "I saw both screen tests. And it was incontrovertible that Nick was the righter choice for that role," says Shanley. "Peter was a very good actor, but Nick just had this eccentricity and this fire."

* * *

In footage from the rehearsal sessions for *Moonstruck*, Cage sits across from Cher in a leather jacket, his hair spiked up haphazardly like he just stumbled

† Coincidentally, Cher's real boyfriend at the time, twenty-two-year-old Robert Camilletti, was an Italian guy who worked in a bagel shop and was the same age as Cage. Cher met him on her fortieth birthday and fell in love with him during the *Moonstruck* shoot. "He had a very similar energy to Nick," Palef says.

in from a Sex Pistols audition. He is surrounded by actors old enough to be his parents. He looks categorically out of place, though isn't that the idea? Would *Moonstruck* have worked if Ronny weren't such a live-wire threat to Loretta's complacency?

"Nick always looked like he'd been shot out of a cannon," says Shanley. "He almost looked like a cartoon character. Incredibly handsome. But there was something larger than life about him—and also about the kinds of characters I was writing."

Cage didn't want to be there. Like Cher, he had not wanted to do *Moonstruck*. "I was angry and rebellious," he said in 1992. "I wanted to make the kind of movies that are essentially punk gestures. I read the screenplay to *Moonstruck* and thought, 'I would never pay money to see this film!' But my agent insisted I do it, practically forced me to do it."[18]

In 1986, Cage wanted to be dangerous; *Moonstruck* must have seemed about as dangerous as the Metropolitan Opera House. He was more enamored with the considerably darker *Vampire's Kiss*, which was already floating around the ether and which his agent, Ed Limato, had all but forbade him from doing. "He said: 'No, you're not going to wear those stupid plastic things. I want you to look handsome! Do *Moonstruck*!' And I said, 'I don't want to do *Moonstruck*!' I wanted to be punk rock," Cage recalled in 2021.[19]

Cage proposed a compromise: if he did *Moonstruck*, would Limato let him do *Vampire's Kiss* right after? The deal was made.

Cage's antipathy toward *Moonstruck* was revealing: it crystallized the desire he felt to separate himself from mainstream Hollywood nearly as soon as such roles became available to him. Cage did not want to be a heartthrob, did not want to be a leading man, did not want to follow in the footsteps of Rob Lowe or Judge Reinhold or other comedy-adjacent stars with whom he had competed for roles. Cage's attitude was rebellious and often petulant, but this stubbornness propelled him into the most daring and unpredictable stretch of his career.

The irony is that Cage's character in *Moonstruck* was anything but anodyne. There are no villains in *Moonstruck*, but Ronny is the film's darkest character by far—a son who doesn't love his mother, a man so consumed by anger that he won't attend his big brother's wedding—played by Cage with a vocabulary of withering glances and explosive outbursts. In this sense, Ronny is a distant ancestor of later Cage characters like Roy from *Matchstick Men* or Robin from *Pig*, broken men who have already withdrawn from society, shattered by all-consuming tragedies in their pasts, long before we meet them.

Figure 6.1. In *Moonstruck* (1987, MGM/UA Communications Co.), Cage plays an opera lover, and his performance reflects the heightened, larger-than-life emotions and gestures that are common in opera.

But what ultimately got Cage interested in the *Moonstruck* character was something small: the wooden hand. Ronny, we learn, lost his real hand five years earlier in an accident, which he blames on his brother, Johnny (Danny Aiello), who distracted him while he was using a bread slicer. All this hurt comes tumbling out the first time he meets Loretta, sweating next to the ovens in that medieval basement (Figure 6.1).

Cage has a certain fascination with portraying physical deformities. It is embedded in his namesake—Luke Cage, the Marvel character, gained his superhuman strength as the result of a botched science experiment. Cage is often drawn to characters with unique deformities of their own: the bandaged face in *Birdy*, the freakish nose in *Never on Tuesday*, the whole ludicrous conceit of *Face/Off*. Sometimes he chooses roles for this reason alone.‡ Maybe

‡ When asked why he starred in *Drive Angry*—a dismal 2011 movie in which he plays a dead man who breaks out of hell to avenge his daughter's death—Cage explained that he liked the fact that his character gets his eyes shot out. "[In] the movie *Season of the Witch*, I wanted to get my eye shot out with a bow and arrow, and the producers didn't go for it," Cage told *Movieline*. "So when [*Drive Angry* director] Patrick Lussier said to me, 'You're going to get your eye shot out in a movie,' I don't know why but I just immediately said 'Yes, I'm in.' "

the challenge lies in interpreting and conveying the psychological weight of a physical disfigurement.

So it was with *Moonstruck*. "I took *Moonstruck* because the character was so romantic and I'm romantic," he claimed to *SPIN* in 1989. "I thought it was great that a man with a deformity could be that confident with a woman. Someday, I'd like to play a romantic lead whose face is covered with scars."[20]

Yet if *Moonstruck* is Cage's most purely romantic film, the secret ingredient was his own romantic baggage, feeding his performance from some half-conscious realm. At the time, Cage was reeling from a breakup with his girlfriend of several years, actress Jenny Wright, with whom he lived in 1985 and 1986. When he filmed the indelible late-night soliloquy—in which Ronny passionately implores Loretta to embrace the intrinsic messiness of love and "*get* in my bed!"—Cage was thinking about Wright, imbuing the breathless Shanley dialogue with the weight of his own heartbreak.

This scene encapsulates *Moonstruck*'s core thesis: a treatise on love's destructive yet insurmountable trance. "Love don't make things nice," Ronny tells Loretta after their date to the opera. "It ruins everything! It breaks your heart. It makes things a mess." Secretly, Cage imagined Wright might hear his pleading, might be turned on by how handsome he looked, gleaming in the moonlight in an expensive tux. "It was like a love letter in a way," Cage reflected in 1990. "I was hoping she would be out there listening."[21]

In his odd way, Cage was putting a personal spin on Lee Strasberg's Method technique of "affective memory," in which actors use memories and emotions from their own lives as psychological seedling for a performance. It was one of many qualities Cage had in common with his idol, Marlon Brando. Like Cage, Brando—once the living embodiment of Method acting—used acting to exorcise his inner turmoil; like Cage, Brando had a way of channeling emotions from his traumatic childhood and personal life as fuel for his greatest performances. "The idea is you learn to use everything that happened in your life and you learn to use it in creating the character you're working on," Brando once said. "You learn to dig into your unconscious."[22]

Cage's conflicted relationship with the Method, his knack for embodying torment, his proclivity for being a character actor even after achieving leading-man stardom—all of this called to mind Brando. "There's something of Brando in the way Cage confronts Cher in *Moonstruck*, wearing a soiled white t-shirt, radiating heartbreaking masculine pathos," the critic Manohla Dargis argued in a 1995 essay about Cage. Dargis continued:

> There's something of Brando as well in the way Cage fully uses his body, now and then, to punishing effect. An important characteristic of Cage's performance style is that he charts the life rolling around inside with his entire physical being. His body tells secrets.[23]

Cage later revealed that he was thinking of one of Brando's signature performances, *On the Waterfront*, when he made *Moonstruck*. It's a curious obscurity of Cage's career that he nearly worked with the director who made that film—indeed, the director who made Brando a star and who first brought the Method to a popular audience—Elia Kazan. "I got a call from Elia Kazan after he saw [*Moonstruck*] and he wanted me to do the sequel to *America America* and play Stavros," Cage said in a 2018 interview, referring to the hero of Kazan's 1963 immigrant epic.[§]

The movie never happened. Nor did Cage's ploy to win back his ex-girlfriend succeed, but his passion endeared him to Cher, who found him at once brilliant and maddening. Cage, in turn, found Cher to be so youthful that he barely felt an age difference.[24]

One day, Shanley recalls, during rehearsals, Cage turned to Cher and opened his mouth to show off a half-chewed bite of sandwich. "And Cher just looked at him like, 'Oh, don't be a brat,'" Shanley says. Other times, Cher made lunch for Cage at her apartment in New York. During one of these lunches, he asked Cher if she was a witch. "He was into that stuff," Cher recalled in 1996. "So I said, 'I am.' He said, 'I thought so.'"[25]

This was a strange couple for moviegoers to take in, but their onscreen chemistry was palpable (Figure 6.2). Cage's ranting and raving formed the perfect counterpoint to Cher's exasperated, hand-wringing pragmatism, and he paired it with an illicit swagger primed to melt her defenses. (Just watch the way he pauses to stroke his hair back after flipping the table over just before their first kiss.) Both actors approached the film with a fearless ferocity, a willingness to sweat and shout and breathe genuine urgency into dialogue that may have looked silly on the page.

Cher came away from the film with deep respect for Cage, but doubt that such an eccentric actor could ever be a mainstream star. "He takes

[§] Kazan spent several years casting and finding locations for this film, which would have been his first in twenty-five years and, in his mind, "the toughest picture of my life." Cage was his star of choice. But the filmmaker lost interest when funding issues arose, and turned the story into a 1994 novel, *Beyond the Aegean*, instead. See Kazan, Elia, and John Lahr. *Kazan on Directing*. Vintage Books, 2010, p. 283.

Figure 6.2. Despite their eighteen-year age gap, Cher loved working with Cage in *Moonstruck* (1987, MGM/UA Communications Co.). "Every time I got angry with him, I'd just look in his eyes," she said.

unbelievable chances and personally I think he's crazy—sometimes he was a blast on the set, other days I'd get real peeved at him," Cher told an interviewer shortly after the movie opened. "And of course, he's got those great eyes. Every time I got angry with him, I'd just look in his eyes."[26]

* * *

By the time he began filming *Moonstruck* in late 1986, Cage was recovering from an illness. He had mononucleosis, or perhaps the flu—nobody can remember exactly. Cher was nervous. "She was afraid of doing a love scene with Nick and getting mono," says first assistant director Lewis Gould. "Norman assured her that he would make sure Nick was well before they got to any of those scenes."

With an eye toward his recovery, Cage did not join the shoot until well into the second week of filming. His first scene was the one where Cher confronts him in the bakery basement. Shanley had intended the scene to take place in a typical bakery, but then Jewison visited Cammareri Bros. Bakery in Brooklyn and decided the scene should be set against the medieval-looking ovens down in the basement. Shanley agreed—he liked the way the grim basement brought out Ronny's fiery nature—and rewrote the scene to take place there. He used the bakery's actual name as Ronny's surname, and Cage trained on how to bake bread.[27]

So, that's where Cage was during his first day on set: shoveling bread into a coal-fired oven. "The very first rehearsal, Nick starts to go into that intense speech. 'I lost my hand!' And he just dead away faints and falls on the ground!" Gould recalls. "And all of us thought, 'He's just coming off of mono,' and, 'Guys, let's get a doctor!' "

The crew rushed to Cage to see if he needed medical attention. "Then he got up and Norman said, 'Are you alright?' And he goes, 'Yeah. That was just my choice. That was what I thought the scene might call for,' " Gould says. "And Norman looked at me—he smiled at me—but he was also kind of saying with his expression, 'What the fuck is going on here?' "

In Gould's recollection, Jewison "very diplomatically brought the intensity down. Of course, it stays an intense scene. But he brought him back from literally fainting. We were all taken aback a bit."

Perhaps fainting was Cage's way of spicing up a movie he did not want to make.** His most significant creative conflict with Jewison, however, emerged more gradually. By the time he made *Moonstruck*, Cage—who was self-conscious about his own voice—was determined to use a new voice for each character he played. Ronny would need a Brooklyn accent, of course, a sharp break from the gee-shucks twang Cage had used in *Raising Arizona*.

But Cage went several steps further. He had become enamored with Jean Cocteau's 1946 *Beauty and the Beast*, a surrealistic precursor to the Disneyfication of the fairy tale, starring Jean Marais as the Beast. Cage saw Ronny Cammareri as a modern-day Beast—hidden away in that bakery basement, muscles bulging, chest hair protruding out of his sweat-stained tank top—and he decided to deliver his lines using the same guttural, growling voice Marais had used for *Beauty and the Beast*.

"I wanted to speak like that, because I had responded to the script that way," Cage said in a 2018 *GQ* interview. "About two weeks into production, I went home for the holidays, and I got a call from the director, Norman Jewison. And he said, 'Nick. The dailies aren't working. I want you to drop

** Bonnie Palef believes that in an earlier draft of the script, Ronny really does pass out when he first meets Loretta. Perhaps that is where Cage got the idea. Shanley, however, disputes this. "Oh, hell no!" he says, when asked if fainting was in the screenplay.

the Jean Marais. This voice you're doing is not working.'"[28] In a separate interview, Cage said, "I knew I had to soften the performance or I was going to be fired."[29] He acquiesced.

As with *Peggy Sue Got Married*, it's possible Cage is exaggerating just how close he was to being let go. Palef is skeptical. "I don't think Nick was going to be fired halfway through the shoot," Palef says. Jewison never mentioned this strife in his director's commentary, nor does it come up in his memoir. (Through an assistant, Jewison declined to be interviewed for this book.) Shanley doesn't recall the conflict at all, though he does remember Jewison having a conversation with Cage regarding his jarring performance in *Peggy Sue*. "It was very clear that he was laying out that he didn't want Nick to come up with a bizarre take," Shanley says.

Jewison tended to guide his actors away from stylized or surreal performances. "Norman always likes to underplay," says Palef. "It's like the old-fashioned Hollywood director who always goes, 'Bring it down, bring it down.'" For Cage, working with this long-established filmmaker whose career stretched back to the fifties was vastly different than working with upstart experimentalists like the Coens. He compared Jewison to an armored car: "You know you'll get there safely and he'll provide good work."[30]

Yet Jewison did indulge one of Cage's wackier ideas. By 1986, the actor had become fascinated with the harsh imagery and sharp, distorted gestures of German Expressionist cinema—one of many cultural interests that put him out of step with the rising stars of his own generation. Eager to absorb such influences in his work, Cage insisted on paying homage to Fritz Lang's *Metropolis*, a futuristic masterpiece of the Expressionist movement, during the scene where Ronny holds his wooden hand aloft as he shouts at Loretta about his heartbreak.

"If you look at *Metropolis*, there's a shot of the scientist who invents the technology to create the robot woman—he shows off the robot hand that he invented. He has it raised up, and I told Norman that I really wanted to approximate that shot," Cage told *Entertainment Weekly* in 1996. "He thought it was nuts, but he went for it."[31]

Drama of a more contentious nature unfolded on the freezing night when Cage and Cher were shooting their romantic scene outside Ronny's apartment. The stars were so cold they could barely move their mouths, and Cher's patience was dwindling after a space heater set her scarf on fire.[32] "It was 2:00 in the morning," Palef says. "Nick was having trouble with the speech, and we were all freezing to death. And Norman came over to me and said, 'Get Shanley here now.' "

Shanley arrived to find Cage objecting to major lines in Ronny's "The stars are perfect . . ." speech. "There was some part of the speech that he didn't want to say," Shanley says. In the original shooting script, before pleading with her to "get in my bed," Ronny persuades Loretta with an extended metaphor about food:

> Don't try to live on milk and cookies when what you want is meat! Red meat just like me! It's wolves run with wolves and nothing else! You're a wolf just like me!

Cage disliked those lines and refused to say them. The whole scene could be cut in half, Cage argued. Shanley sat with him in a trailer and talked it over. Sure, the screenwriter agreed, it *could* be cut in half, and the plot would still work. "But in terms of the entire film, you will not fulfill the philosophical premise of this film if we abbreviate this scene." Cage was silent for a moment. "And Nick said, 'Philosophically? OK, fine!' That was the end of the discussion," Shanley says.

Cage gave in and said the line, but it wound up being cut during editing anyway. "So he'd been right!" Shanley laughs. "These people know! They know what fits in their mouth and what doesn't."

* * *

Moonstruck doesn't have much in common with *Raising Arizona*, but both films depart from the confines of cinematic realism subtly and effortlessly, without asking the audience's permission. They are not fantasy films—not formally, at least—yet they both draw on cultural forms that revel in exaggerated, larger-than-life characters and scenarios. In *Raising Arizona*'s case, that influence lies in the zany pop-surrealism of Warner Bros. cartoons. *Moonstruck*, however, has a more high-brow reference point: opera.

It is no coincidence that Cage plays an opera fanatic who has a vintage poster of Giacomo Puccini's beloved opera *La Bohème* on his wall and who tells Loretta he loves only two things: "I love you, and I love the opera." Nor is it happenstance that the most romantic sequence of the film occurs during and immediately after a date to the opera. As Danny Aiello described it, "The operatic flavor is what gives the movie its air of heightened reality."[33]

Opera is all over this movie, nearly from its first frame. During the opening credits, as Loretta walks to work, the camera pans past her, zooming in on a truck emblazoned with the words "METROPOLITAN OPERA SCENIC SHOP." The truck is shown backing into a parking garage, unloading equipment for that week's performance of *La Bohème*, a performance which will hold great significance for our characters. Later, Puccini's score provides a musical backdrop to emotional moments: when Ronny lifts Loretta and carries her to his bed, for instance, the moment is underlined by the dramatic swells of *La Bohème*'s "O Soave Fanciulla," which rise in volume as they begin making love.

This is mere warm-up for *Moonstruck*'s pivotal scene in which a tuxedo-clad Ronny takes Loretta, who is glowing after a fresh makeover, to the Met for their big date, and her first opera (Figure 6.3). A typical eighties rom-com might set a romantic date at a yuppie club or a Bon Jovi concert or something, but *Moonstruck* sets it at *La Bohème*, where, in one of the film's most rapturous sequences, Loretta is moved to tears by the opera's tragic thrall. These were real tears, Cher recalled in her memoir: "We were looking at an empty stage, listening to the music, while Norman told us the story. He told it so well, I cried."[34]

The unusual foregrounding of opera in *Moonstruck* has been a subject of fascination for opera scholars. In her book *When Opera Meets Film*, musicologist Marcia J. Citron describes *Moonstruck* as "a wacky marriage between Italian-American ethnic comedy and romantic idealism" and argues that opera is key to this juxtaposition. "[T]he dualistic tone of the film is itself operatic and resembles an encounter between *opera buffa* and *verismo*," Citron writes.[35]

All of which brings us to two questions: How on earth did opera become so central to this romantic comedy? And what does this have to do with Nicolas Cage?

Let's start with the first. The way Shanley tells it, it was a bit of a chicken-or-egg situation: he didn't truly fall in love with opera until he noticed critics kept comparing his *own* plays to opera. "People would always say in reviews, 'These characters are bigger than life! It's like opera!'" Shanley says. "So I'm like, 'Oh, something about what I'm doing is operatic!' I got a book of all the opera plots and I read all the plots to try to understand more—and also, was there anything I could steal."

Shanley started going to operas at the Met, taking note of little details—like the way the chandeliers retract when the show begins—to write into his script. The opera that particularly moved him was *La Bohème*. Written by Puccini in the 1890s (based on the novel *Scènes de la Vie de Bohème* by Henri Murger), *La Bohème* was among the most renowned works to emerge from the late Romantic period of Italian opera. For Puccini, it was also his most personal, intended as an emotional farewell to his bohemian youth.

"I was drawn to the idea of people leading a bohemian life," says Shanley. "The Nick Cage character—he's a bohemian! He's listening to opera and baking bread and living a fever dream of a life. Filled with fantasies of revenge and impossible love and having a deformity, like Cyrano."

Jewison shared Shanley's passion for the opera. He saw the opening of the film as the opening of *La Bohème*. In fact, early cuts of *Moonstruck* used music from *La Bohème* during the opening credits, but test screenings were disappointing; audiences didn't quite seem to realize it was a comedy. "It just turned everybody off," Jewison recalled in his commentary track.[36] So Palef went to a record store in New York and found some old records to bring to the film's editor, Lou Lombardo. One of them was "That's Amore," the 1953 Dean Martin hit, which became *Moonstruck*'s quirky overture. "It totally

Figure 6.3. The most romantic sequence of *Moonstruck* (1987, MGM/UA Communications Co.) occurs during and immediately after Ronny and Loretta's date at the opera. As Danny Aiello once wrote, "The operatic flavor is what gives the movie its air of heightened reality."

changed the tone," Palef says. "We played almost the same film to an audience, and they laughed right off the top."

What makes *Moonstruck* operatic is not merely that opera is interwoven into the soundtrack and plot. It's that the film itself revels in the heightened, larger-than-life display of emotion that is core to opera's appeal. In *Moonstruck*, declarations of love and pain are performed by characters with a grandiosity that borders on ridiculous. But in opera, such grandiosity is integral to the art. In opera, realism is not the goal; how could it be when characters literally sing instead of speaking?

Jewison understood this. He even brought the cast to see *La Bohème* while they were shooting in Canada.[37] In his view, *Moonstruck* was an opera because every major character delivers their own passionate soliloquy, or, in opera terms, an aria (a self-contained song in which one character expresses their own emotional perspective). Cage's arias are multiple—his tormented rant in the bakery, his romantic plea to Cher after the opera—whereas Vincent Gardenia's aria might be his impassioned speech about plumbing and copper pipes. "Every one of them has an aria to sing!" Jewison said in a 2006 featurette. "Cher is the soprano, Ronny is the tenor, Danny Aiello is the baritone, Cosmo the father is the bass, Dukakis is the contralto. And grandpa is the Greek chorus!"[38]

So, what does all this have to do with Cage? On a familial level, opera certainly fits with Cage's Italian heritage. The actor has a direct ancestral connection to the art form: his great-grandfather, Francesco Pennino, was a Naples-born musician who got his start playing piano for the popular opera singer Enrico Caruso. (Pennino later wrote the musical mini-drama *Senza Mamma*, which Coppola incorporated into *The Godfather Part II*.)[39]

But on an artistic level, Cage has a certain creative kinship with opera. A great Cage performance, like a great opera, breaks away from naturalism in favor of big, lofty displays of grand emotion. "Western kabuki," "Nouveau Shamanic"—whatever made-up term Cage favors for his performance style, the end result is a form defined by unbridled operatic intensity. And one can witness the early blossoming of this style in Ronny Cammareri holding up his wooden hand, channeling his heartbreak into bellowing cries of rage: *"I lost my hand! I lost my bride!"*

Cage had played a tormented man three years earlier in *Birdy*, but there his monologues were bound by the confines of emotional realism. In *Moonstruck*, he broke into a different realm of intensity.

Critics have often described Cage's best performances (particularly *Moonstruck*, *Leaving Las Vegas*, and *Face/Off*) as operatic, and opera has been a recurring motif in his movies. Several years after *Moonstruck* came *Guarding Tess*, a far worse film in which Cage's character again spends a prominent scene attending an opera. After that came *Leaving Las Vegas*, whose tragic third act is intensified by a distinctly operatic score. David Lynch even asked Cage to sing a bit of opera in 1990's *Wild at Heart*, though the scene was ultimately cut.[40] Instead, he sings multiple tunes by Elvis Presley, who in Cage's mind isn't so different.[††]

La Bohème may depart from the stylistic confines of ordinary life, but the emotions Puccini was expressing in the opera were profoundly real. Cage operates with a similar philosophy: in his mind, oversized, operatic acting is no less truthful than naturalistic acting when it is a conduit for authentic emotional expression. "You can design a performance in terms of the size of it, go outside the box, be operatic, but if there is emotional content in it—if you still have the *feeling*—you can commit to whatever you want," Cage said in a 2014 interview. "I'm not the first one to do it. In the '30s it happened quite a bit. Look at [James] Cagney, was he real? No. Was he truthful? Yes."[41]

Cage chafes when people describe his work as over the top—"There is no 'top' when it comes to the imagination," he told an interviewer in 2009—and so does John Patrick Shanley, the man who put all that opera in *Moonstruck* in the first place.[42] "I had it in one of my plays—I forget which one[‡‡]—but somebody says, 'You're running on a little bigger than life.' And the woman comes back with, 'Maybe *your* life,'" Shanley tells me. "When people said my characters were over the top, bigger than life, I was like, I don't even know what you're talking about. This is what I'm like!"

* * *

If *Moonstruck* is an opera, its final scene—in which Johnny returns from Italy to find his fiancée, her new beau (his estranged brother), and her family all gathered at the kitchen table waiting for him—is the grand crescendo. Here is where the ensemble structure pays off: every major character brought together in a sublime farce of mounting tension and dramatic reveals.

[††] "It's clear to me that Elvis was an opera singer," Cage said recently in a *Los Angeles Times* profile, bringing it all full circle.

[‡‡] The play in question is titled *Women of Manhattan*.

This, Jewison later remarked, was the most difficult scene he had shot in any film.[43] Like most of *Moonstruck*'s interiors, it was filmed on a soundstage in Jewison's hometown of Toronto during the early months of 1987. It was late in the production process, and tensions were high. After hours of missed cues and aborted takes, the actors, many of whom knew each other from the Manhattan theater world, were starting to bicker among themselves.[44] Palef describes it like this: "Actors are like horses. You have six or seven thoroughbreds in a room, you're gonna get some action!"

During the tussle, Cage became so enraged at Julie Bovasso, who played Cher's aunt, that he hurled a chair across the room. "They almost came to blows," says Shanley. "There was an explosive confrontation." A Brooklyn native, Bovasso was credited as the film's dialogue coach, training Cher on her Brooklyn accent. But when she tried to give Cage acting notes—imploring him to deliver a line louder and faster—he snapped. "I threw a chair and I said, 'Don't you dare tell me how to act!' I did apologize later," Cage recalled in 1999.[45] Eventually, the eighty-one-year-old Feodor Chaliapin, Jr., who shone as the confused, dog-wrangling grandpa, rose to restore order.[46]

Cage got along better with the late Danny Aiello, who played his brother, despite a thirty-one-year age difference. Onscreen, they were bitter rivals, but in real life, Aiello enjoyed bonding with Cage, about whom he later raved, "I've never met a nicer kid." Cage earned Aiello's lasting gratitude one night during the New York portion of the shoot, when Aiello learned that his son Rick had passed out while partying at a nightclub downtown. "Nicky heard of my troubles and vaulted into action," Aiello recalled in his 2015 memoir. "He didn't question and didn't hesitate but helped me mount a rescue mission." Cage accompanied Aiello to the club and helped the older man get his son out safely.[47]

A hardened New York actor known for playing tough guys and gangsters, Aiello felt uneasy playing a wimpy mama's boy in *Moonstruck*. After the movie came out, he and Cage had something else in common: a love-hate relationship with the film that lifted both of their careers. "I told people that I hadn't wanted my mother to see the film because I didn't want her to see me as a weakling. I was embarrassed," Aiello wrote, a revealing glimpse of the discomfort some actors feel when playing against type.[48]

Perhaps it was Cage's virility that made Aiello feel emasculated. When one of Aiello's friends, the character actor Robert Costanzo, called to compliment him on the performance, Aiello grew defensive. "I said to him, 'Great performance, Danny! Good to see another side of you,'" Costanzo recalls.

"So Danny says to me, '*Bobby.* If you think for one minute that that kid, that young man, Nick Cage, could take a broad away from me, you're outta your fucking mind!' "

* * *

Love don't make things nice. It ruins everything. Ronny says that. And while the love that audiences and reviewers showed *Moonstruck* did not ruin Cage, it confounded him. It complicated his image. Cage had not wanted to make this big-hearted romantic comedy, and now here it was, racking up Oscar nominations and grossing $80 million, his biggest box office hit of the eighties by far. The film delighted critics and audiences, and became an enduring favorite.

Nobody had expected this. Even the cast had low expectations. Cher had reluctantly fit *Moonstruck* into her schedule, thinking it wouldn't go anywhere; as for Olympia Dukakis, when Jewison told her she would win an Academy Award, she stared at him like he was nuts.[49] But Jewison's prophecy came true. Dukakis did win an Oscar. So did Cher and John Patrick Shanley, making *Moonstruck* one of the few unabashed comedies to receive serious Academy attention during the eighties. To this day, it is the only movie on Cage's resumé to have been nominated for Best Picture.

Cage's own performance was oddly ignored by the Academy—a snub which Shanley still finds astonishing—though it did garner him a Golden Globe nomination and considerable acclaim from critics. (Years later, Cage claimed that some of his best scenes in *Moonstruck* had been cut by Jewison and speculated that he, too, might have received an Oscar nomination had they remained.[50])

For Jewison, the film's success was deeply validating—a sign that, in a sea of formulaic action movies, audiences still cared about "films where people actually talk to one another."[51] For Cage, it was more complicated. Seeing the finished cut of *Moonstruck* did not assuage the reservations he had about the project from the beginning: that it was too mushy, too romantic, and would interfere with the anarchic image he sought to cultivate for himself. It is often frustrating for an artist when audiences respond best to a work the artist did not want to make, and just as Coppola had experienced this conflicting emotion with *Peggy Sue*, Cage now felt it with *Moonstruck*. "I wanted to do some punk movie, some wild, rebellious gesture," he admitted in 1994. "When I saw the movie, I think I hurt Norman Jewison's feelings, because I couldn't say anything. That just wasn't the kind of movie I wanted to do."[52]

Cage's ambivalence can be gleaned in some of the interviews he granted around the time *Moonstruck* came out. "I feel like there's a big, wet fish slapping itself against the inside of my head right now," he told journalist Kristine McKenna in early 1988. McKenna wrote a revealing profile of Cage for the *Los Angeles Times* just as he was trying to make sense of the film's success—and, as McKenna put it, "his newfound sex symbol status." Cage's discomfort with both developments was palpable:

> "Things have changed quite a bit in the past three weeks and I don't know what to make of all the attention the film is receiving," he said, anxiously running his fingers through his hair. "I'm grateful that people seem to like the film, but the whole thing's a little bizarre."

Cage had been press-shy for years, unwittingly letting reporters mischaracterize him as a Brat Pack rich kid surfing on his uncle's fame. Now he welcomed McKenna into his Los Angeles apartment, eager to correct misconceptions about his upbringing and show off his eccentric abode. "Though the apartment décor does include an exotic bug collection and a massive stone lion's head on the mantle, he is nonetheless a reasonable young man who claims to live by night, sleep all day, and be 'not too good at the Hollywood thing,'" McKenna reported.

In her interview, Cage admitted that he had done *Moonstruck* to give himself the creative freedom to take a bigger risk with his next film, the low-budget *Vampire's Kiss* which, he bragged, had little commercial appeal. "He's not interested in having a conventional career," McKenna shrewdly surmised.[53]

Indeed, like a punk band sheepishly distancing themselves from their radio hit, Cage spent the next few years running as far away from *Moonstruck* as he could. When he visited San Francisco in late 1988 to attend a screening of *Vampire's Kiss* at the university where his father taught, Cage was asked whether *Moonstruck II* or "a teen-oriented box-office pleaser" might be in his future. "No, no," Cage told the *San Francisco Examiner* writer who had posed the question. "I've just signed to do a movie with Italian director Giuliano Montaldo in Africa."[54] (*Tempo di uccidere*—or *Time to Kill*, as it was called in English-speaking markets—arrived in 1989 and made little impact.)

Cage seemed perturbed when interviewers described him as a sex symbol. "I won't lie and say it's not great to be in a hit movie," he told the *Examiner* in 1988. "But if that were the main criterion, I would never have taken on *Vampire's Kiss*. . . . Some movies I do for my career, others I do for me."[55]

Cage's discomfort with *Moonstruck* is the key to understanding the bewildering stretch of his career that followed. The deranged yuppie hell of *Vampire's Kiss*, the cartoon-coated wackiness of his *Never on Tuesday* cameo, the out-of-control rockabilly lawlessness of *Wild at Heart*—they all can be understood as different manifestations of the punk gestures Cage craved when he made *Moonstruck*. What other actor spent years trying to wash off the stink of his most beloved movie yet?

* * *

Thirty-five years later, *Moonstruck* stands alone in Cage's filmography. He has done other romantic comedies, but none as indelible as this. He has played other tortured romantics, but nobody quite like Ronny. Never has Cage fused his molten sex appeal and his gift for wild-eyed scenery-chewing bombast quite so deftly.

Moonstruck's appeal is curiously timeless; with its multigenerational cast and Dean Martin soundtrack, it doesn't feel tied down in the late eighties. Maybe that's why its cultural stock has only risen as younger generations discover it. Palef notes with some satisfaction that *The Last Emperor*, the historical epic that beat *Moonstruck* for Best Picture, has not had the same staying power. Fans can't seem to snap out of its spell.

In the early nineties, Cage softened his view and finally came around to the film.[56] By then, *Moonstruck* and *When Harry Met Sally . . .* had ushered in a new era of brainy, New York–centric rom-coms—many of them written and/or directed by Nora Ephron—and Cage was ready to cash in on the rom-com boom with movies like *Honeymoon in Vegas*.

"I'm glad that he took that journey and ended up there," Shanley says of Cage's slow acceptance of *Moonstruck*. "Danny Aiello was very irritated by *Moonstruck* as well. Because he didn't know until he saw the movie that his character was very foolish. He was apparently playing it straight and didn't know people were gonna laugh so much." Like Cage, Aiello eventually embraced it. "He recognized that the movie had done him a tremendous amount of good," Shanley says.

Cage warmed up to *Moonstruck* so much that in 2001, his longtime friend and business partner Jeff Levine, with whom he'd started Saturn Films, was in talks with Chip Miller to develop a *Moonstruck* sequel. The project began life as an original screenplay, co-written by Miller, called *The Seven Fishes*, which was restructured to reboot the *Moonstruck* characters a decade and change later. "Jeff Levine came up with the idea," says Chip Miller, a longtime script doctor whose friendship with Cage began with the aborted Gene Vincent biopic. "They were talking to Cher about doing her role. They were developing a script."

According to Miller, both Cher and Olympia Dukakis expressed interest in reprising their roles, and funding options fell into place. Cage's interest was less certain. That summer, Levine and Miller put off pitching the project to Cage because the actor seemed increasingly insecure about the state of his career following the critical flop of *Captain Corelli's Mandolin*. Then the September 11 attacks shut down film production in New York City and caused a key investor to pull out, and the *Moonstruck* sequel never made it past the development phase.

Shanley was not involved in those discussions, but he has always known he could write a sequel of his own. "Nobody ever asked me," Shanley says. "But if I had written *Moonstruck II*, it would have taken up after they had married and divorced in a fiery divorce. And he wants her back." Instead, Oscar in hand, Shanley wrote and directed the 1990 cult rom-com *Joe Versus the Volcano* and authored dozens more plays, including *Doubt: A Parable*, which he adapted into a celebrated 2008 film starring Philip Seymour Hoffman.

No *Moonstruck* sequel has ever materialized, which is just as well. To make it a franchise would cheapen it. *Moonstruck* is its own thing. Shanley still remembers the first time he saw the finished film. "My reaction was, they should not put this out on videocassette or anything," he says. "They should rerelease this in a year. I think it'd be a hit a second time."

7
Kiss Me Deadly

The story begins with a terrible vacation.

Or perhaps "terrible" is too obvious—*Vampire's Kiss* is not the sort of movie that could have emerged from a jolly seaside honeymoon. It is grim, deranged—a comedy so dark its protagonist, played with wild fervor by Nicolas Cage, literally believes he is allergic to daylight. But these were particularly bad vibes. It was January 1986, and a talented young New York screenwriter named Joseph Minion was miserably depressed. "It was a very bad time," Minion says. "It was very cold. I was in a toxic relationship. From film school to then, it was just festering."

Minion's first film, the darkly funny night-from-hell classic *After Hours*, had originated as a Columbia film school assignment before miraculously catching the eye of Martin Scorsese, who directed it in 1985, bringing Minion's vision of urban alienation to a mass audience. Now his second feature-length script, *Motorama*, was trapped in development hell—thus one cause of his misery. He and his girlfriend, film producer Barbara Zitwer, decided to leave town. They caught a cheap courier flight to Barbados. Even there, Minion couldn't shake his tortured mental state.

Zitwer intervened. "She said, 'Listen. I'm going back to New York. You're in a bad mood. You sit here, write a script,'" Minion recalls. Zitwer, who had met Minion in film school and then risen up the ranks as a location scout and associate producer for the low-budget horror filmmaker Larry Cohen, thought a new script might lift his spirits. "She said, 'Whatever you write, I promise I'll get it made,'" Minion recalls.

Zitwer remembers the conversation differently: "I told him to write a script that would be set in Barbados. We'll shoot it there. I love the Caribbean."

A nice idea, but not one Minion heeded. When he met a stranger at the hotel who loved horror movies, inspiration struck: *People are crazy about horror movies. Why not write a low-budget horror film?* Minion spent two weeks cooped up in a hotel room overlooking palm trees, writing. "I was just alone with my demons," he says. "I rented a typewriter. I pounded it out."

One evening, as the sun was setting, he was staring out the open window and saw a group of bats fly out of an opening in the roof. A sign? "It was like, *Oh my God. This is the universe speaking to me.*"

The result was *Vampire's Kiss*, a darkly comic story about a mentally disturbed literary agent named Peter Loew, whose empty, unfulfilled romantic exploits cause him to rant to his therapist and torment his secretary, Alva. When Peter gets bitten by a vampiric lover named Rachel during a one-night stand that he may or not have hallucinated, he comes to believe he's turning into a vampire and descends into insanity, ranting and raving and begging for death. The film regards Peter's spiraling madness with unflinching fascination, as he kills a woman in a nightclub and hallucinates in the streets. It is not entirely clear what's real and what's imagined, what's meant to be funny and what's simply grim.

The story shared some similarities with *After Hours*—the buzzing urban anxiety, the male protagonist's intense sexual alienation, the bleak view of New York nightlife—but even more twisted.

What *Vampire's Kiss* and *After Hours* really had in common—besides the nocturnal Manhattan milieu—was that both scripts served to exorcise their creator's demons. When he wrote *After Hours*, a black comedy about a guy (Griffin Dunne) who just wants to get home from a disastrous date, Minion was inspired by his own housing frustrations. He couldn't afford an apartment of his own; whenever he did spot an affordable listing, he would call and just miss it. "I remember being consumed with needing a stable apartment," Minion says. "For years, I was just: sublet, sublet. I think that fueled that script in many ways, this sense of, just let me get home. But I don't have a home!"

Vampire's Kiss was even more personal. Minion admits the energy behind the script had to do with "cauterizing this really toxic relationship" with Zitwer, which was consuming his life and mental energy. He planned to direct the movie himself.

Minion tells me all this more than three decades later, at a diner on West 57th Street in Manhattan. He is in his sixties now, with dark glasses and a tattoo of the name "Fellini" on his right forearm. The diner is overpriced. "This is starting to become a rich man's town," he mutters, scanning the menu. It's hardly the Manhattan he wrote about in *After Hours* and *Vampire's Kiss*, a gritty town populated by mohawked punks, art studios, and rampant crime. That city was both thrilling and nightmarish. "Darkness is like my middle name," Minion says. "I have a very dark view. I don't feel very optimistic about anything."

Minion admits he was nervous about meeting me. When people talk about *Vampire's Kiss*, they often treat it as a joke. Several years ago, for instance, he was invited on a podcast to talk about the film. He said yes, but never heard back from the hosts. Eventually, he realized that the podcasters had recorded the episode without him. "For at least an hour, they kept using the word 'bad.' 'This is *so baaad*!' 'This is *awful*, oh my God!' These two guys were basically dissing the movie."

He couldn't understand it. The film is a comedy, but it was never a joke. It's personal—and dark. Cage understood that. "I always saw the movie as a story of a man whose loneliness and inability to find love literally drive him insane," the actor said in his commentary track for the DVD release.

Minion is vaguely aware that *Vampire's Kiss* has found a new life on the internet—that it has become the forefather of endless debates about whether Cage is a good actor; that it's beloved among the sort of weirdos who can recite the alphabet in the exact same cadence as Cage's character; that scenes of Cage bugging his eyes out and terrorizing Alva have inspired endless memes and YouTube supercuts.

He shrugs that off. "It's not *Vampire's Kiss*. *Vampire's Kiss* is a movie that starts frame one and ends frame 12,722 or whatever. I'm not responsible for this meme stuff. I don't really care about [that]. I love films."

* * *

When Minion completed the screenplay in Barbados, he mailed it to Zitwer.

"I was completely horrified," Zitwer says. "Horrified because I was Joe Minion's girlfriend and living with him. And I read it and it was like—this is our relationship. To read someone write about this woman he's in love with who's like a vampire and destroying him." Zitwer saw traces of herself in both Rachel, the woman who torments Peter, and Alva, the woman who's tormented *by* him.

Later, producers even toyed with the idea of casting the same actress in both roles, establishing a subliminal link between the vampire and the secretary, but the idea was scrapped.

Despite her initial shock, Zitwer and her fellow producer, Barry Shils, loved the script and immediately decided to get it made. The two had become close friends while working on Larry Cohen's movies in the mid-eighties. Their circle also included Marcia Shulman, a friend of Zitwer's who became

Vampire's Kiss's associate producer and casting director. They were young, hungry, and dying to make a movie of their own. "I basically gave up my entire career for two years to get *Vampire's Kiss* made," Shulman says. "We all got sucked into the vortex of getting that movie made."

Armed with youthful naïveté and one degree of separation from Martin Scorsese, they found a willing financier in John Daly, the late British film producer, who was gathering a library of films for his own production company, Hemdale Film Corporation. The idea was to make a low-budget movie in the spirit of their mentor, Larry Cohen, who pumped out one blood-splattered B-movie after the other. "The thrill of it was to make the movie really cheap," says *Vampire's Kiss* cinematographer Stefan Czapsky. "Make it for $500,000 and then sell it for a million. It doubled your money. I think that was the original intent."

Casting brought its own drama. Today it's impossible to imagine *Vampire's Kiss* without Cage's unhinged brand of "Cage"-iness. Not so in 1986, when he was a young actor still finding his voice. Early on, Dennis Quaid was cast as the lead. "We got financing because of Dennis," Shulman says. The choice makes sense if you think of *Vampire's Kiss* as *After Hours* 2.0, Shulman theorizes. "In some ways, Dennis would have been the Griffin Dunne way to go—the sort of overwhelmed guy." Instead, Quaid dropped out to star in the Steven Spielberg–backed *Innerspace*. "And then the scramble began," Shulman says.

The producers were introduced to Cage through the actress Lisa Jane Persky, who was crucial in getting *Vampire's Kiss* made, though she never received a producer credit, and was herself promised the role of Alva. Persky had met Cage several years earlier, during *The Cotton Club*, and been impressed by his talent. "You just knew that he was gonna make it work for himself," Persky says. "He had that magic, where he's walking the line between reality and artifice. It's unique to him. And it radiates off of him."

Though the filmmakers were uncertain, Persky believed he was perfect for Peter Loew. "I called Nick and said, basically, 'This is just what you're looking for.' He could put all of himself into that role. He agreed and was super stoked."

As the script circulated around Hollywood, the producers got word that Cage was interested. Shulman says, "I remember sitting with Barbara and Barry and saying, 'We have no idea what it will be. But he'll get the movie made. And he's always interesting." She remembered seeing *Valley Girl* a few years prior and thinking, "Who *is* that guy?"

Cage was approached. Minion, still planning to direct *Vampire's Kiss*, met with him at a speakeasy in Manhattan's West Village. The screenwriter had been skeptical about Cage, but he was immediately struck by the actor's enthusiasm for the part. "[I remember] this look in his eyes, like he was gonna really *do* something," Minion says.

Cage was offered the role. He accepted. Then Minion decided not to direct the film after all—and everything fell apart. "I just had to move on," Minion explains. "The darkness of it—I couldn't inhabit it anymore." He and Zitwer had broken up. It had been a stormy relationship and a dramatic breakup; the two could barely be in the same room, much less on a film set together for months. But there was another reason, one Minion finds difficult to explain. As much as he wanted to be a director, "the energy of that project scared me," he says.

Zitwer and her co-producers immediately began searching for a new director. They settled on a British newcomer named Robert Bierman, who had mostly directed commercials but charmed them with his excitement about *Vampire's Kiss*. Bierman met Cage for a drink at the Polo Lounge in Beverly Hills. But there was a new problem. Cage felt misled when he learned that Minion wasn't directing and dropped out. "I was getting a lot of outside pressure from my agent and people representing me that this was not a good move after *Moonstruck*, to make a movie of this nature with the vampire fangs and going off like that," Cage said in the DVD commentary. "I responded to the pressure and I broke."

The scramble for a star began anew. Bierman had dinner with Judd Nelson. "He was very keen, his agent quoted $1 million, we dropped him immediately," Bierman recalls. Shils swears he once personally handed the script to Steve Martin—"who seemed very interested," Shils adds, "but his agency did not."

The producers were desperate. At one point, they tried to give the part to an unknown actor named Adam Coleman Howard, who walked around Manhattan all night reading the script and auditioned the next morning on no sleep. "I went into the audition and I had such a connection to this subtly sadistic, torn character," says Howard. "I controlled the room. I had no doubt that I had killed them. Like, I had slaughtered their souls."

The producers were impressed with Howard and tried to persuade John Daly. "But [Hemdale] wouldn't finance the movie with him," Shulman says.

* * *

Perhaps Cage sensed it was his destiny to star in *Vampire's Kiss*. The producers heard a rumor that he regretted dropping out. "He was kind of obsessed with the role," Zitwer says.

At lunch with their mentor Larry Cohen, they discussed the dilemma. Zitwer scoffed at the notion of working with Cage after he had already dropped out once. "And Larry looked at her and went, 'What, are you *crazy*? He's gonna be a huge star!' " Shils recalls. Shils left the lunch, found a phone booth at the back of the diner, and immediately called Cage.

It wasn't hard to convince him to rejoin the project. Cage was haunted by the script, obsessing over visions of what he could try with the Peter Loew character.[1] "Ultimately, to his credit, he just couldn't get the part out of his mind," Shulman says.

But it took another year or so to get Cage's signature on a contract. Cage's agent, Ed Limato, didn't want him doing *Vampire's Kiss*. Limato hated the idea of his star client debasing himself in a quirky vampire movie. "They wanted his next film to be a big Hollywood movie," Shulman says—not a low-budget art film produced by a team of nobodies.

Shils claims he had to march onto the set of *Moonstruck* and confront Cage just to get Limato to return his calls. "I said, 'Nicolas, if you don't get your agent to call us back and finalize this deal, we just can't go on,' " remembers Shils. "He picked up the phone. Got Ed on the phone. He said, 'Why aren't we closing this deal? I want to do that movie!' We were on the set of *Moonstruck*, somewhere in midtown."

Late that night, the producers finally got a call from Limato at the mouse-infested loft in Lower Manhattan they were using as an office. They closed the deal.

In retrospect, it makes poetic sense that *Vampire's Kiss* was the movie Cage used to detox himself from the sweetness of *Moonstruck*. The film is almost like *Moonstruck*'s angry little cousin. Both are quintessentially New York movies, both set from within a state of romantic derangement. But while *Moonstruck* is concerned with the strange madness induced by love, *Vampire's Kiss* burrows into a darker, more disturbing place—the madness triggered by love's absence.

Cage was ultimately paid $40,000, a reduced fee, and spent the money on his first sports car, a Corvette Stingray which he jokingly called "my *Vampire's Kiss* car." In a 1989 *SPIN* profile, he regretted nothing. "I did the movie for no money," he said, "because I liked the script and I wanted to try something new with my acting."[2]

This was a profound understatement.

* * *

The most famous story from the set of *Vampire's Kiss* involves a cockroach. A real one. The script had called for Cage's character—deep in the throes of madness—to suck a raw egg. Cage and Bierman, the film's director, both thought this was a little too tame.

"[Cage] said to me, 'The thing I hate most in the world are cockroaches. They are my Room 101. So let me eat a cockroach,'" Bierman recalls. "He wanted to eat the most frightening thing for him. I thought, 'This is terrific!' I sent my prop people down into the boiler room. They brought me a box, divided up into little sections with tissue paper. The cockroaches were there lined up for me to cast. I think they're actually called water bugs—they're bigger than cockroaches."

Cage's horror of cockroaches dated back to his childhood. He had recurring nightmares that his mother's head was attached to a roach's body and the fearsome creature lived in his garage. He decided to conquer this lifelong fear, with the cameras rolling.[3]

What you see on film is all nauseatingly real: Cage snatching a live roach, lifting it tentatively, chewing it like a madman. It is Method acting in the purest sense: we cannot know how much of Cage's jittery convulsions are for effect and how much involuntary bodily response. "I really [wanted] to do something that would shock the audience, something you would never forget," Cage explained in the film's DVD commentary track.

He regarded it entirely as a "business decision," a curious phrase from the lips of a man who took a reduced rate to act in this demented art movie against the wishes of his agent, who was almost certainly fielding more lucrative offers. "I've seen this movie in the theater," Cage added, "and when people see that cockroach go in my mouth, it's like the bus blowing up in *Speed*."

It's the only change Cage made to Joseph Minion's script, which never underwent a single rewrite. "I never would have asked an actor to do that," Minion says of Cage's masochistic stunt. "It's amazing. You set the stage, and he brings it to another level."

Producer Barbara Zitwer was furious. She and Cage did not get along. She was frequently in the position of having to say no to his craziest ideas on set. "I was always infuriated with him but also thought he was completely brilliant," she says. "Bob calls me and says, 'Nicolas wants to eat a water bug instead of sucking on the egg.' I'm like, 'Fuck him! I've *had* it with him.' I said, 'Bob. It's probably full of germs. He could get sick.' Bob says, 'Barbara, I think if Nicolas wants to eat a water bug on film, we should let him.' I said first let's call the doctor. I called the doctor. I said, 'Would he get sick if he eats a water bug?' And the doctor was like, 'OK, that's a weird question.' But he says, 'No. But have him drink some whiskey right after.' "

In Bierman's recollection, Cage swigged 100-proof vodka to wash his mouth out afterward. They shot two takes. "The suspense of shooting it was astounding," says cinematographer Stefan Czapsky. "I remember Nick's face when [the camera operator] said, 'Let's do it again.' He actually ingested the cockroach. And then he quickly did a vodka mouthwash."

When Shils later got a call from a concerned animal rights group, he claimed the doomed cockroach had walked away alive. In reality, it had perished somewhere between Cage's gnashing molars and churning stomach.

That's the energy Cage brought to the film set: frighteningly devoted to his performance and willing to go to extreme lengths to fulfill his creative vision. Sources say he often remained in character off-camera and was obsessive about the role. "He was a little kooky," says the actress and director Kasi Lemmons, who played Peter Loew's initial love interest. "He was very, very into his character. He was not casual."

"He didn't have a trailer or anything," Czapsky adds. "In between scenes, Nick was always by himself. He wasn't hiding. He was just in isolation and preparation for shooting. I remember hearing through a door that he was listening to some kind of weird chanting music. We'd laugh, like, 'Nick's in there, you know.' "

In the nineties, the cockroach-guzzling legend would invariably be mentioned in every glossy profile of Cage; like the teeth-pulling myth, it was catnip for magazine writers, although the cockroach had the benefit of being true. By then, Cage was fond of saying that he had saved the producers a million dollars in special effects. The cockroach, he insisted, was just as thrilling as an explosion.

***

Vampire's Kiss was shot on the streets of New York in seven harried weeks during the fall of 1987, from September 8 until late October. Bierman describes the shoot as "complete chaos, from beginning to end"—but a productive and creative chaos. "Around us was chaos," Bierman tells me. "At that time, Manhattan was full of bums and crazy people and the homeless. When

Nick was on the street, we were shooting back on longer lenses. Some people didn't know who he was. They just thought he was one of the crazy people on the street."

In one harrowing scene, a blood-splattered Cage prowls the streets with a wooden stake, incoherently begging strangers to kill him. Those strangers were not actors. In fact, they had no idea they were being filmed, Bierman claims. "Two of the people he asked were homeless people, who I think were quite frightened of him and ran away. It was a very interesting way of galvanizing his character. He became part of the New York scenery of that time."

"One of the bad neighborhoods you didn't really go into unless you wanted to buy heroin was down on the Lower East Side on Avenue A, B, or C," says Czapsky. "I remember we went down there with Nick for the end scene. I guess the term is we stole stuff. We went down there, and Nick just walked down the street dragging this stake and making cries. He just put himself into this environment of really pitiful people, dragging the stake down the street. I just set the camera up across the street—long lens—and photographed it."

At the time, New York was suffering through the darkest days of the AIDS epidemic, a cocktail of death, fear, and institutional neglect. "It was like the end of the world, AIDS in New York," Bierman recalls. "People would throw hypodermic needles at people. There was a lot of fear that you would literally walk into the streets of Manhattan and get AIDS." In 1987, the year *Vampire's Kiss* was filmed, the national death toll from AIDS rose above 20,000. In New York, hundreds of unclaimed bodies were sent to Hart Island, where burial crews recoiled from the task at hand, fearing that the corpses might remain contagious after death. Galvanized by political inaction, the activist group ACT UP formed that March; by October, it was receiving national coverage for its rousing demonstrations.

Vampire's Kiss does not mention or directly reference the disease. "But it was like an undercurrent—on the streets, there was a dark thing happening," Bierman says. Some critics would later interpret the film, with its visions of blood and biting, of fraught sexual encounters mingled with a specter of doom, to be an opaque metaphor for AIDS. The subject even arose in a 1991 *Entertainment Weekly* profile of Minion.[4] He maintains that AIDS was not on his mind when he wrote the script. "The emphasis on blood and biting," he says, "has to do with the vampires."*

* *Vampire's Kiss* was not the only film to provoke such interpretations during the AIDS era. As Caryn James wrote in a 1997 *New York Times* essay, "For Victorians, the vampire's kiss symbolized forbidden sex; in the age of AIDS, the exchange of blood seems ominous." Curiously, some viewers

The film depicts the city as a nocturnal den of sin and desperation, a frightening place where death swoops down at random and hardened urban bystanders barely take notice. That was true both on- and off-screen. "When we were scouting locations, there was a dead body on the sidewalk," Bierman recalls. "Homeless people would die on the streets, and they would just be left there." Later, during the shoot itself, a dead body was removed from a bar as the crew prepared to shoot a scene there. This vague specter of death was hardly a deliberate choice, but it did contribute to the film's sense of ambient dread.

Bierman shrewdly used visual metaphors to represent what he viewed as Cage's character's descent into hell. For instance, "in the office where he rapes Alva, he descends from his office into the basement," the director says. "Metaphorically, he's going down into his underworld. Mentally, he becomes more deranged down there. When he goes into the club, again, he descends into this kind of underworld. And then when he's being helped—from his psychiatrist—he's up high." Ultimately, the symbolism colludes with Cage's distorted and surreal movements to bring male yuppie angst to its most terrifying extremes.

The film's budget was low—sources say around $2 million—and producers saved money every way possible. They shot the office scenes for free in an empty city government building, which also was used as a makeshift production base. They recorded the eerie score in Budapest, because the orchestra was cheaper there, and then ran out of cash and had to borrow money from teamsters to pay for a Dolby sound mix. A journalist who visited the film set for a *SPIN* article described "long hours, low pay, and a lousy craft services table. . . . It's a risky business, and for everyone involved, a labor of love." For months on end, Zitwer's parents were essentially financing the running of the production office.[5]

"Nick cost me $10,000 by humming Stravinsky's *Petrushka*," Bierman recalls. "The Stravinsky estate was still in copyright. So that's why we didn't have any money at the end." (Cage apparently believed it was in the public domain.)

have noted that Cage's paranoia in *Vampire's Kiss* parallels his subsequent film, *Time to Kill*, in which he plays an Italian soldier who is increasingly distressed at the possibility of having contracted leprosy. Perhaps because it was an Italian production—or because of its appalling treatment of sexual assault—Cage effectively disowned *Time to Kill*. For a lively analysis of its similarity to *Vampire's Kiss*, see Rabin, Nathan. "The Travolta/Cage Project #23 Time To Kill (1989)." *Nathan Rabin's Happy Place*, April 27, 2020, https://www.nathanrabin.com/happy-place/2020/4/27/the-travoltacage-project-23-time-to-kill-1989.

And yet, despite the measly budget and harried shoot, Cage cared deeply about fulfilling his vision and making the madness look credible. One particularly harrowing scene required him to stick a gun in his mouth and pull the trigger, then break down in anguish when he survives the gunshot. Unaware that the gun is filled with blanks, the character takes it as confirmation that he's a vampire. According to Czapsky, the production team had shelled out $400 or $500 a day to hire a specialty prop master with access to cap guns. "It wasn't a gun that you could go and actually use as a weapon," Czapsky explains. "It was a specifically made gun that was modified to put blanks in."

But the gun caused considerable frustration for Cage, who wanted the explosion to look as real as possible and seemed unconcerned about being harmed in the process. On the first take, Cage pulled the trigger, "and nothing really happens," Czapsky recalls. "So Nick is really pissed. Like, 'What the fuck. I went through this whole thing, and this is a joke.'" The prop master was told to amplify the charge, and he did, loading the gun with higher-charge blanks. Still: not enough. "So Nick is super mad. And he's mad that he has to put himself through this performance. He's disappointed—the gunshot, it's a dud. It doesn't support his performance."

The third shot was the charm. Once more, the prop master heightened the charge. "The guy is under pressure to not fuck up again," Czapsky says. "So he loads the gun up. And that's the take that wound up in the movie. Nick sticks the gun through his mouth, he pulls the trigger, and it's way over-the-top. I'm watching it, and smoke is coming out of Nick's ears. Since there's been a couple incidents of actors killing themselves accidentally, there's no production that would allow that to happen today. But that was the extent to which Nick was into it."

Indeed, Bierman may have prevented Cage from putting himself in greater peril. In the DVD commentary, the director recalled having to explain to Cage that "you can't use real blanks, because you can actually kill yourself with the wadding when it comes out." As Cage laughed sheepishly, Bierman added: "You were trying to kill yourself before I'd finished the movie! I just wanted you alive until the end." Such concerns were not unwarranted. Just a few years after *Vampire's Kiss* came out, the actor Brandon Lee was killed in an accident on the set of 1994's *The Crow*: he was shot by a prop gun that fired a bullet fragment from a dummy round into the actor's abdomen.[6]

In *Vampire's Kiss*, Cage's character deals with the failed suicide attempt by letting out a pained, unearthly shriek. It's all one shot—"it was in real time," Czapsky confirms—and thus the vision of smoke wafting out of the actor's head leads into one of the most bizarre outbursts in Cage's entire film career: he gently raises his fists to his chin, contorts his face in pathetic agony, and shrieks the word "*Boo-hoo!*" In fact, he shrieks it twice. "I was always trying to challenge myself, like can you get away with actually saying *Boo-hoo*?" Cage explained in the DVD commentary.[7]

Would any other actor on earth commit to such a preposterous acting challenge? It's the dramatic equivalent of straight-up enunciating the words "bow-wow" while impersonating a dog. Cage does, though. And like much of his surrealistic approach in *Vampire's Kiss*, he strikes the right balance of anguish and absurdity to make it work.

Three decades later, thousands of viewers have encountered the "*Boo-hoo!*" shriek without knowing what movie it's from. The outburst appears widely on YouTube, stripped of its larger context, under various titles: there's "Nic Cage Cry," "Nicolas Cage Crying," and even a ghastly techno remix titled "Nicolas Cage—Going Nuts (BOO HOO Remix)."

* * *

Another source of friction was Cage's dislike of Jennifer Beals, who had been cast as the vampire woman, Rachel, a day before shooting (Figure 7.1). "He hated the idea of Jennifer Beals," says Shulman. "He just didn't think she provided proper motivation—creatively, sexually, in any way."

Cage originally wanted the role to go to his love interest, nineteen-year-old Patricia Arquette. The actor had begun a whirlwind romance with Arquette that year after meeting her in Canter's Deli in Los Angeles and telling her on the spot that he wanted to marry her. When Arquette demurred, saying he was crazy, Cage asked her to send him on a quest to prove his love. Amazingly, she did, asking him to procure a J. D. Salinger autograph (he bought one from an autograph store for $2,500), a black orchid (he bought a purple one and spray-painted it black), and other rare gems.

A stunned Arquette finally agreed to a date with Cage, which turned into a trip to Mexico. Cage apparently had an elaborate—and sinister-sounding—plan to make Arquette his bride, which he later detailed to *Playboy*: "I would get her to go with me to Mexico City, then I would abduct her, take her to Cuba, and marry her while my family was there." Such plans went awry when Cage was held up at the Mexican airport. Arquette soon got cold feet and returned to her previous boyfriend.[8]

Figure 7.1. Cage did not get along with Jennifer Beals during the filming of *Vampire's Kiss* (1989, Hemdale Film Corporation). The film's associate producer had to call Beals's agent and make excuses ("Nicolas is in character").

At some point during or soon after this romance, Cage decided he wanted Arquette to be his fictional lover in *Vampire's Kiss*. The actress auditioned for the role of Rachel, but Bierman turned her down. "Nick, I think, was very disappointed," says Bierman. "He was in love with her."†

Another young actress (Bierman can't recall who) got the part, but dropped out right before filming because her fiancé threatened to break up with her if she made love to Cage onscreen. When Beals took the role, Cage treated her so coldly that Shulman had to call Beals's agent and make excuses ("Nicolas is in character"). Cage eventually warmed up to Beals, but his methods remained bizarre. "To get turned on, Nick asked to have hot yogurt poured over his toes while he was doing a love scene with Jennifer," Shulman recalls. Nobody could comprehend why yogurt got Cage aroused, but the crew obliged. "If you look at the shot, you don't see his feet," Shulman says.

† Cage and Arquette stayed in touch, even as both had children with other partners. In 1995, after they ran into each other again at the same deli, Arquette asked Cage if he still wanted to get married. Despite not having dated since 1987, they were married two weeks later.

Another significant complication was the bat, which swoops into Peter's apartment at the beginning of the film. Producers had hired a special effects designer to transport a mechanical bat from England. Cage hated it. He believed the scene wouldn't be authentic unless the bat were real. "I didn't want this remote-control bat," he admitted in the DVD commentary. "I kind of went off my rocker."[9]

"Shooting the bat drove him crazy," Zitwer confirms. "He didn't understand why we couldn't get a real bat. I tried to explain to him, they have rabies. You can't control them. I did everything. I called the head bat specialist at the bat zoo. I was prepared to take him over there, bring the guy to the set." Cage wouldn't let go. "There was a young production assistant who was assigned just to Nicolas," Zitwer says. "His name was Osman. He sent Osman to Central Park with an ice cooler and a broom to try and capture a bat. And then Osman told us that Nicolas found out you could get bats from Mexico. Probably illegally, of course. We just said, 'OK, this is going too far. We're not gonna FedEx some bat from Mexico.' Except I think they actually looked into it. That was one time that I recall being extremely contentious."

Bierman finally persuaded Cage by explaining that if he got bitten by a bat, he would probably die and the film would be ruined.

Cage considered this the role of a lifetime, and you get the sense he would have happily subjected himself to a bat's fangs for the sake of this film. He has said that he cared more about that performance than any other in his career. It's a master class in unbridled bizarreness. Cage saw *Vampire's Kiss* as a chance to pursue his own experimental mode of acting, a full-throttle rejection of naturalism that owed as much to 1920s German Expressionism as it does opera and slapstick comedy. This performance is the seedling from which every great Cage-loses-his-shit role—the self-destructive pathos of *Leaving Las Vegas*, the high-concept psychological torment of *Face/Off*, the obsessive-compulsive jitters of *Matchstick Men*, the campy absurdity of *The Wicker Man*—subsequently sprouted.

His onscreen outbursts are legendary. When the script called for him to rant about a misfiled contract, he delivered, "I've never misfiled *anything!*" with the vein-bulging fervor of a revivalist preacher. In the therapist's office, Cage uses the full force of his physicality to convey the character's insanity. In one memorable sequence, he not only bellows the entire alphabet but performs increasingly frantic hand movements to accompany each syllable, with Elizabeth Ashley working in perfect counterpart as the exasperated shrink. None of that was random. "It actually is extremely choreographed," Cage said in his commentary. "Every one of those moves was thought out in my hotel room with my cat."[10]

"His creative imagination was just unlike anything I had seen, especially of actors of his generation," says Ashley. "I never felt that Nick was anything but totally, truthfully, deeply into his character. Of course, I knew the character was going mad. And I knew that Nick was also going a little mad, because he's that kind of an actor. But working with him was just one of the best experiences I ever had working with another actor."

It's a common misconception that Cage veered from the script or went apeshit against his director's wishes. In reality, everything except the cockroach was in the script ("every word," Minion insists), and Cage and Bierman worked closely together on his surrealistic movements and mounting intensity. It was the director's idea for Cage to hop onto the desk like a deranged cat when he confronts Alva.

"The actual story has got very low stakes," Bierman explains. "I realized, to keep the story moving, the character that Nick was playing would have to be constantly changing, constantly in a new phase of his derangement, so the audience would never know what they would get."

Not every one of Cage's ideas made it in. When he showed up for the film shoot with a penciled-in mustache reminiscent of John Waters, Bierman convinced him to ditch it. But the director did approve of Peter Loew's faux-British accent, a pretentious touch that was inspired by Cage's father's literary airs. "I'd noticed certain Americans in Britain would speak with this affected accent: a transatlantic cultured accent," Bierman says. "So when Nick did this, I thought, 'Oh, this is great.'"

The producers, however, were horrified; Zitwer remembers thinking, "Oh my God, what the hell is he doing?" She confronted Bierman about the accent during a break, "and Bob said, 'Nicolas and I have been working on this a lot. We chose this, because if he did the role totally straight, the character is so hateful that it would be unwatchable.'" Indeed, the accent renders Peter's verbal abuse of Alva cartoonishly funny and quotable, even as we're repulsed by his rank misogyny and brutality.

When the film was finished, Minion, who had been effectively banned from the set during the shoot, watched it in a Manhattan screening room and was astonished. "I was like, *Oh my God*. He brought it to these heights that exceeded even my expectations in my wildest dreams."

As for Cage, after he saw the completed film, he left a message on Zitwer's answering machine saying it had justified his decision to become an actor.

* * *

On the day *Vampire's Kiss* was released, Barbara Zitwer and Robert Bierman hired a limo and drove around to the few theaters in Manhattan where it was playing. It was a hot day in early June 1989. They tried the Beekman Theatre. "There was no one in the theater," Zitwer says. They tried 42nd Street: all the air conditioners were broken. The AC wasn't working at the Village East either.

"It was a grim experience," says Bierman. "We went to a theater on the Upper West Side and sat in a half-full screening. The old guy I sat next to had a portable TV on his lap. He didn't laugh once!" Shulman was so desperate to attract moviegoers that she personally stood at the door of one of the theaters, handing out plastic fangs.

The film was a flop. It didn't help that Hemdale had kept it on the shelf for eighteen months after filming due to drama with distributors. "John Daly really messed up the distribution," Zitwer says of the late Hemdale founder. Adding insult to injury, the company finally released *Vampire's Kiss* the same month that saw the release of Tim Burton's *Batman*—a big-budget juggernaut that grossed more in one night than *Vampire's Kiss* earned in its entire run. "All the hype was around *Batman*. Plus, it's about bats!" Shils protests. "You're not going to go to a vampire movie and *Batman*."

Cage was dismayed by the compromised state of the film. Hemdale had requested a number of cuts; Bierman reluctantly agreed to remove one of the therapist scenes and several on the streets of Manhattan.‡ Cage, though, was heartbroken. "It was unfair: I was the driving force of that movie," he later told an interviewer. "And it was some of the best work that I have ever done."[11]

Critics weren't receptive. A *Washington Post* review called it "stone-dead bad, incoherently bad."[12] A *New York Times* critic described it as being "dominated and destroyed by Mr. Cage's chaotic, self-indulgent performance" and chided Bierman for not keeping the star's performance under control. "Which was absurd!" says Czapsky. "Because first of all, it was what was great about the film. But also, you couldn't control Nicolas! He was uncontrollable—in the best way."

Many reviewers seemed unsettled by the film's violent denouement; Hemdale's marketing materials presumably did not mention that the protagonist rapes his secretary and longs for death. "Nobody really knew what to make of the film," says Bierman.[13]

‡ The excised scenes were finally restored when MGM released *Vampire's Kiss* on DVD in 2002. "The film you see on DVD now is the original movie," Bierman confirms.

Few critics seemed to consider that Cage's approach was a deliberate rejection of realism rather than clumsy "overacting." Yet Pauline Kael, the great *New Yorker* critic, dissented from the pack. "Nicolas Cage is airily amazing here," Kael wrote, noting that he "does some of the way-out stuff that you love actors in silent movies for doing."[14]

In fact, Cage's performance *was* inspired by silent cinema, particularly Max Schreck's turn as a vampire in *Nosferatu* (1922), F. W. Murnau's spectacularly creepy adaptation of *Dracula*. A staple of 1920s German cinema, Schreck was so frighteningly convincing in the role of Count Orlok (one of the earliest cinematic portrayals of Dracula, though the name was changed) that some audiences wondered if he was a real vampire.[15]

Curiously, Cage had a family connection to silent cinema. Long before he was born, his great-grandfather, Francesco Pennino, managed a movie theater in Brooklyn and was credited with releasing several Italian silent films in the United States.[16]

By 1987, Cage had become profoundly influenced by the work of Schreck and other actors associated with German Expressionist cinema, such as Emil Jannings and Conrad Veidt. That fascination traced back to Cage's childhood. "I saw their movies when I was eight, because my dad would play them on a projector for a class he taught at Cal State Long Beach," Cage later told *Movieline*. "I would see *The Cabinet of Dr. Caligari* or *Nosferatu* and freak out, really get nightmares over them. The problem was how to make a modern movie with some German expressionistic acting. The only way to do it was to play a man who's going nuts, who thinks he's a vampire, with his shoulders going up and eyes bulging" (Figure 7.2).[17]

A fascination with silent cinema that flourished decades before he was born is a recurring motif in Cage's filmography, from *Moonstruck*, with its homage to *Metropolis*, all the way up to the mediocre slasher-comedy hybrid *Willy's Wonderland* (2021), in which Cage's character is entirely mute. For that film, he was inspired by Buster Keaton's ability to deliver a meaningful performance without dialogue.[18]

Others, too, have prominently compared Cage to silent actors. Tom Waits once described him as "Lon Chaney in a Buddy Love corvette," referring to the 1920s screen icon.[19] Martin Scorsese thought of Cage's eyes and face when he read Joe Connelly's novel *Bringing Out the Dead* and decided to give Cage the lead role in his film adaptation. "He has a way of putting his whole body, his whole persona, into a part that harks back to some of the best

Figure 7.2. Cage's outlandish facial expressions in *Vampire's Kiss* (1989, Hemdale Film Corporation), such as his leering eyes, later became the inspiration for countless internet memes.

of silent-film acting," Scorsese observed. During the production, Scorsese learned that Cage was a fan of Lon Chaney. The two men bonded over their shared obsession with silent cinema, and Scorsese screened for Cage his own 35-mm print of *The Phantom of the Opera* (1925).[20]

Yet no actor of the silent age had as great an impact on Cage as Schreck. In *Nosferatu*, Schreck instilled his performance with inflected and grotesque gestures to convey emotion without the use of sound. To Cage, such larger-than-life physical gestures were not only captivating but suggested a way to move beyond naturalism in acting (Figure 7.3). "I thought, 'Wow, that's really wonderfully abstract and poetic,' and I wanted to incorporate them into modern filmmaking,'" Cage told the *Washington Post*.[21] *Vampire's Kiss* was his opportunity, and Bierman let him go for it.

As Cage's character begins to suspect he's a vampire, he carries himself, manipulates his hands, and looks increasingly like the vampire from *Nosferatu*. "I'd had to get the rights [to the 1922 film]," says Bierman.

Indeed, *Vampire's Kiss* is flush with references to the silent classic. During one sexual encounter with Rachel, the camera flits away to reveal a scene

Figure 7.3. Cage's exaggerated physical gestures in *Vampire's Kiss* (1989, Hemdale Film Corporation) were heavily inspired by 1920s German Expressionist films, which his father showed him during his youth.

from *Nosferatu* playing on Peter's flickering TV. Later, as Peter's mental state deteriorates, he stalks through a nightclub in a pair of plastic fangs, his shoulders raised, eyes locked into a permanent grimace. Bierman intended the nightclub to invoke the hellish imagery from Bosch's *The Garden of Earthly Delights*, but Cage's stiff, unnatural movements and facial contortions are clearly modeled after Schreck.

Silent cinema inherently rejects aspirations of realism, since it presents a world in which audible dialogue does not exist. A hallmark of these movies—particularly those associated with German Expressionism—is an emphasis on highly expressive movements and physical gestures on the part of the performers, who must compensate for the medium's lack of sound, resulting in a performance style more akin to opera or stage acting than modern screen acting. In *Vampire's Kiss*, Cage embraces this expressive physical approach as though he were a silent actor sixty-five years earlier.

In her book *National Treasure: Nicolas Cage*, Cage scholar Lindsay Gibb persuasively demonstrates how his exaggerated facial expressions and movements draw on the "presentation style" of silent film. In *Vampire's Kiss*,

Gibb writes, Cage "was trying to get to a 'new expression in acting,' bringing German Expressionism—a high contrast, severe, almost cartoon-like style of acting and filmmaking, which famously rejected realism—into his style." The famous shot of Peter Loew taunting Alva is a perfect example: Cage communicates as much with his eyes, which he makes outrageously large and leering, as with his words. No wonder that shot works so well as a reaction meme, expressing condescension and faux surprise.[22]

Critics charged Cage with overacting, but the claim revealed as much about the critics, who subscribed to a conservative standard of what the "correct" amount of acting ought to be, as it did Cage. They called his work "over-the-top," but "I don't believe in such a thing," Cage explained in his DVD commentary track, describing his performance as a deliberate attempt "to use grand gesture and go bigger."[23]

As Gibb notes, one of *Vampire's Kiss*'s early defenders was an acting instructor and film professor named Carole Zucker, who analyzed Cage's performance in her 1993 article "The Concept of 'Excess' in Film Acting: Notes Toward an Understanding of Non-Naturalistic Performance." Zucker challenges the accepted notion that realism is the acting ideal: "The idea that acting for film should adhere to a standard of gestural and psychological verisimilitude suggests a limited vision of performance," Zucker writes.[24]

Further, Zucker argues that audiences should "recognize 'excess' in performance—not as a negative attribute—but as a challenging, exploratory style of acting," particularly in films that depict a distorted reality. *Vampire's Kiss* certainly fits this criteria. Zucker defends Cage's creative choices as more intentional and considered than critics seemed to recognize:

> Cage's play with vocal intonation, highly choreographed movements, and stylized gestures provide no illusion of spontaneity. Rather, they are resources that exhibit the actor's special skill, and speak to Cage's extraordinary level of competence. . . .[25]

Even when you set aside such academic analyses, *Vampire's Kiss* also stands as one of Cage's most personal performances. It is noteworthy that this and *Rumble Fish*, two films that reflect the overt influence of German Expressionism, both share links to August Coppola, the man who introduced his son to films such as *Nosferatu*. *Vampire's Kiss*, however, is also intimately linked to Cage's mother. The send-up of highbrow literary culture is a homage to August, yet in portraying a man going insane and talking to walls, Cage drew on memories of his mother's mental illness. "She gave me an awareness of all kinds of expressions and possibilities," Cage later told *Interview* magazine, "and . . . in *Vampire's Kiss* I showed a lot of what I had seen her go through."[26]

Critics knew none of this at the time. Cage did virtually no press to promote the movie (perhaps due to frustration with the cuts that had been made), and *Vampire's Kiss* sank. Cage's disappointment was compounded when the film appeared on home video with a goofy cover featuring his face superimposed onto a Dracula cape. "Big business marketed it as some shlock vampire movie, some supernatural piece of shit," he later protested. "I pour my heart into this and then they put me in that stupid cape."[27]

Yet throughout the nineties, the hurt subsided and Cage spoke fondly of *Vampire's Kiss*, often describing it as a pivotal creative breakthrough. The actor's vampire fetish only grew stronger. In the early nineties, he purchased a castle with a gothic décor inspired by *Dracula*; David Lynch joked that the former tenant must have been a vampire.[28] In 2000, Cage produced a feature film about the making of *Nosferatu*, *Shadow of the Vampire*, in which he considered playing Max Schreck before giving the role to Willem Dafoe.[29] Finally, in 2021, he bowed to the inevitable and signed on to play Dracula in Universal's Dracula spinoff *Renfield*.

All the while, Cage's affection for *Vampire's Kiss* hasn't waned. As recently as 2018, he declared it his "favorite movie I've made."[30] He even showed it to a date one evening after his third divorce.[31]

* * *

The commercial failure of *Vampire's Kiss* was a small blip for Cage, whose stardom was already assured by *Moonstruck*. But it was personally and, in some cases, professionally devastating for the people who'd worked relentlessly to get it made. "After *Vampire's Kiss*, I couldn't get anything going," says Zitwer. "I would just cry. I would go to the movies and cry, like, why can't I do this? I love film! I really do." *Vampire's Kiss* had amounted to a brutal education in how difficult and exhausting it is to get a film made at all.

"And then I realized, this is never going to happen again," Zitwer says. "My film was a bomb. No one saw it. No one cared. I'd say it opened my eyes. What I realized is, I don't want to be a film producer." Unwilling to enmesh herself in the corporate gears of Hollywood, Zitwer switched careers; she launched her own literary agency in 1995.

Before 1989, Bierman had a promising film career in the United States. "*Vampire's Kiss* really put the brakes on it quickly," he says. At one point, he was offered the opportunity to direct the Mike Myers comedy *So I Married an Axe Murderer* but turned it down because it seemed too similar to *Vampire's Kiss*. He shifted over to television work in his native England, where the film had been better received.

Minion *did* move to Hollywood, where he lived for most of the 1990s, feeling ludicrously out of place. In 1991, *Motorama*—the film he wrote before *Vampire's Kiss*—finally got made, with Barry Shils directing. After that, Minion's luck began to dry up. Meetings with producers made him feel like he was from a different planet. "I don't have a mainstream sensibility," he says. "Not a bone in my body."

Minion rebelled against Hollywood culture by writing an aggressively bizarre noirish flick called *Trafficking*, which he directed with a cast of unknowns in 1997. The movie is distinctly Minion, with an abrasive narrative that grows increasingly warped as its protagonist, a private investigator, loses his mind. Minion considers it part of a loose trilogy that began with *After Hours* and then *Vampire's Kiss*. "I call it the Anxiety Trilogy," he says. "They all have this quality [of existential anxiety]. I think they got more and more operatic."

But *Trafficking* never found a distributor. "I tried and I tried," Minion says, "until there were no options left." Nor could he scrounge up financing for postproduction. A rough cut of the film now lives in obscurity on Vimeo. For more than two decades, Minion has fantasized about finding a way to distribute it; he's even considered remaking it with a new cast. Mostly, though, he seems to have made peace with the whole nightmare. "That was a new learning phase: 'This is it. This is the end. You've done exactly what you wanted, and it's not right for this world.'"

When I ask what effect *Vampire's Kiss* had on his career, Minion diverges into a lengthy spiel about his filmmaking sensibility and critic J. Hoberman's theory of "Midnight Movies" and his love for transgressive cult films, like the works of George A. Romero. "The people who made those films—you almost got the feeling they were a little bit insane. But in a good way. I loved that! So many times, I feel like things are made by committee and everyone's *too* sane." After *Vampire's Kiss*, Minion came to feel that this unhinged aesthetic wasn't welcome in Hollywood.

Then he stops and remembers my question. "How did it affect me? I dunno. Go ask people who didn't hire me."

* * *

In 2018, Robert Bierman was lecturing at a film school in London. After class, one of his graduate students approached him and said, "I'm sorry I didn't ask you questions in class, but I find it a bit overwhelming being in the same room with you." Bierman asked what he meant. "You know, you directed *Vampire's Kiss*," the student replied. "It's just so overwhelming. This is a legend. All we talk about is this movie."

"He was like a twenty-six-year-old student," Bierman adds. "I realized that this generation of young filmmakers have seen the film in a completely different way." Baby boomers don't particularly register the movie. But when younger fans realize Bierman directed it, "they react like, *Oh my God!*"

Bierman has earned the right to some vindication. The film, he believes, was simply ahead of its time: "There are certain scenes that are so modern—the way women are treated in it, sexuality, the problem with personal mental conditions, particularly with young men who have become obsessed."

Nobody knows exactly when *Vampire's Kiss* became a cult favorite. It began during the nineties, when Jim Carrey was paid millions to channel a more palatable version of the demented slapstick that got Cage vilified. Around then, Kasi Lemmons, who had a small role in *Vampire's Kiss*, ran into Cage in Los Angeles. Cage said something to the effect of, "Hey, how 'bout our little movie? It's kind of like a cult classic now!" Lemmons recalls.

As Cage's profile rose and his body of work deepened, *Vampire's Kiss* began to make sense as a gateway to the experimental side of his career. To whatever extent Cage is known for portraying characters deep in the throes of madness or obsession—for being "unafraid to crawl out on a limb, saw it off and remain suspended in air," as Roger Ebert once put it—*Vampire's Kiss* served as the blueprint, inspiring his own presentation-style discipline of acting, which Cage has dubbed "Nouveau Shamanic."[32]

The film's cultural resurgence crystallized about two decades after its release. In 2010, a film editor named Harry Hanrahan uploaded to YouTube a four-minute supercut titled simply "Nicolas Cage Losing His Shit." The montage included clips of Cage ranting and raving from movies across his career, set to the swelling orchestral music from *Requiem for a Dream*; nearly the entire first minute is taken from *Vampire's Kiss*. "Nicolas Cage Losing His Shit" quickly spread across the internet, delighting Cage fanatics and amassing millions of views. The supercut has been viewed by exponentially more people than went to see *Vampire's Kiss* in theaters.[33]

YouTube also serves as a repository for now-legendary snippets of the film; somehow, a nine-second clip of Cage screaming "I'm a vampire!" has half a million views. "It's almost as if they're little commercials for the movie on the internet," Bierman observes. "The film creates a fanbase through the bits. And then they go, 'Oh, what's the rest of the film like?' "

For years, Cage resented this phenomenon: the out-of-context mish-mash of his performances and outbursts, stripped of meaning and greeted as an absurdist joke. When I interviewed the actor for *Newsweek* in 2015, I asked him about the meme-ification of his work. He gamely answered the question ("I don't even know how to process it. So I try not to think too much about it"), but his handlers were bothered by it. Immediately after the interview, the publicist who had scheduled it became inexplicably upset about the question and pressured me to spike the whole thing (I politely refused).[34]

Eventually, Cage shrugged his shoulders and came to accept the meme world's response to his art.[35] In films like *Mandy* (2018) and *The Unbearable Weight of Massive Talent* (2022), he even seemed to be going out of his way to give the YouTubers more wild-eyed fodder for their highlight reels.

As it turns out, *Vampire's Kiss* seems practically tailor-made for the surrealist meme age; it just arrived a few decades too soon. Those too lazy to seek out the actual film can watch a ten-minute highlight reel titled "Best Scenes from 'Vampire's Kiss,' " which has amassed 1,200,000 views as of this writing. In 2011, a comic drawing of Cage's bugged-out eyes spread as a reaction meme on Reddit and Tumblr, expressing sarcastic faux-surprise, often accompanied by the caption "YOU DON'T SAY." (Cage never actually utters those words in *Vampire's Kiss*.)

"My kids said that's the most popular meme at school," Bierman says. "I think someone at school had told them it was a film I had directed. I don't think they even knew. They'd say, 'Hey, dad, is that one of your movies?' "

The downside of this meme-heavy treatment is that it attracts fans who approach *Vampire's Kiss* solely from an ironic distance. The film gets saddled with condescending labels like "good bad movie," a loathsome term that primarily gives audiences a way to express affection for a movie while asserting their superiority over it. As the writer J. W. McCormack recently argued in a *Baffler* essay, "If moviegoers watch Nicolas Cage with the same kind of smug irony with which they dissect intricately poor movies like *The Room*, they've taken the wrong lesson from his filmography. Cage offers an articulate nada, something untaught, impossible to explain, mimeograph, sanitize, or resist. He's too in touch with his own mayhem to be caught merely trying his best."[36]

Fortunately, since its resurgence, *Vampire's Kiss* has attracted sincere critical attention. In 2012, the movie received a thoughtful reassessment from then-A.V.

Club critic Scott Tobias, who observed that Cage's performance "raises the question of what good acting really means." As Tobias wrote, "Cage's unbridled exuberance is reason enough to cherish *Vampire's Kiss*," but the actor's unhinged approach also serves a narrative purpose:

> As a study of misogyny, the film taps shrewdly into Peter's fear of women. . . . Griffin Dunne shrinks in the face of these fears in *After Hours*, pinballing through a city intent on punishing him for trying to get laid. By contrast, Cage is all raging id, aggressive and demonstrative and unrelenting in his stampede through the night, but he's tortured for it all the same.[37]

It's fair to say that Cage's techniques and self-awareness are more understood in hindsight. In 2016, *Vampire's Kiss*'s producers and director celebrated its cultural resurgence by appearing at a Museum of Modern Art screening of the film. Minion was there, too.

The film has also amassed a portfolio of famous fans, from Simon Helberg, who in 2012 delivered a dazzling impression of the alphabet scene on *Conan*, to Tom Waits, who once listed the cockroach moment among his all-time favorite movie scenes.[§] During the nineties, Shulman worked with John Leguizamo and happened to mention *Vampire's Kiss*. "He was like, 'Oh my God, it's my favorite movie—I watch it every week!'" Shulman recalls. Christian Bale was also rumored to have drawn influence from it when he played Patrick Bateman in *American Psycho*, a similarly disturbing send-up of yuppie emptiness.[38]

Cage, to his credit, seemed to have a prescient sense for the film's eventual cult even before it came out. Speaking to *SPIN* in 1988, when it was still caught in distributor purgatory, he mused about its outré appeal. "Even if the worst happens and it doesn't come out for some reason, it's a movie with integrity," he said. "Someone's going to see it and want to see it again. Maybe it can become a rare movie, like a bootleg record." Cage even offered a preemptive response to the detractors: "I act for myself. I did *Vampire's Kiss* for myself. It was something I had to do whether or not people liked it."[39]

In 1995, Shils encountered Cage at an American Film Institute (AFI) event honoring him. By this point, he had won immense praise for *Leaving Las*

[§] Tom Waits was apparently an early appreciator of *Vampire's Kiss*. In 1988, Cage told *SPIN* that Waits had said *Vampire's Kiss* "was like watching a two-hour train wreck and the last twenty minutes of the film reminded him of listening to Jimi Hendrix." Years later, Cage claimed in a *Playboy* interview that Cher had praised his *Peggy Sue Got Married* performance as "like watching a two-hour car accident." It seems he genuinely enjoyed having his work likened to vehicular disaster.

Vegas. The critics who had dismissed his antics in *Vampire's Kiss* now had to take him seriously. Cage recognized the producer and began rhapsodizing about their experience all those years earlier.

"Nick used to say to me, '*Vampire's Kiss* was like my laboratory for these big studio pictures! That was my laboratory!'" Shils recalls. "He really loved the film. Loved making it. And he was able to explore some crazy shit."

8

Cage and the Curious Case of the Big Rubber Nose

In 1989, seven years after relinquishing the Coppola name, Nicolas Cage decided to make it official.

A formal notice appeared in the *Los Angeles Daily Journal* that summer: Nicolas Kim Coppola, of 450 N. Rossmore, #1001, "has filed an application proposing that his name be changed to Nicolas Kim Cage." Anyone objecting to the legal name change was ordered to appear in court on August 4.[1] Whether Cage's application succeeded remains unclear.*

Cage's desire to formalize his professional identity couldn't have come at a stranger time. From 1987 to 1989, Cage was on a self-imposed strike from mainstream Hollywood, refusing to follow the success of *Moonstruck* with anything remotely palatable to a popular audience. Cage's career choices were wild, even before he starred in a movie with "wild" in the title, and so were his offscreen antics, reports of which spilled over into newspapers and tabloids.

Cage appeared to be disappearing into his weirdness. Rumors spread about his affinity for exotic animals, a reputation which followed him into casting offices. Casting director Valorie Massalas, who cast Cage in *Fire Birds* and *Honeymoon in Vegas*, recalls hearing about his large monitor lizard: "I heard he would keep weird food in his freezer because he would feed it to the pet."

In press clippings, Cage's personal eccentricities began to overshadow his work. When *Playgirl* profiled Cage in 1988—a strange piece in which he bemoaned being alone and invited readers to suggest "a woman who might want to be my wife"—the headline described his growing reputation: "Nicolas Cage: Madman or Mystery?"[2]

* In 2014, Cage told an interviewer that he is "still legally Nicolas Coppola." His divorce paperwork from 2019 seems to confirm this.

The following year, *Playboy* sent a correspondent to interview Cage at his office. "Unaccustomed to self-promotion, he paced the floor like an inmate on death row," the correspondent reported. The subsequent Q&A scarcely mentioned *Vampire's Kiss*—the film he was ostensibly promoting—but did find the actor expounding on money ("I try not to worry or think about money. I just keep spending until I get a phone call from my business manager telling me to stop"), women ("I'm totally mystified by women"), and a nasal problem that was plaguing him. Asked what he was wearing when he had the most fun, Cage offered this anecdote: "I was stealing an aquarium from the Museum of Modern Art and I was with a friend of mine and I think I was wearing a large black trench coat."[3]

Even Cage's neighbors were baffled by him. Front desk staff at the El Royale grumbled about Cage's surly behavior; fellow residents—many of them lawyers or corporate types—wondered about him. Ana Figueroa, a journalist who lived at the historic building during the late 1980s, says Cage wore lots of leather and seemed to be nocturnal. "I just called him the vampire, because I only saw him at night," Figueroa says. "Always with his head down in a leather jacket on this motorcycle, which was weird. He was trying to be James Dean. But it was the eighties."

Late one night, Figueroa heard Cage and his girlfriend outside her window. He was gunning his motorcycle over and over, pretending to run her over, as she playfully screamed, "*Nicolas! Nicolas!*" This went on for an hour, Figueroa says. "And I just remember thinking, 'What is so great about this guy that you're gonna let him run you over in the middle of the night?' "

* * *

The film critic Nathan Rabin has a theory about Cage's "lost years." In an A.V. Club article, Rabin proposes that, during the late eighties and early nineties, Cage's criteria for choosing roles were threefold:

(1) How ridiculous will my accent be? Will it sound like a dialect never spoken by anyone, ever, in the history of time?
(2) How about facial hair? Can it look like fake hair haphazardly placed on me by a blind man with an odd sense of humor?
(3) Will I be called upon to shamelessly overact or go completely fucking nuts?[4]

Swap out facial hair for a prosthetic nose that belongs in the bargain bin of a Halloween shop, and Cage's cameo in the little-seen 1989 sex comedy *Never on Tuesday* fits the bill. *Never on Tuesday* is a sophomoric teen flick that went straight to video and sank into obscurity upon release. No, it's not an essential Cage performance; admittedly, the man appears onscreen for all of sixty seconds. But Cage's cameo in *Never on Tuesday* is revealing of his mindset during this wilderness period: his determination to bring a glowing cloud of surrealism to even the most boilerplate project, as well as his tendency to deliver his most extreme work when the stakes (and pay) were lowest. *Never on Tuesday* demonstrates just how far out Cage was willing to go, even when everyone around him was playing it safe.

The debut feature of a young director named Adam Rifkin, then in his early twenties, *Never on Tuesday* was financed by veteran producer Elliott Kastner and made on the cheap for $800,000. When Rifkin met Kastner in the mid-eighties, Rifkin was seeking funding for a dystopian script he had written called *The Dark Backward.*

But Kastner wasn't interested in *The Dark Backward.* He was exploring the booming straight-to-video market. He wanted a teen flick.

"He said, 'Do you have any scripts that would appeal to the kids?'" Rifkin recalls. Rifkin said yes. When Kastner asked him to bring it in the next day, Rifkin said he needed a few days to polish it up. "I didn't have anything for the kids," Rifkin admits, "but I ran home and wrote *Never on Tuesday* really fast. And I brought it in Monday."

Never on Tuesday is the sort of movie you might show a college class if you're trying to teach the concept of the male gaze. The plot revolves around two college-aged boys from Ohio (Andrew Lauer and Peter Berg) who embark on a road trip to California, eager to score with attractive women. Instead, they get into a minor accident on a remote stretch of highway and find themselves stranded with the other driver, a beautiful blonde photographer named Tuesday (Claudia Christian). The boys desperately hope to fulfill their fantasies with Tuesday, who announces that she is a lesbian, a revelation the boys greet with frustration and disbelief. Like a dime-store *Breakfast Club*, most of the film revolves around these three characters opening up to each other—emotionally, not sexually—in one location.

If *Never on Tuesday* has a redeeming quality, it's the parade of cameos from uncredited Brat Packers, portraying eccentric passersby who encounter the three kids but never actually help them. There's Gilbert Gottfried chewing the scenery as a kooky salesman, Charlie Sheen as a knife-wielding robber, and Judd Nelson as an erratic, giggly cop.

But no cameo shifts the mood as aggressively as Cage's. He pulls up in a Ferrari, and what emerges from the vehicle is a dose of pure, uncut Cage weirdness. His unnamed character wears a red jacket and a large rubber nose. "Is anybody hurt?" he asks in a falsetto voice that sounds like a dying puppet. "Can I give somebody a lift?"

When his offer is rebuffed, Cage flashes a suggestive smile and laughs maniacally before driving away. That's the whole cameo.

* * *

None of this was in the script.

In fact, Cage's entire appearance in *Never on Tuesday* was unplanned. According to Cassian Elwes, the film's other producer (and Kastner's stepson), the cameo was originally given to Rob Lowe. When Lowe backed out at the last moment, Elwes frantically searched for a replacement. A friend of a friend suggested Cage.[5]

"Word came back that Nicolas Cage would be open to doing it on three conditions. He wanted to drive a red Ferrari: OK, no problem. He wanted to be able to do whatever he wanted: OK, no problem. And he wanted to wear a big, fake nose: OK, no problem," Rifkin says. "So Nick shows up, and he was already in this crazy character he was playing before I met him."

This character was not native to the script. Cage had invented it. Andrew Lauer, who played one of the leads, remembers the confusion when Cage, who was flown out to the desert town of Borrego Springs, California, emerged from the makeup trailer. "Doors swing open. And there's this tall guy with this *huge* nose. There's an audible gasp among the crew and the actors. We're just like, 'Whoa, what?' People start filing through the pages of the script that we're going to shoot—no mention of this huge nose. I thought it was just a joke, and then he was going to take the nose off and we were going to rehearse. Doesn't happen!"

The producers had okayed the rubber nose, but the actors were bewildered. Lauer and Peter Berg huddled nervously and discussed what to do. Lauer agreed to approach Cage. Cage answered him in his helium voice. "I was like, 'Oh God. Is he in character??' And he *was*," says Lauer. "I said, 'The nose thing—are you keeping it?' He said, 'Yeah!' Talking just like the character, in that high-pitched voice!"

"I remember Nick's character was so freaky that I didn't feel comfortable giving him direction," says Rifkin, who was only twenty at the time. "I remember being like, well, that's what we get. It was a weird day."

The scene was shot in one or two takes. Cage sped toward the camera in a borrowed Ferrari Testarossa. The vehicle's owner was delighted that a movie star was driving his car. Then Cage missed his mark and smashed into a stack of apple boxes. "The owner of the Ferrari goes white immediately," Rifkin recalls.

Cage emerged from the Ferrari gesticulating like a lobotomized mime and delivering his lines in that high voice, as seen in the film. "Our reactions were totally real," says Lauer. Then Cage veered off-script. In Rifkin's memory, he got a creepy expression on his face and asked, "Got any butthole?"

"Peter Berg said something like, 'No! No, we don't.' Then Nick screams 'Pinocchio!' really loud, and then laughs really hard," Rifkin says. "I think it was like a one-shot deal. We did it once and that was it. Oh, and he wasn't allowed to drive away again because he had hurt the car. We pushed the car out of the shot and added sound effects of him driving away."

Cage's work was complete. To the horror of Lauer, who hoped he would film a more sensible take, Cage returned to the makeup trailer to have the prosthetic nose removed. Then he was gone. "[He] takes all his stuff and disappears and I never had a chance to talk to him," Elwes recalled in a 2019 interview. "The whole thing was bizarre beyond belief!"[6]

Cage did the cameo as a favor to the producers and agreed not to be credited. Like the other cameo actors, he was paid just $360.[7]

* * *

Never on Tuesday never got a theatrical release. Rifkin screened the film for studios and there was interest. But Elliott Kastner had partnered with a fellow producer and home video pioneer named Andre Blay. According to Rifkin, Blay sold the video rights to Paramount and said he would release the film theatrically through his own distribution company, for which Paramount gave him an additional $2 million.

That never happened. "Andre never had any intention of theatrically releasing *Never on Tuesday*," Rifkin says. "He just pocketed the additional $2 million and that was that. I was furious." (Blay died in 2018.)

Meanwhile, Cage's ad-libbed lines were removed: no more butthole, no Pinocchio. "The powers that be made us cut that out because it was so weird,"

Rifkin says. "I would love someday, if it even exists, for a restored version of that movie to come out so people can see the actual lunacy that he created."

Never on Tuesday went straight to VHS in 1989, arguably the most bizarre year in Cage's filmography,[†] and faded into home-video obscurity. It has never been released on DVD.

* * *

Until recently, even hard-core Cage fans couldn't tell you what *Never on Tuesday* was about. So nonexistent was the film's legacy that a 1998 Cage biography mistitled it as *Never on a Tuesday* and called it "an ultra-low-budget horror flick."[8]

Then an obsessive Cage fan named Alex Navarro tracked down a copy. The cameo lodged itself in his brain. In July 2019, Navarro tweeted out the footage of Cage's cameo and wrote: "there is a direct to video movie from the late '80s that Nicolas Cage randomly appears in. this is the entirety of his performance."

Plenty of Cage performances weren't fully embraced until years later, but no film demonstrates this pattern as acutely as *Never on Tuesday*. The clip went viral, amassing tens of thousands of likes, as well as write-ups in publications like the *Washington Post*. Rifkin and Elwes were stunned. "I love the fact that now, because of [Cage], this movie might get a second life," Elwes told me that week.[9]

A week later, Cage did an interview with *Vulture*. He, too, was delighted. Though he was supposed to be promoting a new project, he couldn't stop himself from talking about this thirty-year-old cameo. "I had a whole character worked out for that one scene, a whole subtext, a complete unspoken backstory," Cage told interviewer Charles Bramesco, and explained:

> The character was [supposed to be] some sleazy guy who wanted to pick up a girl in a Ferrari, and that wasn't so interesting to me. So I came up with a concept: This character had a physical deformity. He looked like a freak: long nose, bullied as a kid, called "Pinocchio" in the schoolyard. His father felt bad for him, bought him a nice red Ferrari to make him feel good.

[†] Cage appeared in three roles in 1989: as a rubber-nosed rubbernecker in *Never on Tuesday*, a mentally deteriorating literary agent in *Vampire's Kiss*, and a brutish Italian soldier who rapes an African woman in the little-seen Italian film *Time to Kill*. Two of these never made it to theaters in the U.S.; all three flopped in their own distinct ways.

> He's lonely, and so when he sees these people on the side of the road, he wants to help them and see if they're hurt.[10]

There's an element of Cage's own childhood in this tragic character: he was also bullied as a kid, and was deeply affected by the film *Pinocchio*.[11] Leave it to Cage to devise an imaginary backstory for a character who's onscreen for all of sixty seconds, not share it with the director, and then remember every detail three decades later.

* * *

That Cage concocted this bizarre character for such a low-stakes movie was not a coincidence. As he told *Vulture*, "If I'm in a cameo and I'm not getting paid, just let me do whatever I want and make some of my experimental visions come true. They said 'Go for it,' the three most beautiful words any actor can hear on a set."[12]

This is a revealing glimpse into how Cage thinks about the eternal push-and-pull between creativity and commerce. When the pay is low, his leash is long; he feels emboldened to pursue his wildest ideas. He becomes in essence his own director, sometimes to the chagrin of the *actual* director, who may not be so willing to defer to Cage's experimental impulses.

For a more extreme example of this pattern, let's skip ahead to *Deadfall*, the widely panned 1993 crime drama that reunited Cage with his childhood collaborator, director Christopher Coppola. Like *Never on Tuesday*, *Deadfall* is a B-movie whose profile was considerably lifted by a slate of enviable cameos: Peter Fonda, Charlie Sheen (again), Talia Shire. More to the point, *Never on Tuesday* and *Deadfall* are both relatively straightforward genre exercises—one a teen comedy, the other a neo-noir—thrown from their axes by wild-eyed Cage performances that seem to have been beamed down from a foreign galaxy.

But while Cage's wackiness in *Never on Tuesday* was concentrated to one scene, he swallows up half of *Deadfall* with a performance so chaotic that it feels intended as a sizzle reel, with Cage showing off every accent he could imitate, every expletive he could scream, and every drug he could snort.

In a performance that overpowers its surrounding movie like a hyena chomping into a wildebeest, Cage plays a mustachioed gangster named Eddie, a short-tempered coke fiend who waves an imaginary whip in the air when revving up his convertible and yells things like "*Hi-fuckin'-ya!*" when he pounds anyone who gets in his way. When he's not screaming "*Fuuuuuck!*"

at the top of his lungs in his favorite strip club (elongating its sole syllable into an operatic crescendo of profanity), Cage spends the movie stalking around in a bow-tie, dark shades, mustache, and a horrific toupee, looking like he just robbed the set of the "Sabotage" video shoot (Figure 8.1).

Cage's accent also mutates at random from scene to scene. At one point, he even reverts back to his Pokey voice, holding his boss (James Coburn) at gunpoint and taunting him with a high-pitched, sing-song-y refrain: "*Bull*-shit! *Bull*-shit!"

This was the first time Cage had been directed by his brother Christopher in a professional capacity, and it would be the last. The film's mention still dredges up bad memories for Christopher today.

"It's not what I wanted," Christopher sighs. "My brother just made it about him. That's just what he does."

* * *

Like his younger brother, Christopher Coppola entered the family business, but his path was more circuitous than most. A self-described pretentious kid with few friends, he left high school at sixteen and studied experimental

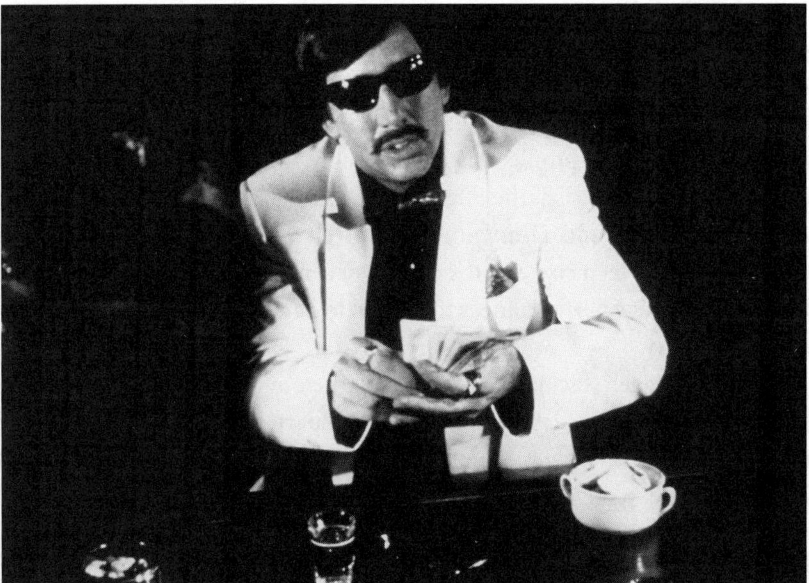

Figure 8.1. Cage's bizarre appearance in *Deadfall* (1993, Trimark Pictures) is reminiscent of Andy Kaufman's alter-ego: sleazy lounge singer Tony Clifton. Note the dark sunglasses, wig, and gaudy jacket.

music at the University of Redlands. Christopher was always a bit miffed when Cage would tell people his name was inspired by John Cage; what did *he* know about John Cage? "That was my world!" Christopher says.

As his younger brother rose to fame and his older brother became a radio personality, Christopher stayed in school, earning a film degree from the San Francisco Art Institute. When Cage saw some of Christopher's art films, he showed them to his then-agent, Ilene Feldman, and said, "Why don't you try out the whole Hollywood thing?" Christopher was skeptical, but he wanted to make feature-length films, so he agreed to give it a shot, leading to a deal with Dino De Laurentiis's production company.

His directorial debut was *Dracula's Widow*, a low-budget vampire thriller he made for De Laurentiis in 1988. "I made it as arty as possible," Christopher says. "It didn't do well."

A few years later, Christopher and Cage started talking about working together. Christopher was writing screenplays with Nick Vallelonga (the future co-writer of *Green Book*) and together they wrote *Deadfall*, a twist-laden crime story inspired by film noir classics and made during a period of neo-noir revival (*Miller's Crossing*, *Bad Lieutenant*, etc.). "We unfortunately got hooked into a so-called producer who so-called put up some money, named Ted Fox, who we both disliked tremendously," Christopher says.

Deadfall found a financer in Trimark, a leading home video company whose CEO, Mark Amin, received a producer credit. "It was pitched to me as a Coppola family movie," Amin says (the project boasted not just Cage and Christopher, but cameos from their brother Marc and aunt Talia Shire). "I think because of their connections, they were able to get an amazing cast together for a very low budget. So they brought this package to us."

Internally, the script did not get a good reaction at Trimark. But Amin didn't care. Back then, his company had a "Jeffrey Katzenberg philosophy": pump out cheap movies that will make money and don't worry about critics or prestige. He knew he could cover the budget of *Deadfall* with foreign pre-sales and home video profits with or without a theatrical release. And because the budget was low, "Chris had total control, and basically told us to stay out of the way," Amin says.

"My background wasn't film school or anything," Amin adds. "All we cared about was whether we can sell this or not. It was all just financial projections. We didn't really pay that much attention."

* * *

Deadfall tells the story of Joe (Michael Biehn), a hardboiled con man in business with his father (James Coburn). After Joe inadvertently kills his dad during a con gone wrong, he must fulfill the old man's dying wish by going out west to locate his dad's estranged brother Lou, also a con man (Coburn again). He starts working for Lou and becomes embroiled with Lou's sleazy, psychopathic flunky Eddie (Cage), who does not take kindly to Joe muscling in on his turf and stealing his girl (Sarah Trigger as an icy femme fatale).

At this point, Cage's performance singlehandedly steers *Deadfall* away from noir and toward high-octane gonzo comedy. But an hour into the film, the character goes ballistic on his boss and dies a gruesome death involving a deep fryer. *Deadfall* tries to shift back into cynical noir realism, but it's too late. Not even cameo appearances by Charlie Sheen or Angus Scrimm (who plays a sinister mob boss with a terrifying metallic claw) can save it from clunky writing and an anemic performance by a miscast Biehn.

Does Cage's outlandish and essentially comic performance ruin the film? Or does it rescue it from sheer tedium? That is up for debate. The way Christopher tells it, though, *Deadfall* was one of those disastrous projects where nothing went as planned. "The whole process of making that film is one of the ugliest periods of my life," he says.

The filmmaker initially planned to have Cage star as Joe, with Tom Waits as Eddie. But Cage insisted on playing the latter character. Waits was "a little irritated with me," Christopher says, but the director felt he needed to go with his brother. So, he cast Val Kilmer as Joe, with a budget set at $8 million and shooting scheduled to begin in July 1992. That month the *Washington Post* published an article hyping the project:

> Kilmer is the hero, and Cage plays a shady con man. This role, in fact, sounds like it could fit nicely into Cage's gallery of cinematic weirdos. "He's a guy that's sort of stuck in the '50s," says Coppola. "He gets his head deep-fried, he always has a full deck of jokers with him, which he hands people and asks them to pick cards, and he says stuff like 'be-bop-a-lula.' And yet there's also something about him that's real tragic and real human."[13]

Then, days before the shooting date, disaster struck. Kilmer broke his contract and backed out, saying he hated the producer. The budget plummeted. The crew felt as if someone had died. The director scrambled for a replacement. But everything felt cursed.

To this day, Christopher wishes he had never continued. "We ended up making the film for like $2.5 million," he says, "but I still had a cast, including my brother and James Coburn. They had to be paid what they were offered.‡ I had a guy come in—Michael Biehn, who I like—but he's not really a leading man. He's no Val Kilmer. But we had to make the film in eighteen days."

Amidst this turmoil, Cage staged a mutiny of one and delivered the most chaotic performance of his career, rendering himself unrecognizable and alienating his co-stars. Perhaps he felt emboldened to go big because his brother was directing. Reflecting in a 1996 interview, Cage framed *Deadfall* as a collaborative endeavor: "That was a chance to work with Christopher, and he let me go for it in the regard that I could have fun with the makeup and disguise myself so I could really take advantage of the opportunity."[14]

But in Christopher's view, he lost control of his own movie. "I just wanted Natural Mr. Cage. I was going for a natural movie," Christopher says. Instead, Cage arrived in a cheap wig, handlebar 'stache, dark shades, and fake nose, vacillating between mumbling his dialogue and screaming it (Figure 8.2).

"My brother basically came to the set wearing what he wanted. I had zero control over him," Christopher says. "I had to fight and say, 'Look, can you just take off your friggin' sunglasses so we can see why you're so insane in the film? Because it's just not real. The only way I can make this real is if your eyes look lost and you've been feeling so much distrust of your world that you become that guy, filled with anxiety, and you need to kill the pain with drugs.' He just wouldn't take off his sunglasses. And twice he finally did, and he literally had a temper tantrum."

"It was a disaster," Christopher adds. "Now, the only reason why I would care to look at the movie is because of his over-the-top performance. And he's good at that. It's fun. I think he did that better in *Vampire's Kiss*. But he just was out of control. I felt bad for James Coburn. He's screaming in his freakin' face! That's James Coburn! Who the hell are *you* to be screaming in his freakin' face? That's what this film means to me."

The *Vampire's Kiss* comparison checks out. As in that film, Cage seems to be on a different plane of physicality than his co-stars—barging into his girlfriend's room, karate-kicking the air, striking a Mick Jagger pose as he rants and raves. But this time Cage improvised heavily, peppering his

‡ Cage was paid "a few hundred thousand," Christopher says—well below his then-asking price, but still a substantial sum. The director, however, deferred his own payment: "I got nothing! I put all my money back into it."

Figure 8.2. While filming *Deadfall* (1993, Trimark Pictures), Cage refused to take off his sunglasses. The director, his brother Christopher Coppola, had to beg him to do so.

outbursts with absurdities like "Vive la *fuckin'* France, man!" and "Here's to Sam fuckin' Peckinpah!"

And unlike *Vampire's Kiss*, *Deadfall* never gives us a sense of how the character has gotten to this state of madness. That was Christopher's great frustration: he wanted to convey Eddie's humanity and anguish. In his mind, Eddie was an orphan who had been taken in by Lou, but Cage played the character like an "angry clown."

Christopher speaks reverently of the rare scenes that offer a glimpse of Eddie's vulnerability—for instance, when he removes his shades during Joe's first meeting with Lou and we see that his eyes are watery with tears. "It's tragic," the director says. "That means something to me. That connects me to that character. And he only did that twice because I begged him."

When producer Amin saw the dailies, he was shocked by Cage's appearance and worried that viewers wouldn't recognize him. "We thought the fake nose made it a little too silly," Amin says. But Cage insisted it was part of the character, and Trimark had promised Christopher creative autonomy. In reality, Christopher felt that his brother was holding the film hostage.[15]

* * *

How should a Cage fan make sense of the actor's brash, unhinged performance in *Deadfall*? I propose two interpretations.

The first is a matter of timing. When Cage made *Deadfall* in 1992, he had just filmed two relatively mainstream studio comedies (*Honeymoon in Vegas*, *Amos & Andrew*) and may have felt restrained. Playing a coked-up wild man offered a chance to let loose.

Several of Cage's most chaotic performances came under similar circumstances. He filmed *Peggy Sue Got Married* after feeling straightjacketed by the one-dimensional *The Boy in Blue*, and he made *Vampire's Kiss* as a reaction to *Moonstruck*.

The other interpretation is that Cage was paying homage to one of his childhood idols, Andy Kaufman. Except Cage was not channeling Kaufman himself. He was channeling Kaufman's belligerent alter ego, Tony Clifton. (Cage has mentioned Kaufman approvingly in interviews, and his high school friend Maria McKee recalls that, as a teenager, he was obsessed with Kaufman.)

The legendary performance artist often opened his own shows in character as Clifton, a fictitious lounge singer who insulted audience members and told incoherent jokes. Clifton's signature look—rumpled tuxedo, filthy mustache, mop of brown hair—oozed nightclub sleaze, and he always wore sunglasses. "Hip audiences simply hated Clifton, probably because audience abuse was the crux of the act," wrote Bill Zehme in the *New York Times*. Similarly, Eddie's repulsive behavior seems designed to alienate everyone around him.[16]

In *Deadfall*, Cage appears to have modeled his look after Clifton, straight down to the porno 'stache and garish suits. And in the scene where Eddie stalks through the strip club, babbling obscenities and abusing bystanders (as Clifton might have done), his voice is highly reminiscent of Clifton's gruff bark.

Several critics have noted the parallel. Christopher says it's plausible—"it's probably part of his building of the character"—but doesn't recall Cage mentioning Tony Clifton. Instead, when the director confronted his brother about what he was wearing, Cage told him, "I'm just fuckin' Joe Namath, man." "I'm like, '*Really*. You're gonna be Joe Namath.' I had zero control."

One of the main plotlines in *Deadfall* involves Joe's attempts to learn why his father and uncle had a falling out. Maybe this is the ultimate irony of *Deadfall*: that a movie about a contentious relationship between two estranged brothers lingers at the center of a contentious relationship between the two brothers who made it.

* * *

Like Clifton during his club appearances, *Deadfall* flopped. It received a limited theatrical release in October 1993, but the critics were vicious. "It got one good review," says Christopher. "Mainly it was like, '*Deadfall* is *dreadful*.' That was cute."

Trimark wasn't upset. The company earned its investment back through video rentals and TV licensing. But Christopher felt ostracized after the film's failure. His lawyer told him to lay low for two years.

Even today, the filmmaker has never really made peace with *Deadfall*. It's his least favorite film he's made. Yet it follows him like an albatross. His students (a passionate educator, he taught for years at the San Francisco Art Institute) often mention it. Some of them love it. "I don't know why," he admits. He wishes people would talk about films of which he is proud, like *Palmer's Pick-Up* (1999), instead.

In 1997, a nu-metal band called Snot even created a song about *Deadfall*. Christopher likes to joke, "Some Coppolas get Oscars. I get Snot."

Like *Never on Tuesday*, *Deadfall* found an unlikely second life decades later. In 2017, Cage reprised the character of Eddie King—hairpiece, mustache, and all—in *Arsenal*, a leaden, gore-filled crime thriller that ranks somewhere near the grime-encrusted sewer of Cage's VOD era. *Arsenal* is sometimes referred to as a *Deadfall* sequel, which is strange, considering (1) it has no other characters from *Deadfall* and (2) hey, didn't Eddie die in a deep fryer? (*Arsenal* simply ignores this complication.)

Arsenal wasn't marketed as a *Deadfall* sequel, though, and many reviewers seemed wholly unaware that Cage was riffing on a character he'd played before. Perhaps only diehard fans recognized the other link to the 1993 film: a cameo by Christopher Coppola himself, playing Eddie's brother, whom Eddie executes in brutal fashion.

Strangely, it was Christopher who encouraged Cage to reprise the character. The idea grew from a conversation he had with Cage in the 2010s, when the actor's career was in a lull. "I told him, 'You're still incredibly relevant to young people. They do those silly memes, whatever they're called. Even though you might think they're making fun of you, they're not doing that with other stars that are struggling,' " Christopher says.

Christopher mentioned that his students loved his *Deadfall* performance and suggested Cage bring him back as an older Eddie. Cage responded, "Well, maybe you should be in it and I kill you," Christopher recalls. "I'm like, 'Well, I know that would probably make you happy. So yeah, sure, it'll be like the great catharsis.'"

Christopher's relationship with his brother has been strained since *Deadfall*. At one point, they didn't speak for ten years. As of this writing, they're again not on speaking terms, a rift that occurred around the 2021 death of their mother.

Despite it all, Christopher praises his brother as a "master artist of acting." He went to see *Pig*. It's now his favorite Cage performance.

* * *

Several years ago, Christopher Coppola was talking to Francis Ford Coppola about *Deadfall*.

"I really wish I never made that friggin' movie," Christopher vented to his uncle, reflecting on old regrets. "It's just been a curse, and people bring it up all the time. I've done so many more things in my life, helping people and teaching and films I like so much more."

He added, "I wonder why my brother did that to me."

According to Christopher's account of the conversation, Francis responded with a hint of commiseration: "Well, that's what you get when you hire Nick Cage."

9

Goofing on Elvis

The first time David Lynch got together with Nicolas Cage and Laura Dern, there was fire.

I don't mean fire in the hacky metaphorical sense: *Their chemistry was so hot. . . .* I mean fire. Arson. Lynch took Cage and Dern, who had not yet met, to dinner at Muse, a celebrity-friendly restaurant on Beverly Boulevard.[1] Several blocks away, a huge fire raged. "There was a very famous theater that was burning down," Lynch says, referring to the May 1989 fire that destroyed Los Angeles's historic Pan Pacific Auditorium, a grotesque spectacle that shot flames 200 feet into the sky.[2] "We didn't see the flames. We heard about it, I think."

A different filmmaker might have considered this a bad omen. For David Lynch, it must have seemed like some depraved initiation ritual for *Wild at Heart*, a movie so obsessed with fire—its searing, incontrovertible power and rage—that its opening credits are literally engulfed in Halloween-orange flames. Or maybe it was a metaphor for the breakneck speed with which *Wild at Heart* had entered production after Lynch wrote the script. "It was one of those things that once it started it was like a fire," Lynch recalled in the mid-nineties. "It just burst into being."[3]

No matter what, that first meeting confirmed what the filmmaker had already suspected: nobody but Nicolas Cage and Laura Dern could possibly play the outlaw couple at the center of Lynch's fifth feature, a romance set in a world aflame, a road movie in which violence and madness leer out from every exit. "Me and Nick and Laura had dinner, and it was one of those things where I knew it was gonna be okay and good," Lynch tells me. "And it was."

* * *

Nicolas Cage and David Lynch were probably bound to work together eventually. This was one of those incendiary pairings, like David Bowie and Brian Eno or Werner Herzog and Klaus Kinski—two visionary spirits, fleetingly fused together at the height of their respective powers.

By the time they made *Wild at Heart*, Cage and Lynch were both known for polarizing audiences and flouting orthodoxy. Each admired this quality in the other. Lynch once described Cage as "the jazz musician of actors" and warned that "if you don't channel him or ride herd on him, it could become frightening music."[4] Cage in turn described Lynch as "like a criminal director. He's not concerned with Establishment laws and rules. . . . A scene can turn into a comedy or into heavy horror in a fraction of a second."[5]

The two artists each possessed antennas finely tuned to the absurdity of life, but they also contained surprising capacities for tenderness, which is filtered through the sun-streaked romance that redeems the brutality of *Wild at Heart*. People who meet Lynch are often taken aback by how normal and earnest the man seems. "When David speaks, he sounds like he just got off the Greyhound bus from Iowa," said the late Steve Golin, who produced *Wild at Heart*. "But underneath that Jimmy Stewart look you find a darker side."[6]

In 1977, Cage was a film-obsessed teenager when Lynch rose to prominence with the grim, desolate *Eraserhead*, which the young filmmaker had labored over intensely for years, even living on the film's set for a period. *Eraserhead* introduced audiences to the disturbing visions that seemed to pour forth from Lynch's mind like bats from a desert cavern, but it wasn't an immediate success. Instead, the film gathered a fanbase slowly but surely, finding popularity on the midnight movie circuit and during a years-long run at the Nuart Theatre in Los Angeles.[7]

Stanley Kubrick was among the film's admirers. So was a young Nicolas Coppola, who raved about *Eraserhead* to classmates and went to see midnight screenings at the Nuart with his friends Crispin Glover and Larry Law.[8] "I remember people would get mad and shout things at the screen and leave the theater," Glover later told author Kristine McKenna.[9]

By the mid-eighties, as Cage's career was taking off, Lynch's was collapsing under the weight of 1984's *Dune*, an expensive flop that rendered Frank Herbert's sci-fi novel about as comprehensible as Tylenol ingredients. Deprived of final cut privilege, Lynch was so appalled by the changes studio executives made that he disowned the film. "I was almost dead," Lynch later recalled. "*Dune* took me off at the knees."[10]

Yet despite the film's failure, the *Dune* debacle was clarifying for Lynch, offering lessons he would carry with him for the rest of his career: avoid big-money studio pictures, and never relinquish creative control in exchange for a higher budget. Lynch was never meant to be a director-for-hire working in service to some financier's vision. This was the kind of philosophy that made him and Cage kindred spirits.

Operating on a much smaller and more personal scale, Lynch redeemed himself with the mystery-noir masterpiece *Blue Velvet*. When critics throw around the term "Lynchian," the thematic obsessions of *Blue Velvet* are what come to mind: small-town malevolence, warped Americana, concealed criminal underworlds, an obsession with bodily deformities, and shocking juxtapositions of violence and retro pop culture kitsch—all filtered through a surrealist haze. In typical Lynch fashion, the result captivated many cinephiles and repulsed others. *Blue Velvet* began Lynch's long working relationship with Laura Dern, and it led into the most prolific stretch of his career, during which Lynch co-created the cult television series *Twin Peaks*. And then, while the show's first season was still in production, along came *Wild at Heart*.

To some observers, it was surprising that, after his hellish experience with *Dune*, Lynch would choose to make another adaptation of a novel. This was hardly the plan. After *Blue Velvet*, Lynch had tried and failed to get several other movies going, including an original screenplay called *Ronnie Rocket*, which he had been trying to get made since the late seventies. *Ronnie Rocket* was to Lynch what *SMiLE* was to Brian Wilson: a long-unrealized dream project. Back in 1981, in fact, Lynch had met with Francis Ford Coppola at his Napa Valley estate regarding Coppola's interest in producing the film through Zoetrope. Coppola apparently gave a copy of the *Ronnie Rocket* script to seventeen-year-old Cage, who gave it to Crispin Glover—a young Lynch fanatic—who adored it.[11]

But Coppola never produced *Ronnie Rocket*. That dream ended when Zoetrope fell into bankruptcy.[12] *Ronnie Rocket* never became viable, neither then nor after *Blue Velvet*, and Lynch gradually realized that the major studios were not eager to work with him.

Then, in 1989, while Lynch was immersed in *Twin Peaks*, his producer friend Monty Montgomery read the manuscript for Barry Gifford's not-yet-published novel *Wild at Heart: The Story of Sailor and Lula*. Gifford was a prolific author and poet who had been heavily influenced by the Beat Generation. This particular novel centered on a sex-crazed outlaw couple, the titular Sailor and Lula, speeding across the country, on the run from a vicious hitman hired by Lula's obsessive mother. Montgomery liked it so much that he and a fellow producer, Sigurjón Sighvatsson—cofounder of Propaganda Films, which had produced *Twin Peaks*—quickly snatched up the film rights. Sighvatsson recalls that he told Montgomery, "David is looking for a film. Why don't we send him the book? It doesn't seem like *Ronnie Rocket* is getting anywhere."

Montgomery's plan was to direct *Wild at Heart* himself. But he asked Lynch if he would consider being executive producer. Jokingly, Lynch responded, "That's great, Monty, but what if I read it and fall in love with it and want to do it myself?" Montgomery said he would step aside in such a case. Then Lynch read the book and did fall in love with it. Montgomery stepped aside and let Lynch direct, with himself, Sighvatsson, and Steve Golin serving as producers.

Lynch found Gifford's novel exhilarating. At the time, he felt like the world around him was spinning out of control, growing crazier and more violent every year—shootings, L.A. gang wars, drugs everywhere. "The book and the violence in America merged in my mind and many different things happened," Lynch told author and filmmaker Chris Rodley.[13] *Wild at Heart* felt disturbingly timely, with a love-drunk romance at its rupturing center and a sprawling road-movie structure that offered myriad possibilities for Lynch to indulge his fondness for sleazy, twisted characters. Taking plenty of creative liberties with Gifford's source material—from changing the ending to inserting a haunting encounter with a delirious car crash victim—Lynch banged out a script.

"I wrote the screenplay in two weeks and then did a rewrite right after that in two weeks," Lynch says. "I saw this as a love story in hell. It's a modern love story, as I said back then, because each person—the man and the woman—has mutual respect for one another. And it's in the middle of a world which, at that time, I thought was crazy. But it's gotten even worse since then."

PolyGram put up the money, and *Wild at Heart* shot into production with absurd speed, befitting the film's kinetic energy. Lynch had grown accustomed to the faster pace of TV production; he wrote the screenplay in April or May 1989 and began principal photography on August 9 in New Orleans. "It was one of the quickest movies I've ever done," says Sighvatsson. "From screenplay to shooting was less than eight weeks."

There was no time for uncertainty in the casting process. Everything fell into place. For Lula—the liberated, Carolina-talkin' blonde with a fierce love for her man—Lynch immediately pictured Laura Dern. Dern had played a more innocent part in *Blue Velvet* as a teenage girl accidentally sucked into a murderous world of crime and voyeurism, but Lynch, who had been stunned by her talents, was eager to give her a role that spotlighted her intense sexuality.[14] Like Cage, Dern had been born under the sign of Hollywood and was not averse to working with her famous relatives: her real-life mother, Diane Ladd, co-stars in *Wild at Heart* as her character's ruthlessly domineering mother, Marietta Fortune.

When it came to casting Sailor—the impulsive, Elvis-loving ex-con with a romantic streak—Lynch could imagine nobody in the world except Cage, whom he had briefly encountered once in a Thrifty Drugs store.[15] He did not consider any other actor. "Same thing with Dennis Hopper and *Blue Velvet*," Lynch tells me. "There's only one person that could be that person, and that was Nick. I don't know why that is." What made the filmmaker so confident in Cage's rightness for the role? Was it a previous performance? "Just the overall essence of him," Lynch explains. "I never had second thoughts, any doubts. Nick is just that person and he did a flawless, perfect job."

"David doesn't see many films, and he doesn't go by performances in other things," says Johanna Ray, Lynch's longtime casting director. "He just goes by what he senses innately in the person when he meets them. That's how he makes his casting decisions." Nor would Cage be burdened this time with screen tests or auditions. "David doesn't do that. He just doesn't believe in it," Ray says. "He goes by his instinct."

At the start of the shoot, Cage was nervous, working with a director whose work he had enthusiastically followed since high school. But Lynch's openness put him at ease. Lynch's sets were known to be peaceful and respectful environments, a mood encouraged by the director's daily meditation practice. As Cage told the *San Francisco Examiner*, "Working with David was the most liberating experience I've had as an actor."[16]

Lynch's instinct proved correct. Who else could have possibly played Sailor? By 1989, Cage seemed to specialize in playing twisted romantics driven to do outrageous things for love. He had even played an ex-con with a romantic side once before, but Sailor was considerably louder and brasher than his *Raising Arizona* counterpart—bringing his girl to ecstasy in bed one moment, defending her honor against a nightclub interloper the next.

In Cage, Lynch found someone who could swerve from the sacred to the profane in seconds, an actor who could karate-kick dance to speed metal with a cigarette dangling from his lips without looking ridiculous—someone willing to try anything. "You give him an idea, and he grabs onto it like crazy," Lynch told *American Film*. "He's like a wild dog on a leash."[17]

* * *

The jacket came first. In the spring of 1989, before filming *Wild at Heart*, Cage found a flamboyant snakeskin jacket at an L.A. vintage shop called Aaardvark's Odd Ark (Figure 9.1). Inspired by its resemblance to the snakeskin coat Marlon Brando had worn in 1960's *The Fugitive Kind*, he began wearing it everywhere, even to the West Coast premiere of *Vampire's Kiss*.[18] "I knew I was going to wear it in some movie," Cage later said.[19]

When *Wild at Heart* came along, Cage's jacket quickly became Sailor's beloved talisman, a signature fit in what is sometimes cited as Lynch's most stylish film. "The way I remember the story, Nick just came to rehearsal at David's house wearing the jacket and David spotted it and said, 'This is a great jacket! This is a Sailor jacket!'" says Sighvatsson. In Lynch's mind, however, Cage was the one who asked if he could wear it in the movie. Lynch not only loved the idea; he wrote it into the script, with Sailor repeatedly proclaiming the jacket "a symbol of my individuality and my belief in personal freedom." Cage's style and Sailor's style had fused into one.

The story epitomizes the freewheeling spontaneity that placed Cage and Lynch on the same wavelength. Like the Coens, Lynch could be obsessively

Figure 9.1. Before filming *Wild at Heart* (1990, The Samuel Goldwyn Company), Cage found a snakeskin jacket at a vintage shop. The jacket became a talisman for Cage's character, Sailor Ripley, who proclaims it "a symbol of my individuality and my belief in personal freedom."

precise about his vision: while filming the scene in which Cage throws a knife-wielding assailant down a flight of stairs, the director kept insisting that the fake blood needed to be blacker.[20] "When you work with David Lynch, there are no problems," Sighvatsson says, "because David Lynch just decides everything."

Yet unlike the Coens, Lynch reveled in improvisation and spur-of-the-moment ideas. When Lynch was told that a woman had approached their set and announced "Hey, y'all need a whore? I'm a real one," he laughed—then asked if they could still get her.[21] The script was never sacred. "Lines change. Thoughts and ideas change. Entire scenes end up different than they were in the script," Cage told the *St. Petersburg Times*.[22]

"When I became his producer, his favorite phrase was, 'Everybody sees a script on the table? Underneath it is a garbage can. Throw it in there,'" says Deepak Nayar, a second AD on *Wild at Heart* who went on to produce *Lost Highway*.

In other words, Cage had found his dream director. He and Dern inhabited their characters so fully that Lynch let them ad-lib, and *Wild at Heart*'s atmosphere of ramshackle, lived-in intimacy was deepened by their improvisations. "When Nick and Laura caught the drift of Sailor and Lula, their ad-libbing is Sailor and Lula," the director said in 1990. "Why am I going to tell them anything? That's Sailor and Lula there." Cage, for instance, tweaked a line in which Lula asks Sailor when he started smoking. The script said, "When I was about six," but Cage enjoyed messing with Lynch by lowering the age in every take, and Lynch used a take in which he said age four.[23]

Wild at Heart's jarring convergence of road movie, romantic fantasia, and violent thriller—with delirious *Wizard of Oz* homage and nods to sixties B-movies along the way—would be difficult for any actor to navigate, but Lynch is effusive about Cage's versatility. "Nick is fearless," the director says. "And he understands the human condition. It's really pretty amazing what he can do." There was, for instance, the time when Lynch surprised Cage by instructing him to sing opera in a scene.[24] Cage assented, "and I think he sang opera in a scene that we cooked up that wasn't in the film," Lynch says.*

"I always thought Nick was a little bit out there," says producer Sighvatsson. "He didn't seem very articulate. He didn't seem very focused. But the minute

* This scene is described in a 1997 *Premiere* article. It was to depict Sailor waking from a dream involving a cotton ball, then discovering a real cotton ball under his bed and singing to it in the darkness. "Now, there are not a lot of people you could talk to about that who would really grab hold of it," Lynch told the magazine, "but Nick just lit up like a Christmas tree." The scene was ultimately cut.

he was on set, he knew his lines. He was completely with what was going on on the set. But off set, it was hard to connect with Nick. He was a little strange."

While Lynch frequently addressed Cage and Dern as "Sailor" and "Lula," the director says Cage did not remain in character throughout the shoot. Yet Cage's essence and Sailor's essence fused so tightly that it was hard for others to tell where the actor ended and the character began. "He's not like Sean Penn, who I worked with, who actually stays in character," says Sighvatsson. "But he very much becomes the person nevertheless. Nick is so infused in his work that he becomes a part of it."

This was apparent to Jeff Litke, bassist for the Minnesota speed metal band Powermad, which was prominently featured in the film. "It seemed like when the snakeskin jacket was on him, he was definitely in character in between takes," says Litke. "Once the snakeskin jacket came off, there was a distinct sea change."

Powermad had entered Lynch's orbit by way of their Warner Bros. A&R rep Kevin Laffey, who was friends with the director. In 1989, Laffey was at Lynch's house for an unrelated meeting and had with him a copy of Powermad's new album. The band had fantasized about having Lynch direct their video, so Laffey nervously asked Lynch if he might take a listen. As Laffey watched, Lynch placed the test pressing on his turntable and was greeted with the menacing power chords of Powermad's song "Slaughterhouse." Silently, Lynch stood up and stopped the record after less than a minute. Then he started it over again. And again.

Laffey was mortified, believing Lynch hated what he was hearing. Instead, Lynch declared that he wanted to put Powermad in his next movie. Not only did those grinding power chords become a recurring motif, but Lynch opted to place Powermad's members onscreen when Sailor and Lula visit a metal club in New Orleans. Soon Litke and his bandmates found themselves on a stage in Los Angeles, playing to a recording of their own music as Cage thrashed wildly in front of them.

Yet when the music stopped, Cage seemed wholly in control. Litke recalls thinking that he and Lynch had that in common. "Even though there was chaos going on behind their collective eyebrows, it seemed their outward presence was very confident and very cool."

Throughout the day's shooting, Powermad guitarist Todd Haug found Cage to be generous and welcoming, but still isn't sure whether he met Nicolas Cage or Sailor. "In my opinion, he never broke character," Haug says.

"He wasn't Nicolas Cage. He was the character in the movie. It was kind of weird, actually. You meet him for the first time, you have a conversation, it's like, who am I talking to here?"

* * *

David Lynch's brain is a mysterious place. Images and ideas enter his mind; often he does not know where they come from. Take *Blue Velvet*, for instance. Fragments of ideas for that film came to Lynch as early as 1973. Years later, a crucial piece of the ending came to him in a dream. "It all comes in from somewhere else, like I was a radio," Lynch explained to author Chris Rodley. "But I'm a bad radio, so sometimes the parts don't hook together."[25]

The bizarre ideas seemed to be coming faster than ever during the making of *Wild at Heart*, and after the cult success of *Blue Velvet* (which had been made on a tight $6 million budget), Lynch now had the confidence and wherewithal to put them into motion. Mr. Reindeer, for instance—a flamboyant crime lord perpetually surrounded by topless women, even while on the toilet—was Lynch's own invention. "I don't know if Mr. Reindeer was in the book and don't know where he came from," Lynch wrote. "He just arrived."[26]

It is equally mysterious how Elvis Presley entered Lynch's brain. At some point during the film's development, the filmmaker became fixated on the idea of a cosmic connection between Sailor and Presley. "I guess it came into my mind reading the book," Lynch says. "That he was like an Elvis guy, and that Laura was kind of a bubblegum-chewing Marilyn Monroe."

Although *Wild at Heart* is ostensibly set in contemporary times, it freely borrows from the iconography of the rockabilly era. In *Blue Velvet*, Lynch had selected Kyle MacLachlan because he projected a kind of 1950s small-town innocence. "In *Wild at Heart*, he was looking for the '*cool*' '50s," *Movieline* reported, "and he went straight for the Elvis he saw in Nicolas Cage."[27]

Music is central to *Wild at Heart*, and the jarring juxtaposition of styles replicates the film's contrast of violence and tenderness. Within the first five minutes alone, the soundtrack shifts violently from an orchestral piece by Richard Strauss to jazz to Powermad's pounding speed metal and back to jazz. Yet no musical icon permeates the film as prominently as Elvis. Where *Blue Velvet* had hooked itself to the swooning balladry of Bobby Vinton as funneled through Isabella Rossellini, *Wild at Heart* was Lynch's rock & roll movie. In both cases, Lynch was fixated on the darker, more sinister underbelly of 1950s culture. "It's a little strange, because Elvis is pretty cliché in

1990—and not necessarily so revered at that time," says Sighvatsson. "But David has this fascination with, let's just say, Americana."†

Cage seized the idea and didn't let go. During rehearsals, he began delivering all of his lines in a thick Elvis purr. He and Lynch and Dern found themselves talking about Elvis and Marilyn Monroe—two American icons. Lynch bought a copy of *Elvis' Golden Records*. After listening to it, he called Cage and told him he needed to sing two Elvis songs in the movie, a wild idea which Lynch promptly wrote into the script, heightening the film's absurdist Americana pastiche.[28]

"I remember somebody asked David if Nick could sing," says Sighvatsson. "To David, it was just the most absurd thing. Because David doesn't think that way."

Cage was nervous about his limited vocal capacities, but he assented. In a quavering croon modeled after the King, he recorded his own renditions of "Love Me" (which Sailor sings to Lula in a metal club, with Powermad pantomiming as his backing band) and "Love Me Tender" (which Sailor croons at the film's fairy-tale climax, swaying and gazing into Lula's eyes while wearing a prosthetic broken nose) to lip-sync to during the shoot. Real session musicians who had worked with Elvis were hired to accompany him. "They went into a studio with Nick and Nick knocked it out of the park," Lynch says. "I mean, the guy was channeling Elvis! It was incredible."

Lynch did not know that he was activating some nascent rockabilly spirit that had been percolating inside of Cage ever since that aborted Gene Vincent biopic. For years, Cage projected the rebel spirit and gangly sex appeal of a fifties rocker, and he had proven himself a capable crooner in *Peggy Sue Got Married*. When *Wild at Heart* came along, his Elvis obsession entered full bloom. "For a while, the Elvis thing was just happening," Cage told *Newsday*. "One night I was watching [1981 documentary] *This Is Elvis* and, by the time we got to him doing the karate in the jumpsuit, I was just howling on the floor at the tragedy and the absurdity of the situation. And that's when I knew I loved Elvis."[29]

Elvis became a kind of guiding light for Sailor. Cage didn't just play Sailor as an Elvis fan; he approached the character as a conscious imitation of the King, a parody of a parody, soaking up Elvis's mannerisms, from the bad-boy

† Despite Elvis's dwindling hipness, David Lynch wasn't the only celebrated American filmmaker indulging this fascination. *Wild at Heart* was closely preceded by Jim Jarmusch's anthology film *Mystery Train*, in which references to Elvis prominently appear throughout three discrete storylines. The two films premiered at Cannes a year apart.

masculinity to the thick-as-molasses Southern-fried accent. When Sailor tells Lula he wants to go out into "the crazy world o' New *Awl'*ns" and eat a "fried banana sandwich" (a nod to Elvis's favorite snack), he sounds like a spooky reincarnation of the King.

Some of the oddest performance decisions Cage makes in *Wild at Heart* make sense when you view them through Elvis-colored glasses. His dancing in the scene where Sailor and Lula visit a metal club, for instance, is bizarre: a flailing explosion of roundhouse kicks, air punches, and erratic kung-fu moves. Even the members of Powermad, who appear in this scene, were puzzled by Cage's moves. "It is very martial arts-based," says guitarist Todd Haug. "But also, no one does that at a metal show. It was kind of confusing to us."

Yet Sailor's wild dancing can be understood as a warped tribute to Elvis's love of karate. The King earned a first-degree black belt in 1960 and was later known to incorporate karate moves into his concert performances.[30]

The downside of Cage's Elvis-inspired approach in *Wild at Heart* is that his performance arrives wrapped in so many layers of parody and homage that it can dim the film's emotional impact: he's always doing a bit. The movie's heart instead belongs to Dern, whose portrayal of Lula as a passionate, vulnerable, fast-talkin' heroine (who, beyond her blonde hair and sexual appetite, doesn't resemble Marilyn Monroe much at all) ranks among her best work ever. Yet for Cage, that was the puzzle: applying an emotional core to an inherently ridiculous caricature. "To do that and actually put a heart beating behind an Elvis rhythm monologue was the challenge I had," he told the *Washington Post* in 1990.[31]

With rare exceptions (*The Boy in Blue*, *World Trade Center*, *Army of One*[‡]), Cage does not usually portray real people. He does not gravitate to biopics or historical dramas the way, say, Leonardo DiCaprio does. But in his mind, riffing on Elvis in *Wild at Heart* was another chance to defy acting norms that others considered sacrosanct.

"I had this epiphany," Cage later told *Interview* magazine. "I was thinking about Andy Warhol, because I believe that what you can do in one art form, you can do in another. He took icons like Mick Jagger and Elvis Presley, and

‡ In this incoherent 2016 comedy, Cage stars as Gary Faulkner, the ponytailed construction worker who traveled to Pakistan with a samurai sword on a mission to capture Osama bin Laden. Cage spends the entire movie speaking in a pinched-nostril voice that sounds like a cross between himself in *Peggy Sue Got Married*, Dustin Hoffman in *Rain Man*, and an agitated chipmunk—a bizarre choice, given that even the real Gary Faulkner does not speak like that.

made collages out of them. I thought, 'Why can't you do that with a film performance?' And then I read the book *An Actor Prepares* by [Konstantin] Stanislavski, and he said that the worst thing an actor can do is copy another actor.[§] I thought it was a rule that should be broken in the spirit of creating a Warhol-like experience." Lynch approved the choice after Cage told him, "I think Sailor has some sort of a connection with Elvis, and that may be the source power that moves him."[32]

Was it Sailor who had a deep connection with Elvis, or was it Cage? Was there a difference? Was it Elvis's music and raw swagger that drew him in? Or was there a deeper identification with Elvis's story: a troubled boy who overcame a childhood riven with family instability and trauma, only to reinvent himself as a performer and sex symbol in his late teens?

Once Elvis's ghost began using Cage as a host body, it did not let go for years. *Wild at Heart* was only the beginning. A month after the film premiered at Cannes, Cage was spotted impersonating Elvis onstage at a club in Greenwich Village.[33] (Embarrassed by the drunken spectacle, he lamented to an interviewer that summer, "I have these musical dreams and I don't know how to manifest them."[34]) Two years later, Cage rebooted his career with the rom-com *Honeymoon in Vegas*. That movie's climax—wherein our hero leaps out of an airplane filled with Elvis impersonators—almost passed for a meta-commentary on how Elvis kept following Cage around. While promoting *Honeymoon* in 1992, Cage hosted an episode of *Saturday Night Live*; among the characters he played was an action-figure-sized Elvis in a sketch called "Tiny Elvis."

Anyone who has loved a Phish fan knows that music fandom can drive a person to extreme lengths. Still, few anticipated that Cage would go from resembling Elvis's long-lost son in *Wild at Heart* to becoming Elvis's actual son-in-law a decade later. In 2001, the newly divorced Cage met Lisa Marie Presley (daughter of Elvis, ex-wife of Michael Jackson) at a party. Their 2002 marriage lasted just four months—the divorce process took significantly longer than the marriage itself—yet helped immortalize Cage's cultural affiliation with Elvis Presley.

If you wade deep enough into Elvis fan communities, you will encounter questionable theories that Cage married Presley purely so he could view

§ More precisely, the book features an acting instructor named Tortsov (a fictionalized version of Stanislavski), who rebukes a student for imitating an acquaintance in a performance. "At that point you went over to sheer imitation, which has nothing to do with creativeness," Tortsov says.

Elvis's private bedroom on the upstairs level of Graceland, which is strictly forbidden to all except members of the Presley family. Elvis's living quarters are said to look exactly as they did on the day he died; Cage is reportedly the only fan who has gotten a peek. One rumor, according to Dylan Jones's book *Elvis Has Left the Building*, holds that around the twenty-fifth anniversary of Elvis's 1977 death, Cage "sat on the King's 'throne,' composed himself in the prone posture in which Elvis died, stretched out on the King's bed, and even tried on one of his leather jackets."[35]

Jones concludes that this rumor is probably just that. That it even falls within the realm of believability suggests that David Lynch was onto something when he asked Cage to sing those Elvis tunes.

* * *

Wild at Heart is not David Lynch's best movie. It's a little too unruly, overstuffed with characters and subplots and tonal shifts—pulpy melodrama and brutal violence and winking artifice all mushed together. By embracing the highway sprawl of a road movie, Lynch loses some of the precision and focus that made *Blue Velvet* so powerful.

But it *is* Lynch's brashest, rockingest, and sexiest movie by a considerable margin, a curious thing for a director whose work is not often described as sexy. In Lynch's other films, sex is often depicted as a source of anxiety and problems (*Eraserhead*) or as a vehicle of power and humiliation (*Blue Velvet*); "sex-positive" is not exactly the vibe. As critic Lauren Carroll Harris has argued, "Lynchian sex is mostly abusive, manipulative, and humiliating—either non-consensual or barely so."[36]

Wild at Heart is the exception, its bubbling cauldron of violence and menace interlaced with plentiful scenes showing Sailor and Lula conjoined in steamy, sensual embrace (Figure 9.2). It captures the euphoric glow of a youthful relationship, when two partners are endlessly turned on by each other and the sex hasn't turned sour. Lula is neither a victim nor some femme fatale cliché: Dern plays her as sex-crazed and uninhibited and achingly earnest all at once. She brings a vulnerability to lines that might read like silly porno-babble on the page ("I swear, baby, you got the sweetest cock," she coos in one postcoital embrace), while Cage serves up his sensitive bad-boy side.

After the dark sadomasochism of *Blue Velvet*, Lynch liked the idea of portraying a healthy sexual union for once, free of malice and exploitation. "There was so much freedom and so much happiness and so much equality in that relationship, as crazy as they were," Lynch told author Chris Rodley.

Figure 9.2. The erotic abandon of *Wild at Heart* (1990, The Samuel Goldwyn Company) was new territory for Cage. The sex scenes represent Sailor and Lula's (Laura Dern) determination to carve out pleasure and love in a hellish world.

"And Nick Cage and Laura Dern were mentally in line with that."[37] Indeed, Cage in 1990 described the film's sex as "very pure. It's not an exploitative kind of sexuality. I think it's a celebration of sexuality. It's kind of like saying, if you're really in love, it's cool to have radical sex."[38]

These sex scenes occur in rundown motel rooms across the American South, and they serve to reinforce Sailor and Lula's determination to carve out pleasure and love in a hellish world (a juxtaposition illustrated by Lynch's pairing of love scenes with violent flashes of fire).

When asked what emotion he was aiming to capture, Lynch says, "Joyful and hot would be two words." After borrowing a lens device from *Elephant Man* cinematographer Freddie Francis, the director drenched these erotic interludes in bright red and yellow hues to capture the dreamlike high of Sailor and Lula's love. "It does sort of the same thing as pre-flashing the film," Lynch says. "That was really cool, to give each love scene a kind of color and intensity."

It's surprising that, for all of his sexual bravado onscreen, Cage had little experience shooting explicit sex scenes before *Wild at Heart*. There were those love scenes in *Vampire's Kiss*, but those were truncated by bats and violence, and the actor largely kept his clothes on. In *Valley Girl*, the action never progresses beyond heavy petting; in *Raising Arizona*, the copulation is artfully implied; in *Moonstruck*, the camera pans away before the clothes come off, as preferred by Cher, who wore a nude bodystocking to avoid showing skin. ("Boy, everybody made it very clear that she was not gonna be naked in that scene!" recalls *Moonstruck* producer Bonnie Palef.) Weirdly, Cage's raunchiest pre-1990 sex scene was buried in the throwaway sporting drama *The Boy in Blue*, in which our hero engages in some animalistic thrusting with Melody Anderson.

So the erotic abandon of *Wild at Heart*, in which he and Dern can be seen ravaging each other's bodies in all sorts of positions, was new territory for Cage, but it was territory he was eager to explore. The actor made no secret of his healthy fascination with the pleasures of sex. "If I were to become a woman for a day, the first thing I would do is masturbate," he informed *Playboy*, seemingly unprompted, in a bizarre 1989 interview.[39]

Early in the film's production, he, Dern, and Lynch chatted openly about their sex lives and discussed their favorite positions, each of which would be incorporated into the film.[40] In a particularly unusual move, Lynch encouraged Cage and Dern to take an actual road trip together to get comfortable with each other before the shoot. The pair journeyed from Los Angeles to Las Vegas in Cage's '67 Corvette, which he had nicknamed the "Blue Shark." "We just opened up [and] cultivated that trust thing," Cage told the *St. Petersburg Times*.[41]

Rumors swirled that the two had become real-life lovers; Cage insisted they were merely good friends, but the divide between character and reality was clearly blurring more than ever. When it came time to choreograph *Wild at Heart*'s erotic interludes, that trust in each other, and in Lynch not to exploit their naked bodies, proved essential. "In reality, some parts of them were close to Sailor and Lula, and so the sex scenes were really wild and fun. They could do anything with each other and it wasn't twisted," Lynch later recalled.[42]

It's a testament to the perverted glory of *Wild at Heart* that, as raunchy as the movie is, some of the raunchiest scenes of all never made it to the screen. "They were just too much," Sighvatsson says laughing. One such scene depicted Lula having an orgasm while describing a dream in which she was ripped apart by a wild animal. In another, Dern apparently improvised having Lula lower herself onto Sailor's face while murmuring, "Take a bite out of Lula." Dern recalled in 1990 that "a couple of people working on the film saw that scene and said they had to hide their eyes."[43] The scene was eventually excised.

Lynch does not seem to remember these cuts, perhaps because more significant to his mind was the decision to remove a major chunk of the scene in which private eye Johnnie Farragut (Harry Dean Stanton) is tortured and killed by homicidal goons. In its original form, this sickening sequence prompted the Motion Picture Association of America to threaten to give the film an X rating and caused about 125 people to walk out of a test screening.[44] Had it stayed in the picture, Lynch says, "there wouldn't have been anybody in the theater."

* * *

After the dismal flops of *Vampire's Kiss* and *Time to Kill*, *Wild at Heart* gave Cage something he had not had in years: a movie people were seeing, talking about, passionately arguing over. When the film premiered at the 1990 Cannes Film Festival—following a frantic editing process which culminated with Lynch and editor Duwayne Dunham completing the film the night before flying to France—its lurid extremities provoked a polarized reaction unique in the festival's history. On the one hand, the movie played to adoring festivalgoers and won the Palme d'Or. On the other, the prize announcement prompted a loud chorus of boos, including from Roger Ebert, whose review slammed the film as "repulsive and manipulative."[45]

Emotions were high. Some critics hailed *Wild at Heart* as a profound statement. Michael Wilmington of the *Los Angeles Times* described it as a "masterpiece of playful American pathology" and suggested that Cage had emerged "as the ace—or, at the very least, joker—of his acting generation."[46] Others were even harsher than Ebert: David Ansen of *Newsweek* accused the film of "opportunistically trafficking in Lynchian grotesqueries" and compared Lynch to "a kid who never got over his first discovery that life is dirty."[47] Lynch was due for a backlash, and *Wild at Heart* became a sort of hyper-charged Rorschach test, confirming whatever suspicions reviewers already held about him or Cage.

Cage, attending his first Cannes since *Raising Arizona*, lapped it all up. Finally, here was the punk gesture he had longed for. That it revitalized his career far more than the desperate mainstream gasp *Fire Birds* (which hit theaters the same week as Cannes) added a delicious irony. At the festival, Cage seemed to encourage the perception that he and Sailor Ripley weren't far apart; one evening, Ansen reported, during a dinner at a swanky hotel, "he leapt on a table and sang 'Love Me Tender' to the surprised wife of festival organizer Gilles Jacob."[48]

By the time of the film's August theatrical release, Cage's media appearances were growing increasingly bizarre. It was almost as if he had siphoned some of Sailor's swagger for himself. He rambled about Boris Karloff in a *Los Angeles Times* profile and declared himself "a man in search of a spooky-ride style of living."[49] He appeared on British TV program *The Word* and encouraged host Terry Christian to get himself a wooden hand so he could turn on as many women as Cage had in *Moonstruck*. (Women dig wooden hands, Cage insisted.)[50]

Most memorable was an August 24 interview with Irish host Terry Wogan, arguably the actor's strangest television appearance ever. A greasy-haired, leather-jacketed Cage made a spectacular entrance, bolting onstage with a full somersault before tossing dollar bills into the audience and unleashing wild karate kicks. Two minutes in, Cage interrupted his host's questions by ripping off his jacket and shirt, punching the air in a shirtless fervor, and gifting Wogan his *Wild at Heart* t-shirt. His jacket draped loosely over his nipples, the actor spent the rest of the interview regaling Wogan with stories of his troubled youth in between aggressive throat-clearing noises. "I used to like the idea of robbing banks," Cage said. "So at least now I don't really have to rob a bank. I can just do it in a movie."[51]

The outlaw image Cage had spent the better part of a decade carving for himself was undeniably potent. With *Wild at Heart* and *Raising Arizona*—two movies in which his character is hauled off to prison within the first five minutes—Cage solidified his reputation for portraying criminals. Within the next seven years, he would play a small-time thief in *Amos & Andrew*, a drifter unwittingly sucked into a criminal underworld in *Red Rock West*, a psychopathic cokehead henchman in *Deadfall*, an equally psychopathic crime boss in *Kiss of Death*, a mullet-haired prisoner in *Con Air*, and a homicidal terrorist-for-hire in *Face/Off*.

For Cage, such roles were as much a lifeline as a creative preference, a release valve for lawless fantasies. Instead of channeling his most volatile urges into real-life transgression, he could channel them into characters. If it weren't for acting, he told a Scottish newspaper in 1996, he would probably have turned to crime. "I have at times felt criminal tendencies," he said, "but because of the work I have been able to release it. I've kept it on film."[52]

* * *

The paradox of *Wild at Heart* is that no other role finds Cage drifting so far into parody and impersonation, and yet no other performance from this era became quite so intermingled with his real-life persona. What this suggests is that, as much as he is commonly praised as a true original, Cage at his core is also a vehicle for homage, a living and breathing wink to his cinematic heroes, whether it be Elvis in *Wild at Heart* or Max Schreck in *Vampire's Kiss*. The real Nicolas Cage is a pop artist. No wonder he has repeatedly called *Wild at Heart* his Andy Warhol performance.

Some critics recognized this fact. When Wilmington profiled Cage for the *Los Angeles Times* in 1990, he argued that Cage's "borrowing from the past makes him, in some ways, both a throwback and an unusually modern movie actor," whose expressionism "connects with the super-media era of electronically manufactured politicians and stars."[53]

"With any number of other actors, the [*Wild at Heart*] performance could be grotesque, a morbid invention stitched together from the dead and the tired, like Frankenstein's monster," wrote critic Manohla Dargis in a 1995 piece for *Sight & Sound*. "That Cage has thus far avoided the dangers of hollow pastiche has everything to do with the fact that in the final reckoning he's a *failure* as a movie star." In Dargis's assessment, Cage's creative success and commercial limitations (in those pre-*The Rock* days) were essentially linked:

> Despite various turns at top billing and the many films that he's had to carry, Cage remains more of a character actor than not. Undoubtedly one reason critics have had difficulty recognizing Cage is that he doesn't make easy sense as a star. Central to this is a performance style that often works outside the Hollywood rule, more along the lines of Brecht than Stanislavsky or Strasberg. . . . [H]is work on screen doesn't always neatly fit the tradition of seamless realism that has dominated American movies since the 50s.[54]

By the time Dargis wrote those words, Cage had spent a few years dabbling in conventional leading-man roles, yet none had the cultural staying power of *Wild at Heart*. It is by far his best-remembered role from the early half of the nineties. Despite its polarized reviews and moderate commercial return, the film boosted Cage's profile during a turbulent period; and it helped make an unlikely celebrity out of Lynch, too, arriving in tandem with the enormous cult appeal of *Twin Peaks*. In October 1990, *Time* magazine placed the filmmaker on its cover, dubbing him the "Czar of Bizarre."[55] Pretty soon, "Lynchian" had entered the popular lexicon, like "Hitchcockian" or "Capraesque."

Like *Eraserhead*, *Wild at Heart*'s influence makes more sense in hindsight. "If you look at the films that came out after *Wild at Heart*, it opened a door to a certain kind of cinema," Lynch says. "And it had to do with the craziness in the world."

Within two years, a young Quentin Tarantino came to prominence with *Reservoir Dogs*, which crackled with a similarly intoxicating meld of eye-popping violence, irony, and vintage pop-culture references. "I say it was like a precursor to Tarantino," Sighvatsson says of *Wild at Heart*. Indeed, Lynch's film had anticipated the arrival of a more brutal, violent strain of American independent cinema, which flourished in the 1990s. Given this influence, it's odd that *Wild at Heart* remains surprisingly unavailable today. It has never gotten the Criterion treatment bestowed upon other Lynch films, and as of this writing, it is not available on any streaming platforms.

Cage promoted *Wild at Heart* with an enthusiasm he afforded few other films during this era.** By 1993, he seemed to consider it his favorite. "It's my only movie which I can still watch and get lost in without thinking about what I had done in playing the character," he said. "I attribute that to David Lynch being a superior director."[56]

Lynch thought equally highly of Cage, and when *Wild at Heart* was released, he publicly expressed his eagerness to work with the actor again.[57] But although he made Dern something of a regular in his work—granting her major roles in 2006's *Inland Empire* and 2017's *Twin Peaks* revival—he and Cage never reunited. The only exception was *Industrial Symphony No. 1: The Dream of the Brokenhearted*, an avant-garde performance piece/short film about a woman who is spurned by her lover and then hallucinates a dreamy flood of music and visuals. Lynch filmed *Industrial Symphony No. 1* very soon after wrapping *Wild at Heart*, and he had Cage and Dern appear in the first three minutes (seemingly still in character as Sailor and Lula, though their identities are never stated) as the couple breaking up.

Industrial Symphony No. 1 was staged in 1989 and released on VHS in 1990, and Lynch has not worked with Cage since. When I ask why, Lynch insists that he has no aversion to reuniting with Cage. "It just wasn't right for some reason," the director says. "And it never happened. But it could happen

** It's likely he would have promoted *Vampire's Kiss* with similar fervor had the film gotten a proper promotional push, and had he not been dismayed by cuts made to his performance.

tomorrow! You never know." That would be an exciting development, I say. "I would love to work with Nick again, are you kidding? I think he's one of the all-time greats."

On numerous occasions, Lynch described Cage as the jazz musician of actors. What did he mean by that?

"The thing is, he can riff on a thing," Lynch says. "He can get into it and keep going! He can keep going!"

* * *

In the spring of 1990, six months after filming *Wild at Heart*, Cage was back in New Orleans, shooting more softcore love scenes in varying degrees of nudity. These weren't reshoots for Lynch's film. This was a different movie, a racy erotic thriller which would eventually be known as *Zandalee*. Heavily flawed, and forgotten by all but the most devout Cage fans, *Zandalee* remains one of the most fascinating and provocative failures in Cage's career—and it offers a dark counterpart to his erotic swagger in *Wild at Heart*.

The surface similarities between *Wild at Heart* and *Zandalee* are striking. Both were made around the same time, set at least partially in New Orleans, and loaded with copious nudity and desire. I've chosen to group the two films into the same chapter for these reasons, yes, but also because they're both products of a more permissive era in which Cage, like other stars of his generation, was pushing himself toward frank, visceral expressions of sexuality.

By 1991, *Wild at Heart* and *Zandalee* contained the two most erotic performances Cage had given by far, yet they seemed to form a deliberate contrast. In *Wild at Heart*, passionate sex nourishes the bond of a committed relationship; in *Zandalee*, it destroys one. In *Wild at Heart*, sexuality is a respite from ruthless violence; in *Zandalee*, it is the cause of violence.

Cage was intrigued by this duality. *Zandalee* "is sort of an exploration of sexuality, but the dark side of it," he told the *Washington Post* in 1990. "*Wild at Heart* was such a happy side to that, I thought. Whereas in [*Zandalee*], it's almost like a religion to this character. He takes it too far. He's an obsessive, a psychotic adulterer. It results in death."[58]

He was also drawn to *Zandalee* as a vehicle to exorcise dark emotions. "That was a movie I made which was a very dark example of sexuality—something that I was living through—and I wanted to express it," he later told an interviewer. "I wouldn't have done it if I had not been getting betrayed in my own personal life. I wanted to be the 'other guy.'"[59]

* * *

Set in the fragrant bohemian culture of New Orleans, *Zandalee* explores a love triangle between three tortured twenty-somethings. Zandalee (Erika Anderson) is a ravishing young woman married to Thierry (Judge Reinhold), a failed poet who has abandoned his dreams to run his recently deceased father's business. Zandalee is bored in the marriage and sexually frustrated; Thierry no longer turns her on. He may even be impotent, though he seems more adrift in a spiritual sense: "I'm just paralyzed—a paraplegic of the soul," he informs Zandalee after an aborted attempt at sex. Thierry spends his time drinking heavily and ruminating on his disillusionment while dressed like a Southern aristocrat in steady decay.

When Thierry's boyhood friend Johnny comes to town, Zandalee is first irritated by him, then intrigued. Johnny (Cage, sporting a horrid goatee that belongs on the wall of fame at a small-town bowling alley) is an impulsive and free-spirited painter who deals drugs on the side. Johnny's only moral code is to pursue pleasure at all costs, without concern for others. He's the type of guy who wears his hair in a flowing mullet and says things like "I wanna shake you naked and eat you alive" to women he desires. And Zandalee is one such woman.

They begin a tumultuous affair, satisfying their dirtiest desires on a washing machine, in a church, and anywhere they can. Eventually, Zandalee tries to pump the brakes and reconcile with her now-suspicious husband. They decide to start clean on a romantic getaway, but Johnny won't relent. He follows the couple to the Louisiana bayou, where his obsessive infatuation with Zandalee leads to a tragic climax.

The film's screenwriter, New Orleans–based Mari Kornhauser, had a long-standing interest in pornographic literature, from Marquis de Sade to Georges Bataille. She loosely based the story on *Thérèse Raquin*, the scandalous 1867 novel by French author Émile Zola. Her working title was *Adios Thierry*.[60]

Kornhauser also drew on her own experiences as a trauma survivor. "I was exploring things like trauma and responsibility between partners, based on things that happened to me, where you're being pushed too far," Kornhauser says. "And then I wanted to make it a noir. It fit into that long lineage."

The screenwriter adds, "I was doing high melodrama and doing what I call the 'sex noir.' One of the things I was examining was the fine line between eroticism and pornography with your lover when you're exploring different spaces in having sex. But all that subtext and metaphor was kind of lost. Because when production goes sideways, those are the things that go."

Kornhauser describes it as an extremely personal script and wonders in retrospect if it ought to have been directed by a woman. "I didn't have enough confidence to even approach directing it at that point. The industry was not female-friendly," she says. So Kornhauser showed the screenplay to her friend and then-manager, William Blaylock, who decided to produce it. A French producer named Nicole Seguin also expressed interest; Seguin's production company, Electric Pictures, took on the project and put up some financing.[61]

Eventually, the film's title morphed into *Zandalee*. "My joke has always been, the film was called *Adios Thierry*, which is great, and then they changed the title to *Zandalee*, so it went from A to Z real fast for me as a writer," Kornhauser says. "I can separate what was supposed to be the film, which is the script, and the actual film because they have separate titles, which is really good for me psychologically."

* * *

Sometimes when Sam Pillsbury reads a script, he can sense in the core of his being that he knows how to make the film work. *Zandalee*, née *Adios Thierry*, was not one of those scripts.

"I never got that feeling when I read it that I knew how to make this movie work," Pillsbury says. "It all came to me about twenty years later. I woke up one morning and thought, 'Ah! That's what I should have done.'"

In 1989, when he was hired to direct *Zandalee*, Pillsbury was a seasoned New Zealand filmmaker new to Hollywood. He had an agent at ICM, where the script made the rounds. *Zandalee* struck him as an interesting challenge. "Nicolas was interested as an ICM client," Pillsbury says. "They put Nicolas and I together and we got on like a house on fire."

Pillsbury assembled an enviable cast, including supporting players Marisa Tomei (as Johnny's girlfriend) and Steve Buscemi (as a deceptively wise beggar), both on the cusp of fame. Cage was the clear choice to play the wild-eyed Johnny, but casting Zandalee proved more difficult. Hundreds of actresses read for the part with Judge Reinhold, but many balked at the copious nudity and sex.

The producers eventually settled on Erika Anderson, a twenty-six-year-old actress and model from Oklahoma whose only feature credit was *A Nightmare on Elm Street 5*. Though inexperienced in the acting department,

Anderson had grown up around art—her father was a sculptor—and was not frightened of the explicit material.[62]

"The script required a great deal. There were love scenes with both actors and they were fairly intense," says Anderson, who recalls auditioning seven times and reading opposite Cage. "They needed somebody who wasn't afraid to do that. That's a tall order for somebody who's new."

Meanwhile, *Zandalee* reunited Cage with Judge Reinhold, who had beaten him out for a role in *Fast Times at Ridgemont High*. By 1990, Reinhold's career in comedy was flailing. His body-reversal comedy *Vice Versa* had been a flop, and roles were drying up.[63] As ludicrous as it seems to write this sentence, *Zandalee* was intended to rescue Reinhold's career and establish his dramatic chops. "I've been hiding behind comedy my whole life," he told a writer for *Premiere* who visited the film set. "Some of the movies I've done I would not have gone to see myself. And this is a movie I am very proud to say I would really run to see."

Reinhold wound up co-producing the film and tweaking the script. He had high hopes. Everyone did: "[T]his is going to be a serious movie, a romantic tragedy," *Premiere* stated, assessing the hopeful vibe on set. "What they are shooting, say the director, the producers, the cameraman, and the actors, is a sort of *Last Tango in New Orleans*."[64]

Maybe that seems like an odd way to talk about a movie in which Nicolas Cage licks whipped cream off a stripper's breasts, but the early nineties were a different galaxy. The success of *Fatal Attraction* (1987) had brought the erotic thriller to the forefront of Hollywood attention, and HBO, coupled with the emerging home video market, had triggered a new demand for soft-core, adult-oriented content. As early as 1986, Cage had mentioned his desire to play "a character that's driven by a very strong sexual impulse, which can possibly lead to doom." At last, he had his chance.[65]

Unlike *Vampire's Kiss*, the money wasn't bad, either: Cage was paid around $1 million, according to producer William Blaylock—a significant chunk of the film's budget, which hovered around $7 million.[††]

Cage requested a meeting with Kornhauser. The screenwriter visited his El Royale apartment. The actor opened the door wearing a velvet robe, like he had just woken up. She sat on the floor and discussed the script. "I just

[††] A *Premiere* feature put the figure at $7 million. Pillsbury says he got ripped off. "I never received my full salary. I've never received a penny in residuals from it," the director says. "[The producers] said it was a $7 million movie and at 1.5 million they stopped the funds flowing. The crew stayed on for another five days and worked for me for free to finish it."

remember feeling really comfortable with Nick and thinking, 'Oh, man, I want this apartment. I want that robe. I hope he wants to do the part—he's perfect,'" Kornhauser recalls.

"In retrospect, I can't imagine anyone else playing it," says Eyal Rimmon, one of the film's producers. "The story called for someone who's rocking her life—pulling her out of her miserable boredom in her married life, lighting this huge fire of passion and decadence." Rimmon had seen *Moonstruck* and *Vampire's Kiss* and knew Cage was his guy: capable of summoning that fervent passion, but also on the short list of stars the financiers would approve. Plus, Rimmon liked the contrast between Cage's muscular, towering figure and Reinhold's slenderer frame.

Initially, though, Cage wasn't available. He had been offered the lead in the helicopter flick *Fire Birds*, and planned to shoot *Wild at Heart* and *Fire Birds* back-to-back during the summer and fall of 1989. The producers wanted Cage so badly that they offered to push the shoot back to 1990 to accommodate his schedule. "I went back to Limato and said, 'If we let him do the other two films, will he commit now to doing ours?'" Blaylock remembers.

That's when Cage signed on for the raciest movie of his career.

* * *

By the time Cage flew to New Orleans in February 1990, he seemed to have absorbed the wild essence of Johnny Collins.

"He assumed the character of that lunatic guy from the moment he arrived," director Pillsbury says. "I picked him up at the airport. I was a bit shocked when I saw him, because he looked so different. He looked like a fucking lunatic."

The film's producers had envisioned Cage being coiffed like his regular self. Instead, Cage showed up wearing hair extensions and a goatee/soul patch monstrosity, looking like he had busted out of the screen at an adult movie house like Jeff Daniels in *The Purple Rose of Cairo*. Somehow, he convinced them this should be the character's look.

Throughout *Zandalee*, Cage displays a flamboyant sexual swagger. He slips in and out of a N'awlins drawl—sounding, in critic Nathan Rabin's estimation, "like a New Orleans Elvis mumbling with a mouthful of peanut butter"—yet never quite commits to the dialect as fully as Judge Reinhold. Still, the Southernness of the character, coupled with the long, flowing hair, makes Johnny Collins seem like the perverted ancestor to Cameron Poe in *Con Air*.[66]

The *Zandalee* production was a spirited affair, headquartered in the French Quarter and seeking to capture the neighborhood's bohemian milieu and cultivation of decay. Producer Eyal Rimmon describes the shoot as a freewheeling experience, soaked with alcohol. "There was a sense of some kind of decadence to it," Rimmon says. "In a way, it was very useful to the movie. The whole story is about this spiral of self-destruction."

Cage was in fine spirits. "We would go out to restaurants and he would stand up on a table and sing songs for the people in the restaurant, which they loved," Pillsbury says.

Yet the actor could also focus when it was time to work. Pillsbury was impressed with the star's professionalism. "Judge Reinhold was a nightmare to work with. Nicolas Cage was a sweetheart," the director recalls. "Go figure."

At the time, Reinhold was a recovering alcoholic facing a declining career. Multiple sources attest that his short temper—perhaps exacerbated by an unspoken rivalry with Cage, which is personified onscreen by a ludicrous dance-off set to Cajun music—made filming difficult. Crew members learned to fear Reinhold's explosions of anger, and Anderson was hurt when he insulted her in front of the whole set, screaming that they should have hired a real actress instead of "some fucking model." Even journalist Phoebe Hoban, visiting the set for *Premiere*, observed that "Reinhold in a rage is not a funny sight." (Reinhold did not respond to interview requests for this book.)[67]

Pillsbury eventually lost patience with Reinhold's tendency for throwing fits. "He just got worse and worse throughout the movie," Pillsbury says. "But he would never behave badly if Nicolas was around. And Nicolas was always a gentleman."

* * *

Zandalee is the horniest film in Cage's filmography. That says a lot, considering his filmography includes *Moonstruck*, *Wild at Heart*, and the bewilderingly bad *Between Worlds*.[‡‡]

Cage was already a reluctant sex symbol by the late 1980s. But in *Zandalee*, he took sensuality to a dark extreme, playing a copulation-crazed maniac who uses sex as an instrument of power and obsession, a source of validation more reliable than his middling art career. If operatic passion is what

‡‡ A 2017 film, in which Cage's character has raucous sex with a woman possessed by the ghost of his dead wife while reciting a poem containing lines like "Your peach juice cascaded over and upon my golden cock."

lets Cage sail away from realism in *Moonstruck*, and insanity is the narrative device that justifies his antics in *Vampire's Kiss*, then insatiable horniness is the drug that activates Cage's overheated lunacy in *Zandalee*. It wraps around his every gesture like a gauze. It is the lens through which to understand this performance.

For this character, sex is a mind-altering substance. It drives him to disturbing and indefensible behavior. It distracts him from work—early on, Johnny describes what it's like to paint nude models: "When that big, red snatch is coming right up against your face like a freight train, it's pretty hard to paint, I'll tell you what!" In the modern parlance, Johnny might be described as a dirtbag.

Appalled by his crude manner, Zandalee shoves off his advances. Then, fed up with Thierry's distant demeanor, she encounters Johnny in a rainstorm and submits to his desires. Soon the sex-starved Zandalee and her new lover are moaning in ecstasy on a mattress in Johnny's studio as a sighing ambient score sets the mood (Figure 9.3).

Figure 9.3. Johnny (Cage) and Zandalee (Erika Anderson) share a steamy embrace in the erotic thriller *Zandalee* (1991, LIVE Entertainment). For the role, Cage was determined to embody a darker side of sexuality—a corrupter of innocence.

Cage's role in this love triangle may evoke *Moonstruck*, but this is no PG rom-com; the sex is vivid and frequent, and Anderson spends much of the film without clothes. Cage told *Premiere* during the filming, "There are the most sex scenes in a movie that I've ever seen. It's just chock-full of sex." While these soft-core interludes are doused in an animalistic lust that sometimes crosses over into goofiness, the lucid intensity of the love scenes—and their variety of moods and backdrops—is what gives the movie its texture and emotional arc.[68]

At his most tender, Johnny fingerpaints Zandalee's breasts in a bizarre postcoital ritual. At his most perverse, he screws her atop a washing machine while Thierry hosts a dinner party in the adjoining room. "Take my dumb, coon-ass prick inside of you with your husband in the next room," he orders. She obeys.

She doesn't love Johnny. She calls out Thierry's name during sex with Johnny, seemingly using the latter's body as a sexual stand-in. But Johnny wants Zandalee all for himself.

Cage clearly relished playing such a depraved character. "I think Johnny is a sort of vampire of innocence," he mused in 1990. "He wants to corrupt innocence because it is very seductive to him. He wants to push all his impulses to the edge, like an orange-juice machine extracting the juice. He's almost like a messenger of temptation."[69]

The film is suffused with religious imagery. Zandalee keeps a wooden cross on her bedroom wall; she later wears a gold cross around her neck as she mourns Thierry at the cemetery. But her faith is desecrated by lust. In a pivotal scene, Johnny follows Zandalee into a church, screams obscenities when she resists his exhortations to leave Thierry, then forces himself on her. "Isn't this the way He really shows Himself to us?" he muses. He enters her from behind in the confessional booth; it is not consensual. "Thank you, Father," Johnny pants, gazing heavenward, as he climaxes.

She flees the sanctuary in guilt and disgust. "I freed you!" Johnny insists. But unlike in *Wild at Heart*, the sex in *Zandalee* brings the opposite of freedom.

From the start, Pillsbury believed that the film ought to depict sex as realistically and unflinchingly as possible. For all three leads, this required baring a good deal of skin. "I think we were all nervous about it," says Anderson.

"One of the things I hate about American films is when they have sex scenes and the guy's in bed with a woman and she has her bra and panties on. It's so ludicrous," Pillsbury says. "I talked to Erika and Nick about this and we agreed we would do these love scenes with no clothes on. We would just be careful about what we showed."

Yet the director was also conscious of Hollywood's eternal double standard: you can show a woman in full-frontal nudity, but not a man. "Nicolas didn't want his genitals to be shown, and I respected that and also think it was probably a good idea," Pillsbury recalls. "I just tried to do [the scenes] in a way that felt real. There was one five-frame bit where you could see his penis in one of the shots, and he was very upset about it. He went to the lab, and we cut those five frames out of the negative.

"The next time we shot a nude scene, he wrapped duct tape around his genitals," Pillsbury adds, laughing. "And it cost us an hour of production time. I hung around after wrap to watch him take the duct tape off because I kind of wanted to see him suffer."

Producer Blaylock recalls viewing dailies of a different sex scene (or perhaps the same) with Cage and Pillsbury. He could see the displeasure on Cage's face. "They'd actually gone too far. They were just a little too graphic," Blaylock says.

Blaylock decided the scene needed to be reshot. "I went to the editor and said, 'Get me all the outtakes from those scenes from last night and the negatives. Put 'em in a box.' "

The next morning, Blaylock got a call from Ed Limato. "William, we got a problem," Limato said, referring to the graphic love scene. Blaylock reassured him that he already put the negatives in a box: "We sealed it. And we're sending it to you. And we'll reshoot everything."

* * *

Among the young notables with a bit part in *Zandalee* was Zach Galligan, a twenty-six-year-old actor best known for starring in the campy horror classic *Gremlins*. Galligan was offered the role of Rog, an art dealer interested in Johnny's work. It was a nothing role—basically a glorified cameo—but Galligan liked the idea of a free trip to New Orleans and jumped at the chance to work with Cage, who had fascinated him since *Birdy*.

"The thing I was struck by before I even met him was, he's one month older than I am," Galligan says. "I never really had a masculine, manly quality. I'm not Robert Mitchum. I'm not Gregory Peck. I'm not Mr. Testosterone Guy. Probably couldn't grow a full beard until I was thirty-two. *Cute, preppy pretty-boy* was what I was type-cast in. So, I was always intrigued by Nick because it just seemed like, he's romancing Cher in *Moonstruck* and the dude's twenty-two years old! He seems like he's *thirty*-two years old! He's big, he's well-built, he's a muscular guy. All of those things were reinforced when I finally met him."

The first time Galligan spotted him in the flesh, Cage was in a makeup trailer on the *Zandalee* set, listening to Elvis Presley. It was March 1990, and *Wild at Heart* had wrapped only a few months prior. By chance, Galligan had also been on an Elvis kick. He started chatting Cage up, asking if he knew certain songs. "He was like, 'Oh my God, you know Elvis?' " Galligan recalls.

Galligan found Cage friendly and charming. The two actors quickly bonded over music and gonzo humor. "I played him this absolutely preposterous Barry White song, which has a line in it where he says, 'I don't wanna feel no clothes / I don't wanna see no panties / And take off that brassiere, my dear,' " Galligan says. "When I played it for him, we sang 'Take off that *brassiere*, my dear' together at the same time. And we laughed hysterically. I thought, 'I'm gonna get along with this guy fine.' "

The two were still giggling to themselves a few moments later when it was time to shoot their first scene together. The scene was just a fleeting interaction where Johnny (Cage) runs into the snooty art dealer (Galligan) on the street. "If you watch it, you can see that he and I still have the giggles, because we're cracking each other up," Galligan says.

After that, Galligan had five days off. He recalls five days of wild boozing and merriment with the cast and crew in New Orleans—hanging around a bar called the Blue Diamond, pounding shots, watching Steve Buscemi take shots, etc.

Cage was at the center of it all, reveling in what he didn't know would be his last shoot before becoming a father. He wasn't inhabiting his character as literally as he was during the *Birdy* days, but Cage still seemed to carry traces of Johnny's aura offscreen. "There was something very powerful about his presence and about his command," Rimmon says. "He was not being [Johnny]. But the intensity and physicality were there. The way that he gestured around. It was always big gestures and emotions and physicality."

In other ways, Cage seemed to be still in character as Sailor Ripley: the Elvis fixation, the singing, even the snakeskin jacket. "He apparently had fallen in love with his suit from *Wild at Heart*. And was wearing it everywhere," Galligan reports. When Cage first strolled into the Blue Diamond, he was dressed like Sailor, Galligan says. "Like, exactly. But nobody had seen the movie, so we weren't like, 'Oh my God, here's this thing from *Wild at Heart*!' "

Rimmon points to Cage's outrageous screen entrance in *Zandalee*, which is pure zonked-out rock-star theatrics: he materializes in the corridor of a strip club, gives a wild hair-flip, and swaggers toward the party. "Even in *Zandalee*," Rimmon says, "there was some aspect of Elvis in the character."

Anderson, though, saw a more sacrilegious element in Cage's look. "Zandalee's supposed to be this upright Catholic girl, but then he shows up looking like Jesus."

* * *

After five days of partying, Zach Galligan returned to set for his second scene—the sequence where Galligan's character, Rog, visits an unstable Johnny, who is at his art studio, distraught, following Thierry's death. In the script, this was a fleeting interaction: Rog assesses Johnny's recent paintings and insults him by praising one of his earlier works instead. "The way it was scripted, [Johnny] goes, 'Alright, man. Cool. Thanks for stopping by,'" Galligan says. "That's the scene."

They rehearsed it a few times in the French Quarter warehouse that passed for Johnny's studio. Then Pillsbury wanted to shoot a take. What happened next occurred so fast that Galligan barely had time to get nervous. "Nick grabs me on the shoulder and goes, 'Hey, um, I might improv a little bit. Is that OK?' We're ten seconds away from going! And I'm like, 'Yeah, that's fine.' He's the star of the movie. He's Nick Cage. I'm on a plane tomorrow."

As the camera rolled, Galligan was focusing on staying in the center of the camera frame But before he had even finished his line encouraging Johnny to return to his earlier style, Cage veered way off-script and let loose a tirade of fury: "Well, in seventy-five years you're gonna be fucking dead and I'm gonna be standing next to *Picasso* and *Vincent*! So get the fuck out of here!" Cage thrust his arms around violently, not unlike the outrageous choreography he'd brought to *Vampire's Kiss*. It was fully ad-libbed.

"He explodes and screams in my face and has a cocaine-induced temper tantrum out of nowhere," Galligan says, referring to the character's coke addiction. "It only takes half a second in the movie. But it probably took 10,000 seconds in my mind. I'm sitting here going, 'What the fuck just happened?'"

His mind spinning wildly, Galligan remained in character, telling Johnny to call him when he had some new work. "To me, it was kind of thrilling," he says, "because it was the first time I had ever done anything on camera where anything could happen."

Remarkably, it was the only take Pillsbury filmed. "That was the print," Galligan says. "One take. That's what's in the movie—the explosion. And [Cage] comes up to me afterwards and goes, 'Is that OK, man? I just felt it, so I went with it.' And the first AD's like, 'Moving on!' "

Galligan's work was done, but he remained on set while Cage filmed the scene where he destroys his paintings, covers himself in black paint, and howls like his gallbladder is on fire. "I stayed and watched him do that. And I was like, 'This guy is one of the most intense people I've ever seen in my life.' And that's saying a lot, because I worked with Ellen Burstyn on a TV movie."

Galligan adds, "Nick was just a supernova of intense focus and concentration, and he seemed to be super-focused on one thing: never wanted to be predictable. Never wanted to know what he was doing. Always wanted the audience to be one step behind him. . . . Nobody I worked with in that period came close in any way, shape, or form to the type of risk-taking and tightrope-walking he was doing."

This stretch of *Zandalee* is indicative of how much Cage's choices shaped the climax. In the most bracing sequence, Johnny smears black paint all over his body and screams in a fit of rage and self-destruction. This remains one of Cage's most operatic onscreen meltdowns. "Nobody knew he was going to do that," says Anderson. "I think people were a little bit frightened. Because it was so intense. But it's also thrilling."

"That wasn't in the script," Pillsbury confirms. "That was his idea." When the director called out cut, he fell on the floor and laughed hysterically.

"Quite a bit of the time in that movie, I was working in the dark," he adds. "As a director, you can't afford to do that very often. You have to know this creature that you're giving birth to has got all its limbs."

* * *

Cage's personal life was in a tumultuous way when he made *Zandalee*. The film offered an escape. He formed a close connection with Anderson, his partner in high-grade smut. "He was in a very, very contentious relationship with Christina Fulton at the time," says Anderson. "It was just madness."

Cage had begun dating Fulton, a young actress and model, in 1988. They moved in together at the El Royale, to the horror of the apartment's rental agents, who eventually sued the couple for causing severe flooding and water damage, apparently from leaking shark tanks. By the early nineties, the relationship was tabloid fodder. The pair would make bets with each other in which the losing partner had to do "something humiliating," Page Six reported; Cage once reportedly made Fulton walk down the street screaming, "Round and round I go, down and down I go!"[70]

When Fulton visited Cage during the filming of *Zandalee*, the actor's mood seemed to shift. "He was more uptight when she was around," says Anderson. "He was tense."

In the meantime, Cage grew close with Anderson. She had far less acting experience than her co-stars, and Pillsbury had to work extensively with her to elicit a convincing performance. "There was a point where we were not 100 percent sure Erika was up to par to play the role," says producer Rimmon. "[Cage] was of the opposite opinion. He felt she was doing a good job. Something about her innocence rubbed off the right way on the film."[71]

Cage opened up to Anderson. One day, he told her about his secret formula for choosing roles. "He would do one film for his agent. He would do one film for himself. And he would do one film for art. That was the pattern he tried to follow," Anderson recalls. "I think we were the art film."

One evening, Cage hung out with Anderson at the townhouse where she was staying. At the end of the night, they wound up turning off all the lights and playing hide-and-seek. "Like children!" Anderson recalls. "It was completely ridiculous. I'm a grown woman, he's a grown man. It was a blast, though."

Other times, Cage would invite Anderson to dinner and not show up. She would get angry, then realize he was stoking her anger for the sake of her performance. "I think it was manipulative," Anderson says. "I think all of it probably fed the script. I don't remember what scene I was doing the next day. But I was really mad. And I think it helped. He didn't do anything awful. It was just little things that would propel the story."

With Reinhold, Anderson tried to develop a rapport similar to their scripted roles: a passionless marriage. They went to dinner and called each other at night, as though obligated. With Cage, everything was wilder and more spontaneous. "There was a rivalry going on between him and Judge that kind of carried on throughout the entire film," Anderson recalls.

As was Cage's tendency, the lines between movie and reality began to blur. Cage was daring and intense, just like Johnny. And Anderson was caught between two men, just like Zandalee. "If it was a rainy day, I would have love scenes with Judge. If it was a sunny day, I would have love scenes with Nick. We shot them all together in a period of three days. I felt kind of compromised," she says.

At times, Anderson sensed both actors vying for her attention. "When I had love scenes with Nick, Judge was nowhere to be found. He was not on set," Anderson says. "If I had gone out with Nick the night before and Judge knew about it, there was just an underlying rivalry."

She and Cage did not have a romantic relationship, she says. But the evidence suggests he was smitten. Toward the end of the shoot, when Anderson was upset with him, he surprised her with a gift—an antique watch ring from the 1920s, engraved with the words *TO EA, FROM NC*. She was amazed.

The actress's collaboration with Cage felt all-consuming and intense. After the shoot, back in Los Angeles, they remained friends. "He called me in the middle of the night one time," Anderson recalls. "He calls at four o'clock in the morning and leaves me this message saying, 'That's it! We're going to Vegas! I'm coming over to get you and we're gonna go to Vegas and we're gonna get married.' Completely enthusiastic, out of nowhere, in the middle of the night. I'm sleeping. Like, *how* am I supposed to explain that?"

Was he serious? "I have no idea," Anderson admits. She was in love with her boyfriend at the time. "I think he saw that as a challenge." She ignored the message.

"He called me another time in the middle of the night freaking out because his cat was having kittens and he didn't know what to do," Anderson says. "So I got in my car and I drove over there and I sat with him in the closet while the cat had babies."

* * *

Sam Pillsbury is the first to admit that *Zandalee* doesn't really work. It wasn't until decades later that the fatal flaw dawned on him: Johnny seems crazy from the beginning. "I hadn't thought about his character arc enough. If I had somehow known better at the time, I would have started him plausible and worked up to that fucking lunatic," Pillsbury says.

He now feels similarly about the love scenes: they were too confrontational, at least for American audiences. "They should have started very gentle and tender. It would have been an interesting journey to watch. It was my mistake. I did not have a good grip on how to make that movie work."[§§]

[§§] The international cut of *Zandalee* is even more explicit than the American version, which was censored to avoid an NC-17 rating. Notably, the international version includes more graphic shots of Johnny violently thrusting into Zandalee during their first lovemaking session, as well as a bizarre sequence in which he mixes olive oil with cocaine and rubs the mixture over Zandalee's nude body. These scenes are omitted from the film on U.S. streaming platforms.

At one test screening, he says, half the audience walked out. Despite receiving a theatrical release in various European countries, *Zandalee* went straight to video in the United States. Critics ridiculed it. "It's quite a while before it sinks in that this movie isn't an *Airplane!*-style send-up of such trash classics as *9½ Weeks*, *Two Moon Junction*, and *Wild Orchid*," wrote Kevin Hennessey in *Movieline*.[72]

Screenwriter Kornhauser was frustrated when reviewers blamed her for the film's shortcomings. "They didn't shoot the script. My version of what the film would be is in the script, because they left so much out," Kornhauser says. "They really are two different animals."

The writer regards *Zandalee* as a missed opportunity. A large portion of her third act—what she describes as "this operatic melodrama as people start to unravel and lose their minds"—was left unfilmed. Over the years, she has had conversations with female directors she wishes had directed the film. "Or I would have directed it and it would have been a hot mess, but at least *I* would have directed and it would have been a hot mess."

In 1991, *Zandalee* became the second Cage film in two years to flop so hard it almost annihilated its director's stateside career. The first was *Vampire's Kiss*, whose British director, Robert Bierman, had a blossoming career in America before *Vampire's Kiss* sucked the blood right out of it, causing him to pivot to BBC dramas. As for Pillsbury, he says he was approached to direct 1993's *Sleepless in Seattle* in the early nineties. "I could have done that movie with my hands tied," Pillsbury says. "Then they saw a cut of *Zandalee* and they just looked at me in horror and said, 'How could you do a movie like that?'"

Pillsbury moved on from the *Zandalee* drubbing, directing a spate of made-for-TV dramas, as well as *Free Willy 3: The Rescue*. But his career never fully recovered. "I had my own independent income," Pillsbury says. "I was fine. I knew I wouldn't be destroyed if [*Zandalee*] was a disaster. But it did pretty much keep me out of the big time." Eventually, he left the business entirely to enjoy a second career as a winemaker.

Anderson, meanwhile, was crushed. *Zandalee* was supposed to be her breakthrough role after years in the modeling trenches. "I thought it was going to get a full theatrical release," Anderson says. "It was a very high-profile role. It had visibility in the industry, and then it just got dropped. At the time, I was really devastated." She starred in a few other straight-to-video releases, but by the end of the nineties, her acting career had dried up.

Cage was largely unscathed. By the time *Zandalee* came out, he was riding high on the success of *Wild at Heart*. Nothing seemed to crack his armor—not the poor reception of *Zandalee*, not the tabloid coverage of his and Fulton's messy breakup, not even an embarrassing incident in which he was nearly jailed for an airplane prank in 1990. (Midway through a flight, Cage commandeered the P.A. system and pretended to be the pilot. As a joke, he said he was feeling unwell and losing control of the aircraft; passengers started screaming. Upon landing, Cage was greeted by six police officers. Remarkably, he "very delicately and politely talked my way out of going to airport jail."[73])

Cage was living—and spending—large. In 1991, a few months after *Zandalee*'s release, Zach Galligan attended a New Year's party at the actor's Hollywood mansion. Also in attendance were Charlie Sheen and Cary Elwes, among other stars of the day.

Galligan was stunned by the opulence in which his friend was living. When Cage saw him waiting to use the bathroom, he shepherded Galligan into the bedroom, where a private bathroom awaited. Galligan stared at the unusual décor. At the foot of Cage's bed was a table holding a plexiglass case. Inside the case was a sculpture of a bumblebee.

"It's a giant bumblebee in a box!" Galligan recalls. "If somebody's like, 'Hey, I want to make a bumblebee but I want to make it fifty times its actual size,' this is what it would look like. I come out of the bathroom and I look at the bee and he goes, 'That's a huge bee, isn't it!' And I go, 'That's a huge bee, yeah!' "

Cage then pressed a secret button, and a flat-screen television clicked into place. "It's one of the earliest plasma TVs I've ever seen," says Galligan. "He had it installed at the foot of his bed and it had this, like, hydraulic lift."

At twenty-seven, Cage was living a life of Hollywood luxury. He also had a new baby to support, and had not appeared in a major box office success in four years. Much as he concealed it from friends, he had a secret: he needed money.

***

Despite its failure, *Zandalee* consummated Cage's unusual connection to New Orleans. There is some mysterious quality about New Orleans that unleashes Cage's most sexually aggressive performances. Maybe it is a molecule found only in Cajun seasoning. He fell in love with the city while filming *Wild at Heart* and *Zandalee* back-to-back. He returned in 2002 to shoot his directorial debut, *Sonny*, a meandering drama that locks in only when Cage himself briefly appears onscreen, as a flamboyant, cane-wielding pimp known as Acid Yellow, who struts around snorting cocaine in a frilly yellow suit.

That was before Cage entered new realms of depravity in a movie with New Orleans in the title: Werner Herzog's hallucinatory *Bad Lieutenant: Port of Call New Orleans* (2009), starring the actor as a crack-addicted cop stalking around post-Katrina New Orleans, threatening, snorting, and fucking everything in his path.

Clearly, Cage's wild side thrives in New Orleans. "My ability coalesces with the genius of a place," he claimed in a *New York Times Magazine* interview. "I've made very good movies in Las Vegas; there's a *genius loci* that is a good match for me. New Orleans has a *genius loci*." He added, "I became a man in New Orleans, if you know what I mean. The city has a soft spot in my heart."[74]

In 2010, Cage bought a white pyramid tomb in New Orleans for $20,000. It is where he intends to be buried.[75]

10
The Sunshine Trilogy

For years, Nicolas Cage had been floating in some nebulous space between character actor and leading man, and that was how he liked it. The rare films where he unambiguously reached for the latter category, where he tried embodying a hunkish, uncomplicated hero—1986's *The Boy in Blue*, 1990's *Fire Birds*—were ones that he regarded as creative failures. But that whole calculus was about to shift.

In 1991, Cage was twenty-seven, a new dad, and beginning to grow tired of the wild-man image. His reputation was solidified—the *Los Angeles Times* had dubbed him "crown prince of the darker realms of absurdity"—but Cage resented that people conflated him with the rogues' gallery of wackos and criminals he had played onscreen.[1] He complained that people thought he really had a wooden hand (he didn't) or wore a snakeskin jacket (he did). He feared his abrasive reputation was costing him worthwhile roles. "I became aware that I was about to intense or weird myself right out of the business, and that I had to find some balance," he later reflected.[2]

Cage yearned to do something light and accessible. He yearned to do comedy.

The result was a string of upbeat, unabashedly mainstream comedies which Cage made in the early nineties and which he would eventually dub his "Sunshine Trilogy": *Honeymoon in Vegas* (1992), *Guarding Tess* (1994), and *It Could Happen to You* (1994).* With lighthearted storylines and sizable budgets in the $20 million range, each of these films sought to rebrand Cage as a kind of benign, everyman hero. At best, this era positioned Cage to reach the family-oriented audiences who weren't shelling out for *Wild at Heart*; at worst, it swathed the actor in a fog of inoffensive mediocrity. Certainly, his career objectives had recalibrated since his days of scoffing at *Moonstruck* in favor of punk expression.

* Cage starred in two additional comedies during this era—the tone-deaf *Amos & Andrew* (1993) and the rancid crime comedy *Trapped in Paradise* (1994)—but he did not count them among his Sunshine Trilogy. Cage didn't seem to want to discuss those movies at all, really, quite understandably.

Cage's stated reasons for swinging toward the mainstream varied depending on the day. In some interviews, he offered a rather sweet explanation: his maternal grandmother, Louise "Divi" Vogelsang, wanted to see her grandson do a nice movie that she and her friends could enjoy. Cage described a conversation in which "my grandmother told me I needed to do a romantic comedy and not play a crazy man for a change."[3]

Other times, he spoke about an epiphany he had experienced while watching an old interview with Jim Morrison. In Cage's telling, he was struck by hearing Morrison say that the Doors had not yet created a song that expressed pure happiness. "And I thought about myself. I thought, 'I should do that. Something that's not so angst-ridden.' "[4]

Whatever the veracity of these stories may be, Cage eventually admitted that financial considerations were at the forefront of his mind. He now had a son to support—his first child, Weston, born to his then-girlfriend, Christina Fulton, at the end of 1990. Cage never married Fulton, but he did want to be a decent father. He worried about Weston seeing him onscreen in violent situations. Parenthood, he said, inspired him to play "roles that will give me the chance to project greater dignity."[5]

And well before he was routinely commanding $6–7 million (his *Con Air* and *Face/Off* salaries), $12 million (his *City of Angels* salary), or even $20 million (*Windtalkers*) per film, Cage's extravagant appetite for real estate was putting a strain on his finances. By 1991, he owned at least two palatial houses. First came a 100-year-old Victorian mansion in the Pacific Heights neighborhood of San Francisco, where the actor installed large aquariums and a carved stone fireplace modeled after a dragon's mouth; antique gargoyles and gilded swans ornamented the living room. Then, in the fall of 1990, he paid a reported $1.5 million for a hilltop castle in the Hollywood Hills, built in the 1920s and boasting panoramic views of the city.[6]

All of which is to say, Cage needed cash. "I hadn't gone bankrupt—OK, I was only three weeks away from it, maybe—when I basically made a decision to go with the big studios," he admitted in 1994. Such an admission reveals that Cage's financial issues began interfering with his career decisions long before this dynamic became common knowledge.[7]

Still, the question was uncertain: Could Nicolas Cage credibly play a . . . normal person? In 1990, he didn't think he could. By 1991, it felt like the grandest challenge of all.

* * *

Before we talk about the Sunshine Trilogy, we need to talk about a military movie called *Fire Birds*. *Fire Birds* (or *Wings of the Apache*, as it was known in international markets) is best remembered for two reasons: (1) it was Cage's first action movie; (2) it was Cage's first bad-movie-that-he-did-because-he-needed-the-paycheck.

Fire Birds, released in May 1990, can also be understood as a dry run for the Sunshine Trilogy, in that it was Cage's first conscious attempt to play a wholesome all-American hero. "I remember him saying specifically, 'I've never done this sort of thing before. I really would love to have a go at this,'" says director David Green. "I think it tickled him because nobody ever offered him anything like that before."

The film was panned by critics as an overheated, pro-America *Top Gun* knock-off. The aerial stunt sequences were mind-numbing at best, and Cage's chemistry with female lead Sean Young, for whom he struggled to feign passion, went down like lukewarm milk. *Fire Birds* sank at the box office, and Cage distanced himself from it almost immediately.[8]

He barely waited until the ink on his check was dry before admitting that *Fire Birds* was a dud. By the late summer of 1990, he was willing to acknowledge that he had been miscast. It's a Hollywood taboo to admit you did a bad movie for the money, but Cage made it clear: he did it for the money, joining that hallowed Coppola tradition of making movies to pay off debts. Presumably, *Vampire's Kiss* (for which he was paid $40,000) and *Never on Tuesday* (total fee: $360) weren't sufficient to cover Cage's real estate costs.

"I had bought this house and I got over my head and I realized I was in serious need of money," he told the *Washington Post* that August. "I wasn't being true to my instincts, but I felt like I wanted to do a role which was this straight American character."

Cage insisted he had wanted to liven up the dull hero, to Cage-ify what was essentially a rote exercise in patriotism: "I started playing it like he had a few problems. I don't think that went over too well with the producers of the movie," he said in the same interview. "I mean, I just seem to find the weirdness in a character."[9]

Whatever weirdness is lurking within military hero Jake Preston doesn't make it to the screen as he deadpans his way through dry military jargon and earnestly says things like "I'd marry that thing!" about a helicopter. *Fire Birds* has been justly forgotten. But the film foreshadowed Cage's desire to try playing straight. He just needed a genre framework where glimmers of absurdity could shine through—not military movie, but comedy.

* * *

Cage wanted to establish himself as a man of mainstream comedy, and he wanted to do something light. He got his chance with *Honeymoon in Vegas*, an outlandish rom-com in which he plays Jack Singer, a private investigator hellbent on winning back his fiancée from a slimy millionaire, who tries to seduce her with riches and trips to Hawaii.

That Jack Singer—a neurotic private investigator who has severe maternal hang-ups and dreams about his dead mother vacuuming naked—was regarded as a normal character by Cage's standards says more about the wackos he'd played previously than it does about *Honeymoon*. But hey, here was a well-meaning character who loves his girlfriend *and* loves his mother. "In all my other films, I've never even had a mother–son relationship," Cage marveled at the time. "Some of those characters you wouldn't even think would have a mother."[10]

With *Honeymoon in Vegas*, Cage entered his short-lived "Tom Hanks period." While Cage was busy swallowingcockroaches, Hanks had mastered the alchemy of Hollywood likability, and Jack Singer—the goofy, Hawaiian-shirt-wearing hero of *Honeymoon in Vegas*—was exactly the kind of role Hanks might go for. (Some reports claimed Hanks was in negotiations to star in the film before Cage signed on in May 1991, though director Andrew Bergman denies this.[11]) Cage saw Jack Singer as a "regular guy," a character not unlike himself, and to prove the point, he used his own voice for the role—no accent or vocal affectation—something he had scarcely done since the mid-eighties.

When we first meet this regular guy, he's at the deathbed of his overbearing mother (Anne Bancroft), whose dying wish is that he never get married. Jack frantically promises as she goes into rigor mortis. Like *Moonstruck*, this is a romantic comedy with a morbid streak, though the tone—established via the animated retro-sixties opening titles—is more madcap than operatic.

Four years later, Jack, a private investigator who spends his days snooping on cheating spouses, hasn't broken his promise. He loves his girlfriend, a kind-hearted schoolteacher named Betsy (a pre-fame Sarah Jessica Parker), but Betsy is hungry for marriage and children, and Jack can't commit. Finally, Betsy gives him a gentle ultimatum: "I won't be a girlfriend forever." In a panic, Jack proposes that they fly to Las Vegas and get married that week.

But no quickie Vegas marriage ever goes according to plan. At their casino resort, Betsy is spotted from afar by slimeball gambling tycoon Tommy Korman (James Caan), who decides that he must marry her because she's the spitting image of his beloved dead wife. Jack, of course, is his obstacle. So

Tommy hatches a sinister plan: he ropes Jack into a high-stakes poker game, and beats him to the tune of $65,000. Jack can't afford to pay, so Tommy offers a deal in exchange for forgiving the debt: "I want," he sleazily intones, "your girlfriend for the weekend" (no sex, just companionship).

Betsy reluctantly agrees to the plan, and Tommy whisks her away to his lavish Kauai getaway, where she begins to fall under his manipulative charm. Jack, meanwhile, spends the film's latter half in a continuous panic attack, sweating through his Hawaiian shirts as he goes to absurd lengths to try to make it to Hawaii to get Betsy back. It's like *Planes, Trains and Automobiles* crossed with a 1930s screwball comedy, juiced up with absurdist gags and a colorful array of cameos: Ben Stein, Peter Boyle, even a five-year-old Bruno Mars.

But it's Cage's high-octane performance that gives the wacky plot a sense of urgency. Cage instills Jack Singer's plight with pathos and wild-eyed desperation, his blood pressure rising, his hairy arms protruding from his garish shirts. His performance kicks into overdrive forty minutes in, when Betsy informs him that Tommy is taking her to Hawaii and Cage prowls around their hotel room in a crazed stupor, gesticulating his paranoid visions with the fervor of a televangelist preacher.

The actor's involvement in the film was not preordained. He had strayed far from comedy since *Moonstruck*. "My agent even said *Honeymoon in Vegas* was a long shot," he reflected later. "Rick Moranis would have fitted better."[12]

When director Andrew Bergman wrote the screenplay, he didn't have a star in mind. A Queens-born writer with a Ph.D. in American history, Bergman had left academia and made a name for himself in the early 1970s comedy trenches when he wrote the story that morphed into Mel Brooks's deliriously profane *Blazing Saddles*. Later, with cult hits like 1979's *The In-Laws* (which he wrote) and 1990's underrated *The Freshman* (which he wrote and directed), Bergman developed a knack for fast-moving comedies about regular guys caught up in outlandish circumstances. He also had a knack for borrowing from Francis Ford Coppola's talent pool: *The Freshman* featured Marlon Brando cheekily riffing on his *Godfather* character, while *Honeymoon in Vegas* cast Coppola pal James Caan and Coppola's own nephew as romantic rivals.

With *Honeymoon*, Bergman aimed for a perverse love story. "I wrote it because I'd been making 'guy-guy' movies," Bergman says. "*The In-Laws*, *Fletch*—*Blazing Saddles* was certainly a guy movie. I wanted to make something resembling a romance. Of course, it was a bizarre premise, which even in those days was sexist. When I suggested the idea to my agent, he said, 'Are you insane? Guy loses his girl in a poker game?' I said, 'It won't be what you think.' And it *wasn't*, because of the personalities involved."

Castle Rock acquired the screenplay, and *Honeymoon in Vegas* entered production in 1991. Sarah Jessica Parker was attached early on, but there was no male lead. Bergman considered Billy Crystal, but he seemed a little old. Then he learned that Cage was interested. He was surprised. "I knew he did these insane, cockroach-eating [characters], but there was just an inherent sweetness about him," Bergman says. "And when he read, I said, 'OK, he's Jack Singer. He *is* this guy.' I didn't have any picture in mind when I wrote him. Just someone in over his head. And Nick's rhythms were so specific."

Others were interested, Bergman says, but when Cage came in to the office and read for the part, it was unshakable. "He showed up and he *was* the guy."

Castle Rock executives, however, were not convinced of Cage's star power.[†] "They didn't think he meant anything at the box office, and they thought he was kind of weird," says producer Mike Lobell. "A lot of people thought he was weird, because he did a lot of weird stuff." Bergman wanted Cage, but studio heads wouldn't approve him without a screen test. In Lobell's recollection, a tense conversation with Ed Limato ensued. "The agent got a little crazy and said, 'He's not gonna test,'" Lobell says. "But evidently he talked to Nick right away and Nick said, 'Of course I'll test.'"

In those days, high-rolling agents like Limato—whose roster of A-list talent included Denzel Washington and Winona Ryder—preferred to think screen tests were beneath their clients. Newcomers did screen tests. Not established stars. "Ed kind of believed that the more you exclude your client from people, the more attractive they are," says casting director Valorie Massalas, who cast Cage in *Honeymoon in Vegas* and *Fire Birds*. "He wasn't the kind of agent that rushed his client into the office. He just didn't do it."

But Cage wanted the role badly and must have understood that he needed to prove his commercial worth. His eccentric genre-hopping had confused studios. "I was a mystery to the powers-that-be in Hollywood," he later recalled. "They didn't know what to do with me."[13]

[†] Lobell says Castle Rock executives were reluctant to give Cage the part. Bergman doesn't remember those conversations and says the studio was "fabulously supportive." Both men, however, say Cage needed to do a screen test.

Just like in the *Moonstruck* days, he did a screen test opposite the female lead. "He was so good," Lobell says. "The two of them had such chemistry, it was a slam dunk."

* * *

For Cage, *Honeymoon in Vegas* was an opportunity to take the exaggerated mannerisms he'd brought to *Vampire's Kiss*—the oversized outbursts, the agitated hand motions, the bug-eyed facial contortions—and make them palatable within the confines of a mainstream comedy. Like Peter Loew, *Honeymoon*'s Jack Singer spends the bulk of the movie in a state of mounting aggravation. But while Peter loses his sanity, Jack loses only his fiancée. His erratic behavior never crosses over into villainy. He never loses the audience's sympathy.

As goofy as the movie is (in ways that sometimes stretch credulity), Cage's physical expression of anguish keeps the material compelling. Consider the scene where Jack gets into a fight at the airport with a droning stiff played by the king of droning stiffs, Ben Stein. Jack is desperate to get to Hawaii, and Stein, questioning the ticket agent in his dry, monotonous voice, is holding up the line. During the altercation with Stein, Cage wiggles his eyebrows and flares his eyes wildly, like his romantic frustration is a sentient animal trying to escape through his face. When the ticket agent reprimands him to get back in line, he erupts into full Cage mania: "Then what!" he screams at her. "I'll be *arrested*? Put in *airport jail*?"

Cage's upper-body choreography here is a direct descendent of the alphabet scene from *Vampire's Kiss*. During the words "airport jail," he thrusts both hands in front of his face and stretches his fingers in perfect coordination with the widening of his eyes. He looks like he's trying to draw literal quotation marks around the words he's screaming. "His exasperation was heavenly, and the whole movie was about torturing this guy for two hours," Bergman says.

Bergman had a tendency to italicize particular words when he wrote dialogue. Cage responded to the italics, letting them guide his most explosive line readings. "Every time it was in italics, he hit it with everything he had," Bergman says.

For example, there is a scene where a frustrated Jack Singer asks to be brought to the vacation home of Tommy Korman and instead winds up at the rundown residence of one Chief Orman. As Jack melts down, his taxi driver (Pat Morita) warns him not to insult the chief because he has considerable influence around here. Cage's line was "Influence? He lives in a *shack*," except he shrieked the word "shack" with so much full-body force that it startled the crew. "In fact, the first take was ruined because the producer laughed when he heard it," Bergman says. "It was so out of the blue. And it was so perfect. This guy's on a hair trigger."

For Cage, this was a revelation. He could use his surrealist intensity to make mainstream audiences laugh. "That was my first chance to bring the wacky behavior that I developed in *Vampire's Kiss* to a commercial form," he later told *Entertainment Weekly*.[14] Sometimes he would ask Bergman if his gestures were too over-the-top. Bergman reassured him, "There's a lot of room at the top here."[15]

* * *

Cage would later describe *Honeymoon in Vegas* as a new beginning, a period "full of potential and possibilities."[16] He had been in an acting lull.

In fact, by the time *Honeymoon* began principal photography in mid-1991, Cage had not been on a film set in more than a year. Instead, he spent the early part of that year adjusting to fatherhood and embarking on a Kerouac-inspired cross-country road trip with his longtime friend Jeff Levine, which Cage wrote about in a strange, meandering essay full of ramblings such as "I wonder if there's a hole in the soul of my generation" and "I am a lizard, a shark, and a heat-seeking panther."

One impetus for the trip was ennui. "I'm just sitting here in Los Angeles getting soft," Cage wrote in the essay, which was published by *Details* magazine. "Twenty-seven years old, balding, and without a shred of inspiration. My representatives tell me to stay in town, so that I can meet people for jobs. I've been doing that for a year. Petting my cat, thinking about exercise, never reading a good script."[17]

And then, in the middle of his road trip, Cage received a good script: *Honeymoon in Vegas*. He moved fast. Shooting began during the late summer of 1991. "We started in New York, then in Vegas, but you know that eventually you're gonna be in paradise," Bergman says, referring to Kauai, where much of the movie was shot on location, and where Cage personally paid for a luau-style wrap party. ("He hired somebody to roast a pig on the beach," says Lobell. "He hired hula girls. He was so generous to do that.")

Cage no longer thought of himself as a Method actor in the living-the-role sense, but he still went to extremes to make his performance authentic. Take the scene where he arrives at the pool to inform Betsy that she's been loaned out to a sleazy millionaire. Cage was determined to look sick with worry. "He smoked a pack of cigarettes before we did it—like ten cigarettes in a row," says Bergman. "He really wanted to look queasy. So there's this sheet of sweat on him that he induced by smoking all these cigarettes, because he had stopped smoking. It really made him nauseous."

He was equally determined to elicit a sincere emotional response for the scene back in his New York office, where a client, played by character actor/comedian Robert Costanzo, is distraught about his wife's affair. The Costanzo character is describing his wife's infidelity in copious detail, but the camera keeps cutting to Jack's face, increasingly anguished as he imagines his own girl with Tommy Korman. Finally, Jack snaps and screams at the client.

While filming the reaction shot, Cage asked Costanzo to use his real girlfriend's name to provoke real jealousy. "He said, 'Bobby, do me a favor, use this woman's name,'" Costanzo says. "And I said, 'Really, who's that? Your girlfriend?' And he kind of gave me a sly smile."‡

Costanzo happily obliged Cage's odd request. "It would really get a reaction outta him. And he would get pissed, and it worked!" he says. In fact, it reminded him of the sneaky acting tricks Robert Duvall played when Costanzo worked with him years earlier. "[Duvall] would say to me, 'Costanzo, you fuckin' Italian piece of shit'—you know, getting me real angry," Costanzo says. "And then at the dailies, he'd say, '*Hey*, Costanzo! I got a real moment outta you!'"

As Costanzo's story shows, Cage's performance in *Honeymoon in Vegas* was at least partially powered by his own romantic angst. Cage wanted to be married, but couldn't make it work.[18] Things had fallen apart between him and Christina Fulton. "It all stems from an emotional base," Lobell says of the performance. At one point, Lobell says Cage approached him and Bergman for relationship advice, "because he knew that he was failing at a lot of them," Lobell says. "And he was very serious about it. Very emotional and sensitive guy, Nick."

Cage sometimes felt that playing Jack Singer was the closest he'd come to playing "the real me."[19] Then he began living the part in a way he hadn't anticipated: a real-life love affair with Sarah Jessica Parker. "He had a crush on Sarah Jessica," recalls Caan. "When it was over, he kept talking to me about, 'I want to go back and visit her.' I'd say, '*Go*, man!'"

‡ Constanzo can't remember the name that Cage asked him to use. Cage reportedly broke up with Christina Fulton—the mother of his child—shortly before the filming of *Honeymoon in Vegas*. In June 1991, a Page Six gossip item claimed that Fulton was suing Cage for child support.

Then twenty-six, years before her *Sex and the City* fame, Parker was at first intimidated by Cage—she expected him to be a brooding nutcase—and then was charmed by his warmth. One crew member remembers Cage raving about Parker and saying things like, "Wouldn't Sarah be the best girlfriend?" By the end of filming, they were a real-life couple. They continued dating for months afterward, and fizzled out in 1992. Two years later, Parker implied that their breakup had been messy but admitted she still had "great affection for Nick."[20]

"They really adored each other," says Bergman. "You see it in the movie, how much they like each other." From the director's perspective, such off-screen romance could only be a good thing. "Unless they're both married, and then it's a disaster. But they were both happily single, and it was wonderful for the movie."

Honeymoon also granted Cage an opportunity to work with one of his uncle's regulars. James Caan had gone to college with Coppola before starring in *The Rain People* and *The Godfather*. Cage not only felt a kinship with Caan's most famous character, the hot-headed Sonny Corleone, but had unsuccessfully lobbied Coppola to play Sonny's son in *The Godfather Part III*. "I think I could play this part," Cage told his uncle. "I just see myself more as James Caan's son."[21]

Caan knew none of this. He was, however, greatly fond of Cage and impressed by his work ethic. "At the time, Nick had the weirdest way of talking to you," Caan says. "He would look at you twice like he was trying to understand what you said through your first sentence and wait for more. He would just be a little late in answering sometimes. He'd do that; I'd just laugh. I thought it was just ridiculous."

During a press day in Las Vegas, Caan decided to play a prank on the younger actor. Caan went in a room with about a dozen reporters, answering their questions, while Cage waited outside. As he wrapped up, Caan told the reporters that Cage had an odd way of speaking and requested that they all "speak very slowly and distinctly" when they interviewed him.

How did Cage react? "He comes out and he goes, 'What the hell's wrong with them people?' " Caan laughs.

* * *

Honeymoon in Vegas was the first of several key movies Cage shot in Las Vegas, a city which would assume a cosmic significance in the actor's life and career. He earned his Oscar there. He began living in Vegas as his primary residence around 2008 (because, he sheepishly admitted in a *Guardian* profile, Nevada has no state tax), and later married his fourth and fifth wives there. *Honeymoon* might as well have been titled *Entering Las Vegas*.[22]

In 1991, Cage was new to this particular den of sin, and vulnerable to its temptations. Many cast and crew members spent their downtime gambling heavily during the shoot. "You're working in that casino for four weeks! It's not an ideal environment," says Bergman, referring to Bally's Las Vegas Hotel and Casino.

Of course, Cage got in on the fun, and so began another strange blurring of movie and reality: Cage's real-life roulette bets started freaking out his co-star. "I was making small bets—$50 on red or black—but wasn't getting off on them so I started going for the bigger numbers," Cage later claimed. "It made Sarah Jessica a little nervous. But I wasn't the guy at the baccarat table betting a million dollars. At one point, I was betting ten grand. She was getting ill. I lost ten grand and couldn't get it back."

Like Jack Singer, Cage realized he was in over his head. He relieved the stress by running on the treadmill for an hour. Then, by his own account, he returned to the table before his next set call. "I went down to the table and bet twenty grand and got all my money back. Then I stopped. I never bet again."[23]

For a director, setting a movie in Las Vegas provides license to heighten the ambient weirdness in every scene: viewers tend to believe any wacky situation is plausible if it's happening in Vegas. In *Honeymoon*, the running gag involves a convention of Elvis Presley impersonators—or "Elvi"—wandering around in full Elvis regalia while Jack and Betsy are in town. Elvis covers dominate the soundtrack, including a rollicking Bruce Springsteen version of "Viva Las Vegas," and the end credits refer to characters like "Black Elvis" and "Oriental Elvis."

"I was a child in the fifties," Bergman says. "Elvis was just this God, arrived on earth." Before he wrote *Honeymoon in Vegas*, the filmmaker had carried around a fascination with Elvis impersonators for years. He envisioned a sea of Elvis lookalikes, in every size and color: "Everywhere you look, Elvis coming out of the elevator, at the bar. When I did this movie, I said, 'This is the place where I can do that!' "

By cosmic coincidence, *Honeymoon in Vegas* became Cage's second film in two years with a prominent Elvis motif. In *Wild at Heart*, he had embodied the spirit of The King. Here, he's the straight man surrounded by Elvis clones—a significant difference.

In an early shot, a gaggle of Elvis lookalikes, clad in rhinestone jumpsuits, floods the hotel lobby as Jack and Betsy watch in bemusement. Later, during Betsy and Tommy's first dinner together, there's a surreal cameo by a child Elvis impersonator crooning "Can't Help Falling in Love" in a blue jumpsuit. That child is played by a puffy-haired, five-year-old Bruno Mars (then Bruno Hernandez), who had become a local sensation in Hawaii and was regarded as the world's youngest Elvis impersonator. "We always joke that we discovered Bruno Mars," says *Honeymoon*'s first assistant director, Yudi Bennett.[§]

That much of the film takes place in Hawaii—where the real Elvis's film career peaked with the hokey 1961 musical *Blue Hawaii*—only heightens the Elvis-ness of it all. Yet the movie doesn't reach peak Elvis until the final act, when our hero is so desperate to get back to Las Vegas to stop his fiancée from marrying Tommy that he hops a small plane full of Elvis impersonators. Unbeknownst to Jack, these are "flying Elvises," and their mission is to skydive from 3,000 feet over Vegas.

Bergman had originally written a more halfhearted ending: Cage's character gets a ride back to Vegas with the legendary tiger-wielding duo Siegfried & Roy and their white tigers on the plane with them. "It was very mild, you know?" Bergman says. "It seemed to me he had to do something heroic." So Bergman had a terrified Jack leap from a plane in full Elvis regalia.

This entailed some of the most daunting physical stunts of Cage's pre-action-hero career. "We hung him from a crane, for crying out loud, and we strapped him into an airplane," says Bennett, the first AD. "This was before the age of visual effects. So all that skydiving stuff was practical: real ropes, skydivers. Literally, he was in an airplane strapped in so he wouldn't fall out the door."

A frenetic feat of editing juxtaposes Cage's white-knuckle descent above Vegas with Betsy's escape from Tommy amid a crowd of spectators. Local Las Vegas skydivers were hired for the actual jump, but Cage had to be hung from a crane for the landing sequence. "He never complained, to my knowledge," Bennett says. Bergman adds, "There was only one bad moment for Nick. We had a shot when he was actually up in the air. And he had the open door. He was pretty nervous about that, as any sentient human being would be. But he was tethered in. He wasn't going anywhere."

[§] How did baby Mars wind up in the film? "I don't know, he showed up with his mother!" says producer Lobell. "His mother would bring him and wait there. There weren't too many five-year-olds who could do that. He was amazing."

Figure 10.1. *Honeymoon in Vegas* (1992, Columbia Pictures) was Cage's second movie in two years with a prominent Elvis motif. But rather than embodying the spirit of the King, as he had in *Wild at Heart*, he's the straight man absorbed into a group of Elvis impersonators.

After his brief stint as an amateur Elvis impersonator, Cage was fascinated to find himself surrounded by real Elvis impersonators (Figure 10.1). Some were eager to initiate Cage into their cult. To his astonishment, they never dropped the accent. "They took to me like I was one of their own," Cage said in an interview with television reporter Bobbie Wygant. "I wasn't sure I liked that so much. After I'd finish a scene, they'd come up to me and say, 'You make a great Elvis in *Wild at Heart*. After you finish up here, we'll get a few beers and talk about E, what do ya think?' I'm like, 'Guys, that's great, thanks a lot, but I gotta go home.'"[24]

Most of the Elvises were not trained actors, but their devotion to the King made Cage's fandom seem casual at best. "We had Elvises show up who knew Elvis," says Bennett. "One guy had a pendant that Elvis had touched. It's really quite a cult."

So, to recap: Cage really was in love with Parker, really was overwhelmed by Elvis impersonators, and really *did* have a gambling streak. No wonder he felt like he was playing himself.

* * *

When *Honeymoon in Vegas* opened during the late summer of 1992, Cage attended two screenings and was startled to hear genuine laughter from the audience. "It was a wonderful sound," he told the *Dallas Morning News*. "Except for *Moonstruck*, I've never had a movie that made people feel good.... *Honeymoon in Vegas* is an outright comedy, and I'm surprised at the amount of joy I'm experiencing from that."[25]

The film became Cage's strongest box office showing since *Moonstruck*, grossing around $35 million and earning mostly positive reviews. It even earned him a Golden Globe nomination. Still, the actor must have been bemused at how much press attention zeroed in on his newfound interest in playing normal.

"I'm growing up a little bit," Cage told a California newspaper that summer. "I'm mellowing out."[26]

Maybe Cage believed that. Maybe he was sending out the bat signal for higher-paying roles. Still, he was insistent: he was going to keep making audiences laugh.

"I like the idea of doing comedies right now," he told Wygant, the television reporter. "I want to make people laugh. I want to make people feel good. I think we need to feel good in this country."[27]

* * *

Cage only made one truly great movie during the long, inconsistent stretch between *Wild at Heart* and *Leaving Las Vegas*, and it was not part of his Sunshine Trilogy. It wasn't even a comedy.

I am referring, of course, to the independent gem *Red Rock West*. Shortly after wrapping *Honeymoon in Vegas* during the fall of 1991, Cage traveled to rural Arizona to star in this taut, perennially underrated neo-noir directed by the filmmaker John Dahl. The film wasn't a mainstream production, and thanks to some distributor turmoil, it nearly didn't get seen at all. But I'm going to argue that Cage's understated performance here is Sunshine Trilogy–adjacent. The reason is simple: Cage plays a fundamentally decent, honest character with no leering eccentricities. Besides, it just seems wrong to write a chapter about Cage's early nineties period and not talk about how good *Red Rock West* is.

So, let's talk about how good *Red Rock West* is. Two parts neo-noir and one part Western, the film wrings devilish suspense from a case of mistaken identity and an obsession with the dark side of small-town America. Cage stars as Michael, an out-of-work drifter bumming around Wyoming, broke and looking for a job. When he wanders into a sleepy bar in the desolate town of Red Rock, the bar's owner (J. T. Walsh) mistakes Michael for the hitman he's hired and gives him a stack of money to kill his wife.** Desperate but conflicted, Michael takes the cash and visits the man's wife, Suzanne (Lara Flynn Boyle), who coolly offers him more money to kill the husband.

Once the real hitman, "Lyle from Dallas" (a diabolical Dennis Hopper), rolls into town, the web of coincidence and betrayal intensifies, and circumstances keep bringing Michael right back to Red Rock. Sharp jolts of black humor and irony enrich the narrative as it spirals toward an inevitable showdown, but Cage plays it straight; he's the ordinary guy caught in a mess of homicidal proportions, while Hopper brings the outsized villainy.

John Dahl and his brother, Rick Dahl, hatched the idea while John was cutting his first film, the 1989 thriller *Kill Me Again*. "We started talking about writing a script," says Rick, who co-wrote *Red Rock West* and served as associate producer. "My brother had this idea: what if a guy just pulls up to a bar, walks in, and the bartender says, 'Are you Lyle from Dallas?' and the guy lies, because he needs a job. We started bouncing ideas back and forth."

A Montana native, John was fascinated by the inner worlds of depressed Western towns. He and his brother quickly drafted a script and approached the production team that had produced *Kill Me Again*, Propaganda Films, which soon optioned *Red Rock West*. They began recruiting a cast. Cage wasn't their first choice. Instead, they wanted Matt Dillon as Michael and Bridget Fonda as Suzanne. "They were completely untouchable," Rick says. "Matt Dillon, in 1991 into '92, was a bigger star than Nick Cage."

Cage's interest in the role was rather fortuitous. By chance, Francis Ford Coppola had recently seen *Kill Me Again* in San Francisco and loved it. He raved about the film over dinner with his nephew.[28] Pretty soon, the Dahl brothers got word that Cage had read the new script and was interested. "He met John and me. And he said, 'My uncle says you're a really good director,'" Rick recalls. That's the kind of praise you don't easily forget.

The brothers set a budget around $7 million and, with Cage attached for a salary of $500,000, managed to secure financing. There was only one problem: they had planned to shoot *Red Rock West* in Montana in September 1991. Then Cage was offered the lead in *Honeymoon in Vegas*, which was to shoot the same month, for a substantially higher salary.

** If you're thinking to yourself, "Hey, that's the same plot set-up as *Beavis and Butt-Head Do America*," you're not nuts—according to a *Rolling Stone* interview, Mike Judge took direct inspiration from *Red Rock West* while writing the *Beavis and Butt-Head* movie.

Cage's manager, Gerry Harrington, called *Red Rock West* producer Sigurjón Sighvatsson, who had worked with Cage two years earlier on *Wild at Heart*, and threatened to pull out unless they more than doubled Cage's salary. Sighvatsson told him that was impossible on such a tight budget. "He was pleading with me," Sighvatsson says. "And he called me two days later and said, 'Listen. Nick is gonna be a big star. And he wants to do *Honeymoon in Vegas*. Why don't you just postpone your movie, and we'll stick to the $500,000?'"

An agreement was reached. Cage would shoot *Honeymoon*, and *Red Rock West* would be pushed back to December, creating a new complication: Montana would be covered in snow by then. A producer had a suggestion: "Go south." They wound up shooting the bulk of the movie in rural Arizona—with Willcox, Arizona, standing in for the fictional town of Red Rock, Wyoming—and filmed the graveyard scenes in a hangar at Santa Monica Airport.

In the DVD commentary track, John Dahl described how Cage, who had just shot *Honeymoon in Vegas*, seemed slightly disarmed by the understated nature of the role. "He kept looking for those big moments," Dahl said. "And it was more like, now we're doing this quiet, not a lot of dialogue, sort of Clint Eastwood [part]."

In Cage's only scene-grabbing outburst, he explodes with frustration at Boyle's character, whose unsavory lies and insistent suggestions that they escape to Mexico with stolen money push him over the edge. "*Fuck* Mexico!" Cage screams, fuming against the striped shadows of the bar office where his ordeal began. Cage delivers restraint throughout the rest of the movie, but there he needed to snap. "It felt really right," Dahl said in his commentary. "Because he had been so suppressed, it was like this spring that was just being coiled and coiled and coiled."[29]

* * *

Among critics, *Red Rock West* is often compared to either David Lynch (the principal cast consists mostly of Lynch favorites, not to mention the Propaganda Films connection) or the Coen brothers (the plot, with its web of murder-for-hire and double-cross, is more than a little similar to *Blood Simple*). All reasonable comparisons, but *Red Rock West* is more than rote imitation. It's a brooding and restrained thriller, quieter and less flashy than the Coens' work but with plenty of style to burn: Dennis Hopper, for instance, gets one of his all-time great screen entrances, swaggering out of a vehicle

Figure 10.2. In the neo-noir gem *Red Rock West* (1994, Roxie Releasing), Cage plays a sympathetic drifter in a town full of psychopaths and killers. The role was perhaps the most introverted character Cage had portrayed, which made his quiet performance atypical.

boot-first blasting Johnny Cash. And Dahl is literate with an eclectic range of cinephile influences, understanding that great noir is more about character-building than visual clichés, while steering toward a climactic showdown that overtly nods to Sergio Leone's Spaghetti Westerns.

But none of this would work if not for the believably sympathetic character at the center (Figure 10.2). Cage had portrayed criminals before, and would do so again, but not here. Here he plays a generally honest, if desperate, man caught up in a web of deceit. And that's what connects *Red Rock West* to *Honeymoon in Vegas* or *Guarding Tess*. Cage isn't the instigator of chaos. He's the straight man, the regular guy in a town chock full of psychopaths and killers. (In classic noir fashion, the only other sympathetic character is the femme fatale, played with smoldering intensity by Boyle.)

Because of the film's botched release, Cage didn't do many interviews about *Red Rock West*, but when he did talk about it in the press, he stressed the working-class, everyman quality of his character. In 1992, he told a San Pedro newspaper that he plays "a blue-collar hero wandering around the country trying to get a job."[30] Similarly, when asked about the character by television reporter Bobbie Wygant, Cage said: "I would say he's more Middle America than even Jack Singer. . . . Particularly with the recession and everything, he's the guy that's looking for his next buck. And I like that guy. I want to make a hero out of that guy."[31]

Cage was trying to slot *Red Rock West* in with his newfound interest in playing normal, likable dudes. And while the movie isn't as wholesome as he made it sound, it does place a peculiar emphasis on Michael's integrity—his status as "a moral guy in an immoral world," as the director put it.[32] When we first meet the character, he botches an interview for an oil job because he admits to a leg injury. Later, he wanders into a rundown gas station and eyes a pile of cash unattended, but doesn't take it. Cage conveys this internal dilemma with nothing but his expressive eyes and a swift turn of the head.

It becomes clear that Cage is not playing one of his usual wackos. His character, Michael, is a loner and a man of few words—the most introverted character Cage had portrayed yet—which is part of what makes Cage's performance so atypical. With no grand *Moonstruck*-esque monologues to fall back on, Cage uses only body language and subtle vocal tics to convey the character's ambiguous motives.

Consider the pivotal scene in which Michael is first mistaken for a hired killer by the sleazy bartender, Wayne. When Wayne starts talking about a "job," Michael perks up and makes a split-second decision to go along with it. "You're Lyle from Dallas, right?" Wayne asks, and Cage pauses half a beat, affixes a slight Texas twang to his voice, and plays along: "Right." Cage remains silent for most of the scene, but as it becomes clear Wayne is talking about murder-for-hire and not a routine bartender job, his blank expression betrays the subtlest hints of discomfort.

Red Rock West is a pulpy noir exercise, not a rom-com, and Dahl slyly plays up the suspense when Michael pays a visit to the woman he's been hired to kill. But once the real hitman enters the picture, Cage blossoms into more of a classic Western hero. "There's a couple of moments in the film where you can see he's doing Clint Eastwood, or doing a Steve McQueen kind of moment.[††] He was very aware of the physicality of acting. Almost like it's Kabuki theatre," Rick Dahl says. "After a take, he would be like, 'Do you want it bigger? Does it need to be smaller?'"

[††] Curiously, Cage cited Steve McQueen as his favorite actor in a 1993 interview with the *San Francisco Chronicle*. He suggested that *Red Rock West* was an attempt to channel the *Great Escape* star: "I've always been so external. Wouldn't it be nice to play a quiet, strong type in the McQueen mold?"

Rick remembers Cage being easygoing and flexible, especially in contrast to Boyle, who disliked veering from the script. In conversations on set, Cage casually talked about his career goals. "[He] really wanted to be a leading man," Rick says. "Wanted to be Tom Hanks or whatever."

Even with no dialogue, Cage captivates during the opening credits, showing off his rugged, denim-clad good looks as his character shaves and rouses himself with push-ups on a desolate highway. "He just got down and started doing one-arms," Rick says. "That wasn't in the script. And he was in really good shape. He wanted to have his shirt off and bust a move."

During the high-octane climax, Michael pours a case full of money from a freight train and leaves Red Rock for good. Cage liked this ending; he admired his character's rejection of blood money. Some of the producers, however, objected. "They were like, 'Dude, he would keep it!' " Rick laughs. It was the first omen that *Red Rock West* would soon be stymied by corporate forces.

A studio test screening went fairly well. But the marketing people at PolyGram, which had produced the film, were concerned. "PolyGram didn't really believe in the film," says producer Sigurjón Sighvatsson. "They felt that the movie was a tweener," Rick adds—meaning it wouldn't have festival appeal, but wasn't considered worthy of wide release, either. In the depressing words of one marketing consultant quoted in the *New York Times*, "The film doesn't fall neatly into any marketable category."[33] At one point, studio heads suggested reshooting the ending with a big mano-a-mano battle between Cage and Hopper on the train. "They just didn't get it," Rick says. "It was a bunch of suits. They were just overthinking it and hand-wringing."

The Dahl brothers were dismayed when the film's owner, Triumph Pictures, decided not to release Red Rock West. Columbia TriStar subsequently sold the domestic rights to cable. In 1993, *Red Rock West* was shown numerous times on HBO, prompting a popular misconception that it was made for TV. ("We would never have gotten Dennis Hopper and Nicolas Cage to agree to be in a cable movie," John Dahl later acknowledged.[34])

In Europe, however, *Red Rock West* played in theaters and impressed the director of the Toronto International Film Festival, who decided to show it at his festival that fall. Roger Ebert saw it at Toronto and loved it. So did a guy named Bill Banning, who owned the Roxie Cinema, an art-house theater in San Francisco, and its distribution arm, Roxie Releasing. In early 1994, Banning asked for a print so he could screen the film at the Roxie.[35]

Before long, this once-abandoned movie was a local success story in San Francisco. "That theater sold out consistently for a month straight—every night," Rick says. "And the film started generating buzz. And [Banning] said, could he release it nationwide? So they worked out a deal."

Red Rock West played at eight more theaters in the Bay Area, eventually expanding to New York and Los Angeles. It was nominated for two Independent Spirit Awards (losing to the then-unstoppable *Pulp Fiction*), and became something of a cause célèbre in the press, a cherished example of how indie distributors and critics could come together to save an underdog film from TV-movie oblivion. It was a kind of *Zandalee*-in-reverse, and Cage was thrilled the film had been rescued from obscurity, particularly by his adopted hometown of San Francisco. "The thing would have gotten completely lost if the Roxie hadn't picked it up," Cage told the *Chronicle*.[36] By 1995, he even planned to reunite with John Dahl for the Minnesota-set thriller *A Simple Plan* (1998), although both men wound up leaving that project when it became stuck in development hell.[37]

As a low-budget neo-noir with an assured style and a reigned-in Cage, *Red Rock West* is an undeniable outlier in the actor's nineties filmography—and a real hidden gem.

But with its casting of Cage as the morally redeemable everyman in a world of immoral goons, it feels like a close cousin of the Sunshine Trilogy. Cage even found his character's integrity aspirational for his own career moves. "*Red Rock West* meant something to me because I was dealing with money in my own life. At the time, I was trying to avoid selling out, or accepting roles I didn't want just because large amounts of money were being offered," he told the *San Francisco Examiner* in 1994. "The dignity in that movie was that [my character] surpassed the money questioned—in the end he basically says, 'Screw the money.'"[38]

Naturally, Cage's next few roles did not reflect this philosophy at all.

* * *

The second film in the Sunshine Trilogy was the weakest of the three, although 1994's *Guarding Tess* (Figure 10.3) does have its moments. It's watchable—particularly if you have a great fondness for Shirley MacLaine, or just want to see a movie where Cage accompanies an older woman to the opera and *doesn't* try to seduce her. But *Guarding Tess*—starring Cage as a perennially aggravated Secret Service agent assigned to protect a perennially aggravating former First Lady—never really lives up to its amusing premise,

Figure 10.3. In *Guarding Tess* (1994, Tri-Star Pictures), Cage plays a prim-and-proper Secret Service agent assigned to an ornery former First Lady (Shirley MacLaine). The role reflected Cage's growing interest in playing likable, even normal characters.

and the film's *Driving-Miss-Daisy*-except-they're-both-white trajectory is predictable at best. It's the rare Cage role that feels like it could have been performed by any decent actor with a likable presence.

Cage, for one, is cast so far against type that it strains credulity. Once again, he's the straight man caught in an unenviable situation with a powerful wacko. But this time, outfitted in a wardrobe of gray suits and dark shades, he's more plain, more buttoned-down, than ever before. A comedy-drama hybrid directed by the late Hugh Wilson, *Guarding Tess* wants you to believe that Nicolas Cage is not just a Secret Service agent, but an uptight, duty-bound, prim-and-proper Secret Service agent named Doug Chesnic, a man who hates nothing more than people who sidestep rules and regulations. How Cage—a guy who projects rigid professionalism about as convincingly as Joe Pesci projects genteel Victorian restraint—landed this role is somewhat of a mystery.

Doug longs for an exciting assignment, like working in the White House protecting the president. Instead, he spends his days in middle-of-nowhere Ohio, guarding a former First Lady named Tess Carlisle (a fifty-nine-year-old

Shirley MacLaine, made to look at least a decade older). The widow of a beloved former president, Tess is a stubborn and cantankerous woman who treats Doug like her servant, making him fetch her snacks at night and pick up golf balls, and who has a defiant disregard for the security protocols he fervently follows.

When we first meet Doug, he talks about Tess in euphemisms—"she has her good days and her bad days," he tells a superior—but we can sense the exasperation and contempt lurking underneath. Doug has reached the end of a three-year tour guarding Tess and is eager to move on, but unbeknownst to him, Tess has needled the current president into keeping Doug in her security detail. They're stuck together.

The film's humor stems from the constant tension, sometimes boiling over into outright animosity, between Doug and the woman he's charged with protecting. There are amusing scenes, such as the battle of wills that results when Doug refuses to let Tess travel until she's positioned in the proper seat of the vehicle. MacLaine is good at playing the mercurial Tess; she talks down to Doug as though addressing an exasperating grandchild and torments him with mind games, but can't conceal occasional glimpses of a sensitive side. Yet the screenwriting is suffused with a dull, noxious reverence for the rituals and emblems of the presidency.

There are a number of reasons why *Guarding Tess* doesn't quite work. As a comedy, it's never quite as funny as it should be. The movie has a tendency to take a moderately funny gag— like Tess insisting on playing golf in freezing weather—and stretch it into an overlong scene devoid of a punch line.

And we never truly get to know Doug, beyond the seriousness with which he takes his job and his yearning for that seriousness to be rewarded. Cage is good at projecting tightly coiled frustration, but the role gives him little to do besides scowl, scold Tess, and look exasperated. There are moments when he explodes in anger, screaming at Tess's driver (Austin Pendleton) and pushing him against a locker. But unlike in *Honeymoon in Vegas*, these outbursts don't bolster the comedy. Rather, they feel like brief, misplaced glimpses of a very different performance.

These flaws may be forgivable, as is the nineties screenwriting dictum that requires that, as *Guarding Tess* progresses, Doug and Tess develop a begrudging understanding for one another. But in its third act, the film lurches into one of the most jarring tonal shifts imaginable. Tess goes missing, and that's when *Guarding Tess*, heretofore happy to lumber along as a quiet comedy-drama, abruptly segues into a dead-eyed kidnapping thriller, with Doug shouting a lot and going rogue, hellbent on saving the day.

It's a clumsy attempt to inject some adrenaline into the otherwise low-key film, and it cements *Guarding Tess*'s status as the least satisfying entry in Cage's Sunshine Trilogy. As the critic Nathan Rabin argues, it's even a harbinger of dismal movies later to come—"dreary, forgettable Nicolas Cage thrillers where the beloved icon runs around wild-eyed and desperate while waving a gun at the bad guys."[39] Suffice to say, when Tess is discovered alive in a grimy cell underneath a farmhouse, there isn't a whole lot of sunshine to be found.

* * *

Though it was hardly his most stimulating role, Cage approached *Guarding Tess* with a journalist's flair for research. He watched *The Bodyguard*, the 1992 Whitney Houston vehicle whose success likely gave *Guarding Tess* a pre-production boost. He interviewed real-life Secret Service agents who had been assigned to former First Ladies and tried to get a feel for the odd roles they found themselves performing. "I remember one told me about having to cook corned-beef stew for, I believe, Mamie Eisenhower," he told the *Philadelphia Inquirer*.[40]

Yet the acting advice Cage received from Secret Service men wasn't exactly stimulating. "They suggested I play Doug very normal, very straight," Cage told the *New York Post*. "There is nothing that eccentric about them."[41]

The origins of *Guarding Tess* are a little hard to trace, owing to the fact that most of the principal players—including writer-director Hugh Wilson, a sitcom veteran who launched a successful movie career with 1984's *Police Academy*, and screenwriter P. J. Torokvei—have since died. We do know that producer Scott Rudin was attached to the project early on. At the time, films like *Driving Miss Daisy* and *The Bodyguard* had whet the commercial appetite for movies about unlikely friendships spanning across socioeconomic or racial barriers. Rudin dropped out when Paramount chairwoman Sherry Lansing wanted to reduce the film's budget dramatically, at which point Wilson brought it to TriStar instead. The budget stayed at a comfortable $20 million.[42]

After spending much of 1992 ensconced in low-budget excursions like the criminally underrated *Red Rock West* and the just plain criminal *Deadfall*, Cage saw *Guarding Tess* as a chance to bolster his mainstream cred after *Honeymoon in Vegas*. He liked that the role signaled restraint and maturity.

"I think Doug Chesnic is about as straightforward as you can get," Cage told a newspaper reporter during the shoot. He added, "I'm ready now to play a role like Doug Chesnic in my own life."[43]

"By the time he did *Guarding Tess*, I think he had really settled down," says Aleta Chappelle, the film's casting director. "He was like a normal human." Chappelle, a former Zoetrope staffer, had first crossed paths with Cage a decade earlier when she witnessed his sophomoric antics on *The Cotton Club* and *Peggy Sue Got Married*. "Once we did *Guarding Tess*, he goes, 'Are you still mad at me?' And I said, 'Yeah. You know, you grew up a little. Let's see.' "

Cage was far more subdued this time around. "He seemed to be in his own world," says actor Dale Dye, who played one of Cage's Secret Service colleagues. "He was kind of a loner. He was working in his head all the time."

Though set in Ohio, *Guarding Tess* was filmed in the Baltimore area during the winter months of 1993, with a historic Mount Washington mansion serving as Tess's residence. Cast and crew members remember it being a smooth, drama-free shoot, save for a historic blizzard that shut down production for several days. Cage was well-prepared and courteous on set, says director of photography Brian J. Reynolds. "I never had any sense of discontent or kooky stuff," says Reynolds. "Early on, when Nick helped carry some gear back to the set, I was like, 'Oh, man. I love this guy.' "

Like *Moonstruck*, *Guarding Tess* gave Cage an opportunity to charm his Hollywood elders—this time Shirley MacLaine, the celebrated actress whose career stretched back to comic classics like *The Trouble with Harry* and *The Apartment* before Cage was born. After four decades in the public eye, MacLaine could relate to Tess's want of privacy and autonomy.

But behind the scenes, MacLaine and Cage—both known eccentrics who gravitated toward character roles instead of typical leads—became surprisingly chummy. "I expected an unkempt, brooding, complicated, dark-spirited young man who was part of some cult even I had never heard of," MacLaine admitted in her 1995 memoir. Instead, she found Cage to be "clean-cut" and "very respectful," though intimidated by her seniority: "I watched him wonder if he could tease me without getting admonished."[44]

MacLaine was relieved when Cage lightened up, and they developed a jokey rapport. MacLaine's spirited cantankerousness reminded Cage of his own grandmother, Divi.[45] The actress teased Cage for having an eighteen-year-old girlfriend (model Kristen Zang, to whom Cage was briefly engaged in 1994) and playfully mimicked his line readings. Cage in turn asked

MacLaine about her long-ago affair with Robert Mitchum,[‡‡] among other topics. "He asked me for advice about everything," MacLaine told the *Los Angeles Times*. "Child-rearing, comedy, what he should do after this. After all, I've lived 3,000 years longer than him."[46]

"He was very intense," says the actor and playwright Austin Pendleton, who portrayed Earl, Tess's rule-defying chauffeur. "His character had an antagonistic relationship with mine. So he told me right from the get-go that he would cultivate an antagonistic relationship toward me so we could bring that. He told me that wasn't how he really felt, but he would do that. I said great, no problem. So we had sort of an edge between us; when we began to shoot the scenes, it was right there." (Pendleton says Cage relaxed that edge as the shoot progressed. They had learned how to establish it on-camera.)

Pendleton is a veteran of the theater who has taught acting at New York's HB Studio since 1969. So I wonder what he makes of Cage's techniques: Does Cage pass muster? Is he a real Method actor? Yes, he says. "But every good actor is in some way or another a Method actor." In Pendleton's view, this has less to do with pursuing attention-grabbing extremes like having your teeth pulled out or remaining in character 24/7 than an overarching commitment to the teachings of Konstantin Stanislavski, whose "system" of training actors provided a groundwork for modern philosophies of acting.

Central to Stanislavski's teachings was the idea that an actor must, in any given scene, be intimately attuned to the "objective," or "task," that his character is aiming to achieve. Only through this psychological effort could the actor arrive at his character's inner emotional truth. "There is no greater harm," Stanislavski wrote in his autobiography, "than the harm in the mechanical forcing of the emotions from outside, without the creation of an inner spiritual stimulation."[47]

‡‡ MacLaine and Mitchum began an intense romance while filming 1962's *Two for the Seesaw*. Cage's interest in Mitchum, however, may have been more personal than MacLaine realized. During his childhood, when his mother was in the throes of mental illness, she lashed out at Cage's father during a heated fight by telling him that Cage wasn't his son and was instead the result of a fling with Mitchum. "She had an old photograph of Mitchum that was signed, 'To Joy, love and kisses, Bob,'" Cage told the *Sunday Mirror* in 1996. "Nothing had happened. She was in a dance troupe at the time and got an autographed picture from a star."

Cage's mother later admitted it was a lie told in the heat of anger. But in Cage's view, his father had really believed he was Mitchum's kid and treated him with disdain as a result. "My dad always said, 'Is Nicky mine?'" Cage told *Movieline* in 1996. "For thirty years my father's been a little angry with me and that's probably why." (Although Dick Cavett once told Cage he had "Mitchum-like looks," a cursory glance at photographs of Cage standing next to his father eases any doubt that they are father and son.)

Understanding the objective is key to the authenticity of a performance. "You pick an objective that keeps encountering obstacles from the other characters," says Pendleton, shifting into teacher mode. "The big phrase is, Play the objective, don't play the emotions. If you play the objective and then you encounter the obstacles, the emotions will just come."

In *Guarding Tess*, Cage's objective was simple: protect Tess. "What Nick would walk around with on set was, *I must protect this woman. I must protect this woman. I must protect this woman,*" Pendleton says. "If he stays with the objective, then every scene automatically presents either large or small threats to that. And that will generate the feeling. We always have an emotional response when we want something and obstacles come up to our ability to achieve it."

Accordingly, every character is either an ally or an obstacle in the way of the objective—hence Cage's premeditated chilliness toward Pendleton, whose character clearly posed an obstacle. Pendleton didn't take it personally. "He walked around in the grip of the objective," Pendleton says.

* * *

Guarding Tess was a modest success, taking first place at the otherwise barren mid-March box office and grossing around $30 million overall. Reviews were mixed, though Cage was again praised for showing a mellower side.

As Cage promoted the movie in the press, he leaned into his wholesome new image. He spoke earnestly about his love for his three-year-old son, whose birth had prompted him to quit smoking, start wearing seat belts, and stop romanticizing the idea of dying young.[48] He admitted that he had not been able to see Robert Altman's *Short Cuts* the prior fall, because he couldn't bear to watch a young boy get hit by a car. He suggested that his swing toward comedy was permanent. "I've decided that people respond better to me in comedies than all that quirky stuff I did in the past," he told a *Philadelphia Inquirer* interviewer.[49]

Yet Cage was also growing frustrated with the loss of creative freedom that seemed to come with big-studio paychecks. *Guarding Tess* was a prime lesson.

One of the film's oddest flaws is that the script is littered with intermittent references to Tess's being diagnosed with an inoperable brain tumor. This plot point is so confusingly unresolved by the end that you might wonder if Tommy Wiseau served as a script consultant. As it turns out, the unexplained cancer subplot is an awkward holdover from an earlier draft of the film, one that existed before studio interference. In the original cut of *Guarding Tess*, the movie culminated with Tess's death. In fact, the whole story was to unfold in flashback during the First Lady's state funeral. But test screenings—that dreaded ritual commonly mandated for studio pictures of a certain budget—revealed that audiences did not like seeing Tess die. TriStar determined that reshoots were in order: Tess would remain alive and well as the credits rolled.

Such money-conscious studio machinations seemed routine to other movie stars, but not Cage, who by 1994 had still spent much of his career in the rarified world of independent cinema. He was frustrated by this brazen intrusion of commerce into filmmaking. A *New York Daily News* profile described him as "an active participant in the fight to preserve *Guarding Tess* in the form originally shot by writer/director Hugh Wilson."

The studio won. The funeral scenes were scrapped, and, just four months before release, Cage reluctantly shot a new ending wherein he escorts Tess out of the hospital after her triumphant rescue.

Still, TriStar's marketing wizards couldn't have been thrilled when Cage made his displeasure clear via the *Daily News* article shortly before the film's release. In the interview, he relayed the wisdom he had gained: "When a movie costs more than $10 million, the control is out of the hands of creative forces." Thus, he would need to keep making the occasional independent movie to feed his wild spirit. "I've got to be able to ruffle my feathers a little," he said, a declaration that foreshadowed the steady push-and-pull between big-budget Hollywood roles (say, *Con Air* or *National Treasure*) and indie excursions (*Leaving Las Vegas*, *The Weather Man*, *Joe*) that would define the next two decades of Cage's career.[50]

* * *

It Could Happen to You, the third and final "Sunshine Trilogy" film, further tested audiences' willingness to accept Cage as a genial leading man, easing into the sort of nonthreatening, everyman roles that could have gone to Tom Hanks or Billy Crystal. Released during the summer of 1994, a few months after *Guarding Tess*, this old-fashioned romantic comedy stars Cage as Charlie Lang, a kindhearted NYPD officer who lives in Queens with his wife Muriel (Rosie Perez), a materialistic woman fed up with their middle-class existence. Unlike Charlie, Muriel is obsessed with getting rich and resents Charlie for being "a working-class stiff."

At a diner, Charlie is served by the beautiful Yvonne (Bridget Fonda), a down-on-her-luck waitress who's been forced to declare bankruptcy due to

Figure 10.4. Cage's performance in *It Could Happen to You* (1994, Tri-Star Pictures) was heavily modeled after James Stewart, particularly in the scenes where good-hearted cop Charlie (Cage) encounters struggling waitress Yvonne (Bridget Fonda).

credit card debt incurred by her estranged husband (Figure 10.4). Charlie doesn't have cash to leave her a tip because he's spent his last few bucks on a lottery ticket, so he makes a deal with her: If his ticket wins the lottery, he'll split half his winnings with Yvonne. If it doesn't, he'll still come back the next day to leave a proper tip. Of course, wouldn't you know it, the ticket wins, and Charlie is true to his word: to Muriel's horror, he splits half of their $4 million lottery winnings with Yvonne, and the story becomes a tabloid sensation.

That much of the plot was based on a true story. In 1984, a cop named Robert Cunningham really did split his lottery winnings with a waitress at a Yonkers pizza joint. But the characters were fictionalized, as was the fairytale latter half of *It Could Happen to You*, in which Cage's character predictably falls in love with the waitress whose life has been changed by his generosity.[51]

That generosity was key to the film, says screenwriter Jane Anderson, who wrote the film on spec. "My dad had just passed away, and he was the most generous man in the world," Anderson says. "I wanted to write a film that would reflect that kind of generosity." Anderson was intrigued by stories of lottery winners and how they were affected by their payday, and, while doing research at a library, came across the story of the cop and waitress. Duly inspired, she wrote a first draft.

Eventually, Tristar picked up the film for distribution, with Andrew Bergman, whose career had been boosted by the success of *Honeymoon in Vegas*, attached to direct. The script was more earnestly romantic than Bergman's previous work, but once he read it, he says, "I just fell in love with it." He agreed to direct on one condition: that it be shot in New York. He also set about making it *look* like New York. "The script I got was set in contemporary New York and everybody was white. I said, 'This is not New York,'" Bergman recalls.

Wanting to make a more racially diverse movie, Bergman gave Charlie Lang a Latino wife and a Black partner in the NYPD, a role for which young rapper 2Pac (Tupac Shakur) came in to read. ("He was the shyest, loveliest guy," Bergman recalls, though the role went to the more seasoned Wendell Pierce.) In an eccentric flourish, soul legend Isaac Hayes pops up periodically as a tabloid photographer who also narrates the film in his butter-smooth voice.

Bergman shepherded the script through seven or eight rewrites. He even had Nora and Delia Ephron pitch in as uncredited script doctors; there is something Ephron-esque about the film's portrayal of New York as a small-town hotbed of meet-cutes. Yet Jane Anderson objected to Bergman getting a writing credit, and a Guild arbitration process resulted in her receiving the sole credit.

Cage was never the obvious choice to play Charlie Lang. Cage's specialty was playing criminals and outcasts, lawless sorts who operated according to their own codes of outlaw ethics: H. I. McDunnough, Sailor Ripley, even Michael from *Red Rock West*. These weren't bad guys, exactly, but they weren't models of upstanding decency. But Charlie Lang? Here was a police officer with a saintly disposition. A creature of the establishment. A man who is good and good all the way through.

"He's sort of a Billy Budd. Not of this earth decent," says Bergman. "Which makes it the fairy tale that it is." Granted, many rom-coms are essentially fairy tales, and this one appeared to be set in a fantasy New York in which NYPD officers spend their days performing acts of kindness and goodwill.

With a $20 million budget, *It Could Happen to You* was a beneficiary of the early-nineties rom-com boom. Midbudget films like *When Harry Met Sally . . .* and *Sleepless in Seattle* had proven to be massive box office draws, and Tristar had high hopes. "They wanted a major star to play the role that Nick played. And we always wanted Nick," says producer Mike Lobell.

As seasoned as he was, Cage's commercial appeal was still uncertain. Several recent outings—*Zandalee*, *Amos & Andrew*—had been humiliating bombs. Studios were suspicious. Bergman remembers considering more palatable stars, like Tom Hanks and Billy Crystal; Lobell says the studio put out an offer to Tom Cruise, who turned it down.

They kept pushing for Cage. Finally, Tristar gave in.

After *Honeymoon*, Bergman was eager to work with Cage again. He wasn't worried about Cage's ability to play a model citizen, a straight-arrow cop. "For all his eccentricities, he's a tremendously decent, loyal human being," Bergman says. "And I swear, the minute I saw him in that [police] uniform, I thought, Jesus Christ. He's perfect!"

* * *

Aside from his uncle, Cage had never worked with the same director twice. On *It Could Happen to You*, he and Bergman were entering a familiar groove. "It didn't take more than a nudge," Bergman says. "Plus, his preparation is stupendous. He is cold on his lines from day one."

Despite dissimilar plots, *Honeymoon* and *It Could Happen to You* are clearly cut from the same stylistic cloth. They're both uncommonly gentle romantic comedies laced with a bright, optimistic sheen that feels a galaxy removed from *Wild at Heart*. They both explore tales of love and money. And they both star Cage as a goodhearted, if conflicted, romantic lead chasing a beautiful blonde love interest. This time, the love interest was played by Bridget Fonda. Years later, when asked if he ever found it hard not to fall in love with his co-stars when playing romantic roles, Cage admitted, "I felt a lot for Bridget Fonda when we were doing *It Could Happen to You*."[52]

"I pretty much fell in love with him while we were working together," says Fonda. "He was just really romantic and, at the same time, sort of undomesticated, which is such an appealing combination."

Like Cage, Fonda (daughter of Peter, granddaughter of Henry) had emerged from a prominent Hollywood family and fought to escape her family's shadow. She viscerally related to Cage's need to separate himself from the Coppola dynasty, though changing her own name never occurred to her: "I just thought, they're gonna find out anyway." By the early 1990s, Fonda had distinguished herself with memorable roles in *The Godfather Part III* and *Single White Female*. Here she projects a more wholesome image, veering from gentle sarcasm to doe-eyed sincerity as the working-class waitress swept off her feet by the kindness of a stranger.

On set, Fonda amused Cage with stories of funny things Carmine Coppola had said to her during *The Godfather Part III*. In between takes, they played Hangman. Both actors bonded over the sheer weirdness of playing normal characters. "It was literally like playing a straight character was this strange role for him," Fonda says.

"Part of it was, 'This is so strange playing somebody who has no edge,' " Fonda adds. "There was [a] pre-sixties sort of no edge, no darkness, not even any grey area. That was such a strange thing to have to play. When we first started with it, I thought that was a challenge. What do you do with somebody who's so vanilla? That's when we came up with the idea that the fact that somebody is so two-dimensional is what makes them a freak and embracing that."

This kindly waitress needs an antagonist, and she gets one in the form of Charlie's money-grubbing wife, played by Rosie Perez at her screechiest. Perez plays a loudmouth materialist who chastises Charlie for giving money to a homeless beggar because she'd rather spend it on pricey fur coats.

The character is overwritten—a concession to Hollywood's demand for a sufficiently hateable villain—but what's noteworthy is how Cage is cast as the reasonable half of a marriage for once. A casting director really looked at Nicolas Cage and said, *He should be the normal one.* Perez does all the gesticulating and screaming. In her 2014 memoir, the Brooklyn-born actress wrote that she nearly didn't get the part because, to her surprise, Bergman "couldn't see me as an annoying bitch." Of Cage, she simply wrote: "Nick Cage is fine as hell and a stand-up guy."[53]

In *It Could Happen to You*, Cage's character embodies modesty in the face of runaway materialism. The film is a lighthearted satire of New York class divisions, fashioned in the gentle spirit of a Frank Capra comedy. Charlie has no qualms about living in working-class Queens and feels alienated by his wife's tax avoidance schemes and outings to Tiffany's.

In reality, while portraying a man of the people onscreen, Cage was becoming increasingly susceptible to extravagant spending in his own life. Not that he had ever made a secret of his desire to grow rich: "I'm doing OK financially, but I can't afford a palatial house yet—and I'm not into being a starving artist," he bluntly told a journalist in 1988.[54] By the mid-nineties, Cage owned not one but two palatial houses, and was soon to acquire a Los Angeles apartment as well, described in *GQ* as "a hushed, baronial downtown pied-à-terre"; it contained sculptures of comic-book villains and was previously owned by the Los Angeles Water Board.[55]

Writers who profiled Cage for major magazines could not help but gush about his arsenal of sports cars (a Lamborghini, a Ferrari, a metallic-blue Corvette Stingray, a Bentley) and the eccentric décor of his Hollywood Hills living room, which contained mounted butterflies, Gothic art, and a large killer bee suspended from the ceiling. Pressed about his lifestyle in a 1996 *Vanity Fair* cover story, Cage admitted, "Sometimes the only way I can feel free is in the mobility I get when I spend money."[56] That same year, he told *Playboy*, "There's one thing I have some difficulty with, and that's hanging on to money. I find ways of spending money that mystify everybody around me."[57]

Those who worked closely with Cage certainly noticed. In 1992, on the set of *Amos & Andrew*, rumors spread that Cage was driving home from set one evening when he passed a Ford showroom, saw a new pickup truck model, and bought one on the spot. According to that film's cinematographer, a camera assistant wound up driving it back to California for him.

While filming *It Could Happen to You* during the summer of 1993, Cage was in a similar spending mood. The film was shot at some 103 locations around New York City.[58] Lobell recalls shooting one day in an office building on Fifth Avenue. There was a break for lunch; Cage wandered out onto the streets of Midtown. "He came back and he rolled up his sleeve and showed us this watch," Lobell says. "So we said to him, 'What is that?' He said, 'It's a Breitling.' Andy and I said, 'What's a Breitling?' I can only tell you he went out to lunch and bought a watch that cost $35,000."

* * *

At the beginning of *It Could Happen to You*, Charlie Lang is in a bathrobe, shaving.

That's not unusual. Cage is often seen shaving in his movies, so much so that author Lindsay Gibb counted and determined that Cage shaves in at least nine films. From *Raising Arizona* (Hi is shown forlornly clutching a razor after he and Ed fail to conceive) to *Honeymoon in Vegas* (Jack frantically rubs an electric razor against his face while en route to Tommy's vacation home), shaving signifies a desperate effort to disguise some anarchy within. Cage characters shave in moments of desperation, as though grooming their face will make them belong.[59]

But that's not why Charlie Lang is shaving. You get the sense Charlie is shaving simply because, well, that's just what he does. This is a normal day, and Charlie's a normal guy. For once, Cage shaves without pathos or terror.

Hell, Charlie may be the single most wholesome character Cage has ever portrayed. When we first meet him, he's doling out baseball lessons to neighborhood kids and helping a blind man cross the street. He's "just a good cop," as Isaac Hayes says in voiceover. Maybe too good—the film's saintly depiction of the NYPD is its worst quality, so shamelessly reverential that it borders on "copaganda." A hokey subplot depicts Charlie heroically rescuing a local deli from an attempted robbery. If you're going to cast Nicolas Cage as a cop, at least have the decency to make him a crack-smoking, iguana-hallucinating cop, as Werner Herzog did.

While *It Could Happen to You* falters when it bows to hero-cop clichés, it's appealing when it swathes Cage and Fonda in a gooey-eyed romantic haze, shot in lush color by Caleb Deschanel. In a fairytale climax, the two lovers dance and sway one stormy evening in the lamplit diner where they first met.

While previous Cage performances had been inspired by misfits and rebels like Elvis Presley and Max Schreck, his work in *It Could Happen to You* was modeled after a more upstanding icon: James Stewart. In his thirties and forties heyday, when he starred in Frank Capra classics like *Mr. Smith Goes to Washington* and *It's a Wonderful Life*, Stewart had embodied a certain ideal of virtuous masculinity. As the film critic David Ansen wrote, "His was a decency, filtered through drawling Midwestern diffidence, that helped a nation define itself."[60]

It's impossible to imagine James Stewart playing, say, Peter Loew, but it's easy to imagine him playing Charlie Lang, who has an aura of earnest, unwavering decency that seems to cut through all cynicism. Charlie even maintains his cool around his shrieking, irritating wife. "You never saw Jimmy Stewart get rattled," notes Lobell.

Indeed, Stewart's name was routinely invoked on set. "I had one direction for [Cage]: 'more Jimmy' or 'less Jimmy,' " Bergman says. As an example, Bergman points to the scene where Yvonne snidely tells Charlie to go get a cat out of a tree, and Charlie responds, without sarcasm: "Well, no, that'd be the fire department." The first time Cage read the line, "he said it just like Jimmy Stewart," Bergman recalls. "I said, 'Maybe a little less Jimmy.' "

Cage knew the comparison was inevitable, and admitted in interviews that his performance was "kind of an homage" to Stewart. "I do think he had what seemed to be a pure American innocence, which trembled on the screen in a way that gave people hope," Cage told a *Los Angeles Times* interviewer. "And there isn't a lot of that right now in movies."[61]

This was far subtler than the cartoonish Elvis affect in *Wild at Heart*, yet both performances find Cage dabbling in conscious imitation of American icons. James Stewart, however, existed in a world apart from the King's boisterous style and sexual provocation. Stewart was praised for his "natural" acting style; one of his co-stars once described him as "so natural, so realistic, that I never knew whether he was talking to me or doing the scene."[62]

For Cage, dabbling in naturalism meant stripping away the layers of surrealist distortion that had colored his performances for years. By 1992, Cage had cycled through so many bizarre accents and vocal affects—in *Peggy Sue Got Married*, *Raising Arizona*, *Vampire's Kiss*, and *Wild at Heart*—that many moviegoers had no idea what his "real" voice sounded like. It is notable that in all three of his Sunshine Trilogy performances he used his own voice without alteration, bringing his old insecurities back to the fore.

He admitted in a 1994 *Newsday* interview that he found it difficult to watch himself onscreen in recent roles "where I'm more me, when I'm not covering myself up with voices or body language, like I did in *Peggy Sue Got Married* or *Vampire's Kiss*. You know how people feel when they hear their voice on tape? Well, imagine that times a billion."[63]

For TriStar, the bid to soften Cage's rough edges paid off. Having won big with *Sleepless in Seattle* the previous summer, the studio viewed the film as a potential hit and subjected it to test screenings. Soon the working title, *Cop Gives Waitress $2 Million Tip*, was nixed.

"That seemed unwieldy, so it was shortened to *Cop Tips Waitress $2 Million*," says Bergman. "Then we began the dreaded preview process. They ask these friggin' groups of people—focus groups—questions. And the first question is, 'How many people like the title *Cop Tips Waitress $2 Million*?' Nobody raises their hand. 'How many people don't like it?' Everybody raises their hands. This is when you start ducking your own responsibility. What you should say is, 'Fuck these people. It's a good title.' "

Instead, Bergman swallowed his pride as the studio chose an "anodyne title," which both he and Fonda disliked but which TriStar executives felt better captured the film's warmth. A nod to the 1940s pop standard of the same name, *It Could Happen to You* conveyed that the film was a throwback to a more innocent era. Then, to Bergman's frustration, the studio pushed back the film's release date from June to July 1994, which placed it in competition with box office juggernauts like *Forrest Gump* and *The Mask*.

In late July, *It Could Happen to You* finally premiered at New York's Paris Theater. At the screening afterparty—attended by quintessential New Yorkers like Tony Bennett and David Dinkins—Cage exchanged pleasantries and handshakes with Bridget Fonda's then-boyfriend: his old *Fast Times* nemesis Eric Stoltz.

It Could Happen to You proved a modest success with audiences and critics; it earned nearly $50 million and gave Cage his biggest box office hit since *Moonstruck*. Though the film has had nowhere near the staying power of that 1987 classic, "it has really held up," Bergman claims. "I see the foreign residuals."

* * *

By the time *It Could Happen to You* came out in mid-1994, an irresistibly fanciful press narrative had congealed around Cage: He was a new man. The wild days were behind him. Fatherhood had mellowed out this beast for good; comedy was his new domain.

Virtually every newspaper profile of Cage from 1994 promoted this narrative. "The new Cage: Nicolas tickles us," trumpeted the headline of a *New York Daily News* article in March, surrounding the release of *Guarding Tess*. ("The formerly surreal-at-heart actor . . . is now avidly courting the favor of the mass moviegoing audience," observed the reporter.[64]) "Now that Nicolas Cage is normal, what's next?" asked the *Philadelphia Inquirer*.[65]

Four months later, the *New York Times* dubbed him "Nicolas Cage, The Sunshine Man" and marveled at his family-friendly persona: "Mr. Cage is 30 now, and the father (by a former girlfriend) of a much-loved three-year-old. Though it makes him a little nervous even to say so . . . he has calmed down."[66] Other outlets similarly attributed this softer tone to parenthood. "He's 30, a Parent, and Taking a Rest from 'Twisted Characters,'" the *Los Angeles Times* proclaimed beneath a photo of Cage looking downright contrite in a suit jacket. In the accompanying article—syndicated from *Newsday*—Cage described himself as "slowing down into a worrywart about society."[67]

It was hard to believe this was the same actor who a few years earlier had boasted to journalists that he was "basically nocturnal."[68] Cage seemed to encourage the perception that his tortured days were behind him. You might have expected him to start appearing in D.A.R.E. commercials by the fall.

Yet in retrospect, the Cage-has-calmed-down headlines seem comically premature, a foolish attempt to ascribe some permanence to Cage's fleeting flirtation with rom-com stardom. Privately, he had already grown disillusioned with his swing toward comedy and was spending months pumping iron and drinking protein shakes in order to play a burly-muscled, psychopathic gangster in Barbet Schroeder's *Kiss of Death* remake. After 1994, he would not appear in a comedy again for six years.[§§]

With the benefit of hindsight, the Sunshine Trilogy seems like simply another experiment for Cage. For all the press chatter about a mainstream awakening, these films (with the possible exception of *Honeymoon*, which spawned a well-received Broadway musical) have had surprisingly little long-term cultural endurance. Who sees Cage's name and thinks, "Ah, the guy from *Guarding Tess*"? This is the demilitarized zone of Cage's nineties filmography: movies that were never destined to accrue the critical and cult cachet of *Wild at Heart* or provide the big-budget action spectacle of *The Rock* and *Con Air*—but nor would they tumble into B-movie oblivion like *Zandalee* or *Deadfall*.

As soon as critics identified Cage's bright new sensibility, he began plotting ways to distance himself from it. By mid-1994, the actor had already quietly signed on to the film that would obliterate his family-friendly image and reboot his career. It was a movie that would bring him back to the city where the Sunshine Trilogy began: Las Vegas. Except this time the only sunshine on his skin was the oppressive glare of daylight, blinding Ben Sanderson's eyes as he stumbled out to score some booze.

[§§] In 1997, Cage was attached to star in and produce a lighthearted film called *Heartbreaker Inc*, apparently based on a story he had written himself in the mid-eighties. The film was to center on a man hired by other men to exact romantic revenge on the women who had dumped them; for unclear reasons, it never got made. In 1998, after his action trilogy, Cage told *Vogue* that he was "dying to do a comedy." Finally, in 2000, he returned to romantic comedy with *The Family Man*, a mediocre, fitfully charming fantasy that feels like a spiritual successor to the Sunshine Trilogy.

11
Drunk in Love

On September 7, 1994, Erin O'Brien wrote a letter to Nicolas Cage. Her brother, the novelist John O'Brien, had been dead for five months. Erin had now learned that Cage was slated to star in an adaptation of her brother's only completed novel, *Leaving Las Vegas*.

She decided she needed to write to the actor.

"We heard you would begin filming *Leaving Las Vegas* this fall," Erin wrote. "I realize the film may be quite different from John's novel, but I can't help feeling a deep personal attachment. Ben is a thinly veiled self-portrait of John. My family and I are anticipating Hollywood's interpretation of John's novel with a strange, melancholy pride. I was delighted to learn you would be playing the part of Ben. The character seems consistent with your work, which I have enjoyed for many years."

"I feel compelled to make connections with the fragments [John] left behind," Erin continued. "You are an unexpected and welcome participant in John's aftermath. As I write this letter on John's computer, I hope you accept this communication for what it is: my way of touching my brother's life."

In the letter, Erin, who is also a writer, wrestled with the unresolved divide between her brother's book, about a doomed alcoholic who decides to drink himself to death, and his life, as a doomed alcoholic who chose to end his life.

"John's life was a bittersweet tragedy," Erin wrote. "I regard *Leaving Las Vegas* as his suicide note."

She mailed the letter to the film's executive producer, Stuart Regen. Eventually, word trickled back: Cage read her letter. He loved it.

* * *

Although John O'Brien's work is known for its brutality and nihilism, the man was not all gloom and doom. He was funny as hell, with a humor that reminded his sister of Robin Williams.

"Johnny was funny in that way," says Erin O'Brien, who was younger by five years. "And you think, a guy like Robin Williams, a guy like Johnny—the membrane that separates this profound sadness and humor, it's so thin."

Perhaps it was this quality that allowed O'Brien to regard his crippling alcoholism with a layer of detached humor. His sister relates an anecdote from the early 1980s, when O'Brien was on "a terrible binge." Realizing that he was experiencing some medical emergency—details unclear—his frightened wife decided to call an ambulance. The paramedics arrived.

"John at this point has curled up in the fetal position in the bathtub," Erin says. "The EMS say to him, 'Mr. O'Brien, Mr. O'Brien. Can you hear us? Mr. O'Brien, what are you doing in the bathtub?' And my brother's response was, 'I couldn't fit in the sink.'" Erin laughs darkly. "He's in this crisis. And he cracks that joke. How else can I deliver what kind of guy he was to you? That was his soul."

Raised in a Cleveland suburb, John O'Brien was a voracious reader, a moody kid who preferred listening to Bob Dylan over playing sports and had trouble making friends in school. Though smart, he refused to go to college. Instead, in August 1979, when he was nineteen, he married his high school girlfriend, Lisa Kirkwood, and began working in law firms as a mail clerk. In 1983, after a wanderlust period, the couple settled in Los Angeles.[1]

The cliché of the alcoholic writer looms large, but O'Brien was consumed by addiction before his literary career began. At twenty, he hid his secret in a clandestine flask at work. In Los Angeles, he spent his evenings at a local bar, swigging beer, then bourbon. He liked to drink until he passed out.[2]

Erin did not realize her brother had a serious problem until 1986. She went out west to visit John and Lisa. One morning, she woke around 6:00 a.m. to use the bathroom. "John was in the kitchen," Erin recalls, "and he was drinking out of a bottle of vodka. And then I knew it wasn't just a lot of drinking. I knew this was something more serious—*Days of Wine and Roses*/*Lost Weekend* territory."

Close friend and neighbor David Baerwald, a musician, later recounted O'Brien's frightening binges. "He got warned several times in hospitals and such that one more drink could pretty well kill him," Baerwald wrote in an *LA Weekly* piece. "Good, he'd think, and drink a fifth of vodka for breakfast. He was pretty serious. One time he was DT-ing, and he swore he saw the devil rip the wall open and lunge in to grab his throat."[3]

For several years, O'Brien bounced in and out of rehab. There were periods of sobriety, but they didn't last. "He was just like the cliché sober guy—bitter, mad at the world that he wasn't drinking," says Erin. "He hated sobriety. He dried out time and time again."

Remarkably, amidst this turmoil, O'Brien managed to launch a literary career. After being fired from a law firm for boozing, he enrolled in a writing class at UCLA. His fiction chronicled the downtrodden world of drunks, lowlifes, outcasts—a world with which he was well acquainted. In 1988, he mailed his parents a short story titled "The Tik." "Here's a story I wrote in January," O'Brien wrote. "Since then, I've been working on a novel."

That novel turned out to be *Leaving Las Vegas*, a shockingly frank dispatch from the damned. The manuscript caught the interest of an old-world literary agent named Ray Powers. After a slew of rejections, *Leaving Las Vegas* was published by a small Wichita-based publisher, Watermark Press, in 1990.[4]

The novel centers on Ben, a terminal alcoholic who spends his days haunting the bars of Los Angeles, drinking to stave off the shakes. After losing both his job and marriage to his drinking, he resolves to move to Las Vegas and drink until he's dead. Once there, he forms a mysterious connection with a beautiful, unflinching sex worker named Sera, who loves him despite his unquenchable thirst, and who agrees never to try to stop his drinking; in turn, he accepts her line of work. Theirs is a romance of two lost souls eking out an oasis of understanding and acceptance amid ruthless self-destruction.

Whether Sera was based on a real prostitute remains unknown. While writing the book, O'Brien frequently visited Vegas for research, "but we never talked about what went on there because I didn't want to know," O'Brien's then-wife, Lisa, told the *Los Angeles Times*.[5]

One does not need to be an alcoholic to write about alcoholism, but *Leaving Las Vegas* chronicles the disease with an intimacy that belies the dark depths of its author's "research." If Hemingway or Bukowski could be accused of glamorizing alcoholism, O'Brien reveals the disease as physically and socially crippling, rendering his character infirm, forced to spend every moment that he is not drinking desperately strategizing as to the source of his next drink.

The early chapters, before the two characters meet, detail Ben's internal monologue as he stumbles in and out of one bar or another, determined to maintain that "elusive mixture of blood and alcohol that makes him feel and act normally happy."[6] He drives drunk with a sense of casual necessity—"Weaving is for amateur drunks, not for him"—though he laments the loss of his independence: "Physically crippled with alcoholism and psychologically afraid of being too far from its source, his walking radius has become the distance from his front door to his car," O'Brien writes.[7]

Like O'Brien, Ben regards his addiction with a kind of detached bemusement. Money—he has received a generous severance check from his ex-employer—is a matter of simple arithmetic. Ben calculates that he has $5,000 in cash and can wring another $5,000 out of his credit cards. "That gives him ten thousand dollars in drinking money," O'Brien writes. "If he drinks one hundred dollars a day—and he can—he's got one hundred days to drink."[8] He is amused to imagine the credit card charges resulting in the eventual discovery of his body, "a trail of American Express charges leading right up to the final room service bottle of bourbon clutched in one stiff fist."[9]

It's bleak stuff. Though disturbed by the novel's content, O'Brien's family greeted its publication with pride and excitement. Strangely enough, Erin was relieved when she read it. "I thought, OK, he has exorcised his demons," she says. "This is him confronting his demons. And this is going to be his road to recovery."

* * *

Sometimes artists must reach a low point before they can conceive their greatest triumph. It's a cliché, but one that occasionally proves true; think of David Lynch making *Blue Velvet* after the humiliating failure of *Dune*, or Paul Simon traveling to South Africa and hatching *Graceland* while mired in the depression of an unsuccessful album and a 1984 divorce.

Accordingly, Nicolas Cage was at a bit of a low point when *Leaving Las Vegas* found him. Not the lowest point of his career—that would come later—but certainly a dead end. It was 1994. His last few movies, *Deadfall* and *Amos & Andrew*, had sunk without a trace. Now Cage was spending the early months of the year freezing in Niagara-on-the-Lake, Ontario, shooting another anemic comedy: *Trapped in Paradise.*

Cage starred in plenty of lackluster movies during the early nineties, but *Trapped in Paradise* (1994), one of many uninspired Christmas comedies that cropped up in *Home Alone*'s wake, may be the worst of them all. Written and directed by George Gallo, a screenwriter best known for *Midnight Run*, *Trapped in Paradise* is one of those films that looks and sounds like a comedy but is mysteriously bereft of discernible jokes.

The movie has the feel of a *Saturday Night Live* skit stretched to 111 interminable minutes. Cage, who veers in and out of a bewildering New York accent, and *SNL* veterans Dana Carvey and Jon Lovitz star as a trio of bumbling brothers who rob a bank in a small Pennsylvania town but change their minds when they witness the kindness of the townsfolk. A rom-com subplot, in which Cage falls in love with a local girl, proves so unconvincing that even the characters appear bored. Like *Guarding Tess*, *Paradise* makes Cage the straight man surrounded by zany characters, but the story never finds a sense of purpose. So inept is the direction that it manages to make the sight of Lovitz teaching yoga to the bank he's holding up unfunny.

"I think Nick knew this was going to be a comedic flop, and he accepted it. He took the money," says Marco Kyris, the man who worked as Cage's full-time stand-in between 1994 and 2004. "The script was terrible. The actors did mock the script."

"I called it *Trapped in Shit*," Lovitz later told the *A.V. Club*. "Nicolas Cage was great and we became friends, but the director just wasn't there. He wasn't directing. . . . Six weeks in, Dana and Nicolas took over." According to Lovitz, Gallo was so out of his depth that Cage effectively directed parts of the film himself.[10]

Trapped in Paradise was a miserable shoot, with weeks of exterior shots in subzero temperatures. By the time it finally wrapped in April 1994, Cage was ready to swear off comedy for years. He even passed up the opportunity to star in *Dumb and Dumber* alongside old friend Jim Carrey, who had rocketed to fame as the animal-loving, anus-talking wacko of *Ace Ventura: Pet Detective*. So hot was Carrey in 1994 that he managed to renegotiate his *Dumb and Dumber* salary up to $7 million after *Ace Ventura*'s success. Cage—in talks to play Harry Dunne—reportedly tried a similar maneuver, increasing his asking price by $2 million. No dice. "New Line balked, Cage walked, and Jeff Daniels got the job," *Variety* reported.[11]

Perhaps Cage thought *Dumb and Dumber* (one of the highest-grossing movies of 1994) would be another *Trapped in Paradise*, another soul-deflating flop. Yet he has never evinced regret for turning it down. Decades later, he recast this decision as a kind of pivot point in his career: "[Jim Carrey] wanted me to be in *Dumb and Dumber* with him. And then I wanted to do a much smaller movie instead called *Leaving Las Vegas*."[12]

In reality, the two shoots don't seem to have overlapped. But maybe the psychic whiplash of jumping from *Dumb and Dumber* to *Leaving Las Vegas* in one summer would have been too much to bear. Or maybe it's just appealing to think of this as one of those fateful, Cage-defining decisions. Two roads diverged in a Hollywood; one pointed the way to a diarrhea sequence in a Farrelly brothers movie, and the other led to an Oscar.

What's clear is that Cage was still mired in the misery of the *Paradise* shoot when he received *Leaving Las Vegas*. "I didn't want to do another big fluffy studio movie that was not going to work," he later told an interviewer. "And I just got angry with myself. I said, 'I can't hold myself with dignity if I do this again.' Then I read *Leaving Las Vegas*."[13]

* * *

Leaving Las Vegas—the book—received modest notice when it was first published, and it caught the attention of an art dealer named Stuart Regen, who found it in a secondhand store. Regen was so moved that he contacted John O'Brien and met the author for coffee in 1991.

"I told him I was interested in making his book into a film and he said he didn't want it turned into a Hollywood movie with a happy ending because that's not what it was about," Regen told the *Los Angeles Times*. Though he seemed skeptical, O'Brien sold Regen an option on the film rights for $2,000. He also busied himself with other work that came his way following the novel's success, such as an assignment to write a remake of the Jack Lemmon film *Days of Wine and Roses*.[14]

By then, O'Brien's condition was deteriorating nearly as fast as his character's. He had been sober while writing *Leaving Las Vegas* but told his wife, Lisa, that he planned to resume drinking in January 1991. He was true to that promise. "Things turned quickly after that," Lisa told the *Los Angeles Times*. In 1992, O'Brien left her for a waitress. "He wanted to drink, and I was getting in the way of that," Lisa explained.[15]

When O'Brien called his sister and said he was getting divorced, she turned to a friend and said, "He's not gonna live six months without her."

The author moved to an apartment in Beverly Hills, where his binges intensified. He resumed his friendship with David Baerwald, who sometimes received distraught calls from his friend at 3:00 a.m.[16] Baerwald was playing in Sheryl Crow's band then and co-wrote a song called "Leaving Las Vegas" on Crow's debut album. O'Brien let Baerwald use the title but asked to be thanked in the liner notes. Baerwald passed the message along, but when Crow's hit album came out, there was no mention of O'Brien. The author was hurt; Baerwald told him it was a mistake that would be rectified on the next pressing.

Then, in March 1994, Crow performed "Leaving Las Vegas" on the *Late Show*. When David Letterman cheerily asked her if the song was autobiographical, Crow indicated that it was. O'Brien, watching from a bar in Venice Beach while drinking himself into a stupor, went ballistic. Crow later said that she did not know about the book or the agreement with O'Brien, and the author's family absolved her of any responsibility in his eventual demise.

"Friends who saw him that night said he just got drunker and drunker and bitterer and bitterer, and finally he broke his lifelong rule against drunk driving and set out to find me and have it out," Baerwald later wrote. "He only made it a few blocks before he got pulled over."

O'Brien was arrested and spent several days in jail. Baerwald never saw his friend again.[17]

* * *

After optioning *Leaving Las Vegas*, Stuart Regen acted fast. He sent the book to his friend Paige Simpson, a producer who was running English filmmaker Mike Figgis's production company. When Figgis read the book at her suggestion, he was stunned by its darkness and black humor.

Figgis excelled at dark dramas and crime films. But he was fed up with Hollywood. His first American film, the Richard Gere vehicle *Internal Affairs* (1990), had been a surprise hit, but a follow-up collaboration with Gere, 1993's *Mr. Jones*, dragged on for two years and was plagued by studio interference. *Mr. Jones* bombed at the box office and left Figgis feeling defeated. He was desperate to leave behind the studio system. *Leaving Las Vegas*—so clearly not a studio picture—looked like a way out.[18]

"I immediately had the idea, I'll shoot it on Super 16, get out of Hollywood," says Figgis, who is also a musician and frequently scores his films himself. "What was exciting was, 'OK, it's gotta be low budget.' And then that became a kind of good energy."

Not that the studios were interested. With Figgis unwilling to deliver a heartwarming recovery narrative, most major and independent U.S. studios, including Miramax, turned the film down, saying it was too dark. "Nobody wanted to finance this film," recalls first assistant director Gary Marcus. Ultimately, the entire budget was financed by a French company called Lumière Pictures, which allowed Figgis final cut.[19]

Figgis became intimately involved with *Leaving Las Vegas* on every level, not only directing, but writing the screenplay, composing the musical score, playing a cameo role, and hand-selecting the leads. Without involvement from O'Brien, he deconstructed the book and condensed its sprawling narratives into a two-hour script centered on Ben and Sera's relationship. Though he tweaked aspects of the story—condensing Sera's backstory with an abusive pimp to a few brief scenes, for instance, and moving a brutal rape scene from the beginning to the end—he was true to the bleakly poetic spirit of O'Brien's novel.

Casting wasn't easy. Here was a low-budget production about an alcoholic and a prostitute, bereft of mainstream moralizing or twelve-step narratives—and hey, did we mention there's not much money? (The budget came to about $3.5 million, and Figgis insists that, after agreeing to a 50 percent deferral, he never received his salary.) Yet Elisabeth Shue was quickly attached to play Sera. Figgis had read her for a different film years earlier and, though Shue was known for more family-friendly roles in movies like *The Karate Kid* and *Adventures in Babysitting*, he sensed some untapped potential in her work, some ability to project profound pain.[20]

Cage he was less sure about. Indeed, the only filmmaker who has ever directed Nicolas Cage to an Academy Award confesses to some early reservations.

"I knew his work. I knew he was quirky, eccentric," Figgis recalls. "But this was one where he was going to have to carry the whole thing. He wasn't just the interesting actor that did the standout performance. The drama was going to be carried with him."

Figgis admired Cage's work—he had previously met with the actor to discuss a role in his 1991 film *Liebestraum*—and was good friends with Ed Limato, Cage's agent ("the last of the old-time proper agents," Figgis says). Figgis's producer, Paige Simpson, meanwhile, had just seen and liked Cage in *Guarding Tess*. So, in March 1994, Figgis sent the script to Limato and conceded that there wouldn't be much money.

The timing was good. Limato knew that Cage was feeling trapped in comedy. Months earlier, Cage had gone to his agent in frustration and said he needed a role that he "could invest my soul in." When Limato read *Leaving Las Vegas*, he told Cage, "This is the answer to all your prayers."[21]

Cage seemed to agree. Advisors told him to skip it, that the film was too dark to win awards, but the actor was determined to play Ben. "The script astounded me," he later told a *Playboy* interviewer. "I was crying when I finished reading it. It is, more than anything, a story about unconditional love. It is definitely one of the coolest relationships I've ever read in a screenplay. There's something about true love that is incredibly elusive. But my character, Ben Sanderson,* found true love."[22]

Figgis quickly got word back: Cage was interested. Hellbent, really. Cage likely saw Figgis as a kindred spirit: here was the most iconoclastic, independent-minded director he had worked with since David Lynch. The

* In the book, Ben's last name is never revealed. In the film, his full name is given as Ben Sanderson.

director remembers receiving a fax from Cage saying something to the effect of: "Please, I beg you. Do not send this to any other actors. I'm gonna do this. I'll do everything I can to make this work."

Figgis had casually discussed the role with other actors—Richard Gere and Andy Garcia both balked—but Cage's enthusiasm won him over. "His response was so overwhelmingly positive and unambiguous that I said, 'OK. That's fine!' "

* * *

Around the same time, in March 1994, John O'Brien's father received a call from a doctor in a Los Angeles detox clinic. Bill O'Brien didn't know his son had a drinking problem. Now he was informed that John was in withdrawal, in chemical shock. He flew to L.A., where he found his son at the hospital, sick and shaking with agonizing delirium tremens.[23]

"The doctors had told him that physiologically he had to stop drinking," Bill later told the *Los Angeles Times*. "He'd lost his job at a coffeehouse, couldn't afford the apartment he was in, and was alone for the first time in his alcoholic life."[24]

Bill tried to talk his son into entering a long-term rehab facility. Failing that, he stayed with John for a week, sleeping on his son's couch, desperately trying to keep him away from booze. They had lunch with John's ex-wife, Lisa. At lunch, when the subject of rehab arose, John told them what Ben tells Sera: "You are never going to stop me drinking."[25]

One day, Bill O'Brien glanced at John's unopened mail and found an important-looking envelope. It was the formal contract for the film rights to *Leaving Las Vegas*, which promised a six-figure check—a sizable sum for an unemployed writer. John signed it that week. Days later, Bill flew back to Ohio and knew, hugging his son goodbye, that he might never see him again.[26]

On April 10, 1994, after gradually disposing of his belongings—much as Ben does in the book—O'Brien died from a self-inflicted gunshot in his Beverly Hills apartment. He had just weeks earlier signed away the film rights. He was thirty-three.

"It was the end of the line," says O'Brien's sister, Erin. "It's the zenith of courage and weakness at the same time. It's when you finally get taken over by the devil or you finally give in to the angels—I don't know. It's just everything happening all at once. It's punctuated by a single bullet."

Figgis, deep into preproduction, was shocked. He considered abandoning the project, then decided to go ahead and honor O'Brien's work. Still, the cast and crew were rattled by the suicide. "I think it had a huge effect on the film," says Elisabeth Shue. "It really grounded all of us in the intensity and reality of the film itself."

Months later, Erin, who began writing herself after John's death and eventually completed several of his unfinished novels, learned that Cage would be playing Ben. "He's a quirky guy," she told her parents. "This is a good guy for the part."

In September, sitting down at her brother's Macintosh Color Classic, she wrote the letter to Cage. She enclosed several photos of John. "I wish you could have met him," she wrote. "Then again, I suppose you will know him in your own way."

* * *

By the mid-nineties, Cage was no longer a Method actor per se, but he still researched his roles with the zeal of a gonzo journalist; for *Con Air*, he even went to Folsom State Prison and asked fearsome-looking inmates about prison life.[27]

For *Leaving Las Vegas*, he dove into character research with typical intensity. He spoke with drunks and asked about their addictions. He spoke to people who ran rehab programs. He tried to understand the hallucinatory agony of delirium tremens.[28]

And he drank. Cage and his friend Phil Roy, a songwriter, embarked on a drinking holiday together. "I felt that since John [O'Brien] was Irish, I should go to his home country to try to understand what it was like to be Irish and very, very drunk," Cage later explained. "So I went to Dublin for a two-week drinking binge."[29]

Cage and Roy hired a driver to shepherd them around the Irish countryside, where they stayed up all night in a haunted castle, waiting in vain for a ghost to appear. More productively, Cage had his friend videotape him when drunk so he could study his movements and speech patterns.[30]

In Elisabeth Shue, Cage found a collaborator equally willing to inhabit the psychology of a character scorned by society. Shue was determined to understand Sera and her profession. "I felt very confident that at the core of her was this deep pain of existential loss in her life and the need to find love with somebody to save her from the pain she had suffered," says Shue. "I think the sexuality of her—how she had to use her sexuality to survive—was a theme

I understood on a deep level, even though obviously I was never a prostitute. I just understood the complexity of what that feels like to feel like your only power could be your sexuality."

Shue spent time talking to call girls and tried to understand the power they derived from feeling nothing during encounters with clients; with Ben, Sera's vulnerability emerges from her willingness to feel for him at all.[31] Shue went so far as to walk around Sunset Boulevard in a short skirt, her husband keeping watch nearby. Shue says, "I think I needed to understand the twisted power that women feel when they sell themselves that way."

As the September 1994 start date approached, Cage's generosity compensated for the meager budget. He made it clear that he was doing the film for fulfillment, not money. "He was basically prepared to do it for nothing," Figgis recalls. Accepting a salary of around $200,000 (a fraction of his typical fee, which hovered between $1 and $2 million per film and would soon rise above $10 million), Cage personally paid for a suite at the Chateau Marmont in Los Angeles, where he and Shue spent several weeks rehearsing with Figgis.[32]

Initially intimidated by Cage's body of work, Shue soon found comfort in Cage's collaborative spirit. "He was always right there with me, never doing his own performance in a vacuum," she says. "We were always completely connected moment to moment."

Shue remembers the exact moment she realized the film would work. It was an early read-through at Figgis's home. She was nervous. Then Figgis went to the piano and began playing a piece of the plaintive score he had written. "It was just a very simple musical phrase that he was repeating, and it was so innocent," Shue says.

Shue looked into Cage's eyes. She had a revelation: despite the sordid circumstances of their lives, the characters' love for each other was innocent and childlike.

"There is a childlike nature to Nick, which is why he's so playful as an actor and able to take such huge risks," she says. "He really comes from such a pure, childlike place in the way he creates. I felt so comfortable. I heard the music, I was looking at him, we were reading, and all of a sudden, I just knew it was going to work."

* * *

Nicolas Cage was thirty when he filmed *Leaving Las Vegas*, but as was his wont, he looked ten years older (Figure 11.1). This suited the film. As Ben

Figure 11.1. Cage was thirty when he filmed *Leaving Las Vegas* (1995, MGM/UA Distribution Co.), but his character, Ben, seemed a decade older. With a balding head and sunken, distant eyes, Ben is in the terminal stages of alcoholism.

Sanderson, Cage is haggard and pale, his arms quivering, his suits ill-fitting. At a bank teller's desk, he sweats and shakes so violently he can't sign the back of a check. Central to this tragedy is the sense that this man used to be somebody—a screenwriter or Hollywood executive of some significance—but his body and reputation have been ravaged by drink.

Cage, who in his thirties would grow self-conscious about his receding hairline, allowed himself to appear conspicuously balding. As Ben's slow-motion suicide progresses, his eyes are sunken and bloodshot, his movements slow and labored. Even in his prime, Cage seemed to excel at playing characters past their primes, men prematurely aged by some unshakable trauma: a war injury (*Birdy*), the loss of one's hand and bride (*Moonstruck*). Here, it's a specter of loss that can't quite be named.

The physical transformation wasn't easy. Just before filming *Leaving Las Vegas*, Cage was in New York, shooting Barbet Schroeder's *Kiss of Death*, a solid if uneven remake of the classic 1947 noir. Cage played the villain, a vicious, goateed thug named Little Junior Brown, who bench-presses strippers and pounds his enemies to dust. *Kiss of Death* never quite lives up to its stacked ensemble, and Cage found the brutality of the role unsettling; while filming a scene in which his character beats a man to death, the other actor fell and cracked his head open, and Cage began crying.[33]

So, after chugging protein shakes and bulking up for *Kiss of Death*, Cage quickly transformed from muscle-bound crime boss to malnourished alcoholic. He binged on candy and pondered the psychic shift. "Little Junior Brown is a character who will kill you if you threaten his environment," Cage told *Drama-Logue* newspaper. "Ben Sanderson is a man who's let go of his pain, his struggles, and his life and has decided to do himself in. The one character is strong and the other is becoming very fragile—which was difficult on my body because I had to pump up and eat and gain weight for Little Junior Brown, and then a week afterwards be a person who was diminishing and becoming this thin wreck."[34]

Kiss of Death wrapped in July 1994. In September, Cage checked into the Gold River Resort & Casino in Laughlin, Nevada, to begin *Leaving Las Vegas*. The resort staff were bewildered by the star's behavior; according to a *People* article, Cage checked in under the name Ben Sanderson and placed a room service order for vodka and cranberry juice. "A lot of people thought he had to be drunk or on drugs because he was so intense," a casino manager named Brad Overfield told the magazine.[35]

Interiors were filmed in Laughlin and in the L.A. area. Various exterior scenes were shot on location in Las Vegas, which proved tricky because—despite the film's title—the Nevada Film Commission refused to cooperate with the production. "They hated us," says Figgis. "[They thought] a film about alcoholism in Las Vegas would be bad for tourism. So we had no permissions at all. They didn't want us to be there."

This complication augmented the film's spirit of underdog ingenuity; crucial scenes, such as Ben's first encounter with Sera on the Vegas Strip (he's a drunk-driver, she a pedestrian), had to be filmed essentially guerrilla-style, without permits. "We just went around stealing those shots where we could," Figgis recalls. The crew learned what property was owned by the casinos and what was owned by the city. "If we were on city sidewalks with a camera and a handheld tripod, they couldn't immediately kick us off," says cinematographer Declan Quinn.

Even the underwater scene, perhaps the most shamelessly stylized sequence in the film, came together on the fly. The crew couldn't afford underwater camera housing, so they sought out a glass-bottomed pool. "We literally drove over to the side of the road, quickly got permission," says first assistant director Gary Marcus. "I remember Mike [Figgis] ran into the bar and bought a Budweiser and gave it to Nick, and he just jumped into the water and started drinking the beer underwater."

Amidst this chaos, Cage and Shue thrived, delivering stellar, fatalistic performances dialed in to the nebulous space between brutality and tenderness—pain and pleasure mingled together like Jack and coke. It was, Shue says, "the most intense, most creative, most challenging, and most satisfying work I've ever gotten to do. . . . I remember that I loved working opposite him, because you never knew what he would do next. There was a certain playful, improvisational quality to how he works. It was very, very natural."

Cage seemed immersed in the essence of Ben Sanderson from day one. "I would say he was semi–in character most of the time he was on set," says Quinn. "When the camera cut, he didn't necessarily turn back into Nick. He would just get quiet and close his eyes and think about what he wants to do in the next take."

* * *

During the early weeks of the production, Cage approached Figgis with a radical idea.

"Nick said to me that he wanted to do the entire film drunk," Figgis recalls. "And he heard that Brando had done a movie where he just had an earpiece and his assistant was feeding him the lines.[†] He wanted to do that. And I said, 'Categorically not.' "

Figgis was adamant that this couldn't work. "We had a very short time to shoot this movie"—a scant twenty-eight days—"so we didn't have time to fuck around. He's very determined, Nick, if he gets it in his head that he wants to do something. I talked him out of being drunk for the whole movie. But he wanted to do at least one scene drunk."

Cage's determination to embody extreme verisimilitude was likely inspired by a survey of cinematic drunks of the past. Before the shoot, he watched famous films about alcoholics and drew slivers of inspiration from each. There was Dudley Moore in 1981's *Arthur*: Cage liked the way the character couldn't seem to modulate his volume. There was Ray Milland in *The*

[†] While filming *Apocalypse Now*, Marlon Brando could not remember his lines and had them fed to him via an earpiece. He used a similar process during the disastrous production of *The Island of Dr. Moreau*, receiving lines through an earpiece obscured by a bucket hat. Reportedly, Brando's receiver would occasionally pick up local police transmissions, prompting the actor to say things like "There is a fire at the local Woolworth's" in the middle of a scene.

Lost Weekend (the rare 1940s film that depicts alcohol addiction as a disease rather than a punch line): he observed how it captured a certain meanness in addiction. Watching Kris Kristofferson in 1976's *A Star Is Born*, he was struck by how the character kept smiling, even as he drank himself to death.[36]

But no performance stunned Cage as much as Albert Finney in 1984's *Under the Volcano*. In this late-career John Huston drama, Finney staggers between sloshed merriment and raving fury as a hard-drinking British consul in Mexico. Like *Leaving Las Vegas*, *Under the Volcano* opens with its hero already in the terminal stages of alcoholism, a state in which drunk and sober are no longer meaningful distinctions; as he slurs to his estranged wife, he is "only drunk in the conventional, incoherent, staggering sense when I haven't had a drink."

Cage was astonished by the gritty verité of Finney's performance. "I saw him walk through the streets of Mexico," he later recalled, "and I went, 'That guy is really drunk.' "[37]

Cage asked Figgis, who was friends with Finney and had recently directed him in a different film, whether Finney was really drinking. "He said no, he certainly wasn't," says Figgis, who mentioned Cage's question at lunch with the *Miller's Crossing* actor. "And then Albert gave me a great piece of advice to tell him: 'If you want to experience being drunk, just have a little tumbler of Scotch on standby. Before each take, put it on your lips, so you have the taste of Scotch on your lips. But do *not* be drunk.' "

Finney also advised against the stereotypical portrayal of a drunk as a clumsy buffoon. "A true drunk puts a glass down like it's a moon landing," Finney told Figgis. "It's so careful; he never knocks anything over."

Figgis passed this wisdom along. Cage, though, decided he needed to go straight to the source by hiring an actual drunk to feed him inspiration on set. At the suggestion of Roman Coppola, Cage hired a poet named Tony Dingman, a longtime friend of the Coppola family who'd had odd jobs on Francis's films dating back to *The Rain People*. Dingman was a self-described drunk, and he'd known Cage since childhood. Now he was hired to be Cage's own, private "drinking coach."[38]

"He's a lovely man," Figgis says. "He was there almost like a buddy for Nick to consult at any point, like, 'Would I do that or would I not do that?' I talked to him, too. He was really useful to me."

Early on, Cage sent Dingman the script, and Dingman offered notes. Cage then proposed that Dingman come to Las Vegas for the shoot. "He didn't really need me, but I was support," Dingman told the *Independent*. "He likes a martini every now and then. But he was not a drunk. So I gave him things to read: Malcolm Lowry's *Under the Volcano*, stuff by Charles Bukowski, and William Holden's life."[39]

To his credit, Dingman may be the only person who has ever benefited an Oscar-winning film simply by getting smashed and passing out in a movie star's trailer. Dingman would stumble in and crash into the makeup mirror while Cage was warming up by playing bongos. Cage observed the poet's binges with a scientific curiosity, and odd phrases he heard Dingman say—"We mustn't kick the bar, we lean *into* the bar," "It's not *vino veritas*, it's *in vino veritas*!"—wound their way into the film, particularly the scene in which Ben gets slugged in a biker bar. It's clear that Dingman was responsible for much of the character's off-kilter comic flavor.

"I just watched Tony," Cage told the *Independent*. "He would go on a bender and pass out, curled up in my trailer in a fetal position. And he would go into these amazing diatribes—and I would put that in the movie. I wanted to give Ben a sort of crumbling elegance. He always takes on a British accent when he's most drunk. And I loved that clue to his flaw."[40]

After the film was released, Cage went out of his way to credit his drinking coach. During his Oscar acceptance speech, Dingman was the fourth individual he thanked.

* * *

Cage did, ultimately, achieve his goal of being filmed piss-drunk in *Leaving Las Vegas*. But only for one scene (Figure 11.2).

The scene is almost operatic in its intensity. Ben and Sera are at a blackjack table in a casino when Ben, who is blackout drunk, starts to nod off. A cocktail waitress rouses him, and after an apparent misunderstanding, Ben becomes enraged and smashes the whole table over while screaming obscenities. He is dragged out by security, all the while screaming and crying in anguish. The once-jazzy musical score rises to a wail of dread. The entire altercation unfolds in one aerial shot, which gives the scene a sense of woozy distance, as though the viewer's powers of observation are impaired by Ben's blackout.

Desperate to match the authenticity he sensed in Albert Finney in *Under the Volcano*, Cage consumed a significant quantity of sambuca, supplied by Dingman, before cameras rolled. "I wanted to be out of control," Cage later told *GQ*. "I didn't know I was gonna go there. I knew I wanted something extraordinary to happen, and they kept it and they put it in the movie."[41]

Figure 11.2. Cage wanted to be drunk throughout the filming of *Leaving Las Vegas* (1995, MGM/UA Distribution Co.), but Mike Figgis refused the idea. Cage, however, was "completely shitfaced" during the scene in which Ben and Sera (Elisabeth Shue) are thrown out of a casino.

Figgis was angry. Cage hadn't told him he would be sloshed. "He got completely shitfaced, and smashed up a casino," Figgis recalls. "It's a good scene. But I think somebody got injured. The pit boss was very unhappy with us. And we had no budget. It's not like we had the luxury of building a set."

The crew was on the verge of being thrown out of the casino; Cage's smashing the equipment was not planned, and the pit boss was furious. Then the extras all broke out in applause, and the pit boss smiled and seemed to cool down.

"I've worked with quite a few method-approach actors, and they all want to do that," Figgis says. "The balance is that he gave a great performance. He's a very, very good actor. So I forgave him. To be honest, I was very angry at the time."

If the casino scene represents Cage going rogue, its uninhibited rage also offers a profound clue to his interpretation of the character. As Ben is being dragged out by security, he screams, "I am his father!" over and over. This was not in the script. O'Brien's book contained no indication that Ben ever had a kid, though the film shows him burning his possessions, including a photograph with a wife and child—a faded relic from happier times.

Cage, then a single father of three-year-old Weston, latched onto this detail with intense interest. Rationalizing Ben's pain to himself, he decided that Ben must have lost custody of his child; that this was the seed, the loss that drove him to drink himself to oblivion. Cage could relate: "Our society in California isn't really geared toward the single father," he told one interviewer.[42] When he screamed in the casino, "that was a sort of primal scream that came out of some part of me that wasn't in the script," Cage later explained.[43]

As ever, Cage was drawing on private pain, private grief (including the death of his cousin, Gian-Carlo Coppola, in 1986), to fuel his performance. Alone in his room at night, he would think about Ben and ruminate on why he wanted to die. "There were some times I would go home from work," he told the *Los Angeles Times*, "and I'd been trying to see the world through Ben's eyes, and then the streetlights on the freeway just suddenly seemed like they were made of cardboard and the freeway itself was made of papier-mâché, and it made me feel like nothing was real and this is all just so temporary."[44]

The whirlwind intensity of the shoot was such that Cage expressed relief that it only lasted four weeks.[45]

* * *

One other significant disagreement arose between Figgis and Cage during the shoot. It involved the ending. In the book, Ben and Sera's relationship is never consummated. Sera visits Ben, who is near death, at his hotel room, where he begins "masturbating furiously"; she takes over until he climaxes. They both fall asleep, and after one final muscle spasm, he is gone.[46] In Figgis's screenplay, however, there is no masturbation. They briefly have sex during their tearful reunion, after which Ben slips off into death—"a properly dark romantic ending," Figgis notes.

On the day this scene was to be shot, Figgis recalls that Cage approached him and said, "I just reread the ending of the book last night. I think I should just masturbate by myself."

Figgis balked. "It's the end of the movie, Nick," he told Cage. "It's quite dark material. To be very British and direct with you, you're suggesting that we should finish this film with you having a wank. I don't think that's the way to go, really."

Figgis stood firm, and Cage eventually bowed to his directorial judgment: no having a wank.

Cage seems to have regarded *Leaving Las Vegas* as a movie with no commercial potential, a low-paying passion project, like *Vampire's Kiss* or *Deadfall*, where he would have free rein to veer off the rails and make the script his own. On low-budget productions, where Cage is bringing the distribution clout, "he probably has a lot of leg-room to do it his way," Figgis says.

But on *Leaving Las Vegas*, Figgis was the director, screenwriter, composer, and part-editor. He was in charge. He had deconstructed the book meticulously and lived with it for a year or two; he had a clear idea of the character.

"I'd made quite a few movies by then," Figgis says. "This was my get-out-of-Hollywood card. I wasn't about to be directed by an actor. . . . So, he came to it with the potential for all kinds of things: 'I want to do the whole film drunk.' No, you're not. 'I want to masturbate at the end of the film.' No, you're not. And that's OK. I think he respected the fact that I was a tough guy. With a lot of actors that I've worked with, that's the only way. And then they respect you for that, and you get an even better performance. Because it's not a bunch of tricks. It's not a bunch of, 'What a zappy, bizarre moment!' It has consistency. And I think that's why he got respect, because he got all the way through a movie very consistent with that character."

* * *

In October 1994, Erin O'Brien, with her parents and husband, flew to Los Angeles to visit the set. "It was an emotional, difficult trip," Erin says.

On a stage in Burbank, the family watched as Cage and Shue filmed the scene in which Ben and Sera reach a non-interference pact; she asks him to move in, and he tells her that she can never ask him to stop drinking. "[The O'Briens] were watching that and they were crying and they just said he embodied their son," Figgis recalls. "They were kind of shocked by how close he was to the character. It was an incredible moment."

Indeed, watching Cage on the monitor as he portrayed Ben was "a moment I will never forget," Erin wrote days later in a letter to Figgis. "He could have been John/Johnny. John the doomed alcoholic, Johnny the soulful poet. . . . Perhaps Johnny was there with us. I felt his presence throughout our trip."

For Cage, the visit was highly affecting. He shook Bill O'Brien's hand and told him that his son's work had moved him deeply. He and Shue each signed a copy of the script for Erin. Shue scrawled a message: "Dear Erin—you have blessed our work."

At times, Cage felt as though he had a telepathic understanding of O'Brien. There was, for instance, the mysterious business of the watch. In the early chapters of the novel, Ben's reliance on his watch is an emblem of his addiction. In Los Angeles, he keeps obsessive track of time, lest he find himself awake when the bars close at two a.m. "Never let two o'clock happen," O'Brien writes, "unless there is more liquor in the house than you could possibly drink in four hours."[47]

So Ben moves to Las Vegas, seduced by the promise of a city where the bars never close. In the film, we see him grinning in a Vegas pawn shop as he unloads his '93 Rolex Daytona for a measly $500. It's a symbolic moment. Ben isn't just cashing in on his last valuable; he's releasing himself from the civilized realm, freeing himself from the world of timekeeping. When time no longer controls the availability of a drink, Ben no longer has need for time.

Cage and O'Brien shared a fondness for luxury watches. O'Brien wore a Rolex. "He valued time so much that he bought the most expensive watch he could afford to keep track of it," Erin says.[‡]

Although the script didn't get too specific, Cage instinctively knew what model watch Ben should wear. When O'Brien's family visited the set, they told him, "That's the same watch John wore."[48]

Cage also selected his character's automobile. One night he called Figgis and insisted that Ben, like most Hollywood bigshots, would drive a black BMW. Figgis assented.[49]

Later, Cage learned that it was the same vehicle O'Brien had driven.[50]

* * *

Hindsight has a way of distorting things and making it seem as though *Leaving Las Vegas* was predestined to deliver Cage enormous acclaim, but in 1994 the perception on set was rather different. Cage himself feared that the movie would not get released.[51]

"There was no part of him that was interested in doing the movie as a way to get attention or acclaim," says Elisabeth Shue. "I thought it was an obscure, teeny, tiny experimental film and that it probably would be a festival film. I never thought it would reach such a broad audience."

"None of us saw this as a mainstream film as we made it," confirms director of photography Declan Quinn. Quinn recalls one afternoon setting up lighting for a scene at the Saharan Motor Hotel, where Ben has a blackout encounter with a prostitute who swipes his wedding ring (the last tangible relic

‡ There is an internet rumor that Cage was wearing O'Brien's *actual* Rolex in the film, but this is false.

of his former life). Quinn and Figgis were on the sidewalk when Cage arrived for the scene. In Quinn's memory, Cage cheerily announced to them, "Well, I just got off the phone with my agent. And I guess I'm working on the least viable film being shot in Hollywood right now!"

"That's total Nick right there," Quinn says. "He made us laugh. But he was genuine. He said, 'I'm really happy to be here.' But he was being told by his agent, 'You're being stupid, this isn't viable.' "

To a cinematographer like Quinn, it was obvious that *Leaving Las Vegas* was not a studio movie. Unlike most mainstream films, which are shot on 35-millimeter, this was being shot on Super 16, which is considerably cheaper. That choice, far from being a mere money-saving decision, had a profound impact on the film.

Super 16 "was chosen because it was a smaller camera," Quinn says, which facilitated a more intimate collaboration between actors and director. Quinn recalls that he and Figgis both owned Super 16-millimeter cameras themselves. In lieu of a typical camera crew, Quinn would shoot one camera and Figgis would shoot the second, usually from a more experimental angle (note, for instance, the way the camera travels in close-up across Sera's face and down her shoulders when she falls asleep in Ben's motel room). The director's camera provided opportunities for more unorthodox coverage.

"While we didn't use that many of Mike's shots in the film, it did give him a way artistically into the scene and to feel the actors' body language up close and to experiment with images," Quinn says. "And the other thing about Super 16 is that there's a grain structure. When you blow it up to the big screen, you see the grain more. It's a little softer, and it has that slightly grittier quality to it."

Cage expressed a fondness for the visual palette, telling an interviewer that it gives the movie "a pastel look . . . like a painting," while Shue liked how small and unobtrusive the camera felt. "That documentary-like feeling to the film helped all of us kind of forget about the cameras a bit," Shue says. "I remember the crew around the camera being small, so I remember enjoying the feeling that we were almost living out these characters' lives. It just felt very intimate."[52]

* * *

With *Leaving Las Vegas*, Figgis made a film that buzzes with contradictions. It is an addiction story, yet there is no predictable recovery narrative. It is a romance, yet largely sexless, with no hope for a lasting love. It is a Vegas movie, yet none of the characters is particularly interested in gambling. It is a character study, yet we are permitted only fleeting glimpses of this man's backstory and what precipitated his death wish. It is a low-budget art film, and yet it became a high-profile award season fixture.

Most surprising is the fizzy tone of Cage's performance. *Leaving Las Vegas* is often described as depressing, even unwatchably so, but Cage brings a chipper, comic air to this portrait of self-annihilation. The movie unfolds in the space between the decision to die and the fulfillment of that idea. Though Ben is severely crippled by his alcoholism—the film hardly romanticizes this fact—in Cage's interpretation, he has already drowned his regrets and let go. Like an emptyheaded animal, he lives only in the present; neither past nor future is of any pertinence anymore. His hedonistic indulgence is the alcoholic's version of a hospice ward.

"And yet he's happy," Cage insisted to *Rolling Stone*. "A man who has made the decision to die is not really fighting anymore. Ben had let go. It's like, 'We're going down the river, and you can try to hold on, but if you just let go, you're riding, you're floating, you're up, you're smiling.' And that seemed to be the way to do it and not have the lines become maudlin."[53]

Cage resisted the urge to deliver a showboating spectacle of despair. "The decision was to not dwell on the sadness or self-pity, but more to explore the freedom and the beauty of no longer struggling. I guess it was in some ways like Zen, in that it's not wanting anymore," he told *GQ*.[54]

In its opening scene, *Leaving Las Vegas* subverts expectations that the film is a downer. As Sting croons "Angel Eyes" (the de facto theme song), Cage whistles, twirls, and boogies down a supermarket aisle, cheerfully grabbing liquor bottles off the shelf. Cage improvised the body movements. "It was meant to be seen much later in the picture," Figgis told *Rolling Stone*, "but we put it in as the opening shot because in one image it establishes that this man is charming, he's pretty energetic, and he's an alcoholic."[55]

From then on, Cage instills the character with a perverse jolliness that livens up the movie and renders his self-destruction bearable. Ben literally goes dancing to his doom: in the liquor aisle, and later at his office, where he woozily slow-dances with a co-worker who is summoning him to his termination meeting. Cage's line readings, too, are pitched toward the absurd. When a woman in a bar suggests he shouldn't drink so much, the script called for Ben to retort, "Maybe I shouldn't breathe so much, Teri. Ha . . . ha." The actor added the equivalent of three exclamation points to the second "ha," which he delivered in a clownish falsetto. Cage may have left comedy to make *Leaving Las Vegas*, but the comedy did not leave Cage.

He also brought in lines of his own—for instance, when Sera asks how Ben, bloodied from a fight, is feeling and Ben blurts out, "Like the kling klang king of the rim ram room!" Figgis was taken aback by that addition. "I shouted as we rolled for the next take, 'Good luck with the improvisation,'" the director told *Entertainment Weekly*. "Well, Nick got a look and said, 'Oh, okay, I'll do a *real straight one* for ya then.' I had made the mistake of thinking it was arbitrary, when in fact he'd worked it all out very careful. He's still very sensitive about the perception that he's wacky, because his performance isn't that. It's all hard work."[56]

In retrospect, Figgis says, "I felt there was tremendous black humor in John O'Brien's novel. I think it was one of the things Nick responded to. . . . I'm British. I come out of that bizarre comedy background, experimental theater. I certainly did not discourage him from going down that direction. He did bring his own ideas. Pretty much what he says, I would say 96 percent is in the script. But then he would add very nice touches: 'We got eggs!' And like a good musician, the improvisations weren't too long-winded."

As Ben inexorably approaches his demise, the film's tone becomes more tragic, its score more operatic. We realize not even true love will save Ben from his chosen fate.

But to Cage, even Ben's death had an optimistic tint. "I really wanted Ben to die saying 'Wow.' When you see death in films, it's always portrayed as being painful and lonely. But we don't know, it could be anything—it could be a roller-coaster ride," the actor explained. "I wanted it to be the beginning of a *trip*."[57]

* * *

By the time *Leaving Las Vegas* opened in October 1995, Cage's life had changed substantially. He had fired Ed Limato, his agent of ten years, reportedly due to frustration with the roles Limato was bringing him, and replaced him with Creative Artists Agency's Richard Lovett.[58] He had broken up with his twenty-year-old fiancée, Kristen Zang, and suddenly married Patricia Arquette, his long-ago paramour, on a romantic impulse.[59]

And now he was receiving the most effusive praise of his career. Critics responded to *Leaving Las Vegas* with rapturous admiration. In *Newsweek*, David Ansen described the film as "a bleak, mesmerizing rhapsody of self-destruction."[60] In *Entertainment Weekly*, Owen Gleiberman hailed Cage's "madly inspired performance as a man spilling over the edges of his own sanity. . . . Cage mingles pain and jubilation until, like Ben himself, we can barely tell the difference."[61] And Roger Ebert emerged as one of the film's champions. Cage, he wrote in the *Chicago Sun-Times*, "a resourceful and daring actor, has never been better."[62]

Leaving Las Vegas eventually earned more than $40 million against its $3.5-million budget. There was rich irony here: Cage's low-budget passion project grossed more than his recent dabblings in mainstream appeal.

For years, Cage had been ignored by the Academy, while his co-stars in *Peggy Sue Got Married* and *Moonstruck* garnered nominations and sometimes wins. Now his luck changed, and he became the third generation of the Coppola family (after Francis and Carmine) to be feted by the Oscars. At the Sixty-eighth Academy Awards, *Leaving Las Vegas* received four nominations: Best Actor, Best Actress (Shue), Best Director (Figgis), and Best Adapted Screenplay (Figgis).

A film as unflinching as *Leaving Las Vegas* could hardly be called Oscar bait, but Cage underestimated the Academy's eternal attraction to able-bodied actors playing characters debilitated by a physical or mental disability. He was also nominated for a Golden Globe, an Independent Spirit Award, and countless other accolades, as was Shue.

"I remember thinking, 'This will maybe make sense in a couple of years' time, but right now it just feels crazy,'" Figgis says. "Not even remotely what I was expecting."

On the day of the Oscars, March 25, 1996, Cage was a nervous wreck, pacing around his Los Angeles penthouse in a Hugo Boss tuxedo. He was the favorite to win Best Actor, having already won the Golden Globe, but his nerves were frayed. He was up against old friend Sean Penn (*Dead Man Walking*), who had just beaten him at the Independent Spirit Awards, where Cage crumpled up his victory speech in disappointment.[63]

At the Dorothy Chandler Pavilion, *Leaving Las Vegas* lost the first three Oscars for which it had been nominated. Figgis silently worried it would lose the fourth as well. Cage squirmed. Then Jessica Lange emerged to present Best Actor, and a sense of calm fell over him. As soon as he heard the first syllable of his name, Cage kissed his wife, leapt from his seat, and arrived onstage, shaking his head in disbelief.[64]

Beaming, with lipstick stains on his face, Cage delivered a mile-a-minute acceptance speech swathed in childlike excitement. Declaring his mission to "blur the line between art and commerce" (a concise thesis statement for his career), he made no effort to hide his bewilderment and delight. A younger Cage had tried to project an image of danger and rebellion. Now, addressing some of the Hollywood power players who had scorned his earlier works, Cage radiated an earnestness and sheer enthusiasm that had always been lurking behind his eccentricities:

> Oh, boy! Oh, boy! Three-and-a-half million-dollar budget, some 16-millimeter film stock thrown in, and I'm holding one of these. I have got to thank the members of the Academy for this, for including me in this group of super-talents, and for helping me blur the line between art and commerce with this award. Well, I know it's not hip to say it, but I just *love* acting, and I hope that there will be more encouragement for alternative movies, where we can experiment and fast-forward into the future of acting.
>
> Let me thank the awesome, multitalented Mike Figgis. My incredible, amazing co-star, Elisabeth Shue. I am going to share this award with both of you! And the late John O'Brien, whose spirit moved me so much. Tony Dingman, Annie Stewart—the producers, Annie Stewart, Stuart Regen, everyone at MGM, UA, Lumière. I'd like to thank Ed Limato. My colleagues, Gerry Harrington, Jeff Levine, Richard Lovett.
>
> And everyone in my family. My gorgeous wife, Patricia. And I just finally want to say, hi Weston, it's Daddy. I love you! Thank you!

After the ceremony, Cage and Arquette proceeded to the Governors Ball, and then to a nearby restaurant, where they spotted Stevie Wonder. Cage introduced Arquette as "my golden lady," and, in a moment of romantic reverie, Wonder sang "Golden Lady" to her. The evening ended at Cage's Hollywood Hills home, where he celebrated with members of his inner circle—cousins Roman and Sofia Coppola, friends Jim Carrey and Phil Roy, agent Richard Lovett, manager Gerry Harrington, Jr.—and nibbled on caviar.[65]

Like many actors, Cage had long insisted he didn't care much about winning an Oscar. But when it happened, he hardly concealed his sense of vindication. As he told *Details*, the success of *Leaving Las Vegas* "shows that I wasn't crazy all these years, that I had a *point*."[66]

* * *

It's strange, perhaps, that Cage and Figgis never worked together again.

It was not for lack of trying. Figgis wanted to cast Cage as a philandering husband in his next film, 1997's *One Night Stand*. Cage declined because, as a newlywed, he felt he wasn't in the right headspace to play a man cheating on his wife.[67]

Then, in 2015, Cage agreed to reunite with Figgis for a Louisiana-set thriller called *Exit 147*. Figgis deferred the shoot for months to accommodate Cage's busy schedule. But during preproduction, Cage suddenly pulled out without explanation.

"We never spoke. I never heard from him," Figgis says. "At the same time, I do know Nick. And I accept him for who he was. He's a very unique guy. And sometimes a little socially challenged."

Figgis was angry. But he seems to have forgiven Cage since then. "Not that I want to hang out with him all the time, but I wish we were in contact," he muses. "I mean, we did a great thing together. Changed both of our lives, absolutely. It's something I'm proud of."

* * *

John O'Brien's family was deeply affected when Cage thanked O'Brien, "whose spirit moved me so much," during his acceptance speech. The author had lived and died in obscurity. Now a movie star was saying his name in front of 44 million people.

Erin O'Brien remembers seeing this moment unfold from her parents' living room, where a small watch party had congregated. It was overwhelming. "I remember that magical thinking enveloping me, thinking: This is John's spirit speaking," Erin says. "This is some gift that he's leaving behind. This is some heavenly reward for him."

Maybe that was preposterous. Erin knew that if John were alive, he would have quibbled with certain creative liberties taken by the film (particularly the decision to move Sera's rape to the third act—"John would have come back to life to bitch about that").

Yet Erin couldn't help but sense her brother's spirit emanating from Cage's performance. There were little moments—the way Ben slips into a wacky British accent just before getting slugged in a biker bar, for example—that summoned John's black humor eerily well. "Maybe he didn't have to smell the vomit to understand the depths of John's alcoholism," Erin says. "To me, watching Cage in that performance, he had to have some depths of understanding of Johnny and what he was trying to convey."

In her letter in 1994, Erin told Cage she regarded *Leaving Las Vegas* as O'Brien's suicide note. Her father told interviewers the same thing. Cage internalized this idea; he told the *Los Angeles Times* that the book "is clearly John O'Brien's suicide letter, and I really felt the weight of portraying a dead man's suicide note."[68]

Today, Erin isn't so sure she still regards it as a suicide note. In reality, O'Brien's death was grim and lonely—not at all like the novel. "Ben died with this beautiful woman fondling him in a hotel room with a bottle of liquor to his lips," Erin says. "*Leaving Las Vegas* was the fantasy. It was the fantasy version of how John wanted to leave the world."

Tellingly, in the film, Ben can't quite believe Sera is real. "What are you," he asks her as they cuddle in bed the morning after his ejection from the casino, "some sort of angel visiting me from one of my drunk fantasies?"

The woozy cinemfatography and editing, its frequent dissolves and fade-outs when Ben is in the throes of delirium tremens, contribute to this sense of dreamlike detachment. Time is never stable; with editor John Smith making use of the then-new Avid editing system, some scenes unfold in slow

Figure 11.3. Despite the film's sordid themes, *Leaving Las Vegas* (1995, MGM/UA Distribution Co.) remains one of Cage's most romantic performances. "What are you," Ben asks Sera, "some sort of angel visiting me from one of my drunk fantasies?"

motion (as when the L.A. sex worker swipes Ben's wedding ring) and others in dizzying acceleration (as when Ben speeds the freeways to Vegas). In the opening credits, Las Vegas glitters in hallucinatory flashes, leaving you unsure if this is a fantasy or nightmare. Just as Ben is unsure if he is drinking as a way to kill himself or killing himself as a way to drink, perhaps it can be both.

* * *

The morning after the Academy Awards unraveled like a dream. Cage, eternally the Hollywood outsider, found himself at the center of the establishment's embrace.

Walking through Los Angeles, he passed a newsstand and spotted his own face on the front page. At a local coffee shop, the cooks applauded him. Then he drove to the beach while listening to "Baby, You're a Rich Man," the song he'd heard in his uncle's car twenty years earlier. Cage was savoring the moment when a police officer pulled him over. Expecting a speeding ticket, he was surprised when the cop simply offered him a congratulations.[69]

Preferential treatment from traffic cops was not the only perk of his prize. In Hollywood, an Oscar is like a legitimizing serum. Your pay rate goes up;[§] your name carries weight; your projects get financed. Cage knew this. "The one thing I had hoped the Oscar would give me more than anything else was that if I came up with an idea that seemed a little left field, you'd just give me five more seconds before you kill it," he later confessed in a *GQ* cover story.[70]

After Cage had his gold statuette, people wondered what he would do next. But by then, the actor's next movie was already in the can.

The decision point had come eight months earlier, during the summer of 1995. Cage was a newlywed then, and had taken an uncharacteristic break from work after wrapping *Leaving Las Vegas*. That summer he flew to New York to meet with Abel Ferrara, the independent filmmaker known for defiantly low-budget crime flicks like *Ms .45* and the original *Bad Lieutenant*. Ferrara was eager to meet with Cage, because Ferrara was eager for Cage to star in his next movie, a crime drama called *The Funeral*, about a family of small-time gangsters. Cage, it seemed, also wanted to star in *The Funeral*. But Cage was at a crossroads. For whatever reason, he couldn't commit.

Later that year, *GQ* published a feature called "Waiting for Nic Cage," which was actually a profile of a paranoid Ferrara desperately trying to

[§] Cage's contract for *Face/Off*, signed in late 1995 or early 1996, stipulated that he would receive a handsome bonus if he won the Oscar for *Leaving Las Vegas*.

secure financing for *The Funeral*, whose "fate currently hinges on Nicolas Cage." Author Scott Raab shadowed Ferrara as he chain-smoked and paced around his studio, waiting for Cage—with whom he had met days earlier—to call back and commit. "Nick's ready to rock and roll," Ferrara told Raab. "But his agents aren't makin' it easy, I'll tell you that. If he backs out now, we're in trouble, man. And they know it."[71]

Days passed. Chris Penn signed on. Isabella Rossellini, too. Ferrara was growing agitated. He needed a star. The start date was pushed back a week, then pushed back again. Where was Cage?

Weeks later, Raab called Ferrara for an update. The news was not good. Ferrara fumed: "It's insane, this whole thing with Cage. Right now he ain't doin' the film. He just calls and says, 'I can't do it.' If he was here right now, there's about nine people that would put a bullet in his *fuckin'* head."[72]

After formally backing out four days before shooting was scheduled to begin, Cage was replaced at the eleventh hour by Christopher Walken. He would not appear in another low-budget film until the new millennium.[73]

In the fall of 1995, Cage began shooting a different movie, for which he was paid a reported salary—$4 million—that exceeded the entire budgets of several previous films by Ferrara. It was called *The Rock*.[74]

Epilogue

In the spring of 2022, while I was finishing a first draft of this book, Nicolas Cage was haunting me.

He was everywhere. On the cover of *GQ*. On *Jimmy Kimmel Live!* Being interviewed in the *New York Times* and *Rolling Stone*. He was even answering fans' questions and telling stories about tubular pasta in a Reddit "Ask Me Anything."

He was embarking on this all-out media blitz in support of a film role that seemed genetically engineered to be Nicolas Cage's most talked-about performance in many years, a role not quite like anything Cage had done before. The movie was *The Unbearable Weight of Massive Talent*—or, as people tended to refer to it in conversation, "the movie where Nicolas Cage plays himself."

By the late 2010s, Cage already seemed to be entering a newly self-referential phase: employing a grating voice reminiscent of Charlie Bodell in 2016's terrorist-hunter comedy *Army of One*, reprising his sleazy *Deadfall* character in 2017's godawful *Arsenal*. In truth, he was over his head in debts stemming from a long string of outlandish real estate purchases—an eighteenth-century castle in England here, an extravagant private island in the Bahamas there. Like his uncle in the eighties, he realized the only way to stave off bankruptcy was to churn out movies at a furious pace. So he did.[1]

It was a difficult period for Cage. He was grieving his father, mourning the end of his third (and then fourth) marriage, and spending thousands a month to keep his mother from re-entering the mental institution. Amid this personal strife, he starred in four, sometimes five, movies a year. And while there were some real gems to be found (2018's *Mandy*, 2021's *Pig*), most of these movies blended together into an undistinguishable straight-to-VOD glop.[2]

But *The Unbearable Weight of Massive Talent*, the curiously meta role that allowed him to finally pay off his debts, offered a new challenge. Cage plays a fictionalized version of himself: an actor by the name of Nick Cage, who, it seems, has starred in all the movies the real Cage has starred in. After losing out on a significant part, this Nick Cage is down on his luck and desperate for cash. So desperate, in fact, that he grudgingly accepts a $1 million offer from a billionaire superfan named Javi (Pedro Pascal), who hires Cage to appear at his birthday party in Mallorca. Once there, Cage discovers that the mysterious Javi is a villainous arms dealer and gets caught up in a convoluted plot to bring him down.

The film earned Cage a reported $7 million salary—six or seven times what he was getting paid for his straight-to-VOD projects and enough to resolve his long-standing financial woes. Its success, coupled with the acclaim for *Pig*, revitalized Cage's career. He resumed landing live-action studio roles for the first time in a decade.[3]

In trailers, *Massive Talent*—which Cage also co-produced—was billed as "the most Nicolas Cage movie ever." The comeback narrative was catnip for journalists, though there was a depressing undercurrent: Cage is still a bankable star, the film's buzz seemed to suggest, but only if he's willing to reprise his past glories in a slick new package.

When I finally got to see it, at a crowded press screening in Times Square, I was at once fascinated and repelled. As an action spectacle, the movie is tedious, and as a meta-comedy in the tradition of Hollywood head-spinners like *Being John Malkovich* and *Adaptation*, it is never as clever or provocative as it wants to be. Instead of subverting Cage's persona or delving deep into his backstory, director Tom Gormican is mostly intent on pushing Cage toward the most manic, self-parodic version of himself. ("You're Nick *fuckinnnnnnnn'* Cage!" Cage's imaginary alter-ego—a younger version of himself, digitally de-aged to resemble his 1990 appearance on *Wogan*—bellows at himself in one trailer-ready moment.)

Yet for a Cage fan, *Massive Talent* is a dizzying work of sensory overload. It is stuffed with blink-and-miss-'em references to Cage's filmography. There's Cage underwater with a drink, recreating a shot from *Leaving Las Vegas*; there's Cage in a car chase, calling back to *Gone in 60 Seconds*. In one scene, Cage comes face to face with a room full of Cage-themed memorabilia: a Castor Troy wax figure from *Face/Off*, the chainsaw from *Mandy*. In another, the film offers a truly unexpected meditation on *Guarding Tess*, for which Javi proclaims his affection in an emotional speech. It's one of the rare moments in which *Massive Talent* acknowledges the quieter side of the actor's work, though it's a testament to his filmography that you could easily swap out those references for a dozen different ones.

Altogether, it amounts to a cynical if fascinating spin on Hollywood's shift to preexisting intellectual property. Instead of rebooting an old franchise or spinning off some beloved side character, *Massive Talent* plops a real icon into a cinematic universe where *Con Air* and *Moonstruck* already exist. You know how when pop stars want to regain control of their masters, they rerecord their old hits with new production techniques? It's like that, with a meta-performance twist. It's a sentient IMDb page of a movie. And to its credit, the crowd at that Times Square screening loved it, howling and laughing at all the intertextual Cage-isms.

While Cage's character in *Massive Talent* is clearly fictionalized (this Cage has a teenage daughter) and heightened for comic effect, there are interesting echoes of the real man. The movie is at its most genuine when it depicts Cage as a nerdy and excitable film lover whose esoteric obsessions sometimes make him an outsider in the modern world. In one scene, he's vying for a big role in David Gordon Green's new movie and eagerly compares the script to the 1949 noir *House of Strangers*. In a recurring motif, he proclaims his love for the 1920 silent classic *The Cabinet of Dr. Caligari*, which the real Cage watched with his father at age ten.[4]

In these moments, Cage is still that same kid marveling at the German Expressionist classics on his father's syllabus. He is still the restless young actor channeling James Dean and Max Schreck and Elvis Presley. He is still a cracked mirror, reflecting a hundred years of cinema history back at anyone willing to squint through the light.

He's still chewing up film classics and spitting them back out anew. Except now the classics are Cage's own.

Acknowledgments

First of all, I have to thank Nicolas Cage for giving so many remarkable performances, enriching the world of cinema, and ensuring that nobody writing a book about his work could ever be bored.

That this particular nobody is writing that book is thanks to my agent, Barbara Zitwer, without whom this would not be possible. My deepest gratitude to Barbara for believing in this project from the beginning, placing it with the right publisher, and providing support and encouragement at every stage.

I'm equally indebted to Norm Hirschy at Oxford University Press for his tremendous faith in this project and for giving me the time and trust to see it through. I owe an additional thanks to project editor Zara Cannon-Mohammed, who helped steer this book to publication, as did Ponneelan at Newgen Knowledge Works.

The idea for this book partially grew out of my experiences writing and reporting a piece about the making of *Vampire's Kiss* in 2019. I am very indebted to Sean Fennessey at *The Ringer* for believing in that piece and bringing it to a passionate audience, as well as the makers of *Vampire's Kiss* for sharing their stories with me.

Throughout the research and writing of this book, I interviewed more than 120 individuals who knew or worked with Cage during his early years. Some are quoted in these pages and some are not, but I want to express my gratitude to all of these sources for generously offering their time, insight, and stories. This book would not exist without them.

I'm obliged to thank by name several individual sources who went above and beyond just an interview. Robert Bierman provided great photos and insights from the filming of *Vampire's Kiss*. Heidi Holicker shared photos and materials pertaining to *Valley Girl* and enthusiastically connected me with other cast and crew members. Across multiple interviews and many emails, Marco Kyris offered invaluable insight into his years working for Cage. Chip Miller provided me with photos and documents relating to the unmade Gene Vincent biopic and answered many follow-up questions over email. Erin O'Brien was a truly indispensable source regarding her brother, the late John

O'Brien, providing me with photos, papers, and letters which I drew on for the *Leaving Las Vegas* chapter. Lisa Jane Persky and Andy Zax sent me valuable information, photos, and yearbook scans from Cage's high school years. Jill Schoelen dug up rare photos from *The Best of Times*. Alice Tompkins was helpful in connecting me with crew members from *Birdy*.

Brian Abrams, Peter Myers, and Rebecca Vaadia each read early chapters of this book and provided invaluable edits, feedback, and all manner of encouragement, for which I am very grateful. Ethan Beck and Sam Sklar helped with interview transcription, as well as moral support.

Many individuals deserve credit, or blame, for encouraging my professional interest in Nicolas Cage. In 2015, Grant Burningham and Cady Drell assigned me to interview Cage for *Newsweek*; the following year, Eric Thurm let me deliver a presentation on Cage for what was then called Drunk TED Talks. Ryan Bort and Paula Mejía greatly encouraged this research in its early stages. Lindsay Gibb's book *National Treasure: Nicolas Cage* was also crucial in getting me to think more deeply about Cage's body of work.

For research assistance, thanks to the New York Public Library for the Performing Arts, the Beverly Hills Public Library, and the LA Law Library. Thanks to Brian Socolow and David Schmerler for their legal expertise. Thanks also to Michael Brennan for his graphic design expertise.

I would also like to humbly thank all the friends who encouraged me during the writing of this book (there are far too many of you to name), the professors and editors who shaped me, the Vaadia family, my grandmother Fran Berger, my uncle Charlie Berger, my whole extended family on both sides, Dash, and Doom.

Finally, for immeasurable love and support during the years I spent writing this book, I am eternally indebted to my family: Elisabeth, Gary, Matt, Sam, and of course Rebecca, who encouraged me always. Thank you.

Zach Schonfeld
January 2023

Source Notes

Introduction

1. Wilmington, Michael. "Nicolas Cage—Wild and Full of Heart." *Los Angeles Times*, August 12, 1990, www.latimes.com/archives/la-xpm-1990-08-12-ca-1096-story.html.
2. Sheff, David. "An Intense Interview with Nicolas Cage." *Playboy*, September 1996, https://www.davidsheff.com/nicolas-cage. Accessed April 11, 2022.
3. Ibid.
4. Ganahl, Jane. "The Wild Heart of Nicolas Cage." *San Francisco Examiner*, August 5, 1990, p. 12. *Newspapers.com*, www.newspapers.com/image/462222916.
5. Horyn, Cathy. "Caged Heat." *Vanity Fair*, July 1996, p. 78.
6. Cowie, Peter. *Coppola: A Biograhy*. Da Capo, 1994, p. 15.
7. Coppola, August. *The Intimacy: A Novel*. Grove Press, 1978.
8. "L.B. Teacher Aids Students in World of Touch." *Redondo Reflex*, July 5, 1972, p. 45. *Newspapers.com*, https://www.newspapers.com/image/621288042/. Accessed October 13, 2022.
9. Sheff, David. "An Intense Interview with Nicolas Cage."
10. "Nicolas Cage." *People*, February 26, 1996, p. 64.
11. Grobel, Lawrence. "Out There with Nicolas Cage." *Movieline*, 1996, p. 44.
12. Tannenbaum, Rob. "Cage Against the Machine." *Details*, June 1996, p. 92.
13. McCoy, Terrence. "Nicolas Cage: 'It Really Sucks to Be Famous.'" *Washington Post*, March 11, 2014, https://www.washingtonpost.com/news/morning-mix/wp/2014/03/11/nicolas-cage-it-really-sucks-to-be-famous/. Accessed February 28, 2022.
14. Wuntch, Philip. "Happily Hopscotching between Eccentrics and Action Heroes." *The Baltimore Sun*, November 21, 2004, www.baltimoresun.com/news/bs-xpm-2004-11-21-0411200330-story.html.
15. Schonfeld, Zach. "Ethan Hawke Discusses 'Blaze,' His Nicolas Cage Obsession and Why He Had to Do 'First Reformed': 'I Felt It in My Bones.'" *Newsweek*, September 6, 2018, www.newsweek.com/2018/09/14/ethan-hawke-interview-first-reformed-blaze-nicolas-cage-1108265.html.
16. Rogers, Katie. "Nicolas Cage Agrees to Return Stolen Dinosaur Skull to Mongolia." *New York Times*, December 22, 2015, https://www.nytimes.com/2015/12/23/arts/design/nicolas-cage-tyrannosaurus-bataar-mongolia.html. Accessed October 17, 2021.
17. Ebert, Roger. "Evolution Is God's Intelligent Design." *RogerEbert.com*, Ebert Digital LLC, September 18, 2008, https://www.rogerebert.com/reviews/great-movie-adaptation-2002.

Chapter 1

1. Coppola, Marc. “Nicolas Cage Interview.” *IHeartRadio*, IHeartMedia, September 29, 2020, www.iheart.com/podcast/1248-the-horrible-truth-49075627/episode/nicolas-cage-interview-72055546/. Accessed January 30, 2022.
2. Itzkoff, Dave. *Robin*. Thorndike Press, 2018, p. 87.
3. Babitz, Eve. “Nicolas Cage.” In her *I Used to Be Charming: The Rest of Eve Babitz*, New York Review Books, 2019, p. 320.
4. Huber, Dean. “A Teenage World in Wild Caricature.” *Sacramento Bee*, July 9, 1981, p. E6. *Newspapers.com*, www.newspapers.com/image/621372560/.
5. Roach, Mary. “The Unlikeliest Action Hero.” *USA Weekend*, June 1, 1997, p. 5. *Newspapers.com*, www.newspapers.com/image/113404803.
6. Thomson, David. “Caged Heat.” *Independent*, January 14, 1996, www.independent.co.uk/arts-entertainment/caged-heat-1323910.html.
7. Tannenbaum, Rob. “Cage Against the Machine.” *Details*, June 1996, p. 92.
8. Winer, Linda. “No Ordinary Joe.” *Newsday*, July 24, 1994, p. 27. *Newspapers.com*, www.newspapers.com/image/725439613.
9. *Women's Wear Daily*, October 2, 1986, p. 11.
10. Schruers, Fred. “Dangerous, Dedicated and Wild at Heart, Nicolas Cage Is a Hollywood Samurai.” *Rolling Stone*, November 16, 1995, p. 96.
11. Markham-Smith, Ian, and Liz Hodgson. *Nicolas Cage: The Unauthorised Biography*. Blake, 2001.
12. Mills, Bart. “Actor Nicolas Cage Lives Roles to Point of Wearing Bandages.” *Kansas City Star*, March 10, 1985, p. 3F. *Newspapers.com*, www.newspapers.com/image/679551162/.
13. Raab, Scott. “Nic Cage's Suburban Nightmare.” *Esquire*, September 1998, https://www.esquire.com/entertainment/movies/a37327688/nic-cage-interview-1998/. Accessed March 10, 2022.
14. Winer, “No Ordinary Joe,” p. 27.
15. Morris, Robert. “Sometimes You Just Have to Break All the Rules.” *Cable Guide*, January 1986, p. 28.
16. Picozzi, Michele. “Andy Grenier Enjoys Teaching Theater in Motion Picture Capital of the U.S.” *Evening Sun*, August 22, 1979, p. B-3. *Newspapers.com*, https://www.newspapers.com/image/520710026/. Accessed July 15, 2022.
17. “‘Fables’ Staged.” *Los Angeles Times*, February 1, 1981, p. 10. *Newspapers.com*, https://www.newspapers.com/image/387617263/. Accessed July 16, 2022.
18. Marchese, David. “Nicolas Cage on His Legacy, His Philosophy of Acting and His Metaphorical—and Literal—Search for the Holy Grail.” *New York Times Magazine*, August 7, 2019, www.nytimes.com/interactive/2019/08/07/magazine/nicolas-cage-interview.html.
19. Hirschfeld, Neal. “A New Face in the Crowd.” *Daily News Magazine*, February 3, 1985, p. 20.
20. Weiss, Jack. “‘Crucible’ Impressive, Professional.” *Highlights*, October 23, 1981.
21. Tannenbaum, “Cage Against the Machine,” pp. 92–93.

22. Puig, Claudia. "He's Up. He's Down. He's Up. He's Down. He's Up for Good?: Nicholas Cage's Movie Career Has Been, Uh Volatile. But He Hit the Jackpot in an Alcoholic Love Story Set in Las Vegas. Will Success Stick? Nothing Is Ever That Simple in Hollywood." *Los Angeles Times*, February 4, 1996, www.latimes.com/archives/la-xpm-1996-02-04-tm-32387-story.html.
23. Sheff, David. "An Intense Interview with Nicolas Cage." *Playboy*, September 1996, www.davidsheff.com/nicolas-cage.
24. Mills, "Actor Nicolas Cage Lives Roles to Point of Wearing Bandages."
25. Stevens, Dana. "Fast Times at Ridgemont High: A Kid's-Eye View," *Criterion Collection*, May 11, 2021, https://www.criterion.com/current/posts/7386-fast-times-at-ridgemont-high-a-kid-s-eye-view.
26. "Fast Times at Ridgemont High." Audio commentary by Amy Heckerling and Cameron Crowe, Universal Studios, 2004.
27. Ibid.
28. Ryan, Patrick. "Nicolas Cage Talks 'Pig' Co-Star, Freezing with Cher during 'Moonstruck' and His Go-to Dinner Recipe." *USA Today*, July 15, 2021, https://www.usatoday.com/story/entertainment/movies/2021/07/15/pig-nicolas-cage-interview/7956840002/. Accessed December 8, 2021.
29. Kenny, J. M., director. *Reliving Our Fast Times at Ridgemont High*. Universal Studios Home Video, 1999.
30. Ryan, "Nicolas Cage Talks 'Pig' Co-Star."
31. Daly, Steve. "High Spirits." *Entertainment Weekly*, March 15, 1996, p. 27.
32. Hall, Carla. "The Wild and Weird Nicolas Cage." *Washington Post*, August 31, 1990, https://www.washingtonpost.com/archive/lifestyle/1990/08/31/the-wild-and-weird-nicolas-cage/214dd456-5317-4186-9c81-6b1e2c64ccbe/. Accessed December 9, 2021.
33. Rickey, Carrie. "Fish Play a Supporting Role in Actor Cage's Life." *Chicago Tribune*, April 23, 1987, https://www.chicagotribune.com/news/ct-xpm-1987-04-23-8701310310-story.html. Accessed December 9, 2021.
34. Kenny, *Reliving Our Fast Times at Ridgemont High*.
35. Rickey, "Fish Play a Supporting Role in Actor Cage's Life.".
36. Whipp, Glenn. "Nicolas Cage Meditates on Movies, Music and What Makes Him Happy." *Los Angeles Times*, January 26, 2022, www.latimes.com/entertainment-arts/awards/story/2022-01-26/nicolas-cage-on-pig-elvis-dracula-and-his-career.
37. McKenna, Kristine. "A 'Moonstruck' Nicolas Cage Opens Up." *Los Angeles Times*, February 21, 1988, www.latimes.com/archives/la-xpm-1988-02-21-ca-44011-story.html.
38. "Mild at Heart." *The List*, February 26, 1993, p. 11, archive.list.co.uk/the-list/1993-02-26/13/.
39. Robb, Brian J. *Nicolas Cage: Hollywood's Wild Talent*. Plexus, 1998. p. 22.
40. Mills, "Actor Nicolas Cage Lives Roles to Point of Wearing Bandages."
41. Lynskey, Dorian. "'You've Got to Be Able to Break the Wall.'" *The Guardian*, February 16, 2007, www.theguardian.com/film/2007/feb/16/1.
42. Mills, "Actor Nicolas Cage Lives Roles to Point of Wearing Bandages."

43. Daly, "High Spirits."
44. Lamagna, Jodi. "Actor's a Little Less Wild at Heart." *News & Record*, May 1, 1993, https://greensboro.com/actors-a-little-less-wild-at-heart/article_eabc1c4d-6428-5527-a197-cbf7d8e7b198.html. Accessed December 21, 2021.
45. Schruers, "Dangerous, Dedicated and Wild at Heart," p. 94.
46. Simon, Alex. "Nicolas Cage: Lord of the Nerds." *Venice Magazine*, October 2005, http://thehollywoodinterview.blogspot.com/2015/05/nicolas-cage-hollywood-flashback.html. Accessed December 22, 2021.
47. "Nicolas Cage: 'Sometimes It's Good to Be Hated.'" *The Talks*, August 13, 2014, https://the-talks.com/interview/nicolas-cage/.
48. Wallace, Amy. "His Truth Is Out There." *Los Angeles Times*, November 12, 2000, https://www.chicagotribune.com/news/ct-xpm-2000-11-12-0011120201-story.html. Accessed January 9, 2022.
49. MacFarquhar, Larissa. "Stranger in Paradise." *Premiere*, June 1997, p. 70.
50. Gibb, Lindsay. *National Treasure: Nicolas Cage*. ECW Press, 2015. p. 12–13.
51. Schruers, Fred. "The Passion of Nicolas Cage." *Rolling Stone*, November 11, 1999, www.rollingstone.com/movies/movie-features/nicolas-cage-1999-cover-story-832684/.
52. Lynskey, " 'You've Got to Be Able to Break the Wall.' "
53. Kaylin, Lucy. "The Rebel at Rest." *GQ*, March 1997, p. 228.
54. "Nicolas Uncaged; The Secret Demons That Drove Star to His Oscar Triumph." *Sunday Mirror*, March 31, 1996, www.thefreelibrary.com/NICOLAS+UNCAGED%3B+The+secret+demons+that+drove+star+to+his+Oscar...-a061180115.
55. McKenna, "A 'Moonstruck' Nicolas Cage Opens Up."

Chapter 2

1. Langway, Lynn, and Sandra Cavazos. "It's Like TUBULAR!" *Newsweek*, August 2, 1982, p. 61.
2. Lane, Christina. *Feminist Hollywood: From Born in Flames to Point Break*. Wayne State University Press, 2000, p. 70.
3. Ibid., p. 67.
4. Chase, Chris. "At the Movies; Three Women and Their Road to Directing." *New York Times*, May 6, 1983, www.nytimes.com/1983/05/06/movies/at-the-movies-three-women-and-their-road-to-directing.html.
5. Attanasio, Paul. "The Road to Hollywood." *Washington Post*, August 7, 1985, www.washingtonpost.com/archive/lifestyle/1985/08/07/the-road-to-hollywood/8cad2099-726c-44dc-b7f2-63b62e68f907/.
6. Lane, *Feminist Hollywood*, p. 78.
7. Spencer, Ashley. "When 'Valley Girl' (and Nicolas Cage) Shook Up Hollywood." *New York Times*, May 11, 2020, www.nytimes.com/2020/05/11/movies/valley-girl.html.
8. Ibid.

9. Ringel, Eleanor. “Kathleen Turner Didn’t Get Harried by Curious Press.” *Atlanta Constitution*, October 19, 1986, p. 5J. *Newspapers.com*, www.newspapers.com/image/399752760.
10. Sheff, David. “An Intense Interview with Nicolas Cage.” *Playboy*, September 1996, www.davidsheff.com/nicolas-cage.
11. Chase, “At the Movies; Three Women and Their Road to Directing.”
12. MacFarquhar, Larissa. “Stranger in Paradise.” *Premiere*, June 1997, p. 103.
13. Taylor, Trey. “Hollyweird: Nicolas Cage’s Crazy Quest to Woo Patricia Arquette.” *Paper*, July 5, 2018, https://www.papermag.com/nicolas-cage-patricia-arquette-2584059371.html. Accessed December 11, 2021.
14. Ganahl, Jane. “The Wild Heart of Nicolas Cage.” *San Francisco Examiner*, August 5, 1990, p. 14. *Newspapers.com*, https://www.newspapers.com/image/462223020. Accessed December 11, 2021.
15. “Kevin Smith and Nicolas Cage Talk about ‘Valley Girl’ | SUNDANCE 2018.” *YouTube*, IMDb, January 20, 2018, www.youtube.com/watch?v=6Qr3DnlteUg.
16. Hirschfeld, Neal. “A New Face in the Crowd.” *Daily News Magazine*, February 3, 1985, p. 14.
17. Rickey, Carrie. “Fish Play a Supporting Role in Actor Cage’s Life.” *Chicago Tribune*, April 23, 1987, www.chicagotribune.com/news/ct-xpm-1987-04-23-8701310310-story.html.
18. Grobel, Lawrence. “Out There with Nicolas Cage.” *Movieline*, 1996, p. 83.
19. Horyn, Cathy. “Caged Head.” *Vanity Fair*, July 1996, p. 79.
20. Spencer, “When ‘Valley Girl’ (and Nicolas Cage) Shook Up Hollywood.”
21. Ibid.
22. Nicholson, Amy. “Quentin Tunes In, Drops Out.” *The Ringer*, Spotify, July 30, 2019, www.theringer.com/2019/7/30/20747034/quentin-tunes-in-drops-out. Accessed November 23, 2021.
23. Ibid.
24. Schonfeld, Zach. “Nicolas Cage: ‘Regret Is a Waste of Time.’” *Newsweek*, September 25, 2015, www.latimes.com/archives/la-xpm-1988-02-21-ca-44011-story.html.
25. “Nicolas Cage on Women Filmmakers He’s Worked With.” *YouTube*, Variety Studio, January 20, 2018, www.youtube.com/watch?v=URxAPUT2GEA.

Chapter 3

1. Caulfield, Deborah. “Summer’s Hot Faces.” *Los Angeles Times*, September 3, 1983, pp. 1–5<. *Newspapers.com*, www.newspapers.com/image/633644682.
2. Ibid.
3. London, Michael. “‘Moon’ Is Lansing’s Balloon.” *Los Angeles Times*, March 23, 1984, pp. 1–9. *Newspapers.com*, www.newspapers.com/image/401316459.
4. Farber, Stephen. “Script to Screeen: A Rockypath.” *New York Times*, November 6, 1983, p. 1, www.nytimes.com/1983/11/06/arts/script-to-screeen-a-rockypath.html.
5. Ibid.

6. Ibid.
7. Daly, Steve. "Nicolas Cage's Discography." *Entertainment Weekly*, March 15, 1996, ew.com/article/1996/03/15/nicolas-cages-discography/.
8. Kelly, Richard T. *Sean Penn: His Life and Times*. Canongate U.S., 2004. p. 94.
9. "Fast Times at Ridgemont High." Audio commentary by Amy Heckerling, and Cameron Crowe, Universal Studios, 2004.
10. Kelly, *Sean Penn*, p. 123.
11. London, Michael. "3 Rising Stars Shoot for 'Moon.'" *Los Angeles Times*, June 29, 1983, pp. 1–4. *Newspapers.com*, www.newspapers.com/image/633684750.
12. Thomson, David. "Caged Heat." *Independent*, 1996, www.independent.co.uk/arts-entertainment/caged-heat-1323910.html.
13. Daly, "Nicolas Cage's Discography."
14. Kelly, *Sean Penn*, p. 124.
15. Kaylin, Lucy. "The Rebel at Rest." *GQ*, March 1997, p. 228.
16. Bull, Debby. "Modine & Cage Are at Head of the Class." *Boston Globe*, April 4, 1985, pp. 8–9. *Newspapers.com*, https://www.newspapers.com/image/437688854. Accessed January 2, 2022.
17. Wilmington, Michael. "Nicolas Cage—Wild and Full of Heart." *Los Angeles Times*, August 12, 1990, www.latimes.com/archives/la-xpm-1990-08-12-ca-1096-story.html.
18. Hirschberg, Lynn. "Restless." *New York Times*, December 27, 1998, p. 20, www.nytimes.com/1998/12/27/magazine/restless.html.
19. "Tough Actors Nicolas Cage, Sean Penn Sling Tough Words." *Tallahassee Democrat*, March 21, 1999, p. 2A. *Newspapers.com*, www.newspapers.com/image/248328168/.
20. Canby, Vincent. "Film: Wartime Pranks, 'Racing with the Moon.'" *New York Times*, March 23, 1984, p. 5, www.nytimes.com/1984/03/23/movies/film-wartime-pranks-racing-with-the-moon.html.
21. Ebert, Roger. "Racing With the Moon." *Chicago Sun-Times*, March 1984, www.rogerebert.com/reviews/racing-with-the-moon-1984.
22. London, " 'Moon' Is Lansing's Balloon."
23. Ibid.
24. Kelly, *Sean Penn*, pp. 136–137.
25. Morris, Robert. "Sometimes You Just Have to Break All the Rules." *Cable Guide*, January 1986, p. 33.
26. Bennetts, Leslie. "'Birdy,': A Difficult Journey to the Screen." *New York Times*, December 23, 1984, p. 2, https://www.nytimes.com/1984/12/23/arts/birdy-a-difficult-journey-to-the-screen.html.
27. Ibid.
28. Streitfeld, David. "The Pain of the Man Behind the Pseudonym." *Washington Post*, October 26, 1989, https://www.washingtonpost.com/archive/lifestyle/1989/10/26/the-pain-of-the-man-behind-the-pseudonym/6ff023f4-36a3-48ee-a84c-05564b2f1fbc/. Accessed December 31, 2021.
29. Parker, Alan. "Birdy: The Making of the Film, Egg by Egg." In his *Alan Parker—Director, Writer, Producer*, 2019, http://alanparker.com/film/birdy/making/.
30. Ibid.

31. Ibid.
32. "The Abstraction of War: Interview with Matthew Modine." Powerhouse Films, 2019.
33. Tully, Jacqi. "Handsome Lowe Working to Dispel 'Kiss of Death.'" *Arizona Daily Star*, 17 July 1985, p. 21.
34. Parker, "Birdy."
35. Hirschfeld, Neal. "A New Face in the Crowd." *Daily News Magazine*, February 3, 1985. p. 20.
36. Daly, "Nicolas Cage's Discography."
37. Parker, "Birdy."
38. Ibid.
39. Sheff, David. "An Intense Interview with Nicolas Cage." *Playboy*, September 1996, www.davidsheff.com/nicolas-cage.
40. Bennetts, "'Birdy,'" p. 2.
41. Sheff, "An Intense Interview with Nicolas Cage."
42. Ibid.
43. Parker, "Birdy."
44. Ibid.
45. Stanislavsky, Konstantin. *An Actor Prepares*. Translated by Reynolds Elizabeth Hapgood, Routledge/Theater Arts Books, 1936, p. 20.
46. Gussow, Mel. "Lee Strasberg of Actors Studio Dead." *New York Times*, February 18, 1982, p. 20, www.nytimes.com/1982/02/18/obituaries/lee-strasberg-of-actors-studio-dead.html.
47. Strasberg, Lee. *A Dream of Passion: The Development of the Method*. Edited by Evangeline Morphos, Methuen Drama, 1987, p. 132.
48. Scott, A. O. "Hollywood Still Matters. These Actors Showed Why." *New York Times*, December 7, 2021, www.nytimes.com/2021/12/07/magazine/great-performers.html.
49. Bose, Swapnil Dhruv. "How Robert De Niro Actually Got an Official Cab Driver Licence for 'Taxi Driver' Role." *Far Out Magazine*, November 2, 2020, faroutmagazine.co.uk/how-robert-de-niro-actually-got-an-official-cab-driver-licence-for-taxi-driver-role/.
50. Yule, Andrew. *Life on the Wire: The Life and Art of Al Pacino*. SPI Books, 1992, p. 80.
51. Rosenfeld, Megan. "Dustin Hoffman, Big Little Man." *Washington Post*, October 1, 1992, www.washingtonpost.com/archive/lifestyle/1992/10/01/dustin-hoffman-big-little-man/10b84f27-176a-4dc5-93e4-37a2dbcd85d7/.
52. Lyman, Rick. "Marlon Brando, Oscar-Winning Actor, Is Dead at 80." *New York Times*, July 2, 2004, https://www.nytimes.com/2004/07/02/movies/marlon-brando-oscar winning-actor-is-dead-at-80.html. Accessed January 26, 2022.
53. Sheff, "An Intense Interview with Nicolas Cage."
54. Hirschfeld, "A New Face in the Crowd," p. 15.
55. Winer, Linda. "No Ordinary Joe." *Newsday*, July 24, 1994, p. 27. *Newspapers.com*, www.newspapers.com/image/725439613/.
56. Flint, Peter B. "Stella Adler, 91, an Actress and Teacher of the Method." *New York Times*, December 22, 1992, p. 10, www.nytimes.com/1992/12/22/obituaries/stella-adler-91-an-actress-and-teacher-of-the-method.html.

57. Bennetts, "'Birdy,'" p. 2.
58. Hirschfeld, "A New Face in the Crowd."
59. Emery, Prudence. *Nanaimo Girl: A Memoir*. Cormorant Books, 2020.
60. Morris, "Sometimes You Just Have to Break All the Rules."
61. Cavett, Dick. "Nicolas Cage on His Acting Technique." *The Dick Cavett Show*, ABC, New York, October 7, 1986.
62. Sheff, "An Intense Interview with Nicolas Cage."
63. Wilkinson, Alissa, and Aja Romano. "Why Nicolas Cage Endures." *Vox*, July 19, 2021, https://www.vox.com/culture/22570234/nic-cage-pig-movie-memes-nicolas.
64. Grobel, Lawrence. "Out There with Nicolas Cage." *Movieline*, 1996, p. 44.
65. Sheff, "An Intense Interview with Nicolas Cage."
66. Grobel, "Out There with Nicolas Cage," p. 44.
67. Sheff, "An Intense Interview with Nicolas Cage."
68. Hirschfeld, "A New Face in the Crowd."
69. Pall, Ellen. "Nicolas Cage, the Sunshine Man." *New York Times*, July 24, 1994, p. 23.
70. Ibid.
71. Mills, Bart. "Actor Nicolas Cage Lives Roles to Point of Wearing Bandages." *Kansas City Star*, March 10, 1985, p. 3F. *Newspapers.com*, www.newspapers.com/image/679551162/.
72. "Nicolas Cage Stars in 'The Boy in Blue.'" 1984.
73. Parker, "Birdy."
74. Collins, Frank. "In a Dream, I'm Trying to Decide What I Am." *Birdy Limited Edition Blu-Ray*, Powerhouse Films, 2019, pp. 13–14.
75. Markham-Smith, Ian, and Liz Hodgson. *Nicolas Cage: The Unauthorised Biography*. Blake, 2001, p. 48.
76. Canby, Vincent. "Film View; 'Birdy' Watching Has Its Rewards." *New York Times*, February 10, 1985, p. 19, www.nytimes.com/1985/02/10/movies/film-view-birdy-watching-has-its-rewards.html.
77. London, Michael. "Will 'Birdy' Fly the Second Time?" *Los Angeles Times*, March 8, 1985, www.latimes.com/archives/la-xpm-1985-03-08-ca-32586-story.html.
78. Ibid.
79. Shulgasser, Barbara. "'Birdy' Had Troubles Taking Off." *San Francisco Examiner*, March 15, 1985, p. E5. *Newspapers.com*, www.newspapers.com/image/460566855/.
80. Hirschfeld, "A New Face in the Crowd," p. 14.
81. Bull, "Modine & Cage Are at Head of the Class."
82. Mills, "Actor Nicolas Cage Lives Roles to Point of Wearing Bandages."
83. Hirschfeld, "A New Face in the Crowd," p. 20.
84. London, "Will 'Birdy' Fly the Second Time?"
85. Higgins, Bill. "Hollywood Flashback: Nicolas Cage First Came to Cannes in 1985 with 'Birdy.'" *Hollywood Reporter*, May 9, 2018, www.hollywoodreporter.com/movies/movie-news/hollywood-flashback-nicolas-cage-first-came-cannes-1985-birdy-1110547/.
86. Gibb, Lindsay. *National Treasure: Nicolas Cage*. ECW Press, 2015. p. 14.

87. Schager, Nick. "Role Recall: Nicolas Cage on His Greatest Films—from 'Raising Arizona' to 'Face/Off' to Trippy New 'Mandy.'" *Yahoo!*, September 13, 2018, https://www.yahoo.com/lifestyle/role-recall-nicolas-cage-greatest-films-raising-arizona-face-off-trippy-new-mandy-141920155.html.
88. Woods, K. W. "Nicolas Cage: Madman or Mystery?" *Playgirl*, January 1988, p. 34.
89. Lipper, Hal. "Cage Has a Lock on Kookiness." *St. Petersburg Times*, August 22, 1990, p. 3D. *Newspapers.com*, www.newspapers.com/image/323214248.
90. Scott, "Hollywood Still Matters."
91. Daly, "Nicolas Cage's Discography."

Chapter 4

1. Tannenbaum, Rob. "Cage Against the Machine." *Details*, June 1996, p. 92.
2. Thomson, David. "Caged Heat." *The Independent*, January 14, 1996, www.independent.co.uk/arts-entertainment/caged-heat-1323910.html.
3. Sheff, David. "An Intense Interview with Nicolas Cage." *Playboy*, September 1996, https://www.davidsheff.com/nicolas-cage.
4. Thomson, "CAGED HEAT."
5. Thomson, David, and Lucy Gray. "Idols of the King: The Outsiders and Rumble Fish." In *Francis Ford Coppola: Interviews*, by Gene D. Phillips and Rodney Hill, University Press of Mississippi, Jackson, 2004, p. 112.
6. Cohen, Rich. "Francis Ford Coppola's Third Act: Italy, Wine, and the Secret of Life." *Vanity Fair*, February 3, 2016, www.vanityfair.com/hollywood/2016/02/francis-ford-coppola-italy-wine-and-the-secret-of-life.
7. Schumacher, Michael. *Francis Ford Coppola: A Filmmaker's Life*. Crown, 1999, pp. 8–9.
8. MacFarquhar, Larissa. "Stranger in Paradise." *Premiere*, June 1997, p. 72.
9. Coppola, August. *The Intimacy*. Grove Press, 1978. p. 119.
10. Rodarmor, William. "Arts and the Man: August Coppola, Dean of Creativity." *San Francisco Examiner*, November 24, 1985, p. 27. *Newspapers.com*, www.newspapers.com/image/461521077/.
11. Cowie, Peter. *Coppola: A Biography*. Da Capo Press, 1994, p. 116.
12. Thomas-Mason, Lee. "Nicolas Cage's 13 Favourite Films of All Time." *Far Out Magazine*, June 3, 2021, https://faroutmagazine.co.uk/nicolas-cage-favourite-films-list-kubrick-coppola/.
13. Paiella, Gabriella. "Nicolas Cage Can Explain It All." *GQ*, March 22, 2022, www.gq.com/story/nicolas-cage-april-cover-profile.
14. Babitz, Eve. "Nicolas Cage." In her *I Used to Be Charming: The Rest of Eve Babitz*, New York Review Books, New York, 2019, p. 319.
15. Grobel, Lawrence. "Out There with Nicolas Cage." *Movieline*, 1996, pp. 43–44.
16. Garratt, Rob. "Nicolas Cage on the Croods." *Time Out Abu Dhabi*, March 26, 2013, https://www.timeoutabudhabi.com/movies/movies-features/39860-nicolas-cage-on-the-croods.

17. Grobel, "Out There with Nicolas Cage."
18. Pall, Ellen. "Film; Nicholas Cage, The Sunshine Man." *New York Times*, July 24, 1994, p. 1,https://www.nytimes.com/1994/07/24/movies/film-nicholas-cage-the-sunshine-man.html. Accessed February 17, 2022.
19. "Mild at Heart." *The List*, February 26, 1993, p. 11, https://archive.list.co.uk/the-list/1993-02-26/13/. Accessed February 17, 2022.
20. Cowie, *Coppola: A Biography*, p. 155.
21. Schumacher, *Francis Ford Coppola*, p. 289.
22. Ibid., p. 296.
23. Ibid., p. 294.
24. Grant, Lee. "Coppola: Dreamer . . . and Doer." *Los Angeles Times*, February 9, 1982. *Newspapers.com*, https://www.newspapers.com/image/389047078/. Accessed February 18, 2022.
25. Schumacher, *Francis Ford Coppola*, p. 313.
26. Cohen, "Francis Ford Coppola's Third Act."
27. Cowie, *Coppola: A Biography*, p. 161.
28. Baron, Zach. "Francis Ford Coppola's $100 Million Bet." *GQ*, February 17, 2022, https://www.gq.com/story/francis-ford-coppola-50-years-after-the-godfather. Accessed February 17, 2022.
29. Murray, Noel. "The Misfit: Nicolas Cage Didn't Fit into the Brat Pack '80s but Found Success Anyway." *UPROXX*, August 28, 2017, https://uproxx.com/movies/nicolas-cage-didnt-fit-into-the-80s-history-career/.
30. Noland, Claire. "August Coppola Dies at 75; Professor Was Father of Nicolas Cage and Brother of Francis Ford Coppola." *Los Angeles Times*, October 30, 2009, www.latimes.com/local/obituaries/la-me-august-coppola30-2009oct30-story.html.
31. Coppola, Marc. "Nicolas Cage Interview." *IHeart*, September 29, 2020, https://www.iheart.com/podcast/1248-the-horrible-truth-49075627/episode/nicolas-cage-interview-72055546. Accessed February 18, 2022.
32. Cowie, *Coppola: A Biography*, p. 168.
33. Ibid., pp. 167–1968.
34. Hoad, Phil. "'Tom Cruise Was an Intense Kid': How Francis Ford Coppola Made The Outsiders." *The Guardian*, November 1, 2021, www.theguardian.com/film/2021/nov/01/how-we-made-the-outsiders-francis-ford-coppola-and-c-thomas-howell.
35. Sheff, "An Intense Interview with Nicolas Cage."
36. Schumacher, *Francis Ford Coppola*, p. 325.
37. Mills, Bart. "Actor Nicolas Cage Lives Roles to Point of Wearing Bandages." *Kansas City Star*, March 10, 1985, p. 3F. *Newspapers.com*, www.newspapers.com/image/679551162/.
38. Coppola, Francis Ford, director. *Rumble Fish: Director's Commentary*. The Criterion Collection, 2017.
39. Reveaux, Anthony. "Stephen H. Burum, ASC and Rumble Fish." *American Cinematographer*, May 1984, ascmag.com/articles/flashback-rumble-fish.
40. Coppola, Francis Ford, *Rumble Fish*.

41. Schumacher, *Francis Ford Coppola*, p. 330.
42. Reveaux, "Stephen H. Burum, ASC and Rumble Fish."
43. Grobel, "Out There with Nicolas Cage."
44. Mills, "Actor Nicolas Cage Lives Roles to Point of Wearing Bandages."
45. Schruers, Fred. "Dangerous, Dedicated and Wild at Heart, Nicolas Cage Is a Hollywood Samurai." *Rolling Stone*, November 16, 1995, p. 94.
46. Hoskyns, Barney. *Lowside of the Road: A Life of Tom Waits*. Faber and Faber, 2009, pp. 271–272.
47. Valania, Jonathan. "The Man Who Howled Wolf." *Magnet*, 1999, www.tomwaitsfan.com/tom%20waits%20library/www.tomwaitslibrary.com/interviews/99-jun-magnet.html.
48. Lanham, Tom. "Tom Waits: All Stripped Down." *Paste Magazine*, December 2004, www.pastemagazine.com/music/tom-waits/tom-waits/.
49. Coppola, Francis Ford, *Rumble Fish*.
50. Lewis, Jon. *Whom God Wishes to Destroy: Francis Coppola and the New Hollywood*. Duke University Press, 1997, p. 101.
51. Ibid., p. 103.
52. Ibid., pp. 104–105.
53. Canby, Vincent. "Film View; A Tale of Two B-Movies: One's Plain, the Other Fancy." *New York Times*, October 23, 1983, p. 19, www.nytimes.com/1983/10/23/arts/film-view-a-tale-of-two-b-movies-one-s-plain-the-other-fancy.html.
54. Thomson and Gray, "Idols of the King," pp. 112–113.
55. Coppola, Francis Ford, *Rumble Fish*.
56. Ibid.
57. Ibid.
58. Thomson and Gray, "Idols of the King," p. 113.
59. Coppola, Francis Ford, *Rumble Fish*.
60. Cowie, *Coppola: A Biography*, p. 173.
61. Cohen, "Francis Ford Coppola's Third Act."
62. Grobel, "Out There with Nicolas Cage."
63. Sheff, "An Intense Interview with Nicolas Cage."
64. "Nicolas Cage, 'Rumble Fish.' " Universal News, 1983.
65. Ibid.
66. Hirschfeld, Neal. "A New Face in the Crowd." *Daily News Magazine*, February 3, 1985, p. 14.
67. Caulfield, Deborah. "Nicolas Cage: 'Valley Girl.'" *Los Angeles Times*, September 3, 1983, p. 5, https://www.newspapers.com/image/633644745. Accessed March 13, 2022.
68. Baron, "Francis Ford Coppola's $100 Million Bet."
69. Lewis, *Whom God Wishes to Destroy*, p. 111.
70. Schumacher, *Francis Ford Coppola*.
71. Ibid., pp. 337–339.
72. Lewis, *Whom God Wishes to Destroy*, p. 117.
73. Schumacher, *Francis Ford Coppola*, p. 340.

74. Ibid., p. 342.
75. Lewis, *Whom God Wishes to Destroy*, pp. 122–123.
76. Barnes, Brooks. "Robert Evans, a Maverick Producer of Hollywood Classics, Dies at 89." *New York Times*, October 28, 2019, https://www.nytimes.com/2019/10/28/arts/robert-evans-dead.html. Accessed March 17, 2022.
77. Schumacher, *Francis Ford Coppola*, p. 333.
78. Ibid., pp. 340–341.
79. Ibid., p. 343.
80. Mayo, Mike. *American Murder: Criminals, Crimes, and the Media*. Visible Ink Press, 2008, pp. 73–74.
81. Silverton, Pete. "Waits Happening." *Beat Magazine*, March 1986. *Tom Waits Library*, tomwaitslibrary.info/biography/interviews/waits-happening/.
82. Morris, Robert. "Nicolas Cage." *Cable Guide*, January 1986, p. 28.
83. Lipton, James. "Inside the Actors Studio: Nicolas Cage." *Cagealot Castle*, April 1, 2011, cagealotcastle.activeboard.com/t42055109/nic-on-inside-the-actors-studio/?page = 1. Accessed April 7, 2022.
84. Sheff, "An Intense Interview with Nicolas Cage."
85. Schumacher, *Francis Ford Coppola*, p. 352.
86. Bull, Debby. "Modine & Cage Are at Head of the Class." *Rolling Stone*, April 4, 1985. *Newspapers.com*, www.newspapers.com/image/437688854.
87. Robb, Brian J. *Nicolas Cage: Hollywood's Wild Talent*. Plexus, 1998, p. 37.
88. Schumacher, *Francis Ford Coppola*, p. 359.
89. Hirschfeld, "A New Face in the Crowd," p. 14.
90. Grobel, "Out There with Nicolas Cage."
91. Lewis, *Whom God Wishes to Destroy*, pp. 140–141.
92. Salmans, Sandra. "'Cotton Club' Is Neither a Smash nor a Disaster." *New York Times*, December 20, 1984, p. 13, https://www.nytimes.com/1984/12/20/movies/cotton-club-is-neither-a-smash-nor-a-disaster.html. Accessed April 13, 2022.
93. Lewis, *Whom God Wishes to Destroy*, p. 139.
94. Schruers, Fred. "The Passion of Nicolas Cage." *Rolling Stone*, November 11, 1999, https://www.rollingstone.com/movies/movie-features/nicolas-cage-1999-cover-story-832684/. Accessed April 13, 2022.
95. Horyn, Cathy. "Caged Heat." *Vanity Fair*, July 1996, p. 144.
96. Lewis, *Whom God Wishes to Destroy*, p. 149.
97. Schumacher, *Francis Ford Coppola*, p. 370.
98. London, Michael. "Winger Injured, Movie Again on Back Burner." *Los Angeles Times*, February 13, 1985, www.latimes.com/archives/la-xpm-1985-02-13-ca-4768-story.html.
99. Cowie, *Coppola: A Biography*, p. 195.
100. Schumacher, *Francis Ford Coppola*, p. 377.
101. Mills, "Actor Nicolas Cage Lives Roles to Point of Wearing Bandages."
102. Herman, Jan. "Here's Looking at You, Kids: The Next Generation of Stars." *Daily News*, June 23, 1985, p. 5. *Newspapers.com*, https://www.newspapers.com/image/487520039. Accessed October 23, 2022.

103. Grobel, Lawrence. “The Good Times of Nicolas Cage.” *Movieline*, June 1998, p. 84.
104. Ibid.
105. Marchese, David. “Nicolas Cage on His Legacy, His Philosophy of Acting and His Metaphorical—and Literal—Search for the Holy Grail.” *New York Times Magazine*, August 7, 2019, www.nytimes.com/interactive/2019/08/07/magazine/nicolas-cage-interview.html.
106. Sheff, “An Intense Interview with Nicolas Cage.”
107. Koski, Lorna. “The Cagey Nicolas Cage.” *Women's Wear Daily*, October 2, 1986, p. 11.
108. MacFarquhar, Larissa. “Stranger in Paradise.” *Premiere*, June 1997, p. 102.
109. Ito, Robert. “Trading Flaming Skull for Inner Dad.” *New York Times*, April 6, 2014, p. 15, www.nytimes.com/2014/04/06/movies/nicolas-cage-returns-to-indie-essentials-with-joe.html.
110. Schumacher, *Francis Ford Coppola*, p. 378.
111. Horyn, Cathy. “Caged Heat.” *Vanity Fair*, July 1996, p. 144.
112. Mills, Bart. “Cage Gets to Drive the Girls Crazy in ‘Peggy Sue.’” *News-Pilot*, October 13, 1986, p. A11. *Newspapers.com*, www.newspapers.com/image/607273142/.
113. Sheff, “An Intense Interview with Nicolas Cage.”
114. Grobel, “The Good Times of Nicolas Cage,” p. 84.
115. Horyn, “Caged Heat,” p. 145.
116. Marchese, “Nicolas Cage on His Legacy.”
117. Daly, Steve. “High Spirits.” *Entertainment Weekly*, March 15, 1996.
118. “Mild at Heart.” *The List*, February 26, 1993, p. 11, https://archive.list.co.uk/the-list/1993-02-26/13/. Accessed February 17, 2022.
119. Marchese, “Nicolas Cage on His Legacy.”
120. Tannenbaum, “Cage Against the Machine,” p. 90.
121. Geller, Lynn. “Moving Images.” *SPIN*, March 1989, p. 53. *Google Books*, https://books.google.com/books?id=bT9Dc3mzdZ8C&q=Cage#v=snippet&q=Cage&f=false. Accessed October 3, 2021.
122. Ganahl, Jane. “The Wild Heart of Nicolas Cage.” *San Francisco Examiner*, August 5, 1990, p. 14. *Newspapers.com*, www.newspapers.com/image/462222969.
123. Marchese, “Nicolas Cage on His Legacy.”
124. Marchese, David. “Kathleen Turner on Trump's ‘Gross’ Handshake and the Co-Star She Slapped.” *Vulture*, August 7, 2018. https://www.vulture.com/2018/08/kathleen-turner-in-conversation.html.
125. Woods, K. W. “Nicolas Cage: Madman or Mystery?” *Playgirl*, January 1988, p. 36.
126. Turner, Kathleen, and Gloria Feldt. *Send Yourself Roses: Thoughts on My Life, Love, and Leading Roles*. 1st ed. Springboard, 2008.
127. Holmwood, Leigh. “Nicolas Cage Wins Libel Battle in High Court over Kathleen Turner's Claims.” *The Guardian*, April 4, 2008, sec. Media. https://www.theguardian.com/media/2008/apr/04/dailymail.medialaw.
128. Gibb, Lindsay. *National Treasure: Nicolas Cage*. ECW Press, 2015, p. 29.
129. Smith, Liz. “‘Rockabilly’ May Rivet, or Just Staple.” *New York Daily News*, September 9, 1983, p. 8. *Newspapers.com*, www.newspapers.com/image/489257757/.

130. "People." *Fresno Bee*, October 6, 1983, p. A2. *Newspapers.com*, www.newspapers.com/image/704801087/.
131. Wilmington, Michael. "Nicolas Cage—Wild and Full of Heart." *Los Angeles Times*, August 12, 1990.
132. Schumacher, *Francis Ford Coppola*, p. 392.
133. Mills, "Cage Gets to Drive the Girls Crazy in 'Peggy Sue.'"
134. Wolf, Jeanne, and Shep Morgan. "Nicolas Cage: He's Normal, to a Point." *Philadelphia Inquirer*, March 6, 1994, pp. F1–F7. *Newspapers.com*, www.newspapers.com/image/175755118.
135. Wallace, Amy. "His Truth Is Out There." *Los Angeles Times*, November 12, 2000, www.chicagotribune.com/news/ct-xpm-2000-11-12-0011120201-story.html.
136. Grobel, "Out There with Nicolas Cage," pp. 84–87.
137. Bierman, Robert, director. *Vampire's Kiss*. Audio Commentary. MGM, 2002.
138. Marchese, "Kathleen Turner on Trump's 'Gross' Handshake and the Co-Star She Slapped."
139. Geller, "Moving Images.".
140. Cavett, Dick. "Nicolas Cage on His Acting Technique." *The Dick Cavett Show*, ABC, New York, October 7, 1986.
141. Grobel, "The Good Times of Nicolas Cage," p. 84.
142. Woods, "Nicolas Cage: Madman or Mystery?," p. 36.
143. Sumner, Mike. "Into the Danger Zone." *The Guardian*, June 30, 1987, p. 9. *Newspapers.com*, https://www.newspapers.com/image/260302574/. Accessed April 21, 2022.
144. Mann, Roderick. "Nicolas Cage Opens Up." *Los Angeles Times*, October 19, 1986, https://www.latimes.com/archives/la-xpm-1986-10-19-ca-5675-story.html. Accessed April 22, 2022.
145. Rickey, Carrie. "Fish Play a Supporting Role in Actor Cage's Life." *Chicago Tribune*, April 23, 1987, https://www.chicagotribune.com/news/ct-xpm-1987-04-23-8701310310-story.html. Accessed April 22, 2022.
146. Woods. "Nicolas Cage: Madman or Mystery?," p. 36.
147. Kempley, Rita. "'Peggy Sue Got Married' (PG-13)." *Washington Post*, October 10, 1986, www.washingtonpost.com/wp-srv/style/longterm/movies/videos/peggysuegotmarriedpg13kempley_a0caec.htm.
148. Schumacher, *Francis Ford Coppola*, p. 392.
149. Attanasio, Paul. "'Peggy Sue Got Married' (PG-13)." *Washington Post*, October 10, 1986, www.washingtonpost.com/wp-srv/style/longterm/movies/videos/peggysuegotmarriedpg13attanasio_a0ad5f.htm.
150. Kearney, Jill. "His Latest Hero Dreamed of Producing a New Automobile. Francis Ford Coppola Simply Wants to Create a Whole New Art Form." *Mother Jones*, September 1988, p. 22, www.maryellenmark.com/text/magazines/mother%20jones/904Y-000-002.html.
151. Schumacher, *Francis Ford Coppola*, p. 392.

152. McKenna, Kristine. "A 'Moonstruck' Nicolas Cage Opens Up." *Los Angeles Times*, February 21, 1988, p. 5. *Newspapers.com*, https://www.newspapers.com/image/404140629. Accessed October 12, 2021.
153. Mills, "Cage Gets to Drive the Girls Crazy in 'Peggy Sue.'"
154. Sheff, "An Intense Interview with Nicolas Cage."

Chapter 5

1. Morris, Robert. "Sometimes You Just Have to Break All the Rules." *Cable Guide*, January 1986, pp. 28–33.
2. Kondrick, Steve, and Izzy Fischer. "Special Interview with Christopher Coppola." *Everything I Learned from Movies Podcast*, PlayerFM, August 23, 2019, player.fm/series/everything-i-learned-from-movies-2361863/special-interview-with-christopher-coppola. Accessed January 12, 2022.
3. Ibid.
4. Coppola, Christopher, director. *Christopher Coppola and Kodak Super 8. Vimeo*, February 29, 2016, vimeo.com/157101111. Accessed January 13, 2022.
5. "Nicolas Cage Breaks Down His Most Iconic Characters." *YouTube*, *GQ*, September 18, 2018, www.youtube.com/watch?v=j_WDLsLnOSM&t=292s.
6. Gritten, David. "The Coen Mystique." *Los Angeles Times*, March 5, 1998, www.latimes.com/archives/la-xpm-1998-mar-05-ca-25488-story.html.
7. Hajari, Nisid. "Talking with Rena Coen." *Entertainment Weekly*, February 28, 1992, ew.com/article/1992/02/28/talking-rena-coen/.
8. Hinson, Hal. "Bloodlines." In *The Coen Brothers: Interviews*, edited by William Rodney Allen. University Press of Mississippi, 2006, p. 8.
9. Ibid.
10. Edelstein, David. "Invasion of the Baby Snatchers." In *The Coen Brothers: Interviews*, pp. 18–19.
11. Hinson, "Bloodlines," p. 15.
12. Richardson, John H. "The Joel and Ethan Story." *Premiere*, October 1989, www.thestacksreader.com/the-joel-and-ethan-story/.
13. Handelman, David. "Joel & Ethan Coen: The Brothers from Another Planet." *Rolling Stone*, May 21, 1987, www.rollingstone.com/movies/movie-features/joel-ethan-coen-the-brothers-from-another-planet-100526/.
14. Pooley, Eric. "Warped in America." *New York*, March 23, 1987, pp. 44–46. books.google.com/books?id = c-QCAAAAMBAJ&pg = PA44&lpg = PA44&dq=#v=onepage&q&f = false.
15. Attanasio, Paul. "Circle Sets Film Deal." *Washington Post*, May 10, 1985, www.washingtonpost.com/archive/lifestyle/1985/05/10/circle-sets-film-deal/d9139baf-d724-4215-af58-38f345641dcc/.
16. Schumacher, Michael. *Francis Ford Coppola: A Filmmaker's Life*. Crown, 1999. p. 381.

17. Woods, K. W. "Nicolas Cage: Madman or Mystery?" *Playgirl*, January 1988, pp. 90–91.
18. "John Trent Killed." *Sun Times*, June 4, 1983, p. 9. *Newspapers.com*, www.newspapers.com/image/728138771/.
19. Woods, "Nicolas Cage: Madman or Mystery?," p. 90.
20. Daly, Steve. "High Spirits." *Entertainment Weekly*, March 15, 1996, p. 27.
21. Mills, Bart. "Cage Gets to Drive the Girls Crazy in 'Peggy Sue.'" *News-Pilot*, October 13, 1986, p. A11. *Newspapers.com*, www.newspapers.com/image/607273142/.
22. Handelman, "Joel & Ethan Coen."
23. Ciment, Michel, and Hubert Niogret. *The Coen Brothers: Interviews*, edited by William Rodney Allen. University Press of Mississippi, Jackson, 2006, p. 27.
24. Strauss, Bob. "Joel and Ethan Coen Go Ga-Ga with Raising Arizona." *Movieline*, March 27, 1987, pp. 36–37.
25. Pooley, "Warped in America," p. 48.
26. Pfefferman, Naomi. "An Eye for Talent." *Jewish Journal*, April 27, 2000, jewishjournal.com/old_stories/2807/.
27. Schager, Nick. "Role Recall: Nicolas Cage on His Greatest Films—from 'Raising Arizona' to 'Face/Off' to Trippy New 'Mandy.'" *Yahoo!*, September 13, 2018, www.yahoo.com/lifestyle/role-recall-nicolas-cage-greatest-films-raising-arizona-face-off-trippy-new-mandy-141920155.html.
28. Richardson, John H. "The Joel and Ethan Story." *Premiere*, October 1989, www.thestacksreader.com/the-joel-and-ethan-story/.
29. Lockhart, Christopher. "Remembering Ed Limato." *Inside Pitch*, Blogspot, July 2, 2010, http://twoadverbs.blogspot.com/2010/07/remembering-ed-limato.html.
30. Wygant, Bobbie. "Nicolas Cage for 'Raising Arizona' 1987—Bobbie Wygant Archive." *YouTube*, May 28, 2020, www.youtube.com/watch?v=oCDwWTC44Xc. Accessed January 28, 2022.
31. Mann, Roderick. "Nicolas Cage Opens Up." *Los Angeles Times*, October 19, 1986, https://www.latimes.com/archives/la-xpm-1986-10-19-ca-5675-story.html.
32. Landau, David, and David Bennett Carren. "First-Person Narrative Screenwriting." In Landau and Carren, *Next Level Screenwriting: Insights, Ideas and Inspiration for the Intermediate Screenwriter*. Routledge, 2019, pp. 66–71.
33. Ciment and Niogret, *The Coen Brothers: Interviews*, p. 25.
34. Nashawaty, Chris. "The First 11 Minutes of Raising Arizona Are the Best Opening to Any Movie Ever Made." *Esquire*, April 29, 2021, https://www.esquire.com/entertainment/movies/a36287882/why-raising-arizona-has-the-best-opening-scene-of-any-movie/. Accessed January 24, 2022.
35. Strauss, "Joel and Ethan Coen Go Ga-Ga," p. 36.
36. Mann, "Nicolas Cage Opens Up."
37. Moorhead, M. V. "Re-Raising Arizona." *PHOENIX*, April 1, 2017, www.phoenixmag.com/2017/04/01/re-raising-arizona/.
38. Pooley, "Warped in America," p. 48.
39. Netter, Sarah. "Nicolas Cage Dares to Be 'Bangkok Dangerous.'" *ABC News*, September 17, 2008, abcnews.go.com/Entertainment/CelebrityCafe/story?id = 5725312&page = 1.

40. Sumner, Mike. "Into the Danger Zone." *The Guardian*, June 30, 1987, p. 9, *Newspapers.com*, www.newspapers.com/image/260302574.
41. Kaylin, Lucy. "The Rebel at Rest." *GQ*, March 1997, p. 229.
42. Ito, Robert. "Trading Flaming Skull for Inner Dad." *New York Times*, April 6, 2014, p. 15, www.nytimes.com/2014/04/06/movies/nicolas-cage-returns-to-indie-essentials-with-joe.html.
43. Edelstein, "Invasion of the Baby Snatchers," p. 21.
44. Ibid.
45. Schager, "Role Recall."
46. Armour, Terry. "Actor's Conundrum: Finding the Truth in Pretense." *Chicago Tribune*, September 11, 2003, p. 6. *Newspapers.com*, www.newspapers.com/image/231438405.
47. Edelstein, "Invasion of the Baby Snatchers," p. 20.
48. Rickey, Carrie. "Fish Play a Supporting Role in Actor Cage's Life." *Chicago Tribune*, April 23, 1987, www.chicagotribune.com/news/ct-xpm-1987-04-23-8701310310-story.html.
49. Handelman, "Joel & Ethan Coen."
50. Sonnenfeld, Barry. *Barry Sonnenfeld, Call Your Mother: Memoirs of a Neurotic Filmmaker*. Hachette Books, 2021.
51. Ciment, and Niogret, *The Coen Brothers: Interviews*, p. 28.
52. Edelstein, "Invasion of the Baby Snatchers," p. 19.
53. Wygant, Bobbie. "Nicolas Cage for 'Raising Arizona' 1987—Bobbie Wygant Archive." *YouTube*, May 28, 2020, www.youtube.com/watch?v=oCDwWTC44Xc. Accessed January 28, 2022.
54. Ebert, Roger. "Raising Arizona." *Chicago Sun-Times*, March 20, 1987, www.rogerebert.com/reviews/raising-arizona-1987.
55. Kehr, Dave. "Unless You Like Snide Films, You Can Skip 'Raising Arizona.'" *Charlotte Observer*, April 8, 1987, p. 19. *Newspapers.com*, www.newspapers.com/image/632622096/.
56. Schager, "Role Recall."
57. MacFarquhar, Larissa. "Stranger in Paradise." *Premiere*, June 1997, p. 74.
58. Nayman, Adam. *The Coen Brothers: This Book Really Ties the Films Together.* Abrams, 2018, p. 44.
59. "Nicolas Cage Breaks Down His Most Iconic Characters."
60. Ciment and Niogret, *The Coen Brothers: Interviews*, p. 29.
61. Grobel, Lawrence. "The Good Times of Nicolas Cage." *Movieline*, June 1998, pp. 48–49.
62. Moorhead, "Re-Raising Arizona."
63. Robson, Eddie. *Coen Brothers*. Virgin Digital, 2011, p. 58.
64. Lipton, James. "Inside the Actor's Studio." *Cagealot Castle*, April 10, 2011, cagealotcastle.activeboard.com/t42055109/nic-on-inside-the-actors-studio/?page = 1. Accessed February 10, 2022.
65. Sumner, "Into the Danger Zone."
66. Mills, "Cage Gets to Drive the Girls Crazy in 'Peggy Sue.'"

67. L.A. Times Archives. "Raising Hackles." *Los Angeles Times*, April 12, 1987, www.latimes.com/archives/la-xpm-1987-04-12-ca-844-story.html.
68. Kael, Pauline. "Manypeeplia Upsidownia." *New Yorker*, April 12, 1987, www.newyorker.com/magazine/1987/04/20/manypeeplia-upsidownia.
69. Rickey, "Fish Play a Supporting Role."
70. McKenna, Kristine. "The Playboy Interview: Joel and Ethan Coen." *Playboy*, November 2001.
71. Shone, Tom. "The Coen Brothers: the Cartographers of Cinema." *The Guardian*, January 27, 2011, www.theguardian.com/film/2011/jan/27/coen-brothers-interview-true-grit.
72. Ganahl, Jane. "The Wild Heart of Nicolas Cage." *San Francisco Examiner*, August 5, 1990, p. 13. *Newspapers.com*, www.newspapers.com/image/462222969.

Chapter 6

1. Handler, Rachel. "Moonstruck Is the Morbid Spaghetti Rom-Com We All Need Right Now." *Vulture*, *New York* magazine, 1 April 1, 2020, www.vulture.com/2020/04/moonstruck-is-the-morbid-spaghetti-rom-com-we-all-need-now.html.
2. "We Should Talk about 'Moonstruck' the Same Way We Talk about 'The Godfather.'" *Esquire*, Hearst Magazines, November 17, 2020, www.esquire.com/entertainment/movies/a34691455/moonstruck-italian-american-movie-essay/.
3. Weaver, Caity. "Dear Academy: Please Give Cher Another Oscar." *New York Times*, December 9, 2020, www.nytimes.com/interactive/2020/12/09/magazine/cher-moonstruck.html.
4. Kenny, J. M., director. *Moonstruck: At the Heart of an Italian Family*. 2006.
5. "Watch Video: Sally Field Reveals She Turned Down 'Moonstruck' Lead on WWHL." *BroadwayWorld.com*, March 11, 2016, www.broadwayworld.com/videoplay/VIDEO-Sally-Field-Reveals-She-Turned-Down-Moonstruck-Lead-on-WWHL-20160311.
6. Kenny, *Moonstruck: At the Heart of an Italian Family*.
7. Gelder, Lawrence Van. "At the Movies." *New York Times*, December 11, 1987, p. 8.
8. Jewison, Norman. *This Terrible Business Has Been Good to Me: An Autobiography*. Key Porter, 2006, pp. 252–253.
9. Wells, Ira. *Norman Jewison: A Director's Life*. Sutherland House, 2021, p. 335.
10. Jewison, *This Terrible Business*, p. 253.
11. Wells, *Norman Jewison*, p. 338.
12. Mills, Bart. "Cage Gets to Drive the Girls Crazy in 'Peggy Sue.'" *News-Pilot*, October 13, 1986, p. A11. *Newspapers.com*, www.newspapers.com/image/607273142/.
13. Cher, and Jeff Coplon. *The First Time*. Simon & Schuster, 1998, p. 231.
14. McKenna, Kristine. "A 'Moonstruck' Nicolas Cage Opens Up." *Los Angeles Times*, February 21, 1988, www.latimes.com/archives/la-xpm-1988-02-21-ca-44011-story.html.
15. Kenny, *Moonstruck: At the Heart of an Italian Family*.
16. Jewison, *This Terrible Business*, p. 255.

17. Cher and Coplon, *The First Time*, p. 231.
18. Wuntch, Philip. "Nicolas Cage Likes to Leave Them Laughing." *The Baltimore Sun*, September 2, 1992, p. 4F. *Newspapers.com*, www.newspapers.com/image/170776647/.
19. Ryan, Patrick. "Nicolas Cage Talks 'Pig' Co-Star, Freezing with Cher during 'Moonstruck' and His Go-to Dinner Recipe." *USA Today*, July 15, 2021, www.usatoday.com/story/entertainment/movies/2021/07/15/pig-nicolas-cage-interview/7956840002/.
20. Geller, Lynn. "Moving Images." *SPIN*, March 1989, p. 80. *Google Books*, https://books.google.com/books?id=bT9Dc3mzdZ8C&q=Cage#v=onepage&q=cage&f=false. Accessed October 3, 2021.
21. Ganahl, Jane. "The Wild Heart of Nicolas Cage." *San Francisco Examiner*, August 5, 1990, p. 14. *Newspapers.com*, www.newspapers.com/image/462223020.
22. Gussow, Mel. "Lee Strasberg of Actors Studio Dead." *New York Times*, February 18, 1982, p. 20, https://www.nytimes.com/1982/02/18/obituaries/lee-strasberg-of-actors-studio-dead.html. Accessed January 26, 2022.
23. Dargis, Manohla. "The Method and Madness of Nicolas Cage." *Sight & Sound*, June 1995, https://www.bfi.org.uk/sight-and-sound/features/method-madness-nicolas-cage. Accessed January 26, 2022.
24. Woods, K. W. "Nicolas Cage: Madman or Mystery?" *Playgirl*, January 1988, p. 36.
25. Horyn, Cathy. "Caged Heat." *Vanity Fair*, July 1996, p. 76.
26. McKenna, "A 'Moonstruck' Nicolas Cage Opens Up," p. 24.
27. Jewison, *This Terrible Business*, p. 255.
28. "Nicolas Cage Breaks Down His Most Iconic Characters." *GQ*, September 18, 2018, https://www.youtube.com/watch?v=j_WDLsLnOSM&app=desktop&persist_app=1. Accessed October 20, 2021.
29. Lynskey, Dorian. "'You've Got to Be Able to Break the Wall.'" *The Guardian*, February 16, 2007, https://www.theguardian.com/film/2007/feb/16/1. Accessed October 20, 2021.
30. Sumner, Mike. "Into the Danger Zone." *The Guardian*, June 30, 1987, p. 9. *Newspapers.com*, www.newspapers.com/image/260302574/.
31. Daly, Steve. "High Spirits." *Entertainment Weekly*, March 15, 1996, p. 28.
32. Jewison, Norman, director. *Moonstruck: Audio Commentary by Norman Jewison, Cher, and John Patrick Shanley*. Criterion Collection, 2020.
33. Aiello, Danny, and Gil Reavill. *I Only Know Who I Am When I Am Somebody Else: My Life on the Street, on the Stage, and in the Movies*. Gallery Books, 2015, p. 194.
34. Cher and Coplon, *The First Time*, p. 231.
35. Citron, Marcia J. *When Opera Meets Film*. Cambridge University Press, 2010, p. 173.
36. Jewison, *Moonstruck: Audio Commentary*.
37. Aiello and Reavill, *I Only Know Who I Am When I Am Somebody Else*, p. 194.
38. Kenny, *Moonstruck: At the Heart of an Italian Family*.
39. Robb, Brian J. *Nicolas Cage: Hollywood's Wild Talent*. Plexus, 1998.
40. Wuntch, Philip. "Nicolas Cage Likes to Leave Them Laughing."
41. "Nicolas Cage: 'Sometimes It's Good to Be Hated.'" *The Talks*, August 13, 2014, https://the-talks.com/interview/nicolas-cage/. Accessed October 19, 2021.

42. Whitty, Stephen. "Nicolas Cage Interview: 'Bad Lieutenant: Port of Call New Orleans' a Return to Form for the Thespian." *Inside Jersey*, November 20, 2009, https://www.nj.com/entertainment/tv/2009/11/nicolas_cage_interview_bad_lie.html. Accessed October 19, 2021.
43. Jewison, *Moonstruck: Audio Commentary*.
44. Wells, *Norman Jewison*, p. 344.
45. Schruers, Fred. "The Passion of Nicolas Cage." *Rolling Stone*, November 11, 1999, https://www.rollingstone.com/movies/movie-features/nicolas-cage-1999-cover-story-832684/. Accessed October 23, 2021.
46. Wells. *Norman Jewison*, p. 344.
47. Aiello and Reavill, *I Only Know Who I Am When I Am Somebody Else*, p. 194.
48. Ibid., p. 195.
49. Harris, Will. "Olympia Dukakis on A Little Game, Moonstruck, Tales of the City, and Death Wish." *The A.V. Club*, February 11, 2015, https://www.avclub.com/olympia-dukakis-on-a-little-game-moonstruck-tales-of-1798276781. Accessed October 24, 2021.
50. Sheff, David. "An Intense Interview with Nicolas Cage." *Playboy*, September 1996, https://www.davidsheff.com/nicolas-cage. Accessed October 25, 2021.
51. Jewison, *This Terrible Business*, p. 256.
52. Winer, Linda. "No Ordinary Joe." *Newsday*, July 24, 1994, p. 27. *Newspapers.com*, https://www.newspapers.com/image/725439613. Accessed October 25, 2021.
53. McKenna, "A 'Moonstruck' Nicolas Cage Opens Up," p. 5.
54. Ganahl, Jane. "The Brooding Nicolas Cage Is the New Type of Leading Man." *San Francisco Examiner*, December 14, 1988. *Newspapers.com*, https://www.newspapers.com/image/155109750/. Accessed October 26, 2021.
55. Ibid.
56. Wuntch, "Nicolas Cage Likes to Leave Them Laughing."

Chapter 7

1. Markham-Smith, Ian, and Liz Hodgson. *Nicolas Cage: The Unauthorised Biography*. Blake, 2001, p. 78.
2. Geller, Lynn. "Moving Images." *SPIN*, March 1989, p. 80. *Google Books*, https://books.google.com/books?id=bT9Dc3mzdZ8C&q=Cage#v=onepage&q=cage&f=false. Accessed October 3, 2021.
3. Tannenbaum, Rob. "Cage Against the Machine." *Details*, June 1996, p. 92.
4. Cagle, Jess. "Joseph Minion's Scripts." *Entertainment Weekly*, July 19, 1991, ew.com/article/1991/07/19/joseph-minions-scripts/.
5. Geller, "Moving Images," p. 53.
6. Harrington, Richard. "Real Bullet Apparently Killed Actor." *Washington Post*, April 2, 1993, www.washingtonpost.com/archive/politics/1993/04/02/real-bullet-apparently-killed-actor/a1ff962b-aff7-497e-a7ca-2edb30a1fe0c/.

7. *Nicolas Cage DVD Audio Commentary Transcript: Vampire's Kiss*, Cagealot Castle, June 26, 2011, cagealotcastle.activeboard.com/t43594194/nicolas-cage-dvd-audio-commentary-transcript-vampires-kiss/.
8. Sheff, David. "An Intense Interview with Nicolas Cage." *Playboy*, September 1996, www.davidsheff.com/nicolas-cage.
9. Ibid.
10. Ibid.
11. Ibid.
12. Hinson, Hal. "The Deadly 'Vampire's Kiss.'" *Washington Post*, June 2, 1989, www.washingtonpost.com/archive/lifestyle/1989/06/02/the-deadly-vampires-kiss/52387051-0004-4a96-95f9-02ed935d390a/.
13. James, Caryn. "Review/Film; The Woman He Adores, It Turns Out, Is a Vampire." *New York Times*, June 2, 1989, www.nytimes.com/1989/06/02/movies/review-film-the-woman-he-adores-it-turns-out-is-a-vampire.html.
14. Kael, Pauline. *5001 Nights at the Movies*. Henry Holt, 2011, p. 812.
15. Kempley, Rita. "'Vampire': A Delicious Chomp in the Dark." *Washington Post*, January 26, 2001, www.washingtonpost.com/archive/lifestyle/2001/01/26/vampire-a-delicious-chomp-in-the-dark/cb52e2e8-f8e0-4c0f-814a-e66b6eb75602/.
16. Schumacher, Michael. *Francis Ford Coppola: A Filmmaker's Life*. Crown, 1999, p. 4.
17. Grobel, Lawrence. "Out There with Nicolas Cage." *Movieline*, 1996, p. 42.
18. Weinbaum, Ted. "Willy's Wonderland Featurette." *Mothmachine Productions*, 2021, mothmachine.com/willy.
19. Geller, "Moving Images," p. 53.
20. Christie, Ian, and David Thompson, editors. *Scorsese on Scorsese*. Faber and Faber, 2003, p. 229.
21. Hall, Carla. "The Wild and Weird Nicolas Cage." *Washington Post*, August 31, 1990, www.washingtonpost.com/archive/lifestyle/1990/08/31/the-wild-and-weird-nicolas-cage/214dd456-5317-4186-9c81-6b1e2c64ccbe/.
22. Gibb, Lindsay. *National Treasure: Nicolas Cage*. ECW Press, 2015, p. 37.
23. *Nicolas Cage DVD Audio Commentary Transcript*.
24. Gibb, *National Treasure*, p. 35.
25. Ibid., p. 34.
26. Marvel, Mark. "No Cage for Nic Cage." *Interview*, August 1994, p. 61.
27. Tannenbaum, "Cage Against the Machine."
28. Ibid.
29. Longsdorf, Amy. "Tales from a Crypt." *The Morning Call*, January 26, 2001, p. D4. *Newspapers.com*, www.newspapers.com/image/279617965.
30. "Nicolas Cage Breaks Down His Most Iconic Characters." *YouTube*, *GQ*, September 18, 2018, www.youtube.com/watch?v=j_WDLsLnOSM.
31. Freeman, Hadley. "Nicolas Cage: 'If I Don't Have a Job to Do, I Can Be Very Self-Destructive.'" *The Guardian*, October 1, 2018, www.theguardian.com/film/2018/oct/01/nicolas-cage-if-i-dont-have-a-job-to-do-it-can-be-very-self-destructive.
32. Ebert, Roger. "Evolution Is God's Intelligent Design." *RogerEbert.com*, September 18, 2008, www.rogerebert.com/reviews/great-movie-adaptation-2002.

33. Goldberg, Matt. "Four Minutes of Nicolas Cage Losing His Shit." *Collider*, Valnet, Inc., November 22, 2010, collider.com/nicolas-cage-losing-his-shit/.
34. Schonfeld, Zach. "Nicolas Cage: 'Regret Is a Waste of Time.'" *Newsweek*, September 25, 2015, www.newsweek.com/nicolas-cage-regret-waste-time-pay-ghost-376290.
35. Paiella, Gabriella. "Culture Nicolas Cage Can Explain It All." *GQ*, March 22, 2022, www.gq.com/story/nicolas-cage-april-cover-profile.
36. McCormack, J. W. "Despite All His Cage." *The Baffler*, July 1, 2022, https://thebaffler.com/latest/despite-all-his-cage-mccormack. Accessed July 2, 2022.
37. Tobias, Scott. "Vampire's Kiss Features One of Nicolas Cage's Best, Most Out-of-Control Performances." *The A. V. Club*, G/O Media, May 24, 2012, www.avclub.com/vampire-s-kiss-features-one-of-nicolas-cage-s-best-mos-1798231471.
38. Rabin, Nathan. "The Travolta/Cage Project #20: Vampire's Kiss (1989)." *Nathan Rabin's Happy Place*, Nathan Rabin's Happy Place, April 8, 2020, www.nathanrabin.com/happy-place/2020/4/8/the-travoltacage-project-20-vampires-kiss-1989.
39. Geller, "Moving Images."

Chapter 8

1. "Order to Show Cause for Change of Name." *Los Angeles Daily Journal*, June 29, 1989, p. 4.
2. Woods, K. W. "Nicolas Cage: Madman or Mystery?" *Playgirl*, January 1988, pp. 34–36.
3. Crane, Robert. "20 Questions for Nicolas Cage." *Playboy*, June 1989, pp. 151–152.
4. Rabin, Nathan. "Nicolas Cagetastic Case File #143: Zandalee." *A. V. Club*, G/O Media, August 5, 2009, https://www.avclub.com/nicolas-cagetastic-case-file-143-zandalee-1798217277.
5. Schonfeld, Zach. "'Never on Tuesday': The Real Story of the Bizarre Nicolas Cage Cameo That Lit Up the Internet." *Gothamist*, WNYC, July 30, 2019, https://gothamist.com/arts-entertainment/never-on-tuesday-the-real-story-of-the-bizarre-nicolas-cage-cameo-that-lit-up-the-internet.
6. Ibid.
7. Easton, Nina J. "Novice Gets Crack at 'Apes' Sequel." *Los Angeles Times*, January 24, 1989, https://www.latimes.com/archives/la-xpm-1989-01-24-ca-1005-story.html. Accessed October 10, 2022.
8. Robb, Brian J. *Nicolas Cage: Hollywood's Wild Talent*. Plexus, 1998. p. 74.
9. Schonfeld, " 'Never on Tuesday.' "
10. Bramesco, Charles. "Nicolas Cage Takes Full Credit for That Prosthetic Nose." *Vulture*, Vox Media, August 6, 2019, https://www.vulture.com/2019/08/nicolas-cage-explains-his-never-on-tuesday-cameo.html.
11. Grobel, Lawrence. "The Good Times of Nicolas Cage." *Movieline*, June 1998, https://lebeauleblog.com/2018/06/25/the-good-times-of-nicolas-cage/2/. Accessed October 12, 2022.
12. Bramesco, "Nicolas Cage Takes Full Credit."

13. Pond, Steve. "Chris Coppola, in Uncle's Footsteps." *Washington Post*, July 17, 1992, https://www.washingtonpost.com/archive/lifestyle/1992/07/17/chris-coppola-in-uncles-footsteps/87fbc4ea-a24b-492b-9d52-3d57b7e61652/. Accessed October 10, 2022.
14. Daly, Steve. "Nicolas Cage's Discography." *Entertainment Weekly*, March 15, 1996, p. 28.
15. Vern, Outlaw. "Deadfall." *Vern's Reviews on the Films of Cinema*, January 15, 2010, https://outlawvern.com/2010/01/15/deadfall/.
16. Zehme, Bill. "Andy Kaufman: The Bug-Eyed Comic Who Saw the Future." *New York Times*, January 16, 2000, https://archive.nytimes.com/www.nytimes.com/library/style/weekend/011600andy-kaufman-tribute.html. Accessed October 19, 2022.

Chapter 9

1. Gold, Jonathan. "Restaurants: Just So You Don't Get Lost or Confused: The '80s' Last Stand." *Los Angeles Times*, March 10, 1991, www.latimes.com/archives/la-xpm-1991-03-10-ca-34-story.html.
2. Lynch, David. *Lynch on Lynch*. Edited by Chris Rodley. Faber and Faber, 1997, p. 195.
3. Ibid., p. 194.
4. Hall, Carla. "The Wild and Weird Nicolas Cage." *Washington Post*, August 31, 1990, www.washingtonpost.com/archive/lifestyle/1990/08/31/the-wild-and-weird-nicolas-cage/214dd456-5317-4186-9c81-6b1e2c64ccbe/.
5. Wilmington, Michael. "Nicolas Cage—Wild and Full of Heart." *Los Angeles Times*, August 12, 1990, www.latimes.com/archives/la-xpm-1990-08-12-ca-1096-story.html.
6. Hutchings, David. "Blue Velvet's David Lynch Views Nicolas Cage and Laura Dern Through a Lens Darkly." *People*, March 19, 1990, http://www.oocities.org/~mikehartmann/wildatheart/wahpeople.html. Accessed November 1, 2021.
7. Lynch, David, and Kristine McKenna. *Room to Dream*. Random House, 2018, p. 113.
8. Manson, Marilyn. "'Cock!': Nicolas Cage and Marilyn Manson in Conversation." *Interview Magazine*, October 20, 2020, https://www.interviewmagazine.com/film/nicolas-cage-marilyn-manson-in-conversation. Accessed October 28, 2021.
9. Lynch and McKenna, *Room to Dream*, p. 113.
10. Lynch, *Lynch on Lynch*, p. 117.
11. Hyman, Nick, et al. "Crispin Glover." *Under the Radar*, December 1, 2006, www.undertheradarmag.com/interviews/crispin_glover_interview_122006.
12. Olson, Greg. *David Lynch: Beautiful Dark*. Scarecrow Press, 2008, p. 144
13. Lynch, *Lynch on Lynch*, p. 193.
14. Lynch and McKenna, *Room to Dream*, p. 284.
15. Campbell, Virginia. "Something Really Wild." *Movieline*, September 1990, lebeauleblog.com/2016/09/11/something-really-wild/.

16. Ganahl, Jane. "The Wild Heart of Nicolas Cage." *San Francisco Examiner*, August 5, 1990, p. 13. *Newspapers.com*, https://www.newspapers.com/image/462222969. Accessed November 2, 2021.
17. Gibb, Lindsay. *National Treasure: Nicolas Cage*. ECW Press, 2015, p. 40.
18. Manson, " 'Cock!' "
19. Arar, Yardena. "'Wild at Heart' Director Orchestrates Creative Chaos." *Austin American-Statesman*, August 21, 1990, p. D5. *Newspapers.com*, https://www.newspapers.com/image/364006756/. Accessed November 6, 2021.
20. Lynch and McKenna. *Room to Dream*, p. 287.
21. Hutchings, "Blue Velvet's David Lynch."
22. Lipper, Hal. "Cage Has a Lock on Kookiness." *St. Petersburg Times*, August 22, 1990, p. 3D. *Newspapers.com*, www.newspapers.com/image/323214248.
23. Arar, " 'Wild at Heart' Director Orchestrates Creative Chaos."
24. MacFarquhar, Larissa. "Stranger in Paradise." *Premiere*, June 1997, p. 68.
25. Lynch, *Lynch on Lynch*, p. 135.
26. Lynch and McKenna, *Room to Dream*, p. 298.
27. Campbell, "Something Really Wild."
28. CBC. "CBC Interview with David Lynch." *Sheep Productions*, https://www.sheepproductions.com/tps/people/dlinterv.txt. Accessed November 3, 2021.
29. Winer, Linda. "No Ordinary Joe." *Newsday*, July 24, 1994, p. 27. *Newspapers.com*, https://www.newspapers.com/image/725439488. Accessed November 3, 2021.
30. "Graceland Announces New Pop-Up Elvis Karate Exhibit to Celebrate the 39th Anniversary of the Opening of the Iconic Property on June 7." Elvis Presley Enterprises, Inc., June 2, 2021, https://www.graceland.com/elvis-news/posts/graceland-announces-new-pop-up-elvis-karate-exhibit.
31. Hall, "The Wild and Weird Nicolas Cage."
32. Manson, " 'Cock!' "
33. *New York Post*, June 25, 1990.
34. Ganahl, "The Wild Heart of Nicolas Cage."
35. Jones, Dylan. *Elvis Has Left the Building: The Day the King Died*. Duckworth Overlook, 2015.
36. Harris, Lauren Carroll. "What Do David Lynch's Movies Say about Sex?" *The Toast*, September 16, 2015, the-toast.net/2015/09/16/david-lynch-movies-sex/.
37. Lynch, *Lynch on Lynch*, p. 199.
38. "Episode #1.3." Brown, Liza, director. *The Word*, performance by Terry Christian, season 1, episode 3, Channel 4, September 7, 1990, www.youtube.com/watch?v=SpB7E7fPg8A.
39. Crane, Robert. "20 Questions: Nicolas Cage." *Playboy*, June 1989, p. 151.
40. "Episode #1.3."
41. Lipper, "Cage Has a Lock on Kookiness."
42. Lynch, *Lynch on Lynch*, p. 199.
43. Campbell, "Something Really Wild."
44. Lynch and McKenna, *Room to Dream*, p. 291.

45. Ebert, Roger. "Wild at Heart." *Chicago Sun-Times*, August 17, 1990, www.rogerebert.com/reviews/wild-at-heart-1990.
46. Wilmington, "Nicolas Cage—Wild and Full of Heart."
47. Ansen, David. "David Lynch's New Peak." *Newsweek*, June 4, 1990, www.newsweek.com/david-lynchs-new-peak-206160.
48. Ibid.
49. Wilmington, "Nicolas Cage—Wild and Full of Heart."
50. "Episode #1.3."
51. "Episode #10.92." *Wogan*, performance by Terry Wogan, season 10, episode 92, BBC, August 24, 1990, www.youtube.com/watch?v=Xf3OgWVkzlI.
52. Thompson, Douglas. "Out of His Cage." *Herald*, July 5, 1996, www.heraldscotland.com/news/12032741.out-of-his-cage/.
53. Wilmington, "Nicolas Cage—Wild and Full of Heart."
54. Dargis, Manohla. "Method Madness." *Sight & Sound*, June 1995, pp. 5–8.
55. Lynch and McKenna, *Room to Dream*, p. 258.
56. Stanley, John. "Nicolas Cage Aims Satirical Stab at Race Relations." *San Francisco Examiner*, February 28, 1993, p. 23. *Newspapers.com*, www.newspapers.com/image/461761342/.
57. Ganahl, "The Wild Heart of Nicolas Cage."
58. Hall, "The Wild and Weird Nicolas Cage."
59. Robb, Brian J. *Nicolas Cage: Hollywood's Wild Talent*. Plexus, 1998. pp. 85–86.
60. Hoban, Phoebe. "Last Tango in New Orleans." *Premiere*, May 1991, pp. 38–41.
61. Ibid., p. 40.
62. Ibid.
63. Rhodes, Joe. "Judge for Yourself: Reinhold Talks about His Rapid Rise and Fall—and His Current Film on Showtime." *Los Angeles Times*, March 15, 1992, www.latimes.com/archives/la-xpm-1992-03-15-tv-6483-story.html.
64. Hoban, "Last Tango in New Orleans," p. 38.
65. Koski, Lorna. "Nicolas Cage." *Women's Wear Daily*, October 2, 1986.
66. Rabin, Nathan. "Nicolas Cagetastic Case File #143: Zandalee." *A.V. Club*, G/O Media, August 5, 2009, https://www.avclub.com/nicolas-cagetastic-case-file-143-zandalee-1798217277.
67. Hoban, "Last Tango in New Orleans," p. 38.
68. Ibid., p. 42.
69. Ibid.
70. DiGiacomo, Frank, and Joanna Molloy. "This an Apartment? It's a Cage." *New York Post*, June 24, 1991, p. 6.
71. Hoban, "Last Tango in New Orleans," p. 41.
72. Hennessey, Kevin. "Zandalee." *Movieline*, 1991, https://web.archive.org/web/20041014154920/http://movieline.standard8media.com/reviews/zandalee.shtml. Accessed December 15, 2022.
73. Taylor, Trey. "Obvious History: Nicolas Cage Almost Sent Charlie Sheen to Jail." *Interview*, May 3, 2018, https://www.interviewmagazine.com/film/obvious-history-nicolas-cage-almost-sent-charlie-sheen-jail. Accessed December 22, 2022.

74. Marchese, David. “Nicolas Cage on His Legacy, His Philosophy of Acting and His Metaphorical—and Literal—Search for the Holy Grail.” *New York Times Magazine*, August 7, 2019, www.nytimes.com/interactive/2019/08/07/magazine/nicolas-cage-interview.html.
75. Paiella, Gabriella. “Nicolas Cage Can Explain It All.” *GQ*, March 22, 2022, https://www.gq.com/story/nicolas-cage-april-cover-profile. Accessed 6 November 6, 2022.

Chapter 10

1. Wilmington, Michael. “Nicolas Cage—Wild and Full of Heart.” *Los Angeles Times*, August 12, 1990, https://www.latimes.com/archives/la-xpm-1990-08-12-ca-1096-story.html. Accessed April 10, 2022.
2. Booe, Martin. “Caged.” *New York Daily News*, August 2, 1998, pp. 1–4.
3. Beck, Marilyn. “Cage Surprised at Fast Success of ‘Guarding Tess.’” *News-Pilot*, March 19, 1994, p. B6. *Newspapers.com*, www.newspapers.com/image/608325495/.
4. Pall, Ellen. “Film; Nicholas Cage, The Sunshine Man.” *New York Times*, July 24, 1994, pp. 1–22, www.nytimes.com/1994/07/24/movies/film-nicholas-cage-the-sunshine-man.html.
5. Stanley, John. “Nicolas Cage Aims Satirical Stab at Race Relations.” *San Francisco Examiner*, February 28, 1993, p. 23. *Newspapers.com*, www.newspapers.com/image/461761342/.
6. “Cage’s Home Is a Hilltop Castle.” *Calgary Herald*, October 22, 1990, p. B8. *Newspapers.com*, www.newspapers.com/image/484805805/.
7. Connelly, Sherryl. “The New Cage: Nicolas Tickles Us.” *New York Daily News*, March 6, 1994. *Newspapers.com*, www.newspapers.com/image/472310129.
8. Lee, Luaine. “No Counterfeit Desire for Fonda, Stoltz.” *Pasadena Star-News*, April 9, 1993, p. 60. *Newspapers.com*, https://www.newspapers.com/image/628335120. Accessed October 3, 2022.
9. Hall, Carla. “The Wild and Weird Nicolas Cage.” *Washington Post*, 31 August 31, 1990, www.washingtonpost.com/archive/lifestyle/1990/08/31/the-wild-and-weird-nicolas-cage/214dd456-5317-4186-9c81-6b1e2c64ccbe/.
10. Wuntch, Philip. “Nicolas Cage Likes to Leave Them Laughing.” *Baltimore Sun*, September 2, 1992, p. 4F. *Newspapers.com*, www.newspapers.com/image/170776647/.
11. “Honeymoon in Vegas (1992).” *AFI Catalog of Feature Films*, American Film Institute, catalog.afi.com/Catalog/MovieDetails/59271.
12. Thompson, Douglas. *Uncaged: The Biography of Nicolas Cage*. Boxtree, 1997, p. 129.
13. Wallace, Amy. “His Truth Is Out There.” *Los Angeles Times*, November 12, 2000, www.chicagotribune.com/news/ct-xpm-2000-11-12-0011120201-story.html.
14. Daly, Steve. “Nicolas Cage’s Discography.” *Entertainment Weekly*, March 15, 1996, ew.com/article/1996/03/15/nicolas-cages-discography/.
15. Thompson, *Uncaged*, p. 130.

16. Rodriguez, Rene. "Committed Cage Insists on Doing Things His Way." *Spokesman-Review*, February 17, 2012, www.spokesman.com/stories/2012/feb/17/committed-cage-insists-on-doing-things-his-way/.
17. Markham-Smith, Ian, and Liz Hodgson. *Nicolas Cage: The Man Behind Captain Corelli*. Blake, 2001, 125–126.
18. Cage, Nicolas. "On the Road with Nicolas Cage." *Details*, July 1991, https://cagealotcastle.activeboard.com/t38067887/on-the-road-with-nicolas-cage/. Accessed January 17, 2022.
19. Markham-Smith and Hodgson, *Nicolas Cage*, p. 129.
20. Costin, Glynis. "Men, Movies & Mayhem." *Vancouver Sun*, September 27, 1994, p. C5. *Newspapers.com*, www.newspapers.com/image/495081659.
21. Keegan, Rebecca. "'Is This Acting or Is This F***Ing Therapy?': Nicolas Cage, Andrew Garfield, Jonathan Majors and the THR Actor Roundtable." *Hollywood Reporter*, January 5, 2022, https://www.hollywoodreporter.com/movies/movie-features/nicolas-cage-andrew-garfield-jonathan-majors-actor-roundtable-1235069392/. Accessed April 15, 2022.
22. Freeman, Hadley. "Nicolas Cage: 'If I Don't Have a Job to Do, I Can Be Very Self-Destructive.'" *The Guardian*, October 1, 2018, www.theguardian.com/film/2018/oct/01/nicolas-cage-if-i-dont-have-a-job-to-do-it-can-be-very-self-destructive.
23. Thompson, *Uncaged*, pp. 130–131.
24. "Nicolas Cage 'Honeymoon in Vegas' 1992—Bobbie Wygant Archive." *YouTube*, September 13, 2020, www.youtube.com/watch?v=TLC-3mH-9tc&t=563s.
25. Wuntch, "Nicolas Cage Likes to Leave Them Laughing," p. 4F. *Newspapers.com*, www.newspapers.com/image/170776647/.
26. Mills, Nancy. "A Kinder, Gentler Cage." *San Pedro News-Pilot*, August 28, 1992, pp. E3–E6. *Newspapers.com*, www.newspapers.com/image/608280151.
27. "Nicolas Cage 'Honeymoon in Vegas' 1992—Bobbie Wygant Archive."
28. Markham-Smith and Hodgson, *Nicolas Cage*, p. 137.
29. Dahl, John, director. *Red Rock West: Audio Commentary*. Roxie Releasing, 2010.
30. Mills, "A Kinder, Gentler Cage."
31. "Nicolas Cage 'Honeymoon in Vegas' 1992—Bobbie Wygant Archive."
32. Natale, Richard. "John Dahl on Making a Killing." *Los Angeles Times*, November 13, 1994, www.latimes.com/archives/la-xpm-1994-11-13-ca-62251-story.html.
33. Hornaday, Ann. "Film; Film Noir, 'Tweener' or Flub?," *New York Times*, April 3, 1994, p. 19, www.nytimes.com/1994/04/03/movies/film-film-noir-tweener-or-flub.html.
34. Dahl, *Red Rock West*. Audio Commentary.
35. Hornaday, "Film; Film Noir, 'Tweener' or Flub?"
36. Markham-Smith and Hodgson, *Nicolas Cage*, p. 141.
37. Armstrong, David. "Leaving Comedy for 'Las Vegas.'" *San Francisco Examiner*, November 8, 1995, pp. C1–C4. *Newspapers.com*, www.newspapers.com/image/462602107.
38. Britt, Bruce. "Nicolas Cage Gets to Play a Good Guy." *San Francisco Examiner*, July 24, 1994, p. 29. *Newspapers.com*, www.newspapers.com/image/461625672/.

39. Rabin, Nathan. "The Travolta/Cage Project #38 Guarding Tess (1994)." *Nathan Rabin's Happy Place*, September 8, 2020, www.nathanrabin.com/happy-place/2020/9/7/the-travoltacage-project-38-guarding-tess-1994.
40. Wolf, Jeanne, and Shep Morgan. "Nicolas Cage: He's Normal, to a Point." *Philadelphia Inquirer*, March 6, 1994, pp. F1–F7. *Newspapers.com*, www.newspapers.com/image/175755118.
41. Schaefer, Stephen. "Cage Breaks Out." *New York Post*, March 7, 1994, p. 29.
42. Markham-Smith and Hodgson, *Nicolas Cage*, p. 150.
43. Lamagna, Jodi. "Cage Embraces a Different Kind of Role." *Deseret News*, April 27, 1993, www.deseret.com/1993/4/27/19044084/cage-embraces-a-different-kind-of-role.
44. MacLaine, Shirley. *My Lucky Stars: A Hollywood Memoir*. Bantam Books, 1996, p. 263.
45. Schruers, Fred. "Dangerous, Dedicated and Wild at Heart, Nicolas Cage Is a Hollywood Samurai." *Rolling Stone*, November 16, 1995.
46. Werner, Laurie. "Shirley MacLaine's Playing 'Old' and Having the Time of Her Life." *Los Angeles Times*, March 12, 1994, www.latimes.com/archives/la-xpm-1994-03-12-ca-33116-story.html.
47. Edwards, Christine. *The Stanislavsky Heritage*. New York University Press, 1965, p. 45.
48. Marvel, Mark. "No Cage for Nic Cage." *Interview*, August 1994, p. 62.
49. Wolf and Morgan, "Nicolas Cage: He's Normal, to a Point."
50. Connelly, "The New Cage: Nicolas Tickles Us."
51. Grogan, David. "After 24 Years Pushing Pizza, Waitress Phyllis Penzo Gets a Tip to Remember: $3 Million." *People*, April 23, 1984, people.com/archive/after-24-years-pushing-pizza-waitress-phyllis-penzo-gets-a-tip-to-remember-3-million-vol-21-no-16/.
52. Manson, Marilyn. "'Cock!': Nicolas Cage and Marilyn Manson in Conversation." *Interview*, October 20, 2020, www.interviewmagazine.com/film/nicolas-cage-marilyn-manson-in-conversation.
53. Perez, Rosie. *Handbook for an Unpredictable Life: How I Survived Sister Renata and My Crazy Mother and Still Came out Smiling (with Great Hair)*. Three Rivers Press, 2015, p. 284.
54. Ganahl, Jane. "Uncaged." *San Francisco Examiner*, March 24, 1996, p. 12. *Newspapers.com*, https://www.newspapers.com/image/461861652. Accessed July 4, 2022.
55. Kaylin, Lucy. "The Rebel at Rest." *GQ*, March 1997, p. 226.
56. Horyn, Cathy. "Caged Heat." *Vanity Fair*, July 1996, pp. 78–144.
57. Sheff, David. "An Intense Interview with Nicolas Cage." *Playboy*, September 1996, www.davidsheff.com/nicolas-cage.
58. Grimes, William. "A Different Sort of Quiet on the Set with Andrew Bergman in Charge." *New York Times*, August 30, 1993, https://www.nytimes.com/1993/08/30/movies/a-different-sort-of-quiet-on-the-set-with-andrew-bergman-in-charge.html.
59. Gibb, Lindsay. *National Treasure: Nicolas Cage*. ECW Press, 2015, p. 41–42.
60. Ansen, David. "The All American Hero." *Newsweek*, July 13, 1997, www.newsweek.com/all-american-hero-174538.

61. Winer-Bernheimer, Linda. "A Castle with a Different Cage: He's 30, a Parent, and Taking a Break from 'Twisted Characters.'" *Los Angeles Times*, July 25, 1994. *Newspapers.com*, www.newspapers.com/image/159925717.
62. "James Stewart, the Hesitant Hero, Dies at 89." *New York Times*, July 3, 1997, p. A20, www.nytimes.com/1997/07/03/movies/james-stewart-the-hesitant-hero-dies-at-89.html.
63. Winer, Linda. "No Ordinary Joe." *Newsday*, July 24, 1994, p. 11. *Newspapers.com*, www.newspapers.com/image/725439497.
64. Connelly, "The New Cage: Nicolas Tickles Us."
65. Wolf and Morgan, "Nicolas Cage: He's Normal, to a Point."
66. Pall, "Film; Nicholas Cage, The Sunshine Man."
67. Winer-Bernheimer, "A Castle with a Different Cage."
68. Lipper, Hal. "Cage Has a Lock on Kookiness." *St. Petersburg Times*, August 22, 1990, pp. ID–3D. *Newspapers.com*, www.newspapers.com/image/323214248.

Chapter 11

1. Katz, Ian. "Living 'Las Vegas.'" *Albuquerque Tribune*, January 29, 1996, p. C5. *Newspapers.com*, www.newspapers.com/image/785168113.
2. O'Brien, Erin. "Interview." *Erin O'Brien*, Blogspot, December 18, 2006, erin-obrien.blogspot.com/2006/12/interview.html.
3. Baerwald, David. *L.A. Weekly*, 1996, www.dbinfosource.com/oldpages/two/lasvegas.htm.
4. Katz, "Living 'Las Vegas.'"
5. McKenna, Kristine. "Movies: Playing the Cards as They're Dealt: Director Mike Figgis Takes a Gamble Adapting a Difficult Tale of Love, Loss in 'Las Vegas.'" *Los Angeles Times*, October 29, 1995, www.latimes.com/archives/la-xpm-1995-10-29-ca-62457-story.html.
6. O'Brien, John. *Leaving Las Vegas*. Grove Press, 1995, p. 79.
7. Ibid., p. 69.
8. Ibid., pp. 66–67.
9. Ibid., p. 102.
10. O'Neal, Sean. "Jon Lovitz." *A.V. Club*, G/O Media, December 29, 2010, www.avclub.com/jon-lovitz-1798223402.
11. "Cagey over Budget." *Variety*, May 16, 1994.
12. Ryan, Mike. "Nicolas Cage on 'Ghost Rider: Spirit of Vengeance,' Almost Starring in 'Dumb and Dumber' and Why He Is Led Zeppelin." *Moviefone*, February 12, 2012, https://web.archive.org/web/20150928050558/http://news.moviefone.com/2012/02/14/nicolas-cage-ghost-rider/.
13. Dudek, Duane. "Suicide's Silver Lining." *Austin American-Statesman*, January 5, 1996, p. E5.
14. McKenna, "Movies: Playing the Cards as They're Dealt."

15. Ibid.
16. Katz, "Living 'Las Vegas.'"
17. Baerwald, *L.A. Weekly*.
18. Hosman, Britta, director. *VPRO's Shot on Location: Leaving Las Vegas. Vimeo*, FrithMedia, March 22, 2013, vimeo.com/62409125. Accessed August 22, 2022.
19. Horn, John. "Rare Despair: A Dark 'Leaving Las Vegas' Rolls the Dice." *Associated Press*, October 27, 1995. *Newspapers.com*, www.newspapers.com/image/legacy/747131701/.
20. Thomson, David. "Caged Heat." *Independent*, January 14, 1996, www.independent.co.uk/arts-entertainment/caged-heat-1323910.html.
21. Horyn, Cathy. "Caged Heat." *Vanity Fair*, July 1996, p. 78.
22. Sheff, David. "An Intense Interview with Nicolas Cage." *Playboy*, September 1996, www.davidsheff.com/nicolas-cage.
23. O'Brien, Erin. "Leaving Las Vegas: Rearview." *Cleveland Free Times*, April 16, 2008.
24. McKenna, "Movies: Playing the Cards as They're Dealt."
25. Katz, "Living 'Las Vegas,'" p. C5.
26. Ibid.
27. Sheff, "An Intense Interview with Nicolas Cage."
28. Ebert, Roger. "Cage Relishes Operatic Role in Tragic `Leaving Las Vegas.'" *Chicago Sun-Times*, November 5, 1995, www.rogerebert.com/interviews/cage-relishes-opera tic-role-in-tragic-leaving-las-vegas.
29. "I Wanted to Know What It's like to Be Irish . . . so I Got Drunk for 2 Weeks; Nic Went on Dublin Binge for Film Role." *Free Library*, 2000, www.thefreelibrary.com/I+wanted+to+know+what+it%27s+like+to+be+Irish..+so+I+got+drunk+for+2...-a06 3960765.
30. Horyn, "Caged Heat," p. 78.
31. Leyva, Ric. "Breakthrough for Shue." *Associated Press*, January 10, 1996, p. D3. *Newspapers.com*, www.newspapers.com/image/legacy/273437586/.
32. Horyn. "Caged Heat," p. 78.
33. Marvel, Mark. "No Cage for Nic Cage." *Interview*, August 1994, p. 62.
34. Siegel, Scott, and Barbara Siegel. "Nicolas Cage." *Drama-Logue*, October 26, 1995, p. 4.
35. Rist, Curtis. "Nicolas Uncaged." *People*, February 26, 1996, pp. 63–64.
36. Heath, Paul. "Looking Back at 'Leaving Las Vegas' & Nicolas Cage's Oscar-Winning Performance." *Hollywood News*, October 31, 2019, www.thehollywoodnews.com/2019/10/31/looking-back-at-leaving-las-vegas-nicolas-cages-oscar-winning-perf ormance/.
37. "Nicolas Cage Breaks Down His Most Iconic Characters." *YouTube*, *GQ*, September 18, 2018, www.youtube.com/watch?v=j_WDLsLnOSM&t=328s.
38. Thomson, "Caged Heat."
39. Ibid.
40. Ibid.
41. "Nicolas Cage Breaks Down His Most Iconic Characters."
42. Tannenbaum, Rob. "Cage Against the Machine." *Details*, June 1996, p. 90.

43. *Inside the Actors Studio*. Performance by James Lipton, season 10, episode Nicolas Cage, Bravo, February 16, 2003, www.youtube.com/watch?v=Yv2VIEkkwtU.
44. Puig, Claudia. "He's Up. He's Down. He's Up. He's Down. He's Up for Good?: Nicholas Cage's Movie Career Has Been, Uh Volatile. But He Hit the Jackpot in an Alcoholic Love Story Set in Las Vegas. Will Success Stick? Nothing Is Ever That Simple in Hollywood." *Los Angeles Times*, February 4, 1996, www.latimes.com/archives/la-xpm-1996-02-04-tm-32387-story.html.
45. Ibid.
46. O'Brien, *Leaving Las Vegas*, pp. 187–188.
47. Ibid., pp. 64–65.
48. Ebert, "Cage Relishes Operatic Role."
49. Daly, Steve. "High Spirits." *Entertainment Weekly*, March 15, 1996.
50. Ebert, "Cage Relishes Operatic Role."
51. Grobel, Lawrence. "Out There with Nicolas Cage." *Movieline*, 1996, p. 42.
52. Ebert, "Cage Relishes Operatic Role."
53. Schruers, Fred. "Dangerous, Dedicated and Wild at Heart, Nicolas Cage Is a Hollywood Samurai." *Rolling Stone*, November 16, 1995, p. 94.
54. Kaylin, Lucy. "The Rebel at Rest." *GQ*, March 1997, p. 226.
55. Schruers, "Dangerous, Dedicated and Wild at Heart," p. 94.
56. Daly, "High Spirits."
57. Tannenbaum, "Cage Against the Machine."
58. *New York Post*, April 1, 1996.
59. Rist, Curtis. "Nicolas Uncaged." *People*, February 26, 1996, p. 66.
60. Ansen, David. "Free Fall In Vegas." *Newsweek*, October 29, 1995, www.newsweek.com/free-fall-vegas-184338.
61. Gleiberman, Owen. "Leaving Las Vegas." *Entertainment Weekly*, October 27, 1995, ew.com/article/1995/10/27/leaving-las-vegas-3/.
62. Ebert, Roger. "Leaving Las Vegas." *Chicago Sun-Times*, November 10, 1995, www.rogerebert.com/reviews/leaving-las-vegas-1995.
63. Sheff, "An Intense Interview with Nicolas Cage."
64. Tannenbaum, "Cage Against the Machine."
65. Horyn, "Caged Heat," p. 145.
66. Tannenbaum. "Cage Against the Machine," p. 90.
67. Kaylin, "The Rebel at Rest," p. 227.
68. McKenna, "Movies: Playing the Cards as They're Dealt."
69. Kaylin, "The Rebel at Rest," p. 225.
70. Kaylin, "The Rebel at Rest," p. 229.
71. Raab, Scott. "Waiting for Nic Cage." *GQ*, October 1995, p. 214.
72. Raab, "Waiting for Nic Cage," p. 217.
73. Rush, George, and Joanna Molloy. "Nick's 11th-Hour Bowing-out Not Fatal to Abel's 'Funeral.'" *New York Daily News*, August 3, 1995, p. 25. *Newspapers.com*, www.newspapers.com/image/legacy/476712306/.
74. Smith, Liz. "Cage Signs on for 'Rock' Cast." *The Palm Beach Post*, July 1, 1995, p. 20. *Newspapers.com*, www.newspapers.com/image/legacy/134192216.

Epilogue

1. Paiella, Gabriella. "Nicolas Cage Can Explain It All." *GQ*, April 2022, https://www.gq.com/story/nicolas-cage-april-cover-profile. Accessed April 25, 2022.
2. Ibid.
3. Kit, Borys. "How 'Pig' Became Nicolas Cage's Cash Cow." *Hollywood Reporter*, October 19, 2022, www.hollywoodreporter.com/movies/movie-features/nicolas-cage-in-demand-films-pig-1235243969/.
4. Puig, Claudia. "He's Up. He's Down. He's Up. He's Down. He's Up for Good?: Nicholas Cage's Movie Career Has Been, Uh Volatile. But He Hit the Jackpot in an Alcoholic Love Story Set in Las Vegas. Will Success Stick? Nothing Is Ever That Simple in Hollywood." *Los Angeles Times*, February 4, 1996, https://www.latimes.com/archives/la-xpm-1996-02-04-tm-32387-story.html. Accessed April 25, 2022.

Index

For the benefit of digital users, indexed terms that span two pages (e.g., 52–53) may, on occasion, appear on only one of those pages.
Figures are indicated by *f* following the page number